Philosophic Pride

Philosophic Pride

STOICISM AND POLITICAL THOUGHT FROM LIPSIUS TO ROUSSEAU

Christopher Brooke

PRINCETON UNIVERSITY PRESS

Princeton and Oxford

Copyright © 2012 by Princeton University Press
Published by Princeton University Press, 41 William Street,
Princeton, New Jersey 08540
In the United Kingdom: Princeton University Press, 6 Oxford Street,
Woodstock, Oxfordshire OX20 1TW

press.princeton.edu

Jacket illustration: *The Four Philosophers*, c. 1611–12 (oil on panel), by Peter Paul
Rubens (1577–1640); Palazzo Pitti, Florence, Italy. Reproduced courtesy of
The Bridgeman Art Library; photo copyright Alinari

Library of Congress Cataloging-in-Publication Data
Brooke, Christopher, 1973–
Philosophic pride : Stoicism and political thought from Lipsius to Rousseau / Christopher
Brooke.
p. cm.
Includes bibliographical references (p. 253) and index.
ISBN 978-0-691-15208-0 (hardcover : alk. paper)   1. Political science—Philosophy—
History.   I. Title.
JA71.B757 2012
320.01—dc23
2011034498

This book has been composed in Sabon LT Std

Printed on acid-free paper. ∞

Printed in the United States of America

10 9 8 7 6 5 4 3 2 1

For Josephine

The Stoic last in philosophic pride,
By him called virtue, and his virtuous man,
Wise, perfect in himself, and all possessing,
Equal to God, oft shames not to prefer,
As fearing God nor man, contemning all
Wealth, pleasure, pain or torment, death and life—
Which, when he lists, he leaves, or boasts he can;
For all his tedious talk is but vain boast,
Or subtle shifts conviction to evade.
Alas! what can they teach, and not mislead,
Ignorant of themselves, of God much more,
And how the World began, and how Man fell,
Degraded by himself, on grace depending?
Much of the Soul they talk, but all awry;
And in themselves seek virtue; and to themselves
All glory arrogate, to God give none;
Rather accuse him under usual names,
Fortune and Fate, as one regardless quite
Of mortal things.

—John Milton, *Paradise Regain'd*, 4.300–318

Contents

Preface

FOR ERNST CASSIRER, writing in American exile during the Second World War, ideas drawn from Stoic philosophy played a vital role in the 'formation of the modern mind and the modern world'. The Greek Stoics had taught that one should live in accordance with a moral law of nature, he observed, and the Roman Stoics had both championed the virtue of *humanitas*, absent from earlier Greek ethics, and argued for a cosmopolitanism that treated the whole world, gods and humans together, as fellow citizens of one great republic. In particular, Cassirer attributed to the Stoics the notion of the fundamental equality of all human beings. Stoic ideas persisted beyond the end of the Stoic school itself, Cassirer suggested, finding a place 'in Roman jurisprudence, in the Fathers of the Church, in scholastic philosophy'. But it was only in the seventeenth and eighteenth centuries that these ideas took on 'tremendous practical significance'. In the world of the Renaissance and the Reformation, the 'unity and the inner harmony of medieval culture had been dissolved', 'the hierarchic chain of being that gave to everything its right, firm, unquestionable place in the general order of things was destroyed', and the 'heliocentric system deprived man of his privileged condition'. The prospects appeared bleak for 'a really universal system of ethics or religion', one 'based upon such principles as could be admitted by every nation, every creed, and every sect'.

> Stoicism alone seemed to be equal to this task. It became the foundation of a 'natural' religion and a system of natural laws. Stoic philosophy could not help man to solve the metaphysical riddles of the universe. But it contained a greater and more important promise: the promise to restore man to his ethical dignity. This dignity, it asserted, cannot be lost; for it does not depend on a dogmatic creed or on any outward revelation. It rests exclusively on the moral will—on the worth that man attributes to himself.[1]

Cassirer thus considered seventeenth-century political philosophy to be in significant measure 'a rejuvenation of Stoic ideas'. He highlighted the importance of works by Justus Lipsius and others, as well as the rapid passage of Neostoic ideas 'from Italy to France; from France to the Netherlands; to England, to the American colonies'. Of the stirring opening phrases of the Declaration of Independence—'We hold these truths to be self-evident, that all men are created equal, that they are endowed by their Creator with certain unalienable Rights, that among these are Life, Liberty and the pursuit of Happiness'—Cassirer claimed that 'When Jefferson wrote these words he was scarcely aware that he was speaking the language of Stoic philosophy'.

What, then, was that Stoic philosophy? Stoicism was one of the philosophical systems that took shape in Athens in the so-called Hellenistic period following the death of Aristotle in 322 BCE. The first Stoic was Zeno from Citium, a Phoenician city on Cyprus, who came to Athens and studied with Crates the Cynic and other philosophers there, subsequently setting up his own school around the turn of the third century. This school met in the middle of Athens at the *Stoa Poikilê*, or the Painted Stoa—a stoa being a roofed colonnade or portico—and it was this structure that gave the philosophy its name. Zeno died in 262 and was succeeded as the head of the school, or scholarch, by Cleanthes, a former boxer. But it was his successor, the third scholarch Chrysippus of Soli, leader of the school during the final decades of the third century, who did more to systematise Zeno's doctrines than any other philosopher, and who gave the Stoic philosophy its definitive form. Stoicism flourished in Athens and spread throughout the Greek and, later, Roman worlds.

Some of the characteristic doctrines of the Stoics were these: that God and the universe are coextensive with one another—a divine fire thoroughly permeates the world of stuff—and this universe is a thoroughly rational totality. The physical world is all that exists, and all events in that world are causally determined. The goal of human existence is to live in accordance with nature, which is to live rationally or virtuously. Virtue is the only genuine good, and it is sufficient for happiness. Other things that we might conventionally call goods, such as health or wealth, are, properly speaking, only 'preferred indifferents'. Vice is the only genuine bad. We must learn to distinguish between those things that are under our own control and those that are not, and train ourselves to be unconcerned about the latter. Most of the emotions that we experience are false judgements, and should be extirpated through Stoic therapies or spiritual exercises. If we can rid ourselves of these emotional responses, then we can live the good life in the passionless state the Stoics called *apatheia*, and to live that ideal life is to be the Stoics' sage. But the Stoics conceded that the sage was rarer than the phoenix and might never in fact have existed. The sage was, they said, both wise and free—a true cosmopolitan, or citizen of the world—and remained happy even under torture.

Stoicism survived as an unbroken tradition in Athens until 529 CE, when the emperor Justinian closed down all of the philosophical schools. Thereafter there was little interest in or detailed knowledge of the Stoics' arguments for about a thousand years.[2] But, as Cassirer indicates, there was a great revival of interest in the Stoics from the time of the Renaissance and the Reformation, when Stoic texts began to be printed and translated, whether from Greek into Latin or from either of these ancient languages into the European vernaculars. That revival of interest in and attention to the Stoic philosophers culminated in the later sixteenth century with the work of the Flemish humanist, Justus Lipsius. His Stoic dialogue *De constantia* was an international best-seller, and he also published the *Politica*, a major work of political theory, as well as an edition of the works of the Roman Stoic Seneca and two handbooks of Stoicism, the *Manuductio ad Stoicam philosophiam* and the *Physiologae Stoicorum*. These last were the first modern works to begin to reconstruct Stoicism in a systematic way, paying attention to both its ethical and physical arguments. Modern scholarship has presented Lipsius as the key figure in an influential intellectual, cultural, and political movement that has been called 'Neostoicism'.

Why has Neostoicism been held to be historically significant? I have already sketched Cassirer's argument about the origins of much modern political philosophy in Stoicism, with the Dutch Neostoics serving as an important conduit, helping to transmit arguments from ancient philosophy to the rest of Western Europe. The German historian Gerhard Oestreich spent his career studying Lipsius and what he called 'the Netherlands movement', and argued extensively for the importance of Lipsius's project for understanding modern politics organised around the centralised and bureaucratic state. 'Lipsius proclaimed the modern state', Oestreich wrote, 'based on order and power, from amid the ruins caused by the religious wars'.[3] More recently, Richard Tuck has proposed that the arguments of Lipsius and Michel de Montaigne, which drew on two of the Hellenistic philosophies, Stoicism and Scepticism, were the inspiration behind much of what he calls the 'new humanism' that spread across Europe in the early decades of the seventeenth century and which in turn formed the crucial intellectual background for the political theories of first Hugo Grotius and later Thomas Hobbes. But we ought not straightforwardly accept any of these interpretations. Cassirer provided an arresting hypothesis and a few broad-brush remarks, but not a properly fleshed-out historical argument. Oestreich's scholarship has been strongly criticised for the extent to which it is implicated in a distinctively National Socialist historiography, and its conclusions thereby have been drawn into question. Tuck's narrative of modern political philosophy has at its heart an interpretation of Grotius as a thinker who drew on an Epicurean understanding of self-love to fashion a reply to Scepticism, but his argument overstates the role of both Scepticism and Epicureanism in Grotius's thinking and radically underplays the significance of Stoicism.

Although these historians have not provided fully persuasive accounts of the place of Stoic argumentation in the development of modern political thought, they are, it seems to me, right in their general contention that the modern engagement with Stoicism was highly significant at key moments in the philosophical story. It was also an extensive engagement, continuing far beyond the 'Neostoic' world of Lipsius and his disciples deep into the seventeenth and eighteenth centuries. As I have just indicated, Grotius's natural jurisprudence has a distinctive foundation in what we might call Ciceronian Stoicism; Thomas Hobbes's fundamental political psychology is the product of a complex dialogue with early modern Stoicism; the ethical systems of the Earl Shaftesbury and Francis Hutcheson are deeply infused with Stoic ideas; and the account of human psychology that Jean-Jacques Rousseau fashioned in his most ambitious book, *Emile*, is strikingly indebted to the Stoics. The principal task of this book, therefore, is to narrate the history of this modern encounter with some of the arguments of the Stoics in the seventeenth and eighteenth centuries, especially as it concerns some of the foundational arguments in modern political philosophy. But to write that historical account also requires the writing of an intertwining narrative, which is the history of anti-Stoicism across the same period and, in particular, of a distinctively Augustinian variety of anti-Stoic criticism.

In an important interpretation of Renaissance thought offered by William J. Bouwsma in 1975, the 'two ideological poles between which Renaissance humanism oscillated may be roughly labeled "Stoicism" and "Augustinianism"'.[4] For too long, he contended, scholars had thought of humanism as an attempt to recover an authentic classicism embodied in Plato or Aristotle, whereas it was the rival philosophies of the Stoics and Augustine that represented 'genuine alternatives for the Renaissance humanists to ponder'.[5] The broad antagonism between Stoicism and Augustinianism had various aspects to it, but the one the Augustinians returned to again and again throughout the entirety of the early modern period concerned the problem of human pride. The core of Augustine's charge against the Stoics had been that their philosophy denied original sin—the sin of Adam and Eve in the Garden of Eden, their disobedience to God's command that grew out of their pride. And the early modern Augustinians redeployed and amplified Augustine's arguments, contending that Stoicism was itself a philosophy for the proud, for those who drastically overestimated the abilities of fallen men and women to act in accordance with reason and virtue in the absence of divine grace.

To put the matter like this might suggest that the story of Stoicism and its Augustinian critics in early modern Europe might be told as a story of secular versus religious ethics. But that would be much too simple. On the one hand, a number of those who engaged sympathetically with Stoicism, from Lipsius in the sixteenth century to Hutcheson in the eighteenth, were trying to produce a distinctively Christian Stoicism, one that could be defended against Augustinian objections. On the other hand, while pride was obviously a concern for religious thinkers, it also became a critically important issue for more secular political thinkers, too. It was central to Hobbes's political philosophy, for example, where it was transposed from being an offence against God to being one against the equality of our fellow human beings, so that when Hobbes explained why his book was called *Leviathan*, he quoted from the 'two last verses of the one and fortieth' chapter of the book of Job, where God calls the great seamonster 'King of all the children of pride'.[6] The vocabulary of pride might have changed according to time and place. Different writers talk of glory, vainglory, self-love, self-liking, honour, *amour-propre*, and so on. But the moral, social, and political anxieties that underlay these various terms were, if not always the same, then certainly possessed of enough commonalities and continuities that they can intelligibly be considered alongside one another—and as we shall see, it is in these arguments that the sharpest thinkers were often working most closely with their competing inheritances from both Stoic and Augustinian traditions.

The book is organised as follows. We begin in late antiquity with a prologue that presents a reading of book 14 of Augustine of Hippo's *De civitate Dei contra paganos* (*The City of God against the Pagans*). This is the part of his text that describes Adam and Eve's rebellion against God's command, the episode that was not only central to Augustine's theological vision as a whole but also the site of his most sustained critical engagement with the categories of Stoic ethics, through which Augustine forged the ideologically powerful link between Stoicism and the notion of original sin that would be restated by his early modern disciples. Before we pick up that modern Augustinian story in the third chapter, however, the first two chapters of the book offer more or less self-contained studies of particular topics in the interpretation of two significant political writers from the Low Countries, Justus Lipsius and Hugo Grotius, to correct distortions in the existing scholarship. The first chapter proposes a new interpretation of Lipsius's political theory through an examination of his six books of *Politica* from 1589. It argues that the significance of this work is not that it introduces Stoic content into modern political thinking so much as that it offers a partial restoration of Stoic political theory in the wake of Machiavelli's devastating attack on Senecan political thought in *The Prince*. The second chapter constitutes an intervention in the ongoing controversies concerning the philosophical foundations of Grotius's natural rights theory, and argues that to understand his system either in terms of self-interest or in terms of sociability is to miss the point of his appeal to the Stoic argument presented by Cicero in book 3 of *De finibus*, where the distinctive Stoic concept of *oikeiosis* serves as an explanation of appropriate action, both self- and other-regarding.

Armed with these improved understandings of the Stoic content of the political theories of both Lipsius and Grotius, in chapter three I return to the Augustinian theme first stated in the prologue. The chapter starts with Lipsius, focusing not, however, on the *Politica* this time but on his popular dialogue *De constantia*, and it navigates a passage from Lipsius to Thomas Hobbes by way of William Shakespeare, Michel de Montaigne, and the contemporary 'Tacitist' literature. Along the way, it illuminates the ways in which the figure of what I call the 'Stoic politician' was often regarded in the late sixteenth century and early seventeenth century with great suspicion. It offers a new approach to Hobbes by suggesting that one of the things he was doing when he fashioned his political argument was generalising this suspicion, so that glory seeking, sedition, and hypocrisy were no longer considered to be the animating vices of a small number of Stoics at, for example, the Jacobean or Caroline courts but far more widespread and deep-seated elements of the human condition. Chapter four outlines the increasing sophistication of the Augustinian anti-Stoic polemic in seventeenth-century France, beginning with the identification of Stoicism with the Pelagian heresy made by Cornelius Jansen and Jean-François Senault and continuing on to the more incisive psychological criticisms developed by Blaise Pascal, Nicolas Malebranche, and La Rochefoucauld. These Augustinians directed their fire above all against the Stoicism to be found in Seneca's philosophical writings, but, as I argue in the chapter's closing section, their critique was not so potent against the Stoicism of the Roman emperor Marcus Aurelius, set out in his *Meditations*. This book, then, could continue to be employed as a resource by those in the seventeenth or eighteenth centuries who sought to expound a Stoicism that could be presented as friendly to the claims of Christianity.

The fifth chapter crosses back across the English Channel in order to examine some of the critical responses to Hobbes—in particular, those of three Anglican bishops, John Bramhall, Richard Cumberland, and Samuel Parker—as background for considering Shaftesbury's fashioning of a more thoroughgoing kind of modern Stoicism in the various pieces that make up his *Characteristics of Men, Matters, Opinions, Times*. The sixth chapter considers the changing fortunes of Stoic physics in the seventeenth and early eighteenth centuries and argues that the appearance of Benedict Spinoza's controversial works prompted a shift in the way Stoic cosmology was classified. Previously understood as a kind of theism, however eccentric, it was thenceforth interpreted with increasing frequency (though never universally) as a variety of atheism.

The penultimate chapter shows how Stoic arguments were refashioned in the early eighteenth century by writers such as Joseph Butler and Francis Hutcheson in order to oppose what they considered to be the modern Epicureanism of Bernard Mandeville, and presents David Hume's philosophy as offering sustained resistance to this Stoicizing current in eighteenth-century British intellectual culture. The final chapter then turns to the philosophy of Jean-Jacques Rousseau and argues that his thinking about human psychology is marked by a shift from a more or less Epicurean perspective in, especially, the *Discourse on the Origins of Inequality* to a far more carefully theorised reworking of Stoicism presented, above all, in what he considered to be his most important book, the educational novel *Emile*. A brief epilogue brings the book to its close.

SOME REMARKS ON METHOD

Obvious problems beset any attempt to write a history of Stoicism and modern thought. 'There is no systematic account of Stoicism in the eighteenth century', Christopher J. Berry has written, 'and one good reason for that is that it would be almost impossible to write it simply because it would have to incorporate and encompass so much of what was written'.[7] This is true, and might be thought especially problematic for this study, which has an even wider chronological range, spanning the period from Lipsius to Rousseau, or from the 1580s to the 1760s. To make my book manageable, therefore, it follows that the treatment of Stoicism is by no means comprehensive. Themes from Stoic ethics, for example, loom much larger than topics in Stoic physics and metaphysics, and even within the sphere of what we might call Stoic political thought I have concentrated above all on certain issues in moral psychology, especially those relating to the foundations of modern natural law, and have neglected (for example) Stoic arguments about cosmopolitanism, or the important question of the relationship between Stoicism and the republican tradition in political theory. Although the argument of the book moves back and forth among a number of centres of intellectual production in early modern Europe, it is also marked by significant geographic limitations. I concentrate here on England and France and, in the earlier chapters, on the Low Countries, but Germany and Scotland are comparatively neglected, and Iberia, Italy, and all of Eastern Europe, including Russia, are ignored. This focus perhaps helps explain why the book culminates in a treatment of Rousseau rather than, say, either Adam Smith or Immanuel Kant, two other major eighteenth-century philosophers whose projects can also be fruitfully interrogated through the lens provided by Stoic philosophy.

Over the last forty years or so, scholars such as A. A. Long, Brad Inwood, Julia Annas, Susanne Bobzien, Malcolm Schofield, Michael Frede, and others have done much to transform our understanding of the technicalities of Stoic philosophy. In the process, the role of Chrysippus in defining the structure and philosophical content of ancient Stoicism has been greatly emphasised. Yet this hard-won appreciation of Chrysippan Stoicism is not especially useful for exploring intellectual life in the early modern period. One reason why the reconstruction of Chrysippus's philosophy has been such a challenging task is that the 705 books he was reputed to have written have all been lost, except for fragments preserved in the reports of later, frequently hostile, authors such as Plutarch. It is thanks to several centuries of increasingly sophisticated textual scholarship, then, that scholars today have a significantly better grip on the nature and subtleties of his Stoicism than was available to anyone in early modern Europe. Nor is it merely the case that Chrysippus's thought was only imperfectly understood by, or not readily available to, early modern writers. Often enough, he was not considered central to Stoicism at all! Diogenes Laertius, the ancient compiler of the *Lives of Eminent Philosophers*, presented his summary of the doctrines held by each philosophical school (or doxography) appended to his biography of its founder. The doxography of Stoicism was therefore attached to the account of the life of Zeno, and early modern writers tended to follow Diogenes Laertius in treating the founder of the school as ipso facto the chief representative of its thought.[8] Some also displayed a marked hostility to Chrysippus, treating him more as a deviant or heterodox Stoic than as any kind of exemplar. Lipsius was one of these, charging that it was Chrysippus 'who first corrupted that grave sect of philosophers with crabbed subtleties of questions'.[9]

There's something of a historical irony here. The Stoics had a reputation in the ancient world for monolithic dogmatism. They argued that their whole philosophical system hung together as a seamless whole. Cicero reports a Stoic view that 'the removal of a single letter' would 'cause the whole edifice to come tumbling down'.[10] But this monolithicity was undercut in a number of ways. The ancient Stoics modified their own doctrines over time, for example; hence the conventional and convenient distinction employed by today's scholars between the periods of the Early, Middle, and Late (or Roman) Stoas. While the school in Athens may have been the home of Stoic orthodoxy, it is an interesting fact that no text written within and for the use of the school itself has survived from antiquity in more than fragmentary form. In the chief sources for Stoic philosophy to which the early moderns had access, furthermore, the idea that Stoicism was a seamless totality is undermined by the multiple voices of the surviving texts, for works by Cicero, Seneca, Plutarch, Epictetus, and Marcus Aurelius are diverse in terms of both philosophical content and literary form.

A further difficulty standing in the way of writing a history of thinking about Stoicism in modern Europe is the lack of the right kind of institutional continuity. A history of the development of Stoic doctrine in antiquity is at least in part a history of the Stoic school itself, and vice versa. By contrast, there is no comparable institution with respect to a narrative of Stoicism in modern Europe that might be employed to provide a coherent structure and a degree of content across time. There was a distinctive 'Neostoic' movement associated with the life and work of Justus Lipsius, and this has been the object of detailed historical studies. Yet although the first chapter of this book considers Lipsius's political thought, the bulk of what follows is concerned with the period after this 'Neostoicism', during which no particular institution—political, academic, or ecclesiastic— ever achieved any kind of recognised hegemony over the legitimate interpretation of Stoicism in Europe.

In the absence of the right kind of institutional structure, we are always in danger of running into the perennial problems associated with tracing intellectual 'influence'. As T. J. Hochstrasser has put it, 'When the notion of "influence" is applied to a long span of time and to a large number of writers it can easily deteriorate into nothing more than the correlation of superficially similar doctrines'.[11] It would clearly be a pedantic and substantially pointless exercise to wade through the corpus of early modern philosophical and political writing looking for any or every moment in which the arguments presented remind the reader of some Stoic thesis or other. Nor is it helpful to label anything that smacks of self-fashioning, self-discipline, fatalism, or imperturbability as Stoic in its inspiration, for such themes are the joint property of various philosophical schools and religious traditions, ancient and modern.[12]

In his own work, Hochstrasser has been able to address the problem of determining intellectual influence in more than an arbitrary manner through his study of 'a range of contemporary sources which discuss self-consciously the relation of contemporary practice to past achievement', in his case the 'histories of morality' that were written in, especially, Germany in the century following Pufendorf's 1678 *De origine et progressu disciplinae juris naturalis*.[13] No single genre of philosophical writing serves as a comparable backbone for this study, but on various occasions in what follows I pay attention to the changing understandings of Stoic philosophy in seventeenth- and eighteenth-century Europe as these are expressed in three kinds of works. First, there are the new editions and vernacular translations of Stoic authors, which provide useful information, especially in their prefaces, about the ways in which scholars and translators were drawn to and thinking about Stoic philosophy. Second, there are the increasingly scholarly works on the history of ancient philosophy, a discipline that develops with great rapidity over the period. These are important works, not only as stores of facts and opinions concerning ancient authors but also, as Hochstrasser himself has shown, as contributions to a long-running argument about the relationship of philosophy to its past. Third, and partially overlapping with this second category, there are the classic reference books of the age of the Enlightenment, for Pierre Bayle's *Dictionnaire historique et critique* (1697) and the *Encyclopédie* of Denis Diderot and Jean le Rond d'Alembert (1751–72) were for many readers basic sources concerning ancient philosophy, and so much else besides. These three kinds of works, taken together, provide a valuable contemporary framework within which, I suggest, particular lines of thinking in relation to the Stoics can be coherently elaborated.

Acknowledgments

I have researched and written this book on two continents, spread over too many years, and have accumulated many debts of gratitude along the way.

Material that appears in this book has appeared previously in a number of places, and I thank the editors and publishers of those pieces for allowing republication here: 'Rousseau's Political Philosophy: Stoic and Augustinian Origins', in Patrick Riley, ed., *The Cambridge Companion to Rousseau* (Cambridge: Cambridge University Press, 2001); 'Stoicism and Anti-Stoicism in the Seventeenth Century', *Grotiana*, vol. 22–23 (2001–2), also published in Hans W. Blom and Laurens C. Winkel, eds., *Grotius and the Stoa* (Assen: Van Gorcum, 2004); 'How the Stoics Became Atheists', *Historical Journal*, vol. 49, no. 2 (June 2006); 'Grotius, Stoicism and Oikeiosis', *Grotiana*, vol. 29 (2008); and 'Rousseau's *Second Discourse*, between Epicureanism and Stoicism', in Stanley Hoffmann and Christie McDonald, eds., *Rousseau and Freedom* (Cambridge: Cambridge University Press, 2010).

Institutions that have sheltered me along the way include Harvard University's Government Department and its Center for Ethics and the Professions; the Classics Department at the University of California, Berkeley; Magdalen College, Balliol College, and the Department of Politics and International Relations in Oxford; and King's College and the Department of Politics and International Studies in Cambridge. For financial support I am grateful to the Andrew W. Mellon Foundation, Harvard's Graduate School of Arts and Sciences and Program on Constitutional Government, and the U.S./UK Fulbright Commission for the award which first took me to the United States in 1995. Research has been conducted in various libraries, in particular the Bodleian, the Rare Books Room of Stanford University's Green Library, the Bancroft Library at Berkeley, Harvard's Houghton Library, the British Library, the libraries at Magdalen and Balliol Colleges, the British School at Rome, and the École Française de Rome. Audiences have listened patiently to me trying to articulate what this project was all about in seminars at Berkeley, Cornell, Harvard, Penn, Oxford (including the Maison Française d'Oxford), Cambridge (including at the Wolfson Humanities Society), Bellagio, St Andrews, the American Political Science Association's 1998 meeting in Atlanta, Jena, Helsinki, and the Institute for Historical Research in London.

Many individuals—teachers, students, friends, and colleagues—have helped me along the way: Arash Abizadeh, Arthur Applbaum, Carolina Armenteros, Rhiannon Ash, Chris Bertram, Hans W. Blom, Daniel Butt, Josh Cherniss, Graham Clure, Sarah Cotterill, Michael Drolet, Michaele Ferguson, Mark Fisher, Luc Foisncau, Peta Fowler, Liz Frazer, the late Ewen Green, Kinch Hoekstra, Bonnie Honig, Istvan Hont, Katherine Ibbett, Terence Irwin, Ben Jackson, Duncan Kelly, Stephen and Joy Kent, Kristy King, Nancy Kokaz, Melissa Lane, Neven Leddy, A. A. Long, Patchen Markell, Sophie Marnette, Christian Maurer, Pratap Bhanu Mehta, Tamara Metz, Jon Miller, Jim Moore, Sarah Mortimer, Russ Muirhead, Sankar Muthu, Isaac Nakhimovsky, Martin O'Neill, John Michael Parrish, Raj Patel, Jennifer Pitts, Sophus Reinert, Patrick Riley, John Robertson, Amelie Oksenberg Rorty, Paul Sagar, Claudia Schaler, Malcolm Schofield, Richard Scholar, Travis Smith, Mike Sonenscher, Peter Stacey, Nick Stargardt, Sandy Stewart, Zosia Stemplowska, Benjamin Straumann, Richard Tuck, Kate Tunstall, Ralph Walker, William Whyte, Brian Young, and Sam Zeitlin, as well as anonymous referees for the *Historical Journal* and *Grotiana*.

Thanks are also owed to the excellent staff at Princeton University Press: in the early stages to Ian Malcolm; later especially to Ben Tate, Debbie Tegarden, and Marjorie Pannell; and to three anonymous readers.

Three groups that deserve particular mention for the contributions they have made to my welfare over the period during which I've been thinking about the Stoics are the inhabitants of 6 Marie Ave, no. 2, in Cambridge, Massachusetts, toward the end of the last century; the staff at Combibos, the best café in Oxford; and my two splendid cats, Andromache and the never-to-be-forgotten Enkidu (2005–9).

I owe most of all to Biddy and Henry Brooke, and to Josephine Quinn.

Philosophic Pride

Prologue

Augustine of Hippo

It is not too much to say that the fourteenth book of Augustine's massive *The City of God against the Pagans* is the pivot on which the rest of the work turns, for it contains the analysis of Adam and Eve's life in the Garden of Eden and their subsequent Fall.[1] This is an episode central not only to his theological project, in that Augustine single-handedly created the doctrine of original sin that dominated the thinking of the Church for so long, but also to his political theory, because it provides the setting for the central categories of the work's overall argument. It is no accident, for example, that the most succinct summary of Augustine's political teaching appears right at the end of book 14. The famous passage that begins 'Two cities, then, have been created by two loves' is Augustine's summary presentation of the position won by the argument of this book, and one that the remaining books will expand upon at very great length.[2] The idea of the existence of two rival cities, earthly and heavenly, has already been richly elaborated by the start of book 14. It is only in the course of this book, however, that the origins and nature of each city—the core theme of the work as a whole—are properly established, the one rooted in disobedience, or in pride rooted in self-love, the other in charity, or love of God 'extending to contempt of self'.

The origins of the cities lie in two different kinds of love, and these loves are central not only to *City of God* but to Augustine's entire body of moral and political philosophy. His theorisation of love, for example, directly shapes his theorisation of justice, the core normative political concept for Augustine as it was for Plato and Cicero before him. It is not simply the case that love of God is good and love of self is bad (though the Jansenists of the seventeenth century, whom we shall encounter later on, did tend to read Augustine in this way), for at least two reasons: first, because the love of self is rooted in the nature of things, and what is natural is created by God and is for that reason good, and second, because the divine commandment to love one's neighbour as oneself itself implies the propriety of a certain kind of self-love.[3] The object of love is significant for Augustine, but more important are the ordering of one's loves and the quality of one's loving, concerns that give rise to Augustine's vocabulary of charitable loving, on the one hand, and passionate loving or lust on the other. The trouble with self-love is not something intrinsic to it but is related to the fact that in practice it so often issues in contempt of God, or pride, which is a misordering of our loves and a denial of the love we owe our Creator. 'Love', wrote Augustine in one of his commentaries on the Psalms, 'but take care what it is you love. . . . Bridle your passion, stir up your charity'.[4] Given this centrality of love to Augustine's ethical theory in general and to the political argument of *City of God* in particular, it is therefore a striking and an important fact about *City of God* that these chapters in book 14 also contain by far the most sustained rumination on Stoic philosophy to be found in the entire work.

Book 14 does not by any means, however, mark the first appearance of the Stoics in the *City of God*. In book 5 Augustine considers the Stoics' account of fate presented by Cicero in his *De fato*, and in book 9 he addresses various topics in Stoic ethics. But neither of these is an especially significant episode in the *City of God*'s overall structure. Insofar as Augustine was critical of Stoic fate, it was to attack their fondness for astrology, an argument best understood as a component part of the more general attack on pagan superstition that dominates so much of the first ten books. Insofar as he was sympathetic, it was to uphold the notion of a universe under the benign governance of an omnipotent deity in possession of perfect foreknowledge, an argument directed against both Cicero and the Pelagians, who worried that the chains of causation that God foreknew were incompatible with the possession of a truly free will by human beings.[5] When Augustine considers the ethics of the Stoics in book 9, furthermore, he is content to repeat Cicero's criticism from *De finibus* about the disagreements between the Stoics and the Peripatetics being linguistic rather than substantial,[6] a complaint that echoes a familiar trope in Christian writings, especially those of Lactantius, about the endless capacity of the philosophers for meaningless disputation.[7] In book 14, by contrast, Augustine expounds a set of Stoic ethical doctrines in order to introduce his analysis of the nature of original sin, and while his verdict on the Stoics is in the end damning, this judgement is passed only after he has signalled his agreement with a very substantial part of the Stoics' approach to moral theory.

The City of God is divided into two unequal halves. The first ten books were written against the Romans and their religion; the last twelve present the history of the citizens of the City of God on their pilgrimage through historical time and a little beyond. These twelve books are further subdivided into three groups of four, on the origin, development, and end of the heavenly city, respectively, so that book 14 is the final book of the first part of the second half, bringing the analysis of the origin of the City of God to a close.[8] The discussion of the Fall is spread over two books, 13 and 14, but the main argument that engages the Stoics is confined to book 14. Book 13 considers the nature of death, which is, Augustine contends, the divine punishment justly incurred for the sin in the Garden, and it presents analyses of some of the metaphysics that arise from thinking about the separation of the soul and the body or the flesh of the saints. This book ends with a discussion of the nature of lust: in the absence of the 'shameless stirrings of those parts which were not subject to the control of the will', how would men 'have begotten offspring if they had remained as they were created, without sin?'[9] Augustine announces that 'so large a subject cannot be treated in so narrow a compass' and that he will end book 13 at this point, so that this important question can be 'treated more appropriately' in the pages that follow. As promised, book 14 does indeed answer the question Augustine has just posed to himself, but only in its second half. The discussion of lust begins in 14.16 and dominates the rest of the book. (This is a passage of argument that contains Augustine's well-known if peculiar claims that in Paradise, men's genitals remained under the strict control of the will, and that the Cynic philosophers who were alleged to have had sexual intercourse in public places could not have done so because 'I believe that such pleasure could not have been achieved under the gaze of human onlookers'.[10]) These passages on lust, however, appear only after a lengthy discussion of Stoic philosophy, which in turn introduces Augustine's presentation of the actual Fall of Adam itself, and it is these chapters that I consider in what follows.

Book 14 opens with a reiteration of the claim, familiar from 12.22 and from so many other Augustinian texts, that 'the individual members of this [human] race would not have been subject to death, had not the first two . . . merited it by their disobedience'. But for the unmerited grace of God, Augustine comments, all men after the Fall would have been 'driven headlong, as their due punishment, into that second death to which there is no end', and it is the existence of this redeeming grace that has led to the 'two orders' of human society, or to the 'two cities'. So far, so familiar, until Augustine appeals to a biblical distinction. Of the two cities, 'The one is made up of men who live according to the flesh [secundum carnem], and the other of those who live according to the spirit [secundum spiritum]'.[11] Book 14.2 clarifies the distinction. Augustine is clear that the Epicureans recommended a life according to the flesh, 'for they place man's highest good in the pleasure of the body'.[12] But Augustine also and immediately insists that the Stoics also belong on the fleshly side of this binary, even though, as he admits, they present virtue as the summum bonum and understand it to be a property of the mind: 'it is clear that all of these [the Stoics] live according to the flesh in the sense intended by Divine Scripture when it uses the expression'. The reason is that the distinction between the flesh and the spirit is not the same as that between the body and the mind, and Augustine provides several examples from scripture where the word flesh is not used 'to mean only the body of an earthly or mortal creature'. The text that provides him with his interpretive key is from Paul:

> Now the works of the flesh are manifest, which are these; Adultery, fornication, uncleanness, lasciviousness, idolatry, witchcraft, hatred, variance, emulations, wrath, strife, seditions, heresies, envyings, murders, drunkenness, revellings, and such like.[13]

Although Paul described these as the works of the flesh, Augustine observes that they are all clearly 'vices of the mind rather than of the body', and to clinch his case, he imagines a man who 'tempers his desire for bodily pleasure out of devotion to an idol, or because of some heretical error'. This man is nevertheless 'still convicted, on the authority of the apostle, of living according to the flesh; yet it is his very abstinence from the pleasures of the flesh that demonstrates that he is engaged in the damnable works of the flesh.'[14] This is the first step in his argument, for having established that the domain of the flesh extends beyond the realm of the body to include what goes on in people's minds, it remains for Augustine to show why the Stoics' account of virtue should be categorised alongside wrath, heresy, or drunkenness.

Two new elements are therefore introduced into the discussion in book 14.3. First, Augustine begins his consideration of the 'disturbances [*perturbationes*] of the mind'. He introduces the theme with reference to a passage from Virgil, who is described as one who 'seems to be expounding Platonic teaching'.[15] The disturbances he goes on to consider, however, are the standard Stoic quartet of desire (*cupiditas*), fear (*timor*), joy (*laetitia*), and grief (*tristitia*),[16] and Augustine departs from Virgil's Platonic view that these disturbances have their origins in the body, asserting as an article of 'our faith' that 'the corruption of the body, which presseth down the soul, was not the cause of the first sin, but its punishment'.[17] Second, Augustine for the first time in book 14 introduces the figure of the devil, who will continue to be a felt presence for the rest of the book. If the Platonic teaching were right, he observes, there would be a problem, for then 'we should absolve the devil from all such vices, since he has no flesh'. Worse still,

> [W]e cannot say that the devil is a fornicator or a drunkard, or that he commits any other such vice pertaining to the pleasures of the flesh,

even though it is he who secretly tempts and incites us to such sins. He is, however, supremely proud and envious [*maxime superbus atque invidus*]; and these vices of pride and envy have so possessed him that he is doomed by them to eternal punishment in the prison of this murky air of ours.[18]

Augustine concludes that 'It is not then, by having flesh, which the devil does not have, that man has become like the devil. Rather, it is by living according to his own self; that is, according to man.'[19] Thus the operative dichotomy in the book shifts yet again: the classical dualism of body and mind was replaced by the biblical binary of the flesh and the spirit; and this binary is now transposed into a distinctively Augustinian key as that between living according to man or to self, on the one hand, and living according to God on the other.

This opposition is further elaborated in 14.4, where Augustine represents living 'according to self' as living 'according to falsehood', because 'man was created righteous, to live according to His Maker and not according to himself', and in 14.5, where he rejects the Platonists' view that ascribes all vice to the nature of the flesh. Each chapter adds a detail to the argument of the book so far and strengthens its Stoic characteristics. The equation of sin with falsehood in the first is coupled with a note that what Cicero calls the four 'disturbances' are more usually rendered as the 'passions' (*pathe*), which can be said to 'embrace all the vices of human conduct'. In locating vice in the mind and identifying it with both passion and falsehood in the second chapter, Augustine is (as he recognises) in agreement with the Stoics and opposed to both the Platonists and the Manichees.[20]

The critique of the Stoics finally begins to take shape in 14.6. Augustine's first line of attack is to insist that there are good as well as bad emotions:

> What is important here is the quality of a man's will [*interest autem qualis sit voluntas hominis*]. For if the will is perverse, the emotions will be perverse; but if it is righteous, the emotions will be not only blameless, but praiseworthy.[21]

Although Augustine's insistence on the importance of will might seem to mark a sharp departure from Stoic theory, his claim here still bears the traces of two very distinctive Stoic claims: first, of Chrysippus's argument that the passions were consequent on poor judgement, rather than vice versa, and second, of Epictetus's emphasis on the importance of the correct use of the faculty of choice (*prohairesis*) in determining right action.[22]

There is a well-rehearsed Stoic response to this kind of objection, that there are good emotions as well as bad ones, and it is one that Augustine acknowledges in 14.8. This is that the sage does indeed show emotion, but that these are healthy emotions, *eupatheiai* or *constantiae*, rather than *pathe*, or 'passions' constituted by error.[23] Augustine's reply to this objection contains four significant elements. First, in 14.8 he peppers his text with a large number of citations, mostly scriptural but some also drawn from Cicero and Terence, in order to draw the conclusion that in the most authoritative literature, the distinction the Stoics insist on is not upheld.[24] Second, he notes that Paul praised the Corinthians for having felt grief 'after a godly manner', although the Stoics not only denied that the wise man feels grief but also refused to supply a corresponding *eupatheia* as a substitute to describe what he does feel.[25] In response to this Pauline argument that 'grief does seem to serve a useful purpose when it gives rise to repentance of sin', Augustine imagines a Stoic reply that would observe that since the wise man does not sin, grief in the service of repentance cannot therefore arise in his mind. In the story of how Alcibiades wept when Socrates showed him how he was miserable because he was foolish, the Stoics had an example of this kind of grief, but it is a grief that the wise man can never experience, precisely because he is wise.[26] (Augustine can allow this response to stand, since the Stoics' dogma that the wise man does not sin is a strand of the rope with which he will hang them a little later in the book.) Third, in 14.9 Augustine argues that the citizens of the heavenly city do feel the four disturbances, but this is 'in a manner consistent with the Holy Scripture and wholesome doctrine; and because their love is righteous, all these emotions are righteous in them'.[27] They may even desire temptation, saying, 'Examine me, O Lord, and prove me; try my reins and my heart', and with reference to the many occasions on which Paul wept and rejoiced and experienced longing, suffering, and jealousy, he proclaims that 'if these emotions and affections, which come from the love of the good and from holy charity, are to be called vices, then let us allow that real vices should be called virtues'.[28] Finally, Augustine reminds his reader that Christ also experienced *pathe* on several occasions.[29] In this final section he also rejects the Stoics' contention that pity is a vice, agreeing with Paul that we should denounce those who are 'without natural affection' and with Cicero that to be entirely free of pain in this world would require the cultivation of 'savagery of mind and stupor of body'.[30]

These last observations pave the way for Augustine's analysis of the central category in Stoic ethics, that of passionlessness or *apatheia*.

> If, then, we are to understand this 'impassibility' [*impassibilitas*] to mean a life without those emotions which arise contrary to reason and

which disturb the mind, it is clearly a good and desirable condition. It does not, however, belong to this present life.[31]

The saints may enjoy *apatheia* in a world to come, but for the moment,

> We live well enough if we live without blame. But if anyone supposes that his life is without sin, he does not avoid sin, but rather forfeits pardon. Moreover, if *apatheia* is to be defined as a condition such that the mind cannot be touched by any emotion whatsoever, who would not judge insensitivity to be the worst of all vices?[32]

The fact that *apatheia* is depicted as a life without fear reinforces the claim that it is unsuited to this world, for on earth we rightly fear God if we wish to live rightly, and only in 'that life of blessedness which, it is promised, is eternal' will that fear come to an end.[33]

Christians need not worry, therefore, that they are fearful or experience the various other disturbances, for 'a righteous life will exhibit all these emotions righteously, whereas a perverse life exhibits them perversely'.[34] The Stoics, on the other hand, are citizens of the earthly city, as the following passage makes clear:

> The city, that is, the fellowship of the ungodly consists of those who live not according to God, but according to man: who, in worshipping false gods and despising the true Divinity, follow the teachings of men or of demons. This city is convulsed by those emotions as if by diseases and upheavals. *And if it has any citizens who seem to control and in some way temper those emotions, they are so proud and elated in their impiety that, for this very reason, their haughtiness increases even as their pain diminishes.* Some of these, *with a vanity as monstrous as it is rare*, are so entranced by their own self-restraint that they are not stirred or excited or swayed or influenced by any emotions at all. *But these rather suffer an entire loss of their humanity than achieve a true tranquillity.* For a thing is not right merely because it is harsh, nor is stolidity the same thing as health.[35]

This, then, is the characteristic vice of the Stoics: their pride leads them to believe that it is in their power to control their emotions. This is impious on two levels. First, it is impious in that it triply fails to recognise that the passions are inevitable (because they are part of the divine punishment for original sin), that there is a proper use of the passions or a righteous way to experience them, and that the correct way of handling the passions comes through a recognition of dependence on God rather than through a doomed attempt to insist that humans can through their own efforts overcome them. Second, it is impious because insofar as a Stoic does falsely believe himself to be in control of his passions, to that extent also his 'haughtiness increases even as his pain diminishes'. Nor is it accidental that the key Stoic vice of pride is the same as was ascribed to the devil a few pages before, as will become increasingly apparent below.

In 14.10, Augustine returns to the First Couple. The chapter title asks 'Whether we are to believe that the first human beings were subject to emotions of any kind when they were placed in Paradise, and before they sinned'. The body of the text poses the question this way: did they feel 'in their animal bodies the kind of emotions which we shall not feel in our spiritual bodies when all sin has been purged and ended'? Augustine answers that they did not:

> The love of the pair for God and for one another was undisturbed [*inperturbatus*], and they lived in a faithful and sincere fellowship which brought great gladness to them, for what they loved was always at hand for their enjoyment. There was a tranquil avoidance of sin [*erat devitatio tranquilla peccati*]; and, as long as this continued, no evil of any kind intruded, from any source, to bring them sadness.[36]

They had been forbidden to eat from the tree, but Augustine is clear that they did not desire the fruit against God's decree and abstain from it 'merely from fear of punishment'. Nor was theirs a righteous fear of the kind discussed in the previous chapter: they abstained out of righteousness, pure and simple, and they lived without the disturbances of fear and desire. 'How happy, then, were the first human beings, neither troubled by any disturbance of the mind nor pained by any disorder of the body!'[37]

Is this a description of Stoic *apatheia*? Marcia Colish has argued that it is not, for if Adam and Eve had possessed *apatheia*, then 'they could not have felt the desire for the forbidden fruit'. 'It is only in the next life', she continues, 'in which the saints will be free from the capacity to sin, that *apatheia* will be possible for man'.[38] But is this correct? Augustine does not make the point that Colish ascribes to him in 14.10, to which her footnote refers, and it is not clear what is gained by denying that Adam and Eve lived in a state of *apatheia*. As we have seen, by contrast, he is quite clear that they lived without any kind of emotional disturbance, the defining characteristic of *apatheia* both in the Stoic tradition and in his own account in 14.9. There Augustine affirms that 'This condition of *apatheia* will only come to pass when there is no sin in man', and in his description of Eden, Augustine is adamant that there was no sin present:

> God forbid, I say, that before all sin, there already existed that sin, committed in respect of a tree, of which, when committed in respect of

a woman, the Lord said, 'Whosoever looketh on a woman to lust after her hath committed adultery with her already in his heart.'[39]

Augustine certainly draws a distinction between the situation of Adam and Eve and the eternal blessedness of the saints, in that the latter enjoy the 'certain assurance that no one would sin and no one would die',[40] but he does not suggest that this is a reason for affirming that the saints enjoy *apatheia* in a way that the first human beings do not. Given Augustine's repeated and deliberate use of Stoic categories and vocabulary to describe the predicament of Adam and Eve—admittedly, without using the word *apatheia* or *impassibilitas* itself—it would be odd to conclude that he is here trying to deny that this is a genuine example of Stoic *apatheia*, indeed, the only instance there will ever be of human beings in such a state.

In 14.11, Augustine turns to the Fall itself. God made man with a good will, and 'a good will is the work of God, since man was created with it by God'.

> On the other hand, the first evil act of the will, since it preceded all other evil acts in man, consisted rather in its falling away from the work of God to its own works than in any one work. And those works of the will were evil because they were according to itself and not according to God.[41]

The will that Adam and Eve possessed was genuinely free, for 'the choice of the will . . . is truly free only when it is not the slave of vices and sins', and theirs was not.[42] They lived in a corporeal and spiritual paradise. 'But then came that proud angel, envious by reason of that same pride which had induced him to turn away from God and follow himself'. Even if Eve's status as a kind of Stoic sage—always a masculine ideal—is thrown into doubt by her inability to resist the serpent's temptation, Adam's is not, for Augustine is emphatic that he sinned knowingly. He had not been deceived (as Paul told the Romans); rather, he 'did not wish to be separated from his only companion, even at the cost of sharing in her sin'.[43]

In the case of sinning knowingly, it is a logical truth that the evil will had to precede the evil act, and in 14.13 Augustine asks, 'What but pride can have been the beginning of their evil will?'[44]

> And what is pride but an appetite for a perverse kind of elevation? For it is a perverse kind of elevation indeed to forsake the foundation upon which the mind should rest, and to become and remain, as it were, one's own foundation. This occurs when a man is too pleased with himself.[45]

And then, a little later,

> It is clear, therefore, that the Devil would not have been able to lure
> man into the manifest and open sin of doing what God had prohibited
> had not man already begun to be pleased with himself. That is why
> Adam was delighted when it was said, 'Ye shall be as gods'.[46]

The origins of sin lie therefore in Adam and Eve becoming pleased with
themselves. This is the beginning of self-love, which is the root of pride,
which in turn is the fountainhead of sin.

We have seen how Augustine's descriptions of the Stoics in book 14
consign them to membership of the earthly city. They live 'according to
the flesh', and pride is their defining vice. The devil also concentrates on
the works of the flesh, and is supremely proud. To live according to the
flesh is to live according to man or to self and not according to God; the
original sin was itself a choice to live according to self, and was rooted in
being 'pleased with oneself', in self-love, or in pride. In this Augustinian
schema, therefore, to bring to mind the pride of the Stoics with their high
valuations of self-sufficiency and autonomy is to be reminded immediately of the devil, on the one hand, and of Adam's transgression on the
other. In one sense, there is nothing remarkable about this. *Any* sin can
swiftly be related to the original sin—that is, after all, a part of the point
of the latter category. But Stoicism is more thoroughly implicated in original sin than this. The obvious mistake the Stoics make, from this Christian point of view, is to think that postlapsarian humans can live without
being troubled by the disturbances, and therefore without sin. Christians
have it as an article of faith that they cannot, and therefore that the claim
of the Stoics appears ridiculous, impious, and prideful, insofar as it denies
human dependence on God.

According to Augustine's narration of the Eden story, furthermore, it is
not just the case that the Stoics mistakenly suppose something to be possible when it is not. For even when it was once possible for a human being
to live as a Stoic sage, untroubled by emotions and therefore in possession of a genuinely free will, Adam nevertheless became 'pleased with
himself', before the perpetration of any 'external' sin, and it was *this* that
led to his disobedience of the divine command not to eat the fruit of the
tree. It is clear that humans cannot enjoy Stoic *apatheia* in this life because of original sin; it is not too fanciful to think that Augustine is here
suggesting that original sin was incurred in part because Adam had lived
in a state of *apatheia*, which precisely helped to induce and then to nur-
ture this feeling of pride. For Augustine, this *apatheia* isn't quite the same
as the truly utopian state the saints will enjoy—concerning which he
stresses their unshakable love of God even more than their freedom of

the will or their lack of troubling disturbances.[47] The *apatheia* of Eden doesn't solve or even address the question of the possible perversity of the will, yet the control of their wills that the First Couple enjoyed fostered, like Scarpia confronted by Tosca, a forgetfulness of God—and in book 13 Augustine is emphatic that Adam forsook God before God forsook Adam.[48]

We have to be cautious here. Augustine is careful not to make a causal argument of any kind about the effects on Adam and Eve that their environment or their predicament might have had. As with the theft of the pears in book 2 of his *Confessions*, itself closely modelled on the episode in the Garden, he deliberately strips away any rational or explicable motive for the sin, until only the fact of transgression undertaken for its own sake remains.[49] But as in the case of the earlier Fall, that of the devil, the set of associations Augustine constructs between *apatheia*, becoming 'pleased with oneself' or proud, and a fall through the perpetration of sin is unmistakable, as is the way in which these associations are subsequently echoed in a shadowy and erroneous fashion in the vanity of the Stoics of the earthly city.

There is, then, a significant philosophical critique of the Stoics in these pages, but it is less important when set beside the ideological or polemical work that the book has performed on them. Far from the Stoics being in any way preferable to the Epicureans owing to their agreement with the Christians that virtue properly belongs to the mind, their philosophy has been relegated to the realm of the flesh, implicated in original sin, and found guilty of the same sins as those perpetrated by the devil, sins that were committed, furthermore, for exactly the same reasons. The familiar Ciceronian objections to Stoic *apatheia* are repeated (that it is both an impossible and an undesirable state of affairs at which to aim), but they are given new force through the way Augustine situates them on his broad—indeed, vast—theological canvas. From Cicero's point of view, to declare oneself a Stoic was to make a number of significant philosophical mistakes; from Augustine's, it was also in a way to declare war on God.

CHAPTER ONE

Justus Lipsius and the Post-Machiavellian Prince

IN HIS FINE 1991 STUDY OF NEOSTOIC IDEOLOGY and the painting of
Peter Paul Rubens, the classicist Mark Morford wrote that Justus Lipsius
'is now little known except to students of Seneca and Tacitus and to intellectual historians of the northern Renaissance'.[1] Given the growing number of studies devoted to Lipsius and his various legacies since Morford's
book appeared, we might want to add students of early modern political
thought and some scholars of literature to his list. Outside these particular corners of the academy, however, levels of Lipsius consciousness remain fairly low. He returned to the heart of European political life, in a
manner of speaking, when the Justus Lipsius Building in Brussels opened
in 1995, providing a new home for the European Union's Council of
Ministers. One might have thought it appropriate that such a building be
named for a distinguished Belgian political writer who argued against the
excesses of patriotism and in support of a European peace based on principles of mutual toleration, and whose books circulated extensively
throughout the greater part of the territory of today's EU. According to
an EU press release, however, the building was in fact named for the Brussels street that used to connect rue de la Loi and rue Belliard and had
been demolished to make way for its construction.[2]

Who was Justus Lipsius? He was born in 1547 in Overijse in Brabant.[3]
He studied at the Jesuit college in Cologne from 1559 and was for a short
while, from 1562 to 1564, a novice member of the order. Having obtained a bachelor's degree in arts, he moved to Louvain in 1564 to study
law, though at this time he seems to have concentrated instead on his
humanist studies, developing a reputation as an acute Latin philologist
and publishing four books of *Variae lectiones* in 1568. In that year he
joined Cardinal Granvelle's staff and travelled through Italy to Rome,
where he studied the Tacitus manuscripts in the Vatican Library. A period
of migration followed. Lipsius was back in Louvain in 1570, but he left
again in 1571, visiting Liège, Vienna, and Leipzig before being appointed
in 1572 to the chair in history at the university in Jena, a Lutheran foundation. He returned to Cologne to marry the recently widowed Anna van
den Calstere in 1573, and in 1574 he published his great edition of Tacitus and left his post at Jena to return to Louvain, where he finally com-

pleted his law degree. Moving to a chair at the new Calvinist college in Leiden in 1578, Lipsius there published his two most significant original works, the philosophical dialogue *De constantia* in two books in 1583 and the six books of *Politica* in 1589. The publication of the *Politica* provoked a sharp public exchange in 1590–91 with Dirck Koornhert, who had accused Lipsius of favouring the methods of the Spanish Inquisition and of Machiavellism ('*ille machiavellisat*'). In the wake of this controversy, Lipsius left Leiden in 1591, reconverted to Catholicism in Mainz, and took up a chair in ancient history and Latin in Louvain the following year. His great work of this final period was his edition of Seneca, published in 1605; he also compiled two handbooks of Stoic philosophy, the *Manuductio*, on ethics, and the *Physiologia Stoicorum*, on physics; there were other works on ancient Rome, especially on its military affairs, and a new book on politics, the *Monita et exempla*, in 1605. Lipsius died in Louvain in March 1606; legend has it that he rejected the consolation of Stoicism on his deathbed and gestured at a crucifix, insisting 'haec est vera patientia'.

The scholarship on Justus Lipsius as a moral and political thinker dates above all from the publication in 1914 of Léontine Zanta's *La renaissance du stoïcisme au XVIᵉ siècle*. This book charted the translation and dissemination of classical texts and the increasing use of Stoic tropes, arguments, and values in the writings of moralists of the time, and presented in its second part an anatomy of the main ideas of the Neostoic 'triumvirate' of Justus Lipsius, Guillaume du Vair, and Pierre Charron, whose books did much to systematise and popularise this Stoic current in the late sixteenth and early seventeenth centuries. Anthony Levi observed in 1964 that the book 'was a pioneer work, but its assumptions about the stoicism of the moralists have today sometimes to be questioned'.[4] That is true enough, but with a long look back it is the first part of this verdict that resonates the most. Zanta was not the first to argue for the historical and intellectual significance of Lipsius and the other Neostoics. Wilhelm Dilthey had earlier paid considerable attention to them as a part of his explorations of changing conceptions of rationality, the transformation of individual consciousness, and the development of the modern scientific worldview,[5] and Fortunat Strowski had considered the sixteenth-century Stoic moralists in the second chapter of his classic 1907 study of Pascal's intellectual contexts.[6] Where Strowski offered a sketch, however, Zanta constructed a far more solid framework for the study of sixteenth-century Stoicizing moral theory in her book, paying attention in particular to the more technical Stoic works of Lipsius such as the *Manuductio*. She also successfully defended her work at the Sorbonne in May 1914, with *La renaissance* becoming the first thesis on a philosophical subject by a woman to be accepted by a French university for the degree of *docteur d'État*. Zanta was a significant feminist: she published her *Psychologie du féminisme* in 1922, for example, and campaigned for the rights of professional women in the interwar French press. She was also an inspirational figure for the young Simone de Beauvoir.[7]

Zanta's book helped to recover Lipsius the Christian Stoic moralist—the Lipsius above all of *De constantia*—forging a path along which subsequent scholars of the history of ethics would follow. Lipsius the political theorist—the Lipsius of the *Politica*—was by contrast comparatively neglected. J. W. Allen's 1928 study, *A History of Political Thought in the Sixteenth Century*, for example, contains no mention of Lipsius or of any of the other major Neostoic authors, nor any consideration of the influence or function of ancient Stoicism concerning the political thinking of the period.[8] Jason Lewis Saunders's 1955 book-length study of Lipsius, the first in English, presented a biographical sketch of his writing career and detailed expositions of the main arguments of the Stoic writings on ethics and physics in *De constantia*, the *Manuductio*, and the *Physiologia Stoicorum*, but passed over the *Politica* and the other explicitly political writings altogether.[9] It is not difficult to come up with reasons why it might have been so easy for the *Politica* to be substantially ignored. First, in comparison with *De constantia* especially, *Politica* appears to be a considerably less original work. The bulk of the text is made up of quotations from classical authorities, giving the work something of the feel of a commonplace book. (It was this aspect of the book that provoked Montaigne's description of it as 'ce docte et laborieux tissu', and opinion differs down to the present over whether this was intended as a compliment or not.)[10] Second, and in contrast to all three of the works that Saunders examined in his book, for example, *Politica* does not advertise itself as having anything in particular to do with Stoicism, making it a less attractive object of study for those interested above all in Lipsius as the protagonist in a 'Stoic revival'. The author most frequently quoted in the *Politica*, for example, is Tacitus, who was no kind of Stoic; Stoicism itself is unmentioned throughout.

The scholar who did the most to draw attention to Lipsius's political thought was the historian Gerhard Oestreich, who died in 1978 and whose final book, *Neostoicism and the Early Modern State*, was published posthumously.[11] For Oestreich, Lipsius's importance was many-sided. His books, in particular *De constantia* and the *Politica*, provided the definitive statement of a political ideology that found its inspiration in a number of mostly Latin texts and foregrounded themes of power, self-inspection, discipline, toleration, and moderation. 'Lipsius proclaimed the modern state, based on order and power, from amid the ruins caused by the religious wars', Oestreich wrote. 'The spirit it embodied and its exceedingly practical orientation derived from the Neostoic philosophy of the state, which was itself eminently practical'.[12] As well as helping to give shape to this ideology, Lipsius was also a prominent propagandist for it, and Oestreich stressed his role as a popular teacher, especially during his period in Leiden; his seven hundred correspondents, scattered all over Western Europe; and the fact that his books were sixteenth-century best-sellers, going rapidly through many editions and being translated into all the major European languages.[13] At the heart of Oestreich's account lies a reading of the *Politica*, whose contents are summarised in the third chapter of *Neostoicism*. His epitome gives particular attention to the fourth book, on actual constitutional practice,[14] with its discussions of religious uniformity, the rise and fall of governments, and 'the troublesome question of *prudentia mixta* or "reason of state"',[15] as well as to the fifth book, on military affairs, above all to its account of discipline.[16] Indeed, Oestreich considered this book central to the interpretation of the *Politica*, for in his view, 'The Leiden professor saw military force (*vis*) as the real foundation of the state.'[17]

Oestreich's claims for the historical significance of Lipsius's project were not small. In his view, the new emphasis on discipline on the part of the writers who contributed to the Netherlands movement played a key role in the military revolution that transformed first European warfare and then the internal organisation of the European states themselves. Prince Maurice of Orange had been one of Lipsius's students in Leiden in 1583–84, Oestreich observed, and he 'always referred to Lipsius as his teacher.'[18] Neostoicism was credited with being one of the major forces behind the consolidation of absolutist ideology, to the extent that it might be said to mark the moment when the national security state came to supplant the free city republic as the focus of political theorists' attention and loyalties.[19] Max Weber had argued for the importance of a Protestant ethic associated above all with Calvinism for understanding the increasing intensification of processes of rationalisation in early modern Europe that helped to stabilise early capitalist relations of production,[20] and Otto Hintze had gone on to suggest that there was an affinity between Calvinism and modern *raison d'état* arguments.[21] Oestreich offered a variation on the theme, suggesting that it might have been Neostoic ideology that had helped to spread an ethic of duty that bordered on asceticism, and that in the context of the early modern absolutist monarchies, furthermore, it made more sense to ascribe significant social and economic effects to this secular ideology than to any religious doctrine.[22] Oestreich's presentation of Lipsius and his interpretation of the political content of Neostoicism has been a very influential one, and his work continues to be cited down to the present (recently, for example, in Charles Taylor's large book on the history of the possibility of a secular society).[23] His position, however, is an increasingly awkward one. In particular, his critics are not persuaded that his argument about Lipsius's political thought has much to do with Stoicism at all, that his grander historical claims are sound, or that the historiographical tradition within which he was working was free from the taint of National Socialist ideology.

In the introduction to his recent edition and translation of the *Politica*, Jan Waszink expresses scepticism about the contribution of Stoic philosophy to Lipsius's argument. In this work, he notes, important Neostoic themes such as the reconciliation of Christian and Stoic doctrine or the desirability of suppressing the emotions do not make any noteworthy appearance; '[t]he Neostoic key virtue of *Constantia* is given no particular prominence'; and Epictetus and Marcus Aurelius are 'entirely absent'.[24] Indeed, Waszink canvasses the mischievous suggestion that Lipsius's book might reasonably be considered an anti-Stoic argument, for a central claim of Stoic political theory was the identification of what was honourable (*honestum*) with what was useful (*utile*), which is one that Lipsius seems to deny. At the start of the famous discussion of 'mixed prudence' in 4.13, he asks whether it is 'allowed that I mix it [prudence] a little, and add a bit of the sediment of deceit?', and he answers that it is ('*ego puto*'), 'in spite of the disapproval of some Zenos, who *only approve that straight road which leads with virtue to honour*' and who 'do not think it permissible that *Reason, given by the Gods with good intentions, is used for deceit and malice*'.[25] 'We might of course define Lipsius' entire body of thought as "Neostoic",' Waszink observes, 'but in that case "Neostoic" must be taken as a mere synonym for "Lipsian", rather than as a reference to the recreation of the Roman Stoa'.[26]

With regard to Oestreich's historical claims, Philip S. Gorski notes the biographical connection that links Maurice to Lipsius and agrees that 'it seems reasonable to conclude that his own study of classical precedents was at least partly inspired by his mentor'. But he is sceptical about stronger claims of influence over the nature and content of the army reforms themselves, remarking that 'the intellectual impetus for the reforms came from William Louis rather than from Maurice' and noting that the reforms were set in motion years before 1595, when Lipsius published his compendium on ancient military affairs, *De militia Romana*. In line with the broader thesis of his book *The Disciplinary Revolution*, which defends Max Weber's original contentions about the importance of the Reformation in shaping subsequent social transformations against the criticism of Norbert Elias and Michel Foucault, Gorski suggests that the Dutch interest in military discipline owed more to Calvinism than to any Neostoicism, and that there may 'have been a psychological connection—an elective affinity—between their religious ethos and their military reforms because both placed so much stress on discipline, both as a value and as a practice.'[27]

The most far-reaching—and the most disturbing—challenge to Oest-reich's argument about Neostoicism has been made by Peter N. Miller in his 2002 article, 'Nazis and Neostoics', which discusses the historical writings of Gerhard Oestreich and Otto Brunner.[28] Miller contends that understanding Oestreich's 1940 article, 'Vom Wesen der Wehrgeschichte' (On the Essence of Military History), 'is vital in order to appreciate why his post-war scholarship took the shape that it did'. In that article, the young Oestreich set out a wide-ranging and interdisciplinary research agenda to bring out the way in which 'the military in its manifold forms and expressions is ever more the guarantee of the life of the people in their conflicts with other states and peoples'.[29] Miller's central charge is that in his postwar work on Lipsius, Oestreich was to execute this re-search project without ever drawing attention to its Nazi origins and emphases, and that his transition to working on a structural history of early modern state building could be considered 'a more or less conscious attempt to efface the ideological position-taking' of his work in the Nazi period.[30] 'It is striking', Miller observes, 'that Oestreich's evocation of Lipsius's idea of discipline', which was central to his overall interpreta-tion of Lipsius's political thought, 'seems to pick up every single nuance and echo of the National Socialist language of *Erziehung zum Wehrwil-len*' (that is, education of the will to war).[31] Oestreich's readings of Lip-sius's works were distorted and distorting. It is implausible, for example, to reduce the argument of *De constantia* to the claim that 'by fighting many battles are won, but none by flight',[32] and in a cutting phrase Miller refers to the way in which Oestreich 'evoked, rather than quoted' Lipsius in the *Politica*.[33] By fashioning a concept of *Sozialdisziplinierung* and ar-guing that Lipsian theory became first Dutch and then Prussian practice, Oestreich could work to 'turn Prussia from the great European exception (militarized and bureaucratized to the hilt) into the great European exem-plar—the paradigmatic modern state'.[34]

An account like Miller's always runs the risk of a kind of ideological reductionism, placing too much weight on the values of National Social-ist historiography in explaining the contours and content of Oestreich's postwar project. But even if we are tempted by that thought, it is worth emphasising that it is not just Miller who considers Oestreich to present a one-sided reading of the *Politica*. Waszink is another recent commenta-tor who finds Oestreich's discussion perplexing in this regard. For while Lipsius did indeed agree with Machiavelli that the army was an impor-tant political institution—hence his devoting an entire book to the sub-ject—'it appears untenable to say, as Gerhard Oestreich did, that Lipsius "saw military force as the real foundation of the state"'. If military affairs and military discipline were as important to interpreting the *Politica* as Oestreich had suggested, then we would expect to see military concerns shaping Lipsius's treatment of other topics in his political discussion, whereas, as Waszink observes, the only time the army is mentioned outside *Politica 5* is in a brief discussion of the use of soldiers in peacetime in 4.7. 'The military', he concludes, 'is not central to the *Politica* at all'.[35] Miller's critique invites us to be suspicious of Oestreich's interpretation of Lipsius and of Neostoic political theory, and our examination of Lipsius's work needs to proceed as far as possible by working outside the interpretive framework that Oestreich did so much to provide.

One way of doing this is to pick up on a remark of Oestreich's concerning Lipsius and Machiavelli. 'This is not the place to continue the comparison between Lipsius and his great predecessor', he wrote, 'by investigating the concept of *patria* and the meaning of *virtù, fortuna, fatum* and *necessità* in their respective writings.'[36] But to continue to develop comparisons like these, it seems to me, may be an excellent way of moving out of Oestreich's shadow. Several scholars have been attracted by the project of trying to establish where Lipsius stands with respect to Machiavelli's political thought, among others, Martin Van Gelderen,[37] Richard Tuck,[38] Robert Bireley,[39] Jan Waszink,[40] and Jan Papy.[41] Machiavelli's *Prince* in particular provides a familiar benchmark against which to assess Lipsius's own argument; although Machiavelli was writing seventy years before Lipsius, 'Machiavellian' argument was both topical and controversial in the aftermath of the Massacre of St Bartholomew; and Lipsius himself, as we shall see, took the relationship between his own book and Machiavelli's political ideas to be an important one.

One clear account of the relationship between Lipsius and Machiavelli is that fashioned by Robert Bireley, which presents Lipsius as the founder, along with Giovanni Botero, of a specifically Catholic 'anti-Machiavellian' tradition of political thought. According to Bireley, Lipsius's chief concern was to 'elaborate a vision of practical politics, in response to Machiavelli, that would be moral, Christian, and effective in the circumstances of the late sixteenth century'.[42] He emphasises Lipsius's doctrine of providence, to which I return later in this chapter, rightly remarking that this 'is most important if he is to be understood as an anti-Machiavellian'.[43] But in general, his attempts to find anti-Machiavellian political theory in Lipsius's work are not especially convincing. He quotes from *Monita et exempla*, for example, on how a good precept is to

> be just and virtuous, and from the depths of the heart will issue forth upright [*honesta*] and useful [*utilia*] counsels. Let us not separate these two, that is, the upright from the useful. The doctor from Italy errs who teaches otherwise, who creates petty tyrants, not legitimate kings or princes.[44]

But as we have already seen, Lipsius equivocates on the Stoic equation of the *honestum* and the *utile* with his remarks in *Politica* 4.13 against 'some Zenos', and Bireley seems all too aware of the limits of his own argument. He writes that Lipsius's pragmatism 'brought him perilously close to Machiavellism himself',[45] and that with respect to the discussion of *prudentia mixta*, while '[a]t first blush he might seem to approve what could be understood as Machiavellian procedures', a 'careful analysis combined with a look at his later statements seems to preclude this conclusion *except perhaps in one or two instances*'.[46] So perhaps he is not so decisively such an anti-Machiavellian theorist after all.

The best response to Bireley's argument concerning both the Roman Catholic character of Lipsius's political thought and its 'anti-Machiavellian' aspect, however, has come from the files of the Vatican's Sacred Congregation of the Index (*Sancta Congregatio Indicis*), which were opened to researchers in 1998 and have allowed Jan Waszink to reconstruct in some detail the saga of the *Politica*'s flirtation with the Index of Forbidden Books (*Index Librorum Prohibitorum*). The *Politica* was first published in 1589 and placed on Sixtus V's Index in 1590, but this document was retracted after the pope's death that same year and never circulated widely.[47] In Rome, Laelius Peregrinus was asked to vet the text of the *Politica*, and it seems that his *censura* was available to the Congregation at its meeting of 10 October 1592, which discussed Lipsius's book,[48] with Lipsius having in the meantime returned to the Catholic fold. That meeting decided to remove the *Politica* from the Index that was being prepared, a decision that was reversed two weeks later[49]—but the Index that was supposed to appear in 1593 was delayed, and it was during this delay that Lipsius agreed to expurgate the text of the *Politica* and the Vatican agreed not to include it on the Index after all. Both the new Index and the new version of the *Politica* were published in 1596.

Bireley discusses this sequence of events in passing and remarks of the alterations to the 1596 text that '[t]hese elaborations and changes must be taken into account in any discussion of the *Politics*, but none of them amounted to a change in his [i.e., Lipsius's] role as an anti-Machiavellian'.[50] What Waszink has demonstrated, however, is that the corrections Lipsius made to the text addressed neither of Rome's major objections to his argument, concerning religion and Machiavellism, in light of which, as Waszink gently puts it, 'one may find it surprising that the *Politica* indeed disappeared from the *Index Librorum Prohibitorum*'.[51] On religion, Peregrinus's *censura* had objected to Lipsius's subordination of religion to politics in 4.3,[52] a strikingly Machiavellian move that aligned Lipsius with the *politiques* and to which the Church authorities were bound to object, but the objection was one that Lipsius ignored when he came to revise his text.[53] On Machiavellism, Lipsius agreed to cosmetic changes, which served to mask rather than to remove the Machiavellian component of his argument. Marginalia were altered in the introductory section, 'De consilio et forma nostri operis', for example, so that the words 'Machiavelli impresses me / though he sometimes goes against morality' were changed to 'Machiavelli is shrewd / but often immoral' (Machiavellus argutus / Sed saepe pravus). The main text these marginalia served to illustrate, however, remained unchanged.[54] Similarly, in 4.13, the final sentence calling for Machiavelli not to 'be so categorically condemned' (for 'whose hand is not flogging the poor man these days?') was removed, but Lipsius left untouched the Machiavellian argument about 'mixed prudence' that had itself provoked this concluding reflection. Concerning *Politica* 4.14, Peregrinus had objected to Lipsius's defence of the prince lying for the sake of the common good, and Lipsius once again ignored his objection.[55] If the *Politica* stayed off the Roman Index, it seems that this owed more to Cardinal Bellarmine's behind-the-scenes interventions on Lipsius's behalf than to any perception that it was an orthodox piece of Catholic, let alone 'anti-Machiavellian', political theory.

If we reject Bireley's particular interpretation of Lipsius as an anti-Machiavellian political theorist, a frequent alternative view that we find in the literature is that Lipsius gives us, to borrow Jan Papy's words, 'an attempt to produce a synthesis between the traditional mirror of princes, a popular genre among humanists, and Machiavelli's *Prince*'.[56] There is obviously something correct about this view, but we should pause for a moment and allow ourselves to be puzzled by this idea a bit more than scholars usually are. If the point is just that the typical Renaissance 'mirror for princes' praises the prince for his possession of conventional moral virtues, whereas Machiavelli teaches the need for the prince to learn how to be bad, then there would not seem to be any real difficulty at all. We might say it is just a matter of repositioning the mirror so that aspects of the prince's face that were formerly cast in shadow are brought into the light. But *The Prince* is itself a kind of mirror for princes, which complicates the question of just what it might be to produce a synthesis of this particular work with that particular genre. Quentin Skinner noted thirty years ago, for example, that *The Prince* was itself a 'recognisable contribution' to the mirror-for-princes literature, and he argued that Machiavelli 'may have had the further intention to question or even to ridicule' some of its humanist authors' values,[57] suggesting also that he was engaged in 'demolishing the usual scale of values underlying the mirror-for-princes literature'.[58] If *The Prince* borrows the literary form of the mirror for princes in order to attack its political content, then the question of what the synthesis of Machiavelli and the mirror-for-princes genre might be like recurs; we can no longer talk of simply repositioning the mirror because on this reading, Machiavelli has already done just that, so we may end up saying, with Jan Waszink, that the two writers are basically engaged in the same enterprise: 'like Machiavelli, Lipsius employs the mirror-for-princes format to criticise the political morality conventionally connected with it'.[59]

How deep is Machiavelli's challenge to the mirror-for-princes literature? In his recent book, *Roman Monarchy and the Renaissance Prince*, Peter Stacey has shown that it is an extremely deep attack.[60] It runs deep, furthermore, in a way that might be thought to pose a significant challenge for Lipsius in particular, if we do think that what Lipsius was doing in his *Politica* might have had something to do with Stoicism after all. For what Stacey has shown is, first, the political thought of the mirror-for-princes genre was always fundamentally Senecan, and therefore Stoic, and second, Machiavelli's *Prince* is at its core a thoroughgoing and quite systematic repudiation of that Senecan tradition of political thought. Neither thought is especially original to Stacey. The connection between Seneca's *De clementia* and the Renaissance mirror-for-princes literature has often been noted, and Richard Tuck observed in passing years ago with *De clementia* in mind that Machiavelli's 'criticism of conventional notions of a virtuous prince is largely an indirect criticism of Seneca rather than Cicero'.[61] Nevertheless, Stacey has certainly done more than anyone else to show how fruitful these thoughts can be in constructing a persuasive overall interpretation of Machiavelli's book. Rather than seeing Lipsius as someone who introduces patterns of Stoic argument in general and Senecan argument in particular into the political theories of the sixteenth century, as we have so often been encouraged to do, it seems to me that we need to learn to see him as someone who is attempting to salvage a version of Senecan or Stoic political theory and to reconstitute the mirror for princes in the wake of Machiavelli's shattering critique. The resultant argument does indeed combine or synthesise elements of the traditional mirror for princes and of Machiavellian political argument, but we need to peer a little closer at its architecture to see just how Lipsius went about trying to bring off this ambitious project. So: first Seneca and Machiavelli (largely following Stacey, in both cases), and then I shall turn my attention back to Lipsius.

Seneca's *De clementia* was written around the year 56 and takes the form of an address to the youthful new *princeps*, Nero, who had ascended the throne in 54. The work is not complete. What has come down to us is all of book 1, which constitutes a treatise on kingship, and a fragment of book 2, which offers praise of the virtue of *clementia*. We might see *De clementia* as doing two things in particular: first, attempting to impress on the new prince virtuous habits of rule, and second, providing a systematic defence of the Roman principate against republican criticism. In setting about the first task, Seneca deploys the idea of the mirror (*speculum*), which he uses to 'show you to yourself' (*te tibi ostenderem*)—or, as Stacey puts it, 'Nero is initially shown what he is through an impersonation, and is then praised for being identical to the person that is held out to him; but the praise is valid only if Nero recognizes himself to be the person which Seneca shows him to be'.[62] The second task is that of replying to the charge that the Romans had recently passed from a state of political freedom under the republic to one of subjection under Augustus Caesar and his successors. In place of this version of the recent history of Rome, Seneca offers his own narrative of a passage from republican corruption to rational principate. In the late republic, the Romans had lost their ability to live in accordance with true *ius* and thereby could no longer be said to be properly free; under the rule of the Caesars, on the other hand, the body politic was restored to health through the guidance of its virtuous ruler—'you are the mind of your *res publica* and it is your body'[63]—and *libertas* was thereby restored to the people.

Seneca's argument is fashioned out of Stoic themes. In Stacey's words, 'the fundamental theoretical movement pervading his text is Seneca's consistent application of the monological concept of Stoic *ratio* to his material'.[64] The rational Stoic community, however, is the world city or *cosmopolis*, and so the boundaries of the Roman principate are extended to the ends of the earth in order for Nero to become a universal monarch with unlimited jurisdiction.[65] If the state is to be rationally directed, furthermore, and its monarchy legitimate, then the *princeps* must be entirely virtuous, ruling in accordance with the Stoics' cosmic natural law.[66] And if the life of the community is regulated according to reason, then the people can plausibly be considered to be free.[67] Nero (of all people!) has thus become the functional analogue of the Stoics' wise man (*vir sapiens*), 'born to assist the community and promote the common good',[68] and hence the image in the mirror that Seneca presents to the new *princeps* has to be a quite extraordinarily idealising one. The ruler must always act in accordance with the providential reason that pervades the world, and acting in such a way necessarily promotes the general good, which means there is no troubling gap between the requirements of what is worthy (*dignum*) and what is useful (*utile*).[69]

We might think that if everything is providentially ordered, which means there is no room in the Stoic scheme for any kind of contingency, then there is no room either for the idea of fortune to be playing any role in this account. If we did think that, however, we'd be in for a surprise, as *fortuna* is something of a key word for Seneca; as Stacey writes, 'the centrality of *fortuna* to his thought requires some explication'.[70] Most generally, what we ascribe to *fortuna* is what appears to us to be contingent, but it isn't really: *fortuna* is just providence misunderstood. Nature, Fate, and Fortune are the same (and, Stacey observes, understood this way, fortune is 'characterised as divine, rational and male').[71] There is also, however, a more specific use of the language of *fortuna*, this time coded as female, that is repeatedly invoked to describe the apparent irrationalities we experience as good and bad luck in the moral life. What appears contingent or random is still providential, of course, but with the sage understanding that such setbacks in particular offer an opportunity to exercise or to test his virtue.[72] Seneca presents lurid descriptions of these encounters in strikingly gendered language, as the capricious goddess *Fortuna* struggles with the *virtus* of Roman heroes—and *virtus*, of course, is a distinctively manly affair.[73] The critical struggle, however, is not that of the particular agent against the world so much as the internal struggle for self-mastery, and the *virtus* that matters relates not to any external heroics but to psychological strength[74]—in particular, to the ability 'to be peaceful and calm, looking down from above at injuries or affronts'. To achieve this goal, the political ruler must above all cultivate the critical qualities of *magnanimitas* and *clementia*,[75] and it is when he is indeed the master of himself—and therefore not tyrannised by irrational *Fortuna*— that his people will enjoy peace, remain safe, and be free.[76]

Such is the outline of the Stoic argument that lies at the heart of Seneca's *De clementia*, whose main elements remain in place throughout the history of the mirror-for-princes literature and which is, as Stacey has shown, the central target of Machiavelli's criticism in *The Prince*, even if Seneca is not mentioned by name in the book. References to Seneca or to the Senecan tradition are, however, frequent. Machiavelli picks up on Seneca's medical metaphor when he prescribes the use of '*medicine forti*' (strong medicines) by the prince, in contrast to Seneca's '*mollis medicina*' (gentle medicine), and the examples he uses directly contradict Senecan teaching. 'Seneca and his Renaissance enthusiasts . . . had rigorously lauded the act of sparing conquered royalty on the grounds that it brought the conquering prince unparalleled glory', whereas Machiavelli advises killing them.[77] But the differences between Machiavellian and Senecan political theory are not just a matter of the one being more tough-mindedly ruthless than the other; rather, they develop out of a radically different approach to princely politics itself. The ideological fulcrum of Seneca's argument was his claim that the introduction of the principate had restored to the Romans their freedom. The opening sentence of Machiavelli's book, on the other hand, sharply separates principalities from republics—'All states, all dominions that have held and do hold empire over men have been and are either republics or principalities'—and Machiavelli nowhere suggests that a principality can ever be a free regime.[78] Seneca's argument had depicted the prince as the 'mind' of the 'body politic', whereas Machiavelli's princes are never integrated into the states they rule but always remain external to them, as his language of princes 'acquiring' states tends to suggest. These differences in turn are generated by Machiavelli's total rejection of the Stoic providential rationalism that underpins Seneca's entire political theory. In Machiavelli's view, not only is Stoic providentialism false but belief in its truth fosters a debilitating psychology, which in turn generates disastrous politics.

On the level of metaphysics, Machiavelli denies Stoic determinism. Chapter 25 begins with Machiavelli noting that he is 'not unaware that many people have held and hold today the opinion that things of the world are governed by *fortuna* and by God in such a way that men have no power to correct them with their prudence'. Such people, he suggests, subscribe to a version of what is known as the 'lazy argument' that has been deployed against the Stoics since antiquity: 'and for this reason they could judge that there is no point in sweating much over things: better to leave oneself to be governed by fate [ma lasciarsi governare alla sorte]'.[79] Machiavelli rejects this view, 'so as not to rule out our free will', implicitly denying the Stoic claim that it is submission to providence that guarantees our freedom, and goes on to state his famous opinion, 'I judge that it might be true that fortune is arbiter of half of our actions, but also that she leaves the other half, or close to it, for us to govern'.[80] *Fortuna* becomes pure contingency once more, and politics correspondingly becomes a far more uncertain and unstable kind of activity. When it comes to political psychology, writes Stacey, 'For Machiavelli, the Senecan view of *Fortuna* so widely endorsed is the height of imprudence, a psychological debility inextricably caught up in the doctrine of princely servitude', the error being 'one of counting so heavily upon a benign rationality that you effectively commit yourself to a slavish dependency upon an illusory master', an attitude that 'threatens to make you dependent on others in a very literal sense.'[81] Seneca's confidence in an underlying moral order and divine benevolence generated a politics of constancy, stressing the importance of holding to one's course in the face of apparent—but only apparent—difficulties and trials. For Machiavelli, by contrast, Stoic constancy precisely disables political prudence; the fundamental truth of politics is that times change, and the prince must know when and how to change with the political weather.[82] Constancy can be another word for obstinacy. There are times when it pays to be 'circumspect' (*respettivo*) and times when one must be impetuous (*impetuoso*). For Seneca, as noted above, *virtus* was a matter of internal fortitude rather than external heroics; Machiavelli shows just how far his vision of princely politics stands from Seneca's when he ultimately declares his preference for the *impetuoso* young prince (to which I return below).[83] To borrow Stacey's words once more, and for the last time, Machiavelli's theory 'violently turns back the tropes of the Senecan account. Machiavelli's prince is not armed with virtue. His virtue is to be armed.'[84]

If Machiavelli's political theory as it is presented in *The Prince* is such a systematic repudiation of the Senecan tradition, at every level from deep metaphysics to what we might call particular policy recommendations, the question arises as to how we might best understand Lipsius's *Politica* as some kind of reply to the Florentine. The first thing to note is that the basic framework of Lipsius's argument looks like the traditional Senecan theory, with a number of familiar themes from that tradition presented and discussed above all in books 1 and 2. So, for example, the very first chapter contains a characteristically Senecan claim about the relationship between virtue and fortune:

> So let us take refuge in virtue, as in an asylum, for virtue alone is quiet and safe, and within *its own power, while everything else is subjected to the tyranny of fortune* [Auct. ad Heren. 4.17]. *Against virtue, however, misfortune, losses and injustice are as powerless as a cloud against the sun* [Seneca, Ep. 92.18.3].

The fourth chapter of the first book presents Lipsius's account of fate, or that '*According to the laws of which the immutable pattern of human affairs is woven*'.[85] The virtues themselves are often treated in conventional ways, too, especially in the second book, which is dominated by a discussion of justice and clemency, described as 'the sun' and 'the moon' of the princely virtues.[86] (The account of the latter is lavishly and unsurprisingly illustrated with quotations from Seneca's *De clementia*.) As in the Senecan tradition, and in opposition to Machiavelli's argument, the prince is again described as being the mind of the body politic, and the address to the world's rulers in the preface posits a direct link between the morals of the prince and those of the people, again a familiar ingredient of the Senecan tradition of political thought: 'Does he lead the way to virtue? We follow. To vice? We retreat. Does he perform his duties well and felicitously? We flourish. Unsuccessfully? We fall or perish with him.'[87]

One way to interpret these aspects of Lipsius's presentation is significantly to discount them—to consider them as superficial or largely rhetorical elements, and to read much of the first three books of the *Politica* as a conventional fireworks display of humanist erudition rather than as any kind of distinctive, interesting, or original political argument. What Lipsius gives us, on this view, is a variation on the Machiavellian theme, but one disguised in Senecan clothing. As Waszink puts it, 'Having carved

out for himself a good moral persona, or "ethos", by carefully adhering
to traditional morality, Lipsius in the last three books comes to discuss
and defend practical prudence, reason of state (though not by that word),
prudentia mixta, and a limited use of deceit if it serves the common
good'.[88] It is the second half of the *Politica*—Waszink calls this 'the real-
istic half of the book'—and especially the argument of book 4 that present the most distinctively Lipsian political thought; indeed, on this view,
the first chapter of book 4 can be read as a 'new preface', introducing the
theme of the prince's own personal prudence, with which Lipsius will be
preoccupied for the rest of the work.[89]

To a considerable extent, this is an attractive way to read the *Politica*.
Some of the early discussions do tend towards the platitudinous, for example, that of clemency in book 2. Lipsius begins book 1 by patiently
setting out a series of distinctions in the characteristic manner of the
sixteenth-century logician Peter Ramus. Virtue is divided into two
branches, faith and goodness; faith in turn is divided into belief and worship, and its 'two shoots' are the acceptance of fate and conscience, and
so on. But it is plausible to think that these are not to be taken especially
seriously, for the distinctions themselves do not play much of a role in the
political argument that follows, and elsewhere Lipsius wrote that 'never
will he be great for whom Ramus is great'.[90] Insofar as the view we are
considering prioritises the argument of *Politica* 4, and therefore the more
'Machiavellian' aspects of Lipsius's theory of politics, we should recall
Lipsius's disinclination to alter the text of key passages on lying and religion in response to the objections of the Vatican. There are other ways,
too, in which the more conventionally anti-Machiavellian moments of
the earlier part of the work give way to something else a little later. Machiavelli's critics had been alarmed by his separation of prudence from
conventional ideas about moral virtue,[91] and it appears from book 1 of
the *Politica* that Lipsius agreed with them and was anxious to present his
two 'Leaders' (*Rectores*) of civil life, 'Prudence and Virtue', as being
closely intertwined. Virtue, we are told in 1.1, is a necessary condition for
prudence, for in the absence of virtue what would otherwise be called
prudence can only be 'cunning and malice' (*calliditas ea sit et malitia*).[92]
Prudence, we are told in 1.7, is a necessary condition for virtue ('what
Virtue can there be without Prudence?'), given that 'Virtue consists entirely in Selection and Moderation', and, '[s]ince these cannot exist without Prudence, Virtue cannot'.[93] On the other hand, one of the component
parts of virtue is 'goodness', which Lipsius considers 'does not strictly
speaking belong to this structure of politics' (1.6, quia in hoc Civili aedi-
ficio proprie non ei locus), and in the third book he threatens to undermine his own analytic separation of prudence and virtue altogether when

he quotes Aristotle approvingly as saying that 'prudence is the ruler's characteristic and sole virtue'.[94]

It would be too swift, however, to dismiss these conventional elements in the *Politica* as just so much rhetoric concealing the true Machiavellian teaching. To do so would be to obscure the way in which these components of the argument do not constitute a pure restatement of the traditional Senecan political theory but rather are building blocks in the construction of a modified Senecan framework, which in fact is what allows the text to function both as a critical response to as well as a partial appropriation of Machiavellian political theory.

Take Lipsius's treatment of fate in 1.4. As we have seen, Machiavelli rejected Stoic determinism in the twenty-fifth chapter of *The Prince*, 'so that our free will not be eliminated'.[95] Lipsius's approach to fate, by contrast, is to yoke the question of its existence to Christian piety rather than to Stoic physics. The acceptance of fate is one of the 'shoots' of faith 'which rise up under this tree'; it 'clearly originates in Belief'.[96] Lipsius denies that he is making an argument about strict causal determinism. Indeed, he says of those who do make such an argument, or who prefer to appeal to astrology, that 'they rave' (*delirant*).[97] Lipsius emphasises the role of God, '[f]or if God rules and directs, then He also foresees and decides', so that fate is, in Augustine's words in *The City of God* 5.9, the 'decree and the voice so to speak of the divine order'. The utility of linking the question of fate to divine decree and divine foreknowledge rather than to any kind of physical necessity is that this move gave Lipsius enough space to assert that he was not denying free will at all, an insistence that was strengthened in the later editions after the Vatican objected that 1.4 was still a bit too Stoic for its liking.[98] We saw earlier how Machiavelli gestured at the so-called lazy argument against Stoic fate. In the chapter on fate, as if by way of reply, Lipsius presents a standard Stoic reply to this objection (as he had done in the parallel discussion of Stoic fate in the earlier *De constantia* 1.22, though in the *Politica* he does not employ the technical Stoic language of 'co-fatedness'):

> Then what? You will ask. Should I do nothing, and leave everything to fate? A foolish thought. Yes indeed, you will tread the path which leads to your destiny, and this too happens out of necessity.[99]

As with Machiavelli's earlier treatment of the same topic, there is nothing philosophically deep here, but where Machiavelli's remarks formed part of his campaign to weaken one of the pillars of the Senecan worldview, Lipsius moves to provide some support, chiefly by making it harder to oppose providentialism without being openly irreligious, but also by denying that the consequences follow that so many have found objection-able: the denial of free will, on the one hand, or the point of trying to do anything at all on the other.

Or take the Senecan claim that the prince is in an important sense the mind of the body politic. In *De clementia* this was a part of an argument whose conclusion was that the Romans were still free, though living under kings, because the *princeps* provided rational direction to the po-litical community. This was an argument, furthermore, which also re-quired the idea that this Roman monarchy enjoyed universal jurisdiction, on the grounds that if it did not, the structural analogy of the prince to the Stoic wise man (*sapiens*) would be bound to fail. Lipsius accepts the analogy, but in his hands it may not be much more than an analogy. So, for example, in the epistle dedicated to the world's rulers, in a passage referred to earlier, he asserts that 'just as in a body the spirit cannot be healthy or unhealthy without strength or weakness at the same time tak-ing hold of its functions, neither can the Prince be well or ill, without similar consequences'.[100] Or, as part of his defence of monarchy in 2.2, Lipsius remarks that '*it seems that one body politic should be governed by one soul. Like one ship by one captain.*'[101] Lipsius does not, however, embrace either of the strong Stoic claims. We might say, with Waszink, that Lipsius 'transferred Stoic ideas about the universality of mankind, governed by a cosmic plan, to the universality of the realm, governed by a prudent prince', for he nowhere suggests that the prince is a universal monarch, let alone any kind of sage.[102] He never claims, furthermore, that the subjects of princely rule are free, a striking agreement with Machia-velli's argument in *The Prince*. (This particular point was obscured to English readers of the *Politica*, for William Jones rendered a fragment of Seneca in 2.6 as 'the thraldome of thy subiects is not committed unto thee, but their libertie, defence and protection', though the word *libertas* did not appear in the original text [civium non servitutem tibi traditam, sed tutelam].[103] As various commentators have observed, Lipsius has lit-tle to say about liberty in his political writings.)

But this is about as far as the Machiavellism goes here. Machiavelli's denial that the subjects of a prince retain their liberty is part of his effort to drive a wedge between the prince and his principality and to treat the former as standing outside the latter and owing nothing to it. The prince and his principality do not make up a harmonious whole; rather, the one 'acquires' the other and uses it in the service of his—not its—ends. Al-though Lipsius may agree that the prince's subjects are not politically free, he nevertheless still insists, against Machiavelli, that the well-constituted state is an integrated unity of the prince and the people. Machiavelli in *The Prince* is chiefly interested in the 'new prince' who comes to power either through *virtù* (which is to say, by dint of his own arms) or *fortuna* (by dint of other people's), and he has little to say about hereditary principalities. Lipsius, by contrast, is only interested in considering the prince who obtains his throne through the operation of the appropriate domestic constitutional mechanisms, 'in accordance with law and custom', either by election or through legitimate succession.[104] 'Whichever of these is the right one', Lipsius contends, 'all other ways are not right: for *no one has by good means exercised a power that he had obtained disgracefully*'.[105] The Machiavellian prince treats his principality as a resource to be exploited in his quest for glory; the Lipsian prince ought to work, by contrast and fully in line with the Senecan tradition, for the '*bonum publicum*' which is 'nothing other than the subjects' welfare, safety, and salvation',[106] and to have, in Cicero's words, 'the happy life of its citizens for his aim'.[107]

In the famous discussion of 'mixed prudence'—that is, of prudence mixed with some kind of deceit—Lipsius argues that it is permissible for the prince 'to depart slightly from human laws; but only in order to preserve his position, never to extend it. For *Necessity, being a great defender of the weakness of man, breaks every law*.'[108] Richard Tuck acutely commented on this passage that here 'Lipsius captured exactly the difference between these late sixteenth-century theorists and Machiavelli, or what they took the difference to be', that '[l]aws could be broken for *preservation*, but not for any other reason, such as the enhancement of a ruler's or his country's *glory*'.[109] That is correct, though it seems to me that this position flows fairly straightforwardly from the modified Senecan standpoint I've sketched above, one that urges on the prince the pursuit of the common good, which is understood specifically in terms of the safety of the subject population. For Tuck, by contrast, it is Lipsius's 'sympathy with scepticism' that generates above all his interest in prioritising preservation (and especially self-preservation) over other goods,[110] but this is a view that seems problematic to me in at least two respects. First, Tuck had suggested that the argument about fate or providence in *De constantia* was 'dependent in some ways on the notion of self-interest: for Lipsius was concerned to stress that the sheer intractability of external events means that men are usually *necessitated* to act in certain ways—the necessitation coming from the combination of unalterable fate and the need to protect oneself'.[111] Yet it is hard to make the claim that *De constantia* champions a politics of self-preservation in quite this way, given that the character 'Lipsius' in the dialogue is presented as someone whose concern for self-preservation is precisely what has induced him to leave the war-torn Low Countries for the safety of Vienna, and it is the argument of his interlocutor 'Langius' that aims to persuade him that self-mastery, in particular the control of the passions and the cultivation of the virtue of constancy, is a significantly more important goal than any mere considerations of bodily self-preservation: death, for example, is described in properly Stoic fashion as one of the 'false evils'.[112] Second, as Anthony Levi has argued, it is more plausible to interpret Lipsius's occasional favourable references to Sceptical arguments not as indicating any broadly sympathetic orientation towards Scepticism of his own but rather specifically as a tactical move to downplay or deny the most obviously un-Christian implications of the more Stoic arguments he was advancing elsewhere—concerning the omnipotence of the wise man, for example, or the impossibility of his sinning.[113]

What, then, of Machiavelli's charge that Stoic politics disables prudence? We have seen part of Lipsius's reply already: prudence is a matter of choice, but where Machiavelli charged that Stoic fate denies the exercise of choice, Lipsius denied this, with his assertion of the compatibility of fate and free will through his emphasis on understanding fate in terms of divine foreknowledge rather than causal determinism. Machiavelli's further charge was that the distinctive Stoic virtue of constancy was disastrous for prudence, as good politics requires the kind of flexibility constancy precludes. Lipsius's countersuggestion is that Stoic constancy is distinctively the virtue of the *subject*, as he had argued in *De constantia* and as he reminds his reader at the start of the *Politica*, where he writes that in that work, he has 'equipped citizens for endurance and obedience',[114] or a virtue of the *counsellor*, arguing in 3.5 that there are five specific virtues a good counsellor needs to cultivate, these being faith (*pietas*), independence (*libertas*), constancy (*constantia*), modesty (*modestia*), and discretion (*silentio*).[115] Lipsius also requests that the character of the government (*forma imperii*) be 'Stern, Constant and Limited'.[116] What he means by constancy here is conservatism with respect to legislation: the prince is exhorted not to tamper with existing laws unless it is absolutely necessary to do so.[117] In the sphere of policy rather than legislation, however, Lipsius nowhere suggests that the kind of constancy that the older Senecan tradition had celebrated and Machiavelli had despised was any kind of specifically princely virtue.

For both Lipsius and Machiavelli, as for other writers, prudence is the art of making good choices. Lipsius indeed defines prudence as 'the understanding and choosing of what is to be sought or avoided, both in private and in public';[118] prudence, suggests Machiavelli, 'consists in knowing how to recognize the qualities of inconveniences, and in picking the less bad as good'.[119] Again, for Machiavelli, for Lipsius, and for other humanists, the cultivation of prudence requires above all knowledge of and reflection on history, especially classical history. Machiavelli's masterpiece was—to give it its full title—*Discourses on the First Decade of Titus Livy*. Lipsius had written in his dedication of his 1574 edition of

Tacitus to Emperor Maximilian that 'Tacitus is a penetrating writer, God knows, and a prudent one: and if ever there was a time when men could profit from reading him, it is now',[120] and there are over five hundred quotations from his writings in the *Politica*—more than twice as many as from Seneca, the next most frequently quoted author—243 from the *Annals*, 219 from the *Histories*, 44 from the *Agricola*, and 22 from the Germania.[121]

Machiavelli and Lipsius agree that the study of the ancient historians is a vital element in the cultivation of prudence, and that whereas reflection on history can generate valuable maxims for the prince, these are maxims, not general rules with universal application. Part of prudence is knowing good maxims, and an even more important part of prudence is knowing when to act on them and when not. 'The Prudence I want to be in the Prince himself', writes Lipsius at the start of book 4, 'is hard to bind down to rules', for 'of particular affairs, there is an infinite number', and because 'what we call Prudence is in reality unstable and changeable in every respect', '[f]or what else is it, than a selecting and combining of things which relate to each other now in this way, then in that way?'[122] Political enquiry cannot manufacture anything that we could plausibly call knowledge, which deals in certainties; nevertheless, although Lipsius 'and other writers grope about in darkness', he refuses to 'remain silent' but will do the best he can.[123] For Machiavelli, too, the study of history can generate maxims, and *The Prince* and the *Discourses* are full of these, but more important than maxims are the examples of political leaders to imitate (or not, as the case may be).[124]

The personal prudence of the prince is critically important for both writers, but the Lipsian prince receives far more assistance from outside sources. In Lipsius's rendering of prudence, its 'parents' are *use* (experience) and *memory* or *remembrance* (*memoria*), and much of the latter can be codified and presented to the prince in books such as the *Politica*. Since the Lipsian prince is less likely to be a man of singular excellence— Lipsius favours hereditary succession, after all, which is not known to be a reliable mechanism for securing outstanding political qualities in the ruler—one thing the prince does need to learn is how to take good advice, and much of book 3 of the *Politica* is devoted to examining the roles of ministers and counsellors. Machiavelli's interest is in the new prince who comes to power through his own arms, in other words, one who is far more likely to possess striking political abilities, and he cautions against the prince relying on advice from anybody. Either the counsellor will be more prudent than the prince, in which case he cannot be trusted not to take advantage of his boss, or he will be less prudent, in which case there is nothing to be gained by listening to his advice, let alone by acting on it.[125] It would be a gross exaggeration to think that Lipsius gives us a description of the workings of an impersonal state bureaucracy, for his prince remains the central political actor, but his account nevertheless marks a departure from Machiavelli's single-minded emphasis on the rule, and role, of *uno solo*.

Machiavelli and Lipsius clearly disagree on the ends of political action, as we have seen. Lipsius's prince aims at serving the common good, understood in terms of the security and welfare of the subject population; Machiavelli's prince acts to secure his own glory. These divergent ends shape the kind of princely behaviour that each writer encourages, to the extent, I think, that it is reasonable to employ one of Machaivelli's own distinctions to illuminate the contrast. In the twenty-fifth chapter of *The Prince*, in the celebrated discussion of *Fortuna*, Machiavelli describes two kinds of princes, one who proceeds 'with caution' (*con respetto*), the other 'with impetuosity' (*con impeto*),[126] and whether each flourishes or fails depends entirely on what Machiavelli calls 'the quality of the times'. An ideal prince would be one who could choose to be either *respettivo* or *impetuoso* according to the nature of the times in which he found himself embroiled, but Machiavelli thinks this is impossible: no man is 'so prudent as to know how to accommodate himself to this, whether because he cannot deviate from what nature inclines him to or also because, when one has always flourished by walking on one path, he cannot be persuaded to depart from it'.[127] Given that a prince has to be one or the other and that neither disposition can be guaranteed to succeed, Machiavelli plumps unhesitatingly for the latter, notoriously because

> fortune is a woman: and it is necessary, if one wants to hold her down, to beat her and strike her down. And one sees that she lets herself be won more by the impetuous than by those who proceed coldly. And so, always like a woman, she is the friend of the young, because they are less cautious, more ferocious, and command her with more audacity.[128]

There's nothing in the *Politica* to suggest that Lipsius favours this kind of impetuosity. Indeed, his stern warnings against temerity might very well stand in for his opinions on the Machaivellian *impetuoso* prince. In the longest discussion of temerity, in 5.5, Lipsius insists that rashness (*temeritas*) 'must be absent from the beginnings of war', asserting, 'War is a matter of great weight: it demands deliberation, and slow deliberation',[129] and reporting various classical authorities as saying, 'be sure that every war is started easily, but is then very difficult to end', 'that even a just war must be abhorred', and that one should 'neither provoke war, nor fear it'.[130] When it comes to waging war, one must act with caution.

Machiavelli criticises *temerità*, too, but a survey of his examples suggests that the two writers deploy the notion in significantly different ways. Machiavelli uses the language of rashness in a number of ways, but most characteristically to describe courses of action that create situations in which the prince is quite unnecessarily exposed to great danger or puts himself into the power of another. In *The Prince*, for example, Machiavelli criticises the Venetians' rashness for bringing the far more powerful king of France into Italy, so that while they secured a small amount of new territory in Lombardy, he grabbed much of the rest of northern Italy;[131] or Antoninus Caracalla, who 'had put to death with disgrace a brother of that centurion, and threatened him every day; yet he kept him in his bodyguard, which was a rash policy likely to bring ruin, as happened to him', when the centurion subsequently killed him.[132] The *Discourses* contain the marvellous story of Pope Julius II and Giavampagolo Baglioni, the tyrant of Perugia. The impeccably *impetuoso* Julius, 'carried along by that fury with which he governed all things', 'put himself with a single guard in the hands of his enemy', so that the 'prudent men who were with the pope'—these included Machiavelli himself—thought the pope to have shown *temerità* for exposing himself to such danger and Giovampagolo *viltà* (cowardice) for not having taken advantage of the situation and killing the pope when he was in his power.[133] The judgement of *temerità*, however, pertains not to the pope's characteristic hastiness or aggressiveness in general, however much these qualities might have helped to generate his behaviour at Bologna, but specifically to his making himself vulnerable to his enemy. Lipsius's notion of *temeritas* is far broader than that, including many of what Machiavelli would consider the most praiseworthy elements of impetuosity itself.

We might say, then, that one substantial difference between Machiavelli and Lipsius when it comes to political prudence concerns their respective attitudes to risk. Both can agree that 'when times are quiet' the prince ought to be building the metaphorical 'dikes and dams' against the possibility of the river of fortune flooding its banks.[134] But having made these kinds of preparations, the most impressive prince for Machiavelli is the one who plays for the highest stakes and who is prepared to bet everything on an uncertain outcome, especially when it involves audacious belligerence. Lipsius's prince isn't enjoined to engage in anything like this kind of high-stakes aggression, and when he writes (to quote the fine words of William Jones's English translation) that 'All things yeeld obedience vnto Prudence, euen Fortune her selfe',[135] one can't help thinking that this is nothing like Machiavelli's counsel for the *impetuoso* prince with respect to *Fortuna* but rather the prudence he is recommending is that which systematically contains the risks the *respettivo* prince faces, playing the percentages in order to grind out a victory against fortune over the long run.

CODA: SITUATING LIPSIUS

In his well-known lecture of 1 February 1978, Michel Foucault gave an account of what he called the 'enormous literature on government' that 'explodes in the middle of the sixteenth century', and we are now well placed to see where Lipsius's *Politica* stands in relation to that body of work.[136] It is always tempting, after all, to draw connections between Lipsius's project and Foucault's. In *Discipline and Punish*, for example, the earliest examples of the disciplinary model of social institutions that Foucault considers are military manuals from the late sixteenth and early seventeenth century, which were to some extent plagiarised from Lipsius's writings on warfare, though Lipsius is not mentioned in that book,[137] and it is striking that Foucault told his audience at the Collège de France at the start of the lecture on governmentality that '[t]he sixteenth century return to Stoicism revolves around this reactualization of the problem of how to govern oneself'.[138] Foucault describes the literature on government, furthermore, as standing in a self-consciously critical relationship to Machiavelli's *Prince*, which he calls a '*point de répulsion*' for the genre.[139] In particular, the works on government rejected the idea that 'the Prince exists in a relationship of singularity and externality, of transcendence, to his principality',[140] such that, for Machiavelli, 'What is to be protected is the principality as the relationship of the Prince to his subjects and his territory, and not directly, immediately, fundamentally, or primarily, the territory and its inhabitants'.[141]

So far, so Lipsian, but perhaps not that much farther, as it is at about this point that the discontinuities between the government literature as Foucault describes it and the *Politica* become apparent. The works on government 'do not exactly present themselves as advice to the prince, nor yet as political science', though this is a phrase that does work quite well as a rough description of the *Politica*. For Foucault, 'The art of government essentially appears in this literature as having to answer the question of how to introduce economy—that is to say, the proper way of managing individuals, goods, and wealth . . . —how to introduce this meticulous attention, this type of relationship between the father and the family, into the management of the state?'[142] Lipsius, on the other hand, is almost completely silent about economic life and says nothing about the management of other parts of the society, whether fathers governing their families or with respect to any other kind of what Rousseau would much later call 'partial associations'. Concerning the literature on government, Foucault describes the way in which the juridical language of sovereignty and the common good gets replaced by a language of arranging things in the right way in order to lead them to 'an end suitable for each of the things to be governed'[143]—yet as we have seen, Lipsius repeatedly deploys the language of the common or public good in the *Politica*.

Even here, however, we can plausibly read the *Politica* as a transitional text, rooted in the advice-to-princes literature but leaning strongly towards the literature on government. First, Lipsius may not say much—indeed, anything at all—about economic life, but he is clear that *commercium* does make up one-half of civil life, just not the half that will be considered in the *Politica*, which is *imperium*.[144] Second, Foucault considered the jurists' notions of sovereignty generated a circle: '[W]hat does this common good ... which is regularly invoked by jurists and laid down as the very end of sovereignty comprise?', he asked, and answered, 'They say that the common good exists when all subjects obey the law without fail', so that 'the end of sovereignty is circular; it refers back to the exercise of sovereignty', something that he thought was 'not so far removed from Machiavelli saying that the Prince's main objective must be to preserve his principality; we always come back to this circular relationship of sovereignty, or the principality, to itself'.[145] It's hard to convict the *Politica* of the same kind of circularity: the juridical language of sovereignty isn't much in evidence, and when Lipsius does appeal to the idea of the common good, his appeal lacks this circular structure, defining the common good in terms of 'welfare, safety, and salvation' (*commodum, securitas, salus*),[146] goals not far removed from what Foucault would go on to call the terrain of biopolitics. There is, in truth, not much on the laws in the *Politica*, beyond Lipsius's appeal to the prince to keep them much as they are.[147]

If the key concern of governmentality is, as Gorski has put it, 'the manner in which the conduct of an ensemble of individuals becomes implicated to a greater and greater degree in the exercise of state power',[148] it is striking to note just how little Lipsius has to say about conduct. He says almost nothing about the way in which civilians will or ought to behave in a well-governed principality, and while interpreters like Oestreich have suggested that for Lipsius, the army is a template for the organisation of the rest of society, we ought to reject this view. Lipsius does explain how discipline is to be achieved in the army in book 5 of the *Politica*, but it is a strange kind of wishful thinking, substantially short of textual evidence, to project this explanation onto the body of the society as a whole. Lipsius might have recommended the importance of citizens' disciplining their own passions in the earlier *De constantia*, with various military metaphors in play throughout that work, but what is described there is a story about the capacities of rational citizens to discipline themselves, not a story in which state power is implicated in the disciplining of the population to any significant degree. Indeed, contrary to Lipsius's reputation as a social disciplinarian, we might plausibly think that his combination in the *Politica* of a relative silence about the lives of ordinary citizens together with his insistence on the merits of a professional standing army in place of any citizen militia in practice reduces the state's disciplinary role vis-à-vis the bulk of the male citizenry, who will not, after all, periodically be having to appear on the parade ground for military drill.

While the *Politica* has affinities with the literature on government, then, and perhaps even a significant tendency in that direction, it belongs far more comfortably within somewhat old-fashioned notions of the mainstream of the tradition of political thought, poised theoretically as well as chronologically between Machiavelli and Hobbes. With respect to Machiavelli, we have explored the ways in which Lipsius can be read as offering a reply to the Florentine's critique of Senecan political thought. With respect to Hobbes, we have seen any number of proto-Hobbesian themes in play in Lipsius's argument, whether the concern for peace and the physical security of the population, or the development of a prudence around the notions of use and memory, or the disinclination to consider the subjects of a sovereign as being free in anything like the traditional republican sense, or support for the state's authority over the religious sphere, or the strong opposition to a politics and psychology of glory. Before considering the passage from Lipsius to Hobbes in the third chapter, however, we need to turn our attention to Hugo Grotius and to the origins of the modern natural rights tradition in a reworking of Ciceronian Stoicism. This is the subject of the second chapter.

Grotius, Stoicism, and *Oikeiosis*

THERE HAS BEEN CONSIDERABLE DISAGREEMENT over the interpretation of Grotius over the past thirty years, especially concerning the foundations of his system of natural law, revolving in particular around the arguments that have been put forward by Richard Tuck in a series of articles and books over the course of his career.[1] Tuck has emphasised the role of self-interest in anchoring Grotius's system, especially when self-interest is understood specifically as the desire for self-preservation, conceding only a minimal role to any kind of principle of sociability. Grotius argued like this, Tuck suggests, to meet the challenge of contemporary scepticism by providing an account of natural law whose foundations were sufficiently uncontroversial that even a thoroughgoing sceptic would have to acknowledge their validity. While this interpretation has been highly influential over the past quarter century,[2] both of its major components have also been heavily criticised. Perez Zagorin and Thomas Mautner, for example, have challenged the idea that Grotius's project had anything to do with scepticism at all;[3] Robert Shaver has argued that Grotius 'grounds natural law in sociableness rather than self-interest';[4] and Brian Tierney has suggested that 'his doctrine of natural law and natural rights was built around these two principles—self-love and sociability—not only or primarily on the first one'.[5]

In the passage in the *Prolegomena* to *De Jure Belli ac Pacis* (hereafter *DJBP*) that stands at the heart of these controversies, Grotius made his famous claim about *appetitus societatis*. In the 1631 edition of his book he identified this *appetitus societatis* with the Stoics' *oikeiosis*, and it may be that understanding Grotius's use of this Stoic concept is crucial to coming to a satisfactory overall characterization of his argument. Here are his words, in the 1738 English translation:

> Now amongst the Things peculiar to Man is his Desire of Society, that is, a certain Inclination to live with those of his own Kind, not in any Manner whatever, but peaceably, and in a Community regulated according to the best of his Understanding; which Disposition the Stoicks termed *oikeiosis*. Therefore the Saying, that every Creature is led by

Nature to seek its own private Advantage, expressed thus universally, must not be granted.[6]

It was never the case that Stoicism was absent from Tuck's account of Grotius. His 1993 *Philosophy and Government* sketches an important story about a passage from the Stoic-inflected 'new humanism' of Justus Lipsius and Michel de Montaigne to the foundations of Grotius's system.[7] In this story, however, the contribution of Stoicism concerns the importance of self-preservation and the achievement of a certain kind of psychic tranquillity rather than any kind of distinctively Stoic sociability. With regard to the arguments about sociability, whether concerning the ancient authors or the early moderns, Tuck's approach has been either to minimise or to draw attention away from the possible contribution of the Stoics, and often to play up by way of contrast an Epicurean strand of thinking about the natural society of the human race. We can see this especially in another of Tuck's books, *The Rights of War and Peace*, in two places: first in the footnote on *oikeiosis* itself in the chapter on humanism, and second in the later treatment of Grotius.

Tuck's footnote read as follows:

> For an account of the Stoic concept, see S. G. Pembroke, 'Oikeiosis', in *Problems in Stoicism*, ed. A. A. Long (University of London Press, 1971), 114–49. As Pembroke makes clear, the Stoic concept is highly complex: at one point it touches on Epicureanism (as Carneades the sceptic in fact alleged—p.129, while at another it touches on Aristotelianism (pp. 132–6)). Renaissance accounts of the matter are equally confused, and little is to be gained by attributing to any writer a 'Stoic' notion of natural sociability, without a great deal of further exposition about what they might actually have believed.[8]

The final warning here is sound, and one of the tasks of this chapter is precisely to try to set out in some detail just what Grotius might have believed on this score. The earlier invocation of Epicureanism, however, is not quite right. What Pembroke implies in the passage to which Tuck refers is that any link between *oikeiosis* and the Epicureans existed in the imaginations of their Sceptical critics rather than in any philosophical reality, and it was not Carneades who was specifically associated with this criticism. What the remark about an affinity with Epicureanism helps to obscure, furthermore, is a far more important fact about the Stoics' *oikeiosis*, repeated across the major sources, namely, the role it played as a building block in the Stoics' fundamental argument *against* the Epicureans. A few sentences into his exposition of *oikeiosis*, for example, Diogenes Laertius observes that the Stoics 'hold it false to say, as some people do [that is, the Epicureans], that pleasure is the object of animals' first impulse', and Cicero has his character 'Cato' remark in *De finibus* that 'the Stoics point out that babies seek what is good for them and avoid the opposite before they ever feel pleasure or pain'.[9]

When it comes to Tuck's discussion of Grotius in the same book, Epicureanism is again placed in the foreground. First, the argument of *De Jure Praedae* is identified as broadly Epicurean:

> So when Grotius talked about human sociability in the *De Indis* [i.e., *De Jure Praedae*], he did not mean . . . that natural men were sociable in anything like the *Aristotelian* sense. Instead, we might say that they were sociable in the *Epicurean* sense, for . . . Epicureanism did permit a thin notion of human sociability.[10]

The argument of the first, 1625 edition of *DJBP* is then identified as being 'in fact an expansion of the arguments of the *De Indis*',[11] but two things combined, according to Tuck, to make it harder for Grotius's readers to understand the theory in its true, Epicurean colours. First, 'Grotius did not make it anything like as clear as he had done in his earlier work what the theoretical foundations of his argument were',[12] and second, the changes Grotius made to the text of the *Prolegomena* of the 1631 edition (when he was 'trying extremely hard to move back to the United Provinces' and therefore sought to make his 'views appear more acceptable to the Aristotelian, Calvinist culture of his opponents'[13]) further obscured the real character of his argument, with one of the major changes being the explicit invocation of Stoic *oikeiosis* (or, as it was misspelled in that edition, *aikeiosin*). Tuck's argument about the extent and significance of the various changes to the text has been contested in the recent literature.[14] My concern here, however, is a slightly different one, for much depends on the plausibility of the 'Epicurean' reading of the argument of *DJBP*. Indeed, we might say that to the extent that Grotius's argument of 1625 can be plausibly understood as a kind of Stoic argument, to that same extent the introduction of explicit language of Stoic sociability in 1631 functions better as an accurate description of the argument of the first edition than as any attempt to obscure anything about it.

J. B. Schneewind, who writes on Grotius somewhat under the influence of Tuck's interpretation, has warned against the attempt to find too much Stoicism in *DJBP*:

> Cicero had sketched a Stoic theory of natural law in two works whose influence was not lessened by the fact that they were preserved only in fragmentary form. Since Grotius of course knew these fragments, it is tempting to think that he was developing a Stoic doctrine of natural

law for modern times. Yet I think this would be a serious mistake. We do not see him appealing to any of the metaphysics behind Stoic ethics. He refuses to say anything, in the development of his theory of natural law, about the relation of our reason and the divine mind. He sets aside, as I have noted, questions of the highest good and of the best form of the state, both of which Cicero discusses at length. He does not assure us that all apparent evils are truly goods or at least matters of indifference to us; he offers no therapy; and he says nothing about individual perfection.[15]

Much of this is quite right. It would be foolish to claim that Grotius is any kind of pure Stoic, given the various omissions Schneewind mentions here. It is also clear that other philosophical frameworks can be helpful for elucidating aspects of Grotius's project. Annabel Brett's discussion of Grotius as a civic philosopher, for example, tracing out the details of his exploitation of Connanus's theory of justice, is illuminating.[16] But while it is true that Grotius does not supply from Stoic sources the various items on Schneewind's list, it is not too strong to suggest that he *is* 'developing a Stoic doctrine of natural law for modern times', or, perhaps better, to say that the doctrine of natural law he is developing is shot through with distinctively Stoic content, and that we would do well to map the contours of that Stoic element in more detail than we have managed thus far.

A small number of scholars have been exploring the Stoic aspects of Grotius's theory. Max Pohlenz's pioneering work on reconstructing Stoic ethics made him interested in Grotius's appropriation of *oikeiosis*,[17] and Matija Berljak devoted a major part of her short study of Grotius to a consideration of 'lo stoicismo come ispirazione di Ugo Grozio', with particular attention to the references she found in Grotius's argument to the later Roman Stoicism of, especially, the emperor Marcus Aurelius.[18] It is only recently, however, that the matter has attracted the most detailed attention. It is perhaps curious that the collection of essays called *Grotius and the Stoa* does not offer a significant examination of Grotius and *oikeiosis*. Jon Miller touches on the subject in his chapter on innate ideas,[19] and although he suggests there that 'other chapters in this book will explore ... Grotius's version of that Stoic doctrine',[20] in fact they do not. Reinhard Brandt's contribution to the same volume, an essay on the tradition of *oikeiosis* in the modern age, for example, concentrates overwhelmingly on Locke.[21] Three recent contributions from Laurens C. Winkel, Jon Miller, and Benjamin Straumann have, however, offered detailed discussion of the Stoic thematic in Grotius. Winkel's essay concentrates on a narrow philological assignment, the ancient origins of the phrase *appetitus societatis*, and he presents the various threads of argument that link it back to the Stoic tradition, ultimately tracing the phrase itself to texts by Cicero and Seneca.[22] The other two essays—Jon Miller's essay on moral deliberation in Grotius and Spinoza and Benjamin Straumann's article on *appetitus societatis / oikeiosis* as central to Grotius's argument on behalf of just war—are properly philosophical. Both of these papers engage directly with the controversies over self-interest and sociability mentioned above: Miller is 'not convinced that it is necessary to decide whether, for Grotius, self-interest or "sociableness" was the more basic instinct', owing to his belief that 'Grotius took self-interest and the desire for society to be aspects of one fundamental human impulse';[23] Straumann concludes his essay by asserting that for Grotius, 'self-preservation is in accordance with natural law only to the extent that such self-preservation is just', so that 'Tuck's view that self-preservation is the foundation of Grotius's natural law must thus be contested'.[24]

This chapter aims to be a contribution to this last body of literature. First I present an outline of a Stoic theory of natural law, following Cicero (mostly) from among the ancients and Julia Annas (mostly) from among the more recent commentators, but I also draw particular attention (here following A. A. Long) to the connection between the argument about *oikeiosis* and the argument about private property ownership. I then present some of the evidence to suggest that Grotius's argument in *DJBP* fits this model quite closely.

An Outline of a Stoic Natural Law Argument

Two Methodological Preambles

The following discussion frequently refers to Cicero and to the idea of 'Ciceronian Stoicism'. This label is problematic, for one obvious reason. Cicero was not a Stoic, claiming instead an allegiance to the New Academy. This does not mean, however, that the term is vacuous. Cicero's works are among the most important sources for our knowledge of (especially) the ethics of the Hellenistic Stoics, in large part through texts such as *De finibus*, in which Cicero presents a lengthy discussion of those ethics through the mouth of a spokesman (in this case Cato the Younger).[25] It is also clear that Cicero's major political writings draw heavily from Stoic sources, most obviously in *De officiis*, which is heavily indebted to Panaetius's lost Stoic treatise *Peri tou kathekontos*, but also other works, such as *De re publica* or *De legibus*, which have a strong Stoic influence, especially when it comes to the arguments these texts present on behalf of natural law. 'Ciceronian Stoicism' is a term that may be used, then, even if it must always be used with some care.

The second methodological preamble is that in what follows, I draw to a considerable extent on what Julia Annas has written about *oikeiosis* in her book, *The Morality of Happiness*.[26] In a world in which the shelves heave with various scholars' rival expositions of Stoic ethics, it is worth saying one or two things about this choice. The first, shared among a number of other commentators, is that her discussion of *oikeiosis* gives pride of place to the long passage from *De finibus* 3.16–21, which is also the Stoic text that is doing the most work in *DJBP*.[27] The second reason for putting Annas's account in the spotlight owes to her determination to write about Hellenistic ethics substantially detached from the sects' wider claims about logic and physics. This has been a controversial decision, as her subsequent exchange with John Cooper demonstrates,[28] but it is helpful in the present context. This is one in which the key ancient text is *De finibus*, a work that presupposes one can have meaningful discussions of ethics in the absence of, for example, considerations of cosmology; in which we are considering the reception of Stoic argument in an early modern world whose grasp of ancient philosophical doctrine was often uncertain and quite eclectic; and in which the particular problem to hand concerns a thinker who appears to be attracted to Cicero's (or, rather, 'Cato's') argument precisely so that he might be able to stress the origins of natural law in human nature, and who inserted his notorious *etiamsi daremus* clause to signal that the argument could stand independently of wider claims about the nature of the universe and God's place in that universe. A third reason for finding Annas a particularly helpful guide is her insistence on the separation of 'personal' from 'social' *oikeiosis*.[29] This is, as she acknowledges, a controversial move that many commentators reject, and nothing in what I say is intended to endorse her interpretation of the Stoics' *oikeiosis* on this point against her rivals'. It is, however, a helpful distinction to bear in mind when considering the passage from Cicero to Grotius, first, because what Annas calls 'personal' and what she calls 'social' *oikeiosis* are neatly separated by space in 'Cato's' account in *De finibus* 3, with the former being discussed at 3.16–21 and the latter at 3.62–71, and second, because when we turn to consider Grotius's argument, the terminology of 'personal' and 'social' *oikeiosis* remains quite useful in analysing what he has to say about the foundations of natural law.

Oikeiosis

It is often reckoned that the idea of *oikeiosis* stands near the centre of Stoic ethics.[30] As Annas notes, *oikeiosis* 'can seem more mysterious than it really is, because there is no good single English equivalent'. She prefers 'familiarization'; others (including Long and Sedley, for example) prefer 'appropriation', or 'orientation'.[31] Curiously, the problem of translation doesn't apply to its antonym, *allotriosis*, which can be unproblematically rendered as 'alienation', a term that resonates powerfully through the history of legal thought and, later, social theory. *Oikeiosis* is a process in which nature is the active agent and through which a person becomes familiarized with him- or herself, on the one hand, and with other human beings on the other.[32] 'An animal's first impulse', wrote Diogenes Laertius, reporting the Stoic view, 'is to self-preservation'.[33] *Oikeiosis* does incorporate a kind of self-love, but what the Stoics insisted on is that *oikeiosis* includes both the tendency to look after ourselves *and* the tendency to develop concern for the interests and the well-being of others. This is why Miller's Stoic interpretation of Grotius, for example, can lead him to judge that self-interest and sociability might be 'aspects of one fundamental human impulse'.[34]

The story about self-love is a developmental story that begins with a description of the way in which infants are born with an instinctive desire for self-preservation, shown by the ease with which they learn to feed from their mother, pursue warmth, and so on. Through their natural development they come to possess a sense of their own identity, especially as being temporally extended creatures, and their search for natural goods to keep them going is also the setting for their first experience of the value of practical reason in obtaining those goods, as they gradually learn when to assent and when to refuse to assent to the appearances with which they are confronted. We come to acquire habits of reasoning, and we learn to reason consistently and to make comparisons across relevantly similar cases. Initially, we value the utility of practical reason solely as a means to obtaining natural goods. But 'it often happens', Cicero's 'Cato' tells us, 'that when one is introduced to someone, one comes to value that person more highly than one does the person who made the introduction'.[35] According to the Stoic story, the natural maturation of reason leads to individuals first discovering that they don't *just* value practical reasoning as a means (so that they prefer to achieve their ends through the use of reason, as opposed to by any other means), and later to an understanding that not only is the exercise of practical reason to be valued for its own sake, we prefer its exercise to the possession of the goods it helps to secure—or, as Annas puts it, that the reasons why we act on a matter are more important than the consequences of acting on those reasons.[36] The culmination of the process of personal *oikeiosis* is the fully rational human being's knowledge that, properly understood, the exercise of practical reason is the *only* good, and coincides perfectly with both virtue and the life according to nature—all of which are different ways of describing the same thing. It is important to recognise, though, that when one is acting rationally, one is still acting to obtain the kinds of things we might have been seeking to obtain before—self-preservation, health, security, wealth, and so on. It's just that we now think of these ends as being preferred indifferents, to use the Stoics' distinctive technical term, rather than as strictly goods, a term that is now restricted to virtue—to rational activity itself.

The story about how we come to have concern for other human beings by a parallel process of natural rational development is the story of what Annas calls social *oikeiosis*. If the primal instinct that gets things going in the earlier narrative is the infant's concern for its own self-preservation, social *oikeiosis* is similarly grounded (psychologically, at least) in the concern that a parent has for its own offspring. Plutarch thought this was ludicrous, and ridiculed Chrysippus for the suggestion that we have concern for our offspring as soon as we ourselves are born,[37] but, as Annas remarks, 'there is no problem if we take the point to be that at birth we have primitive forms of the instincts for both self-concern and for other-concern', even if the latter is one that 'will not come into play until we have offspring'. If and when it does, 'it is a form of primitive instinct, not something learned'.[38] The Stoics' thought is that care for our own offspring is instinctual, but that the same instinct can lead us to care for the well-being of others who are close to us, too. As with the story about personal *oikeiosis*, concerns for self-interest in the form of mutual advantage can play a role in the initial fostering of such a concern, but the relationship that comes into being, if it develops properly—naturally, rationally—isn't then one that is wholly reducible to that mutual advantage. The Stoics' contention is that once this process begins, there is no rational place for it to stop, so that the human being with the most fully developed rationality—in other words, the Stoics' celebrated sage—will be someone who is able to treat everyone's concerns as having equal weight in his or her deliberations just because of their human identity. Borrowing Annas's words again, 'this attitude, of impartial concern for the interests of others, is the basis of justice and of communal life',[39] and the attitude of the Stoic sage is the fullest expression of Stoic cosmopolitanism. If *De finibus* 3 offers an exemplary presentation of personal *oikeiosis*, the richest description of the operation of social *oikeiosis* is perhaps found in the well-known 'concentric circles' passage from Hierocles,[40] though this passage is philosophically problematic,[41] and, as I discuss below, it is interesting that Grotius does not exploit this passage in his own work.

Whether or not we ought to understand personal and social *oikeiosis* as being basically separable processes or not, it is worth seeing how elements in the two different stories interact to reinforce one another. Personal *oikeiosis* includes the development from valuing practical reason instrumentally in the pursuit of what we take to be goods to the valuing of practical reason for its own sake, as we happen to continue in the pursuit of preferred indifferents. Social *oikeiosis* then tells us that while we might be acting to secure the appropriate preferred indifferents for a human being, it doesn't matter from the point of view of living rationally whether we are securing those preferred indifferents for ourselves or for others. The result of all this is that (to employ anachronistic modern categories) Stoic ethics comes to resemble a strange amalgam of elements familiar to us from utilitarianism and Kantian ethics. On the one hand, because the life according to nature is one in which we ought to act in ways likely to secure more rather than fewer preferred indifferents, and because the cosmopolitan sage is unconcerned about prioritising the securing of preferred indifferents for him- or herself rather than for other people, it's not implausible to see the sage as engaging in the kinds of calculations utilitarians make about the likely real-world welfare consequences of the actions they are considering performing. And just as there is a debate within utilitarian ethics as to whether utilitarianism is best understood in terms of acts or rules, there is a debate within the Stoicism literature about whether the Stoics thought that 'natural laws' were general, universal, and exceptionless (as Julia Annas, Phillip Mitsis, and Gisela Striker contend) or whether they are better understood as heuristics, which the Stoic sage would have set aside when it was appropriate so to do (which is the view of A. A. Long and Brad Inwood).[42] On the other hand, the Stoics agree with Kantian moralists that two otherwise identical actions can have entirely different moral values, since morality is relevant to the intentions or dispositions with which a person acts and has nothing to do with the actual consequences of one's actions. To put it another way, this time employing the Stoics' characteristic terminology, the securing of good consequences in the form of preferred indifferents might be the *objective* of moral action (*propositum*), but it is not the *aim* (*telos* or *finis*), they insist that while the morally worthy actions of the sage (*katorthomata*) are phenomenologically identical to the duties (*kathekonta*, *officia*) that the rest of humanity can only aspire to perform, the former have moral worth in a way that the latter do not.

The process of *oikeiosis*, as we have seen, generates a rational concern for oneself and for others. How, then, does this play out in the kinds of practical deliberation the Stoics recommend? In an illuminating discussion of how the Stoics recommend to non-sages (that is, all of us) appropriate ways of living our lives, Tad Brennan draws attention to a saying of Chrysippus about running in a race:[43]

> Runners in a race ought to compete and strive to win as hard as they can, but by no means should they trip their competitors or give them a shove. So too in life; it is not wrong for each person to seek after the

things useful for life; but to do so by depriving someone else is not just.[44]

Brennan calls this the 'no shoving' rule and suggests that the Stoics are best understood as advocating a 'three-round deliberation, in which my pursuit of my interest is curbed by my commitment to avoiding harm to others, especially the diminution of their lawful property, while both of these considerations can and should be overridden by the utility of the whole society'.[45] Brennan himself is allergic to the idea of understanding practical Stoic ethics through the language of laws, let alone that of natural laws, and there are strong grounds for his technical objections.[46] Nevertheless, the origins of what becomes the natural law tradition do seem to stem from something like this argument, with the norms that govern the second and third elements of Brennan's deliberation becoming understood as natural laws prohibiting certain kinds of actions in order to prevent us infringing on either the fundamental interests of others or the common good. To reach into the contemporary lexicon once again, we might think that such a natural law theory comes reasonably close to a Nozickian argument about rights as side constraints.[47]

The Stoics on Justice and Private Property

As in Nozick's theory, and as the remark about 'lawful property' might begin to suggest, concerns about property play a crucial role in this Stoic-derived natural law tradition. Cicero's interest in the defence of private property—to the extent that he considered that the tribune Philippus ought to have been stripped of his citizenship merely for proposing an agrarian law[48]—no doubt owes much to a generally conservative disposition in politics, but it also finds considerable support in the Stoic philosophical tradition. Earlier I sketched an outline of the doctrine of *oikeiosis* without specific reference to property, but looked at from another point of view, concern with property stands at the heart of the argument. This is perhaps easier to appreciate if we think in terms of the language of 'appropriation' rather than 'familiarization'; as Long and Sedley observe, the Greek root *oik-* 'connotes ownership, what belongs to something'.[49] In this retelling of the *oikeiosis* story, what we have is a gradual progression from the fundamental fact and experience of *self-ownership*—which A. A. Long calls 'the Stoics' most far-reaching contribution to their reflections on society, justice, and personal freedom'[50]—through to the development of property relationships in external objects.

In the Stoics' conception, every human being had the power to give or withhold assent to impressions, a faculty they called *synkatathesis*, or *as-*

sensio in Cicero's Latin. This thought stands at the centre of Stoic teaching about individual autonomy (it is most prominent in Epictetus) and, together with the language of *oikeiosis*, which suggests a taking possession of oneself, or a familiarization of oneself to oneself, an argument about the fundamental nature and importance of self-ownership can be elaborated, an argument that in turn was key to the Stoics' denial of any doctrine of natural slavery. *Oikeiosis*, the Stoics thought, explains how we come to have a conception of our personal identity that persists through time: Diogenes Laertius tells us that *oikeiosis* produces not only an animal's affinity for its own constitution but also a consciousness of that constitution, and Seneca provides the most detailed Stoic reflections on what later becomes called the problem of personal identity in his *Letter* 121.[51] The activity of pursuing one's self-preservation and of establishing one's identity—we might say, of finding a home for oneself in the world—on this account naturally involves the appropriation and use of pieces of the material world around us. As Long puts it, for the Stoics, 'just as we need to love ourselves and to forge affectionate ties with other human beings, in order to become well-functioning personalities, so too the appropriation of private property is a natural human tendency and one that helps to establish the individual's identity as such'.[52] It is because property plays an important role in relation to this foundational Stoic concern with *oikeiosis* that the protection of property plays such an important role in Stoic thinking about justice. Here is Long again, expounding Cicero's position:

> Individuals and society have a common interest in the preservation of justice—that is to say in this context, the right of individuals to retain their own property without interference from others: 'Nature (i.e. reason) prescribes that a human being should want to consider the interest of another human being, whoever he is, simply because he is a human being.' I take it that three assumptions underlie this premise. First, the community of reason: if something is rational for me, it will also be rational for you; second, the rationality of self-interest: if it is rational for me to want to promote my own interests, reason constrains me to attribute the same line of thought to you; and third, the universality of interest in ownership: if I am interested in preserving my property (however property is construed), reason requires me to attribute the same interest to you. All human beings, then, have individual interests including interests in their own property. Cicero concludes that justice—scrupulous respect for another's interests—is an interest common to all, and therefore, since it is grounded in the community of rational human nature or natural law, it is binding on all.[53]

What Ciceronian Stoicism requires, on this view, is that humans acknowledge one another's property rights and live with economic arrangements that both preserve, protect, and defend existing property holdings and enable individuals and groups to promote the common good. Obviously, a great deal of detail needs to be filled in before we have a fully fleshed out theory of property or political justice, about the extent of those property rights, the regulations governing accumulation or appropriation, or the question of what social or legal property regimes are acceptable in the sight of this natural law. But the basic shape of the overarching theory is reasonably clear, and reasonably familiar—and we might also note here that, among the Hellenistic schools, the concern with property is quite characteristically Stoic; the Epicurean tradition, by contrast, has little to say about property, just as it says little about politics more generally.

GROTIUS AS STOIC NATURAL LAW THEORIST

When we consider Grotius's argument in *DJBP*, we need to be careful about the state of the text in its various editions, partly because the passages that are most relevant to the analysis of Grotius's use of the Stoics were among those most heavily altered and partly because the significance of such changes as were made has been contested in the scholarly literature. Very roughly speaking, the 1631 edition revised the text of the *Prolegomena* to a considerable extent, including for the first time the identification of *appetitus societatis* with Stoic *oikeiosis*, as well as introducing some other minor changes elsewhere in the main text. The 1642 edition introduced a series of footnote references to a variety of ancient and ecclesiastical authorities that purported to offer further support for Grotius's argument.[54] Any attempt to demonstrate that Grotius's argument has a substantially Stoic component, however, or any suggestion that the argument about sociability has distinctively Stoic characteristics, needs above all to be grounded in a plausible reading of the text of the original 1625 edition. In what follows, I first consider Grotius's use of *De finibus* in the second chapter of the first book of *DJBP*, next move on to discuss the text of the 1625 *Prolegomena*, then turn to the reworked 1631 text, and finally present a brief concluding discussion.

Book 1, Chapter 2, of De Jure Belli ac Pacis

Given that Grotius's book announces its concern with the *ius* of war, the second chapter is clearly a key part of the overall argument, addressing the question 'whether it is ever lawful to make war'. As is characteristic of Grotius's writing, most of the chapter is taken up with the presentation of evidence in support of his argument from classical and scriptural sources, but the opening sections of the chapter present the core philosophical argument, which is where Grotius draws centrally on the passage of Cicero that was considered above, *De finibus* 3.16–23.

Having viewed the Sources of Right, let us proceed to the first and most general Question, which is, Whether any War be Just, or, Whether 'tis ever Lawful to make War?

1.1. But this Question, as well as those which follow, is to be first examined by the Law of Nature. *Cicero* learnedly proves, both in the third Book of *His Bounds of Good and Evil*, and in other Places, from the Writings of the Stoicks, that there are two Sorts of *natural Principles*; some that go before, [and are called by the Greeks Τὰ πρῶτα κατὰ φύσιν,][55] *The first Impressions of Nature*; and others that come after, but ought to be the Rule of our Actions, preferably to the former. What he calls *The first Impressions of Nature*, is that Instinct whereby every Animal seeks its own Preservation, and loves its Condition, and whatever tends to maintain it; but on the other Hand, avoids its Destruction, and every Thing that seems to threaten it. Hence comes it, says he, that there's no Man left to his Choice, who had not rather have all the Members of his Body perfect and well shaped, than maimed and deformed. And that 'tis the first Duty of every one to preserve himself in his natural State, to seek after those Things which are agreeable to Nature, and to avert those which are repugnant.

1.2. After that follows, (*according to the same Author*) the Knowledge of the Conformity of Things with Reason, which is a Faculty more excellent than the Body; and this Conformity, in which *Decorum* consists [*in qua honestum sit propositum*], ought (*says he*) to be preferred to those Things, which mere natural Desire at first prompts us to; because, tho' the first Impressions of Nature recommend us to Right Reason; yet Right Reason should still be dearer to us than that natural Instinct. Since these Things are undoubtedly true, and easily allowed by Men of solid Judgment, without any farther Demonstration, we must then, in examining the Law of Nature, first consider whether the Point in Question be conformable to the first Impressions of Nature, and afterwards, whether it agrees with the other natural Principle, which, tho' posterior, is more excellent, and ought not only to be embraced when it presents itself, but also by all Means to be sought after.[56]

To get a sense of the extent to which Grotius is following Cicero, here is the first paragraph (1.1) again, in the Latin of the 1625 edition, and with the direct quotations, or virtually identical wordings, italicised and with references to *De finibus* inserted in square brackets:

> M. Tullius Cicero tum tertio de Finibus, tum alijs locis, ex Stoicorum libris erudite disserit esse quaedam prima naturae, quaedam consequentia, sed quae illis primis praferenda sint. Prima naturae vocat, quod *simulatque natum est animal, ipsum sibi conciliatur & commendatur ad se conservandum, atque ad suum statum & ad ea quae conservantia sunt eius status diligenda: alienatur autem ab interitu iisque rebus quae interitum videantur afferre* [3.16]. Hinc etiam ait fieri ut *nemo sit, quin cum utrumuis liceat, aptas malit & integras omnes partes corporis, quam easdem usu imminutas aut detortas habere* [3.17]: *primumque esse officium ut se quis conservet in naturae statu, deinceps ut ea teneat quae secundum naturam sint, pellatque contraria* [3.20].[57]

The second paragraph, 1.2, follows both Cicero's Latin and his argument slightly less closely, but it still has a quite distinctively Ciceronian content and flavour. In particular the reference to how 'the first Impressions of Nature recommend us to Right Reason; yet Right Reason should still be dearer to us than that natural Instinct' comes from 'Cato's' argument: Grotius's '*sed ipsa recta ratio carior nobis esse debeat quam illa sint a quibus ad hanc venerimus*' is straightforwardly modelled on Cicero's '*post autem ipsam sapientiam nobis cariorem fieri quam illa sint a quibus hanc venerimus*' (3.23).

That is a bare summary of what Grotius is taking most directly from Cicero's presentation. What is he eliding, or passing over in silence? In between the first quotation in 1.1 (introduced by *vocat, quod*) and the second (introduced by *ait*), Grotius skips over about one hundred words in 3.16–17 that allude to the connection between *oikeiosis* and self-consciousness, report the claim that self-love provides the primary motivation to action, and present 'Cato's' endorsement of the anti-Epicurean insistence that pleasure is not one of the primary objects of desire. More striking is the matter of what gets elided between the second and the third passages that Grotius quotes directly, a gap that covers most of 3.17–20 and is not flagged at all in Grotius's text, as the two quotations are separated only by a colon between *habere* and *primumque*. Here Grotius passes quickly past the outline of a couple of points of Stoic doctrine: the account of *katalepsis* in Stoic epistemology, and, in particular, at 3.20 the beginning of the presentation of the Stoic theory of value (*axia*). It's significant that Grotius avoids picking up on the more technical parts of

'Cato's' exposition; little specifically Stoic jargon apart from the *prima naturae* finds its way into this part of *DJBP*, and we should, I think, be fully aware of the extent to which Grotius is cherry-picking from that discussion and avoiding the parts of it that engage the most distinctively Stoic parts of the argument in the greatest detail.

The absence of any serious consideration of the Stoic theory of value in Grotius is important in its own right. It means that whatever else Grotius is doing with this passage, he isn't attempting to do anything like what Cicero/'Cato' was doing, as the major purpose of 'Cato's' exposition is to build up to a defence of the Stoic claim that what is *honestum* is the appropriate objective (*telos, finis*) of human action, the discussion of the 'ends of good and bad' being the main subject matter of *De finibus* itself. In Grotius's recycling of some of Cicero's words there is no claim that acting in accordance with practical reason is something to be done for its own sake, let alone (as Schneewind noted; see above) a claim that this is the highest good, or the only good. In the absence of a specifically Stoic theory of value, in fact, we might think that this is one place where Grotius's argument really does foreshadow Hobbes's later theory, in which, on the one hand, human beings are always expected to pursue the goods that pertain to self-preservation, while on the other hand, no particular *summum bonum* is acknowledged, nor is the absence of such considered to derail the project of setting suitable rules to govern practical reasoning.

It would be wrong, however, to conclude from all this that Grotius is gutting this Ciceronian argument of any interesting Stoic content. The most strikingly Stoic moment in his exposition is his retention of the link between the two motivations for action. Although *recta ratio* is to be preferred to acting on the 'first Impressions of Nature', it is the latter that 'recommend us to Right Reason' in the first place. In the Stoic account presented by 'Cato', the infant and the mature rational adult are still acting in pursuit of the same kinds of things—security, health, self-preservation, and so on—is the main difference being the adult's consistency in reasoning and an understanding that the real good is to be obtained through the exercise of practical reason for its own sake, rather than through the realisation of those particular kinds of things. In Grotius's account, likewise, the 'first Impressions of Nature' refer to, for example, 'the Preservation of Life or Limbs',[58] and the later, second stage of reasoning specifically includes considerations of sociability—ruling out, as Grotius goes on to explain, only that 'Manner of Violence . . . which is repugnant to Society'.[59]

What is noteworthy here is that Grotius appears to have passed from the realm of what Annas calls personal *oikeiosis* to that of social *oikeiosis*. The material he has taken from Cicero speaks entirely to her discussion of the former, as 'Cato' explains how an infant's instinctive action comes to be replaced by consistent, rationally deliberated action in the adult human being, with, as noted above, a discussion of the explicitly social aspects of *oikeiosis* postponed until 3.62, and yet here we have explicit claims being made about the demands of human sociability. It does not seem plausible that sociability here is being understood in terms of a rather poorly worked out account of mutual advantage, and therefore ultimately reducible to a story about the development of personal *oikeiosis* (perhaps something akin to what de Tocqueville would later call 'self-interest rightly understood'). This is so for a cluster of reasons: first, because the same text that Grotius is exploiting in this chapter itself rejects the idea that justice might be adopted for the sake of utility;[60] second, because Grotius himself makes a similar denial in the *Prolegomena* to *DJBP*; third, because Grotius quotes approvingly from Cicero's *De officiis* 3.5 towards the end of the chapter section in order to emphasise the centrality of the defence of property to sociability; and fourth, because in this discussion Grotius does not consider any of the more obvious difficulties that arise if we do go down a simple justice-as-mutual-advantage avenue. Instead, we would seem to have either a Grotius who sides with Annas's critics against her separation of personal from social *oikeiosis* and who considers that the process of *oikeiosis* that engineers the transition from the *prima naturae* of 1.2.1.1 to the *recta ratio* of 1.2.1.2 also generates a distinctive concern for society as a whole (which seems to me to be more likely), or a Grotius who observes the distinction but is silently presupposing the kind of material that Cicero sets out at 3.62–71 (which seems to me to be less likely). In either case, the identification of *appetitus societatis* (from the *Prolegomena*) with *oikeiosis* as set out by Cicero's 'Cato' appears to be secure.

In both these last cases, the puzzle remains that Grotius seems to be fairly cavalier about the origins of justice, at least insofar as it manages to obtain any kind of grip on human psychology. For the Stoics, as we have seen, these origins lay in the parental instinct, and while Grotius does briefly discuss such an instinct in both versions of his *Prolegomena*, he never gives it any kind of foundational role in his exposition. Indeed, Grotius more generally does not appear to be interested in the particular psychological mechanisms that generate and sustain what Annas calls social *oikeiosis*. One reason for this might be that he failed to find Cicero's discussion at 3.62–71 stimulating, and preferred to short-circuit the entire discussion of how we are to relate to other people with an appeal to straightforwardly impersonal law in the context of the most general concerns about social *oikeiosis*. That seems to me to be plausible. An alternative explanation could presumably be that the distinction set out in 1.2.1.1–2 has nothing to do with the concern for the 'Design of Society' presented in 1.2.1.3,[61] but in that case Grotius's approach in the chapter would be odd; it would not be at all clear, for example, why *De finibus* was being exploited at all, if there were an independent argument for the bindingness of certain social norms, such as respect for property holdings.

Reflecting on these matters brings up a further point of interest, which is that Grotius nowhere employs the passage from Hierocles about concentric circles, which presents the most detailed account of how one might work on extending the range of one's social *oikeiosis* and which has become fairly well known today, in particular thanks to Martha Nussbaum's enthusiastic sponsorship.[62] It is not that Grotius did not have access to this passage. Although parts of Hierocles were unknown to his age, owing to their being preserved on as yet undiscovered bits of papyrus,[63] the concentric circles passage itself is preserved in Stobaeus, and Grotius knew Stobaeus's text intimately.[64] Indeed, he published his own edition of the *Dicta poetarum* preserved in Stobaeus's anthology, and in his major books frequently quoted from texts preserved by Stobaeus. Jon Miller has demonstrated one important conclusion, namely, that nowhere in his writings does Grotius draw on the epitome of Stoic ethics by Arius Didymus and preserved in Stobaeus 2.7 (which is not to say that he didn't know the text; just that he never used it).[65] Here it is worth adding two reasons why he might not have used Hierocles, even though the concentric circles passage speaks directly to relevant concerns of *DJBP*: first, although Hierocles' discussion is universally taken today to be of relevance to understanding the Stoics' *oikeiosis*, the word itself nowhere appears in the decisive passages, and so it is easy to think that it would not have been recognised as a relevant text to understanding the Stoics' argument; second, and perhaps relatedly, Hierocles was not himself taken to be a Stoic philosopher in Grotius's time, and so there is no particular reason to think that Grotius would have had any reason to attempt to exploit this text in this context. (As Gloria Vivenza has observed, it was Max Pohlenz whose work was most important in transforming our understanding of Hierocles.)[66]

The 1625 Prolegomena

The original 1625 text of the *Prolegomena* provides further evidence of a Stoic argument in Grotius's book. The most important passage begins with the best-known portion, here reproduced in Richard Tuck's translation:

> For though man is an animal, he is one of a special kind, further removed from the rest than each of the other species is from one an-

other—for which there is testimony from many actions unique to the human species. Among the things which are unique to man is the desire for society [*appetitus societatis*], that is, for community with those who belong to his species—though not a community of any kind, but one at peace, and with a rational order [*pro sui intellectus modo ordinate*].[67]

Obviously, this passage *can* be read as a piece of Stoicism, especially in light of the final phrase, but it is the argumentation that follows that is most interesting for our purposes, both for where it corresponds with and for where it departs from what we might call the Stoic template. First of all, the saying that 'nature drives each animal to seek its own interests' is qualified: it applies uncomplicatedly to other animals and to children ('man before he came to the use of that which is special to man', that is, fully developed reason), clearly tracking the concerns in the Stoic texts on *oikeiosis* of setting out how adult humans are different from, on the one hand, nonhuman animal life, and on the other hand, infant humans.[68]

The analysis of those differences, however, departs from that of the Stoics. Grotius observes that insofar as nonhuman animals seem to show 'a regard partly for their own offspring, and partly for the other members of their species', this owes not to any natural sociability but to 'some extrinsic principle of intelligence' (which Barbeyrac, commenting on the same passage in the 1631 text, plausibly glosses as God).[69] Grotius's reasoning here is that 'a similar intelligence does not appear in other actions of theirs which are equally difficult'. It is not at all obvious why altruistic behaviour or care for offspring should be viewed as especially *difficult*; perhaps the thought is more directed towards the *complexity* of, for example, a parent's care for its young. The Stoics, of course, explained such behaviour through animal *oikeiosis* itself. The key point for our purposes is that Grotius seems to be asserting that social *oikeiosis* is unique to human beings: 'In the case of men, however, when they perform such actions [care for offspring or otherwise undertake altruistic actions], it is reasonable to suppose that they stem from some internal principle, which is associated with qualities belonging not to all animals but to human nature alone'. When Grotius considers what follows from this parenting or otherwise altruistic instinct, now described as a 'care for society', he certainly does not describe anything that sounds like what we would associate with, especially, child-rearing activity, but claims that

This care for society in accordance with the human intellect, which we have roughly sketched, is the source of *ius*, properly so called, to which belong abstaining from another's possessions, restoring anything which belongs to another (or the profit from it), being obliged to keep promises, giving compensation for culpable damage, and incurring human punishment.[70]

As earlier, the reluctance to say much about the role of parenting in this argument for natural justice is quite striking. Grotius slides quickly from the authentic Stoic concern with the parental instinct to some wider conclusions about the nature of justice and its embodiment in strict respect for general rules. On this occasion, however, the concern with parenting is present in this presentation of social *oikeiosis* in a way that it was not before, and here again it plays out in just the way we would expect from our earlier examination of the Ciceronian Stoic natural law argument, with social *oikeiosis* being understood in thoroughly Stoic fashion as the origin of *ius*. Grotius might himself qualify this final judgement a little later on in the *Prolegomena*, but his qualification itself has a Stoic dimension, for he notes that if the origin of *ius* is in our nature, we can also attribute it to God, 'since he willed that there should be such principles in us', and that 'it was in this sense that Chrysippus and the Stoics said that one should simply seek the origin of *ius* in Jove himself'.[71]

The 1631 Prolegomena

The 1631 *Prolegomena* introduced the explicit language of *oikeiosis* to the discussion of *appetitus societatis*. Shortly after the word itself appears, the argument we were examining earlier begins to diverge from that of the 1625 edition with the insertion of a new discussion of human infants.

> The same [as is said of nonhuman animals] may be said of Infants, in whom is to be seen a Propensity to do Good to others, before they are capable of Instruction, as Plutarch well observes; and Compassion likewise discovers itself upon every Occasion in that tender Age.[72]

Barbeyrac had trouble finding a relevant citation from Plutarch, and judged that the reference was to his *Consolatio ad uxorem*, remarking that in that work he was writing of his daughter, and emphatically not of 'the common Inclination of all Children'. In any case, this insertion is not of particular importance: the earlier edition clearly indicated that human children were to be considered relevantly similar to nonhuman animals, and here Grotius explicitly spells out the inference that was left implicit in that first edition, namely, any apparently altruistic behaviour is to be explained non-Stoically, with reference to the 'extrinsick intelligent Principle'.[73]

The argument continues to depart from the earlier text:

But it must be owned that a Man grown up, being capable of acting in the same Manner with respect to Things that are alike [*cum circa similia similiter agere norit*], has, besides an exquisite Desire of Society [*cum societatis appetitu excellente*], for the Satisfaction of which he alone of all Animals has received from Nature a peculiar Instrument, viz., the Use of Speech; I say that he has, besides that, a Faculty of knowing and acting, according to some general Principles [*secundum generalia praecepta*]; so that what relates to this Faculty is not common to all Animals, but properly and peculiarly agrees to Mankind.[74]

The most interesting indication that Grotius is again at least in part following the Stoics here is the way in which the different aspects of *oikeiosis*—personal and social—are juxtaposed along the way in the same set of claims. The adult human is 'capable of acting in the same Manner with respect to Things that are alike', writes Grotius, closely paraphrasing Cicero on a key aspect of personal *oikeiosis*, which is the achievement of consistency in the selections one makes.[75] Grotius then slides over to social *oikeiosis*, invoking *appetitus societatis* again, and then he repeats his reference to personal *oikeiosis*, reminding the reader that only human beings can act according to *generalia praecepta*.

CONCLUSIONS

Considerable recent scholarship has been keen to emphasise the pronounced Stoic character of Grotius's argument. For Benjamin Straumann, 'the reason why Cicero's arguments in favor of a natural law lent themselves to Grotius was that both Cicero's and Grotius's doctrines originally stem from an attempt to legally defend imperial expansion', with Cicero's argument in *De re publica* being set out specifically as a response to the arguments of Carneades.[76] Jon Miller has explored Grotius's natural law theory in light of a disagreement in the recent literature on Stoicism mentioned above, between those whom he calls 'generalists', who see natural laws as providing a universal and deductive framework for moral deliberation, and those whom he calls 'particularists', who consider Stoic natural laws to be better understood as heuristics because they are at most conditionals, 'the antecedent of which contains an indefinitely long condition that, because it is indefinite, can never be proven true',[77] and his interest in Grotius's 'generalist' argument owes in part to his plausible belief that Grotius's own interpretation of Stoicism on this issue then substantially shaped the way in which later philosophers in the seventeenth century themselves read the Stoics. Stephen Buckle's *Natural Law and the Theory of Property* also stresses the Ciceronian character of much of Grotius's argument, the Stoic sources of his natural law doctrine, and the centrality of the argument about property rights to the overall natural law theory, emphasising the 'important role' in Grotius 'played by the notion of "what is another's", or, more generally, what can be said to be "one's own"'. For Buckle, as for the argument in this chapter, Grotian 'sociableness does not imply the absorption of separate individuals into an amorphous social whole' (although we might wonder whether anyone has ever thought that it does?) 'but requires instead the clear delineation of what is one's own and what is another's, of what is due to each',[78] and the notion of the *suum*, of what is properly regarded as one's own, plays an important role in his discussion.[79]

This chapter adds to the recent literature on Grotius and the Stoics three particular emphases. First, I have argued not only that parts of the argument have plausible Stoic sources or are generally 'Ciceronian' in their character but also that there is a close fit between the general structure of a Ciceronian Stoic natural law theory and the argument that Grotius builds in *DJBP*, the most prominent point of similarity being the organising role that *appetitus societatis* / *oikeiosis* plays in connecting the arguments about self-interest with the argument about sociability and the argument about property rights. Second, I note that the Stoic concern with autonomy combined with the use of something like what Brennan calls the 'no shoving' rule as a way of regulating practical deliberation is what gives us this distinctive argument, in which strong claims about the natural *sociability* of human beings end up issuing in a theory characterised above all by rights that separate people and their property off from one another, rather than in any strong doctrines mandating altruism, charity, or even mutual aid. It's a particular *kind* of sociability argument, and one that should not be mistaken for an especially 'thin' theory of natural human sociability or for a doctrine with substantially Epicurean roots. The third emphasis is also related to the reason why there has been so much disagreement over whether Grotius's theory is to be characterised as a theory dominated by an argument about self-interest, or an argument about sociability, or some particular combination or permutation of the two. Although Grotius calls *oikeiosis* the *appetitus societatis*, which makes it sound as if the other-regarding, sociability aspect of *oikeiosis* will be pushed to the forefront of the analysis, he in fact works far more closely with Stoic sources on the side of personal *oikeiosis* rather than on the side of social *oikeiosis*. With regard to the latter, he never specifically identifies the parental instinct as the (empirical, psychological) origin of justice, and he never explores any argument about the psychological mechanisms through which other-regarding natural sentiment can be strengthened and generalised; instead, he habitually takes a shortcut that bypasses much of what the ancient sources actually report about what comes in between the natural parental instinct and the operation of natural laws. Both his microlevel starting point (*appetitus societatis*) and his macrolevel end point (natural laws concentrated around the rights of noninterference, especially with regard to property) have much in common with the Stoic ideas we find in Cicero's presentation, but the connections between the two are not fully worked out, and one result is that this lopsided account of *oikeiosis* invites misunderstanding.

CHAPTER THREE

From Lipsius to Hobbes

LIPSIUS, MONTAIGNE, SHAKESPEARE

The Stoic virtue of constancy was celebrated above all by Seneca in his essay *De constantia sapientis* (On the constancy of the sage). In Jacqueline Lagrée's words, Senecan constancy 'exhibits the specific quality of the wisdom that is the coherent life lived in accordance with nature and reason' and is 'the virtue that responds to the onslaughts of fortune', representing 'the stability of the sage's soul when faced with the absolute exteriority of fortune, which signifies the changeability of events outside us'.[1] It is not difficult to imagine why constancy might have been a virtue to command attention amid the violent chaos of the religious wars of the sixteenth century. Indeed, when Lipsius published his own *De constantia* in 1584, the wars formed the explicit backdrop to the dialogue he described. When the book begins, the narrator—who is himself called 'Lipsius'—is travelling to Vienna, but stops off in Liège, where he visits his older friend, 'Langius'. Asked about his journey, 'Lipsius' confesses that he is fleeing from the wars in the Low Countries, 'for, said I, who is of so hard and flinty a heart that he can any longer endure these evils?'[2] In reply, 'Langius' upbraids him for his 'childishness' and sets about his explanation, which takes up the entire book, of how 'Our minds must be so confirmed and conformed, that we may be at rest in troubles, and have peace even in the midst of war.'[3]

To be constant is, among other things, to be self-controlled, in particular with regard to one's emotional responses; and, as we have seen in the prologue, Augustine had diagnosed a belief in the possibility of such self-control as a symptom of pride. In this light, it is perhaps not surprising that Lipsius's own presentation of constancy is carefully tailored to avoid this most straightforward Augustinian criticism. 'Langius' defines constancy in the fourth chapter of the first book as 'a right and immovable strength of the mind, neither lifted up nor pressed down with external or casual accidents' (rectum et immotum animi robur non elati externis aut fortuitis, non depressi).[4] 'Strength' is then glossed as 'a steadfastness not from Opinion, but from judgement and sound Reason', and constancy itself is distinguished from 'obstinacy', 'which is a certain hardness of a stubborn mind, proceeding from pride or vainglory'.[5] The obstinate

> can hardly be pressed down but are very easily lifted up, not unlike to a blown bladder, which you cannot without much ado thrust under water, but is ready to leap upwards of itself without help. Even such is the lighthardiness of those men, springing of pride and too much estimation of themselves, and therefore from Opinion.[6]

The contrast is clear. Pride, or vainglory, which is a false opinion about one's own superiority, generates not the virtue of constancy but the vice of obstinacy. Constancy, on the other hand, is based not on opinion but on 'judgement and sound Reason'; and, 'Langius' continues, 'the true mother of Constancy is Patience, and lowliness of mind'.[7] And just as we need to distinguish between obstinacy and constancy, so too patience needs to be distinguished from a vice that can look quite similar, 'a certain abjection and baseness of a dastardly mind', which is 'a foul vice, proceeding from the vile unworthiness of a man's own person'.[8]

Lipsius may have hoped to deter Augustinian criticism through this grounding of constancy in the distinctively Christian virtues of patience and humility, but there were other parts of his argument that remained heterodox, and invited objection. In his consideration of what he calls Lipsius's '(sort of) Christianized Stoicism', for example, Charles Taylor notes two respects in which Lipsius 'leans to the Stoic side'.[9] One is that Lipsius endorses a version of the Stoics' critique of pity in the twelfth chapter of the first book of De constantia, rejecting (in Taylor's words) 'miseratio, or misericordia, the compassion of feeling, in favour of the compassion of active intervention, but on the basis of a full inner detachment'. Christ himself was not so detached—we saw earlier how Augustine drew attention to Christ's experiences with pathe—and criticism from theologians led to the offending claims being withdrawn from the book's Spanish translation.[10]

The other issue concerns grace. Lipsius's argument is not purely secular, or what Taylor calls an 'exclusive humanism', insofar as God is presented as 'the source of the ratio on which we base our lives', and the theorisation of a Christianized account of a Stoic providence is central to the second half of the dialogue. But there is no role here for divine grace in enabling nonsinful human action.[11] The flow of recognisably Augustinian objection to and abuse of the Stoics, therefore, continued through the late sixteenth and into the early seventeenth century. Joseph Marston, for example, in one of the satires in his Scourge of Villanie from 1598, had this to say: 'Peace Seneca, thou belchest blasphemy / To live from God, but to live happily / (I heare thee boast,) from thy Phylosophie'.[12] Simon

Goulart, who translated the *Politica* into French in 1594, could write that 'As long as man glorifies himself and is unaware of the infinite extent of his own misery and the benefit of his Savior, everything he says about God, providence, justice, kindness, and the good life will be but empty and vain prattle.'[13] Joseph Hall, who was regarded as the 'English Seneca' and who argued in favour of a Senecan virtue of tranquillity in his *Heaven upon Earth*, also insisted that this could not be achieved through 'the naturall temper of the soule, so ordered by humane wisdom, as that it should not be affected with any casuall events'.[14]

But there was also a secular critique of Stoic constancy, and one that predated Lipsius, for Montaigne's essays that touch on the subject were published in 1580, well before *De constantia* first appeared.[15] Montaigne in fact wrote an essay of his own called 'Of Constancy', a short and more or less sympathetic piece that describes constancy in terms of 'patiently and firm-footedly bearing misfortunes for which there is no remedy'.[16] Other early essays, however, have a more critical edge. The second book of Montaigne's *Essays* begins with 'On the Inconstancy of Our Actions', and Montaigne's thought that the inconsistency of human nature means that one cannot seriously aspire to be constantly constant is developed in the following essay, 'On Drunkenness'. This essay is engaged with Stoicism from start to finish. The essay begins with the observation that 'vices are all the same in that they are vices—and doubtless the Stoics understand matters after that fashion: but even though they are equally vices they are not equal vices',[17] and it concludes with the reflection, 'When we hear such Stoic paradoxes as, "I would rather be raging mad than a voluptuary" . . . who does not conclude that those are the cries of a mind which is leaping out of its lodgings?'[18] In what falls in between, Montaigne deploys paralepsis—'Let us leave aside that other School which makes an express profession of pride'[19]—before going on to suggest that Stoic self-command is really a kind of derangement. Reviewing some famous examples of constancy in action—Anaxarchus being beaten to death with blows from an iron pestle, 'our Christian martyrs' who cry out 'It is well roasted on this side . . . it is cooked just right: now start on the other side'—Montaigne remarks that 'we have to admit that there is some change for the worse in their souls, some frenzy, no matter how holy'.[20]

Constancy, whether Stoic or Neostoic, was not universally admired, then, even by writers like Montaigne, who were in other respects quite gripped by the ethics of the Roman Stoics, but was the subject of a critical discourse. The argument concerned not just what we might call late Tudor or early Stuart moral psychology, it was also a debate about politics. One way to appreciate this is by way of William Shakespeare's most thoroughgoingly political play, *Coriolanus*, which is plausibly read—and

Geoffrey Miles so reads it—as a meditation on the uses and disadvantages of Roman constancy.[21] Although the ancient authors never present Coriolanus as a Stoic, the chief source that Shakespeare used for his play was Thomas North's English translation of Jacques Amyot's French translation of Plutarch's Greek *Lives*; it was Amyot who put Plutarch's *apatheian* into the contemporary Neostoic language of constancy, and this language found its way from there into North's English version.[22] Early on in the life of Coriolanus, for example, North describes 'men marueling much at his constancy, that he was neuer ouercome with pleasure, nor money, and howe he would endure easely all manner of paynes and trauailles: thereupon they well liked and commended his stowtnes and temperancie',[23] and later a marginal note on Coriolanus's banishment from Rome refers to his 'constant minde in aduersitie'.[24] What is at issue, however, is the nature and character of this constancy. As Miles puts the matter, 'Though Martius' patience in adversity seems to resemble that of Brutus or Portia, Plutarch insists that this is a parody of true constancy, arising not from reason but from an excess of emotion'.[25] And in Shakespeare's play itself, what Coriolanus takes to be his own exemplary constancy is persistently interpreted by his political enemies, the tribunes of the plebs, as his remarkable pride.

When Machiavelli in the *Discourses* discusses Coriolanus, with reference not to Plutarch but to Livy's narration of the story in the second book of his history of Rome, his chief comment is to praise the Romans for having 'an outlet with their laws to vent the anger that the collectivity conceives against one citizen', for he judges the alternative outcome to be Coriolanus being killed 'in a tumult', which would have had strongly adverse consequences for Rome, giving rise to the kind of partisanship that destroys cities.[26] If we turn from the *Discourses* to *The Prince*, however, and consider again Machiavelli's distinction between the *respettivo* and the *impetuoso* political and military leader, then it is clear that Shakespeare's Coriolanus is an example of the latter, not least by virtue of his conduct in the fighting at Corioli, through which he earns his toponymic title in the play's first act. In the case of Coriolanus, furthermore, Machiavelli's criticisms of the politics of constancy canvassed earlier strike home. For it is precisely his inability to navigate successfully the passage from the demands of wartime to those of peace, or more generally to adapt himself and his conduct to his circumstances, that ultimately seals his downfall—just as Machiavelli could have predicted, and as the Volscian general Tullus Aufidius observes in the fourth act, when he considers his archrival Coriolanus's 'nature, / Not to be other than one thing, not moving / From the casque to the cushion, but commanding peace / Even with the same austerity and garb / As he controll'd the war',[27] proceeding to draw the Machiavellian conclusion a few lines later: 'So our virtues / Lie in the interpretation of the time'.[28] When the banished Coriolanus leads an army of Volscians against Rome towards the end of the play, the particular worry some Jacobean writers had about Stoicism, that somehow it worked to generate faction, sedition, and rebellion, is brought into focus.

TACITUS, STOICISM, AND SEDITION

Why should this be the case? We might think it puzzling if we follow the earlier scholarship that treats the political Stoicisms of the late sixteenth century chiefly as a philosophy of obedience in opposition to the fashionable resistance theories of the day. Examining the Stoic politics of Montaigne, Lipsius, and du Vair in the second volume of his *Foundations of Modern Political Thought*, for example, Quentin Skinner writes that 'The chief lesson these moralists preach is the need to remain steadfast in the face of Fortune's changeability'[29] and that this outlook 'carried with it a distinctive set of political implications, the most important being the idea that everyone has a duty to submit himself to the existing order of things, never resisting the prevailing government but accepting and where necessary enduring it with fortitude',[30] something he later calls 'this cardinal duty of submission'.[31] Lipsius himself struck a similar note when he quoted approvingly Aulus Gellius's reduction of Epictetus's teaching to the maxim, '*contine et abstine*'.[32] This is not, however, all that there is to say on the matter. The general Augustinian worry, as we've already seen, associated Stoicism with pride, and therefore with original sin, that is, with an act of rebellion against God, which is, among other things, a matter of disobedience to legitimate authority. But there was a secular worry about Stoicism and sedition, too, which spilled out of the pages of Tacitus, the historian of what has come to be known as the 'Stoic opposition' to the emperors. That phrase has entered the historiography, though it should not be taken to imply that Stoic philosophers were opposed to imperial authority as any kind of coherent group, for they were not. But, as Miriam Griffin has noted, the Stoic tradition offered various resources to shape 'the style and vocabulary in which a Roman senator expressed his political attitudes', from the comparatively trivial up to and including tyrannicide, for all of which 'there were venerated Stoic models as well as Stoic formulae'.[33]

In the final sections of Tacitus's *Annals* that survive, books 14 to 16, which cover the years 59 to 66, the Stoic senator Thrasea Paetus is one of the major characters in the narrative—indeed, the extant manuscript breaks off in the middle of a sentence portraying his death scene, the senator having been ordered by Nero to commit suicide. Nero's mother,

Agrippina, had been killed—again, on Nero's orders—in 59, and on hearing the news, various senators proposed suitable ways of commemorating the occasion, whether with annual games, the setting up of a golden representation of Minerva in the Senate-house, or declaring Agrippina's birthday a 'disqualified day', one on which no public business could be transacted. These deliberations prompted Thrasea Paetus to withdraw from the Senate-house, with Tacitus commenting that in so doing he was 'providing grounds for danger to himself but not presenting the others with their entry to freedom'.[34]

This last remark in fact captures something of the historian's ambivalence towards the Stoic politicians he will go on to describe in the pages that follow. On the one hand, he comes across as sympathetic to their political vision of senatorial independence, and he finds much to praise in Thrasea Paetus's conduct; on the other hand, he is alert to the characteristic vices alleged against those who professed a public Stoicism, and he frequently ensures that less sympathetic interpretations of their conduct are made available to his readers.[35] The same line of thought expressed by this remark about Thrasea Paetus had also been suggested by Tacitus in his earlier work, the *Agricola*. There he had praised his father-in-law for his refusal to court fame 'by parading his virtues',[36] and what may well be an implicit contrast with the Stoic martyrs under Domitian was made more explicit towards the end of the book, when Tacitus praised 'the good sense of Agricola, on the grounds that he was

> not one to court renown and ruin by defiance and an empty parade of freedom. Those whose habit it is to admire what is forbidden ought to know that there can be great men even under bad emperors, and that duty and discretion, if coupled with energy and a career of action, will bring a man to no less glorious summits than are attained by perilous paths and ostentatious deaths that do not benefit the Commonwealth.[37]

(With reference to 'great Thrasea and consummate Cato', who bought 'fame with easy blood' by 'rushing bare-breasted upon drawn swords', the poet Martial expressed a similar preference 'for him who can win glory without dying'.)[38]

The next time Thrasea Paetus appears in the narrative of the *Annals*, Tacitus observes that his move in the Senate to save the praetor Antistius from a death sentence for libelling the *princeps* with his poetry was motivated by a concern 'lest his glory should fall out of sight',[39] just as in the *Histories*, where Tacitus remarks of Thrasea Paetus's son-in-law Helvidius Priscus, at the start of his period of opposition to Vespasian, that 'the passion for glory is that from which even philosophers last divest themselves'.[40] This is an observation that may itself have a powerful early modern echo. It has been plausibly suggested as the origin for John Milton's lines in *Lycidas*, 'Fame is the spur that the clear spirit doth raise / (That last infirmity of noble mind) / To scorn delights and live laborious days'.[41] As Nero is described moving against his enemies, real or imagined, Tacitus reports without comment the opinion of Tigellinus, prefect of the Praetorian Guard, that another Stoic politician, Rubellius Plautus, had been 'adopting too the arrogance of the Stoics' sect, which made men disruptive and hungry for action'.[42] In the aftermath of the failed Pisonian conspiracy in 65, Nero ordered the deaths of, among others, both his tutor Seneca and the philosopher's nephew, the poet Lucan,[43] and Colish has suggested that Tacitus 'observes that Lucan, in his last moments, chose to recite a passage from his own *Pharsalia* which recalled a similar death, a choice suggesting a note of pretentious self-advertisement even in Lucan's ultimate hour'.[44]

The final pages of the surviving portion of the *Annals* portray Nero's attempt 'to extirpate virtue itself' with the death of Thrasea Paetus,[45] who kills himself in the classic fashion—Griffin has identified theatricality, the presence of friends, and calm deliberation as the three constitutive elements of a traditional Roman suicide.[46] But it is noteworthy that even in these passages on the death of a Stoic hero, there are three moments in Tacitus's presentation that set out elements of a case against what we might call political Stoicism. First, there is Capito Cossutianus's argument at the time the charges were drawn up against Thrasea Paetus that Stoicism breeds the kind of men who, in order to 'overturn the empire, they make a parade of freedom; but, if they overthrow it, they will attack freedom itself'.[47] Second, when Thrasea Paetus deliberates with his friends about whether to appear in the Senate to confront the charges in public or wait at home for the order to kill himself, the advice he is offered is shaped by considerations of how to cultivate his posthumous reputation. Those who encourage him to go to the Senate urge that 'he would say nothing except what would augment his glory', for it 'was the sluggish and the panic-stricken who surrounded their final moments with secrecy; let the people gaze on a true man facing death'.[48] Third, we are also introduced in these sections to a different kind of Stoic politician, Publius Egnatius, when he appears as a witness against another of Nero's Stoic victims, Barea Soranus. Egnatius 'had been parading the authority of the Stoic sect, disciplined to display an image of honesty in demeanor and voice but in reality faithless and guileful at heart, concealing his greed and lust',[49] vices that 'had been exposed by money', so that 'he exemplified the fact that the guard one takes against those enveloped in intrigue or stained by iniquity needs to be matched by that against those treacherous in their show of good features and traitorous in friendship'.[50]

All three of these allegations—sedition, glory seeking, and hypocrisy—
were regularly to reappear on the charge sheet drawn up against Stoics
down the ages that followed.

The most entertaining redeployment of the tropes of glory seeking and
hypocrisy in an early modern Tacitist context came in 1612, from Traiano
Boccalini in his *Ragguagli di Parnasso*, later translated into English as
Advertisements from Parnassus, which presents a comic account of how
Lipsius had been received into Parnassus. Apollo had ordained that he
ride in the procession 'between Moral Seneca and Politick Tacitus', the
two authors he had edited in his lifetime.[51] 'But there happen'd a mighty
Dispute between these two great Men' as to who should ride on the fa-
voured right-hand side, because while Tacitus hitherto had always de-
ferred to the older man, now 'he contended so hotly with him for it'. With
the 'Moralists siding with Seneca, and the Politicians with Tacitus', things
would have ended in violence had the former not backed down, it being
'to no purpose to Cope with Politicians, who would be sure to gain the
Victory; if not by force, at least by Fraud and Circumvention.' The question was adjudicated by the censors, who 'decided the affair in favour of
Tacitus; telling Seneca, though his Morals had long been respected in the
World, they were now grown somewhat musty; therefore he must now be
Contented to give place to the Politick *Tacitus*'.[52] 'Seneca obey'd the Censors Commands', Boccalini remarks, 'tho' much against his will', for the
moral philosophers, despite their outward show of humility, were in fact
possessed of the vice of '*una intensissima ambizione*'.[53]

As is now well known, a variety of Tacitisms existed in early modern
Europe. In the sixteenth century, Francesco Guicciardini had picked up
on the way in which Tacitus might communicate differently with different audiences when he commented that the Roman historian 'was very
good at teaching subjects how to live and act prudently, just as he teaches
tyrants how to establish tyranny'.[54] In the 1920s, Giuseppe Toffanin distinguished between a *Tacitismo rosso*, or disguised republicanism, and a
Tacitismo nero, or disguised Machiavellianism.[55] More recently, Richard
Tuck has drawn attention to the specificities of the discourse of Tacitism
in various national contexts.[56]

Although Lipsius was himself very heavily invested in both Tacitus and
Roman Stoicism, and was supposed to have written a text celebrating
Thrasea Paetus called *Thrasea sive De contemptu mortis*, it is striking
that the politics of the 'Stoic opposition' barely registers in the *Politica*.[57]
The closest Lipsius comes is in discussing tyranny in the fifth chapter of
book 6, where he observes there are two remedies against it, 'Removing
it, or Bearing it', and of the first remedy he says that it is 'the mark of the
more upright spirit, to whom it seems preferable *to die than to look at the
face of a tyrant*', quoting from Cicero's *De officiis*.[58] Although Lipsius

immediately commented that he did not himself 'oppose the use of this remedy', he then proceeded to distance himself from it, observing that he 'consider[ed] that other remedy more in accordance with the rules of Wisdom, and even more often in the public interest', and, quoting from Livy, he advised those subjected to tyrants to '*take up the shield rather than the sword*'.[59] But perhaps this disinclination to embrace the politics of Stoic opposition should not be too surprising: the *Politica* is ostentatiously intended for princes, rather than for any kind of opposition politician. In *De constantia*, there is one explicit reference to Thrasea Paetus and Helvidius Priscus, which comes towards the end of the book, but their era is invoked to make the point that while things in present-day Europe might be bad, they have been very bad before, and the point is made in the service of an argument that the present discontents are to be endured, not that these senators provide any kind of practical model of conduct for sixteenth-century emulation.[60] Indeed, it is perhaps worth observing here that one of the most dramatic episodes involving the Stoic opposition to the emperors does not feature prominently in the more overtly Tacitist literature. Helvidius Priscus's celebrated exchange with Vespasian as reported by Epictetus is recycled as a model of senatorial conduct by the more Ciceronian authors. Thus, in France, Guillaume du Vair in his *Moral Philosophie of the Stoicks* describes the scene to illustrate the thought that 'contempt of death is the true and liuely source of all noble and commendable actions', and in England the poet Barnabe Barnes remarks, by way of introducing the Helvidius story in his *Foure bookes of offices*, that 'The part of a Senatour therefore is vprightly to discharge a good conscience: and hee that restraineth truth in feare of any mans hatred, deserueth not his place in this Counsell'.[61]

In England, according to J.H.M. Salmon, 'Seneca and Tacitus became cult figures for many writers on the fringe of court politics'.[62] Sir Philip Sidney had been one of the chief conduits through which French and Dutch Neostoic ideas reached the world of elite English politics. He had corresponded with Lipsius, who dedicated his book on Latin pronunciation to him, calling him the 'bright star of Britannia',[63] and he and other members of his circle engaged in translating and publishing works by Seneca or other contemporary Stoic-inflected writers, such as Philippe Duplessis-Mornay.[64] Sidney died after having been badly wounded by a musket-ball at Zutphen in the Netherlands in the autumn of 1586, whereupon, Salmon writes, 'the entry of Tacitean politics into English Neostoicism was accomplished by those who inherited the tradition of the Sidney ... for Sidney left not only his sword and his widow to [Robert Devereux, the Earl of] Essex, but also his support of the international Protestant cause and his following of friends and clients'.[65] Francis Bacon once observed in a discussion of superstition that it was 'not the Schoole of Epicurus, but the Porch of the Stoiques that hath perturbed ancient states',[66] but the affinity between Stoicism and sedition was by no means purely a matter of ancient history in the later years of Elizabeth's reign and the Jacobean period. After Essex's rebellion and execution in February 1601, one of the early political issues faced by King James, after his accession to the English throne in 1603, was how to deal with his Tacitist associates. These included leading courtiers, among them Fulke Greville and Bacon himself, who had betrayed his former patron when he testified against him at his trial for treason in Westminster Hall.[67]

However much Seneca and Tacitus might have flourished on the fringes of English court politics, they were distrusted at its very centre. James forgave Bacon, Greville, and the others, and would later reward members of the Essex circle with high office, but he was never keen on those who struck a Stoic pose in public life. Even before becoming king of England he had referred dismissively in his *Basilikon Doron* to 'that Stoick insensible stupiditie that proud inconstant LIPSIVS perswadeth in his *Constantia*', the charge of inconstancy being a contemptuous reference to Lipsius's frequent change of religious affiliation.[68] For editions of the book published around the time of James's accession to the English throne and afterwards, the specific reference to Lipsius was replaced with a general charge of hypocrisy directed at 'manie in our daies', who, 'preassing to win honor, in imitating that auncient sect, by their inconstant behauiour in their owne liues, belyes their profession'.[69] The king was not alone in his concern. Andrew Shifflett has described some of the anxieties that grew up around the figure of the Stoic politician, locating James's remarks in a cluster that also included Roger Ascham's identification of the origins of the distinctively Stoic literary style in a 'singular pride in themselves, or some special malice of other, or for some private and partial matter, either in Religion or other kind of learning'; Robert Johnson's verdict that the Stoics were 'busie-headed and turbulent'; and Fulke Greville's 1622 poem, *An Inquisition on Fame and Honour*, which 'stated the problem well . . . when he reflected on the political consequences of one who trusts only in a "self-constellation" and "makes himself his end": "Selfnesse [is] even apt to teare it self asunder: / All governments, like man himself within / Being restlesse compositions of the sinne."'[70] Political philosophers from Cicero to John Rawls have held that a well-ordered political community is one in which the citizens share an appropriate conception of justice, and the perennial anxiety regarding those who present themselves as Stoics is that however assiduously they may be seen to be performing their various offices, they threaten to disrupt the smooth workings of a hierarchical political regime, substituting their own scale of values—regarding justice or honour, for example—for those that are officially recognised and socially sanctioned, and always placing their paramount concern with their own virtue above what others take to be the needs of the commonwealth for orderly, stable government. 'No matter how indifferent to the world he claimed to be', Shifflett concludes, 'the Stoic was held to be a dangerous political animal'.[71] If the self-presentation of the Stoic politician was itself hypocritical—and, if Montaigne had been right about the fundamental inconstancy of human nature, it could hardly help but be—then the possibilities for sedition were multiplied.

THOMAS HOBBES

An intriguing visual connection between Lipsius and Hobbes was forged in 1672, when Richard Royston republished Nathaniel Wanley's recent translation of *De constantia*, which was given the new title, *War and peace reconciled*. For this edition, Royston recycled the frontispiece that Robert Vaughan had prepared for the edition of Hobbes's *Philosophical Rudiments concerning government and society* that he had earlier published in 1651, with the peculiar result that a portrait of Hobbes, flanked by representations of 'Dominion' and 'Liberty', stood at the front of an edition of Lipsius.[72] But perhaps this was not as strange as it sounds. As I noted at the end of the first chapter, there are a number of ways in which Hobbes's theoretical project, culminating in the *Leviathan* of 1651, can be read as continuing to work with central themes from Lipsius's political thought. Both writers agreed with Augustine that the goal of political life was to secure an earthly peace, but they disagreed with the Augustinian tradition through their 'politique' defence of the subordination of religious concerns to those of politics. Both Hobbes and Lipsius were more or less sceptical with respect to traditional arguments about the value of republican freedom, and both defended an account of determinism in human affairs, whether Lipsius's 'fate' or Hobbes's materialist physics. More recently, a number of scholars have fleshed out some historical connections between Lipsius and Hobbes. Richard Tuck's *Philosophy and Government*, for example, tells an interesting and influential story about the trajectory of what he calls 'the new humanism' of Lipsius and Montaigne, a sceptical, Neostoic discourse that was transformed once by Grotius into modern natural rights theory and again by Thomas Hobbes into the language of social contract theory.[73] Others have traced a series of further connections between the Lipsian and the Hobbesian disciplined citizen.[74]

Hobbes's psychological theory also shows a kind of continuity with Stoic theory. As noted by Richard Tuck, 'Our entire emotional life, according to Hobbes, extraordinary as this might seem, is in fact a complicated set of beliefs about the best way of securing ourselves against our fellow men, with all the familiar complexities of love, pride and laughter in the end reducible simply to a set of ideas about our own relative safety from other people's power'.[75] The reduction of emotion to belief is characteristic of Hellenistic philosophy, and when Hobbes argued that the bad effects of the more antisocial passions were specifically produced by mistaken judgements, he was arguing on distinctively Stoic terrain. Here again, his account may owe something to Lipsius's Neostoic presentation. As we saw earlier, Lipsius had distinguished 'obstinacy' from 'constancy' by arguing that the former was grounded in pride, which was a false opinion of one's own superiority. This was one of the more Augustinian moments in his moral psychology. But where it is sensible to read Lipsius here as engaging in a preemptive defence of his account of constancy by seeking to insulate it from the most obvious line of anticipated Augustinian attack, Hobbes took this kind of thought about the rootedness of passion in belief or judgement and made it a major element of his psychological and, thereby, political theory.

There is an obvious and sharp asymmetry between Hobbes and the Stoics with respect to the emotions.[76] For the Stoics, the project of replacing the erroneous passions, or *pathe*, with their rational counterparts, the *eupatheiai*, was bound up with the goal of living according to nature and achieving the *summum bonum*. For Hobbes, by contrast, it was axiomatic that there was no such thing as the *summum bonum*. But if we focus not on the *summum bonum* but on avoiding the *summum malum*, the war of all against all, through the construction of civil peace, then the architectural resemblance between Hobbes's theory and Stoicism persists. In place of the individual practicing Stoic therapies with an eye to the extirpation of the passions, it is the Hobbesian sovereign who maintains the conditions under which it becomes possible for citizens to be able to live peaceably together through their obedience to the sovereign's commands. Considered from this point of view, Hobbes's theory looks quite a bit like those of the Neostoic moralists as presented by Quentin Skinner, with 'this cardinal duty of submission' at its core. But if we can read Hobbes here as a kind of Neostoic submission theorist, we can also read him as someone who is taking the Jacobean or the Tacitist critique of the Stoic politician very seriously indeed. It is this perspective that I want to explore in the pages that follow.

Hobbes was notoriously reluctant in his own published writings to acknowledge the sources that shaped his philosophical project, but recent scholarship has reconstructed a contemporary Tacitean context that can illuminate the development of his political thought. When Hobbes was in

Venice from the autumn of 1614 to the spring of the following year, while travelling with William Cavendish, he met the friar Fulgenzio Micanzio and other local humanists. Following his return to England, a correspondence between Cavendish and Micanzio lasted until 1628, the year in which Cavendish died, with Hobbes translating Micanzio's letters from Italian into English.[77] The three men shared an interest in Bacon's ideas. During the latter part of his time in Italy, Cavendish probably translated the 1612 edition of Bacon's *Essays* into Italian—perhaps with assistance from Hobbes—and presented a copy to Micanzio;[78] he later helped put Micanzio in touch with Bacon;[79] and when Micanzio encouraged Cavendish to provide Bacon with an amanuensis, it may have been Hobbes himself who discharged this function.[80] John Aubrey, at any rate, records that 'His lordship would often say that he better liked Mr Hobbes's taking his thoughts, than any of the other, because he understood what he wrote, which the others not understanding, my lord would any times have hard task to make sense of what they writ.'[81]

Students of Hobbes's intellectual development have long been interested in the 1620 volume of seventeen essays written in the Baconian style called *Horae subsecivae*.[82] After studying a manuscript of fourteen of these essays among the papers at Chatsworth in 1934, 'as far as I can judge, written in Hobbes's hand', Leo Strauss opined that even if 'this manuscript is not the earliest writing of Hobbes himself, his was the decisive influence in its composition'.[83] Computer wordprint analysis carried out under Noel Reynolds at Brigham Young University has indicated that three of the essays in *Horae subsecivae* may very well be by Hobbes— not any of the fourteen in the Chatsworth manuscript itself, as it happens, but the other three items in the printed collection: one 'A Discourse of Lawes'; the second a travelogue, 'Of Rome'; and the third a far more substantial discourse, 'Upon the Beginning of Tacitus', an examination of Roman politics in the age of Augustus that focuses on the first four chapters of the first book of the *Annals*.[84] The identification of these essays as being by Hobbes is controversial. Noel Malcolm, for example, has written that 'there is more than one reason for doubting it', citing worries about the reliability of the wordprint technique and concerns about the content of the essays: 'the description of Rome was the sort of exercise normally performed on an educational Grand Tour by the pupil, not the tutor, and the opinions expressed in the "Discourse of Lawes" differ significantly from Hobbes's later views', though he goes on to remark that in the discourse on Tacitus one does find 'here and there, some touches of Hobbesian phrasing'.[85] But even if Hobbes were not in fact the author of the discourse on Tacitus, this text still provides evidence of a Tacitist context for the development of his political thinking, as the most likely author would then appear to be his pupil Cavendish, with his tutor Hobbes supervising its composition and perhaps providing the distinctively Hobbesian phraseology that Malcolm is content to acknowledge.

In his examination of this text, Jürgen Overhoff does not use the language of 'red' and 'black' Tacitism, but he squarely aligns the author of the 'Discourse of Lawes' with the absolutist Tacitists, in opposition here to the Venetian republicans;[86] he emphasises the importance of Lipsius's edition of Tacitus and of his *Politica* for the discourse of early seventeenth-century Tacitism;[87] and he draws attention in particular to Lipsian claims that find a powerful echo in Hobbesian political theory, namely, that 'human beings were rebellious by nature, that their unbridled conduct caused discontent and civil war, and that therefore the sovereign judgment of all things belonged to princes, not to private individuals'.[88] Overhoff seems to me to be right to connect the Tacitism of Lipsius's *Politica* to the discourse 'Upon the Beginning of Tacitus', but here I want to press a little harder on the link between Lipsius's use of Tacitus and Hobbes's later political theories in order to bring out the themes that I have been considering in this chapter about the contemporary polemics swirling around Stoicism and politics.

Andrew Shifflett has said that the Stoic could be held to be a 'dangerous political animal', and we have seen some of the reasons from Tacitus or from Jacobean politics as to why that might be so. But in both Tacitus and, for example, the *Basilikon Doron*, the problem is merely that *some* politicians are Stoics, and their rulers must be very careful in their dealings with them. There is no particular reason to think that there are that many of them, however, and there's no reason in principle as to why they cannot be identified and neutralised politically. Politicians who profess Stoicism are a little local difficulty for rulers, but not much more than that, if handled well. But now consider a moment in the *Politica*, at 6.4.[89] Lipsius quotes a line from Tacitus about how the 'instigators of civil war' will do various things, 'gathering all the basest men in nightly meetings', 'utter complaints and ambiguous remarks about the Prince' and, 'when they have attracted other helpers of the rebellion as well' they proceed 'in a more daring way: and profess liberty and precious words as their motive':

> But how falsely they do so! Because *in order to overthrow the government, they pretend to defend freedom; and when they have overthrown it, they attack freedom as well.*[90]

The last words from Tacitus in Lipsius's text come from *Annals* 16.22.[91] They are not, however, presented in that text as an opinion of the historian himself but are put into Capito Cossutianus's mouth, and Capito

Cossutianus was not so much reflecting in general on the activities of those who would start civil wars as he was specifically criticising Stoic politicians, as part of the justification he offers to Nero for seeking to kill off Thrasea Paetus. It is not clear to me how much we should make of this kind of thing, or of the extent to which we should think that a good strategy for reading Lipsius involves considering the various *sententiae* that he quotes in their original contexts before making an attempt to establish his illocutionary point. But the move that Lipsius is making here, generalising particular criticism aimed at the Stoics to cover a much wider range of actors in political life, is a somewhat trivial example of what becomes one of Hobbes's major strategies in the construction of his mature political thought. The figure of the potentially destabilising, glory-seeking Stoic senator or courtier, with his own scale of values and his own private judgement, moves from the margins of Jacobean or Tacitist political thought to the centre of the problems of political life, for Hobbes thought that in a republic, almost all politicians, whether in the aristocratic court or the popular assembly, vying one with another for superiority, could pose the same danger as the Jacobeans' Stoic, fomenting social disunity, generating faction, and ultimately provoking civil war and a return to the state of nature.

Lipsius had been a critic of a politics of glory, but the glory in question was that of the prince, who was permitted to dispense with ordinary morality for the sake of his principality's security, but not for the sake of its aggrandisement or for his own personal glory. For Hobbes, however, the problem posed by glory was not so much that of reining in the excesses of the Machiavellian prince as of disciplining potentially unruly subjects. Tacitus might have considered Helvidius Priscus's conduct ultimately to be motivated by his passion for glory, and James criticised the Stoics around him who were 'preassing to win honor', but Hobbes's suggestion was that the overriding concern for glory and honour was not so much a characteristically Stoic vice as a general feature of the human condition, and one of the chief reasons a solution as drastic as the Leviathan sovereign was required in the face of the problems of politics. For Hobbes, 'Glory, or internal gloriation or triumph of the mind', was defined in *The Elements of Law* as 'that passion which proceedeth from the imagination or conception of our own power, above the power of him that contendeth with us.'[92] To honour someone, relatedly, was 'to conceive or acknowledge, that that man hath the odds or excess of power above him that contendeth or compareth himself'.[93] Nor was glorying any kind of incidental pleasure in our lives. In *De cive*, Hobbes made his most sweeping claim about the significance of glory in our emotional lives, writing, 'Every pleasure of the mind is either glory (or a good opinion of oneself), or ultimately relates to glory'.[94] And in that same passage from *De cive*,

Hobbes gives his crispest explanation of why glory posed a problem for politics, for 'no large or lasting society can be based upon the passion for glory', insofar as 'glorying, like honour, is nothing if everyone has it, since it consists in comparison and preeminence'.

Glory is perhaps less important to the human psychology that Hobbes presents in *Leviathan* than it is in these two earlier presentations of Hobbes's political ideas, although even here it is presented as one of the three causes of war in the state of nature, alongside 'competition' and 'diffidence'.[95] Hobbes has more to say about what he calls 'vain-glory', which he defines as joy, but joy when it is 'grounded on the flattery of others; or onely supposed by himself, for delight in the consequences of it'.[96] Overestimating their own power and abilities, the vainglorious are 'enclined to rash engaging',[97] and vainglory is one of the passions that 'most frequently are the causes of Crime'.[98] Its 'violence, or continuance maketh Madness', Hobbes tells us, and it is 'commonly called Pride'.[99] Pride, however, is forbidden by the natural law, for, 'If Nature therefore have made men equall; that equalitie is to be acknowledged', and 'if Nature have made men unequall; yet because men that think themselves equall, will not enter into conditions of Peace, but upon Equall terms, such equalitie must be admitted'. What Hobbes calls the ninth law of nature, therefore, demands '*That every man acknowledge other for his Equall by Nature*', and the 'breach of this Precept is *Pride*'.[100] The proud— those who consider themselves superior to others, those who glory over others, and demand to be honoured—are a perennial threat to stable government, which requires their expulsion from the arena of politics altogether so that they can do no harm to the body politic. It might be God who humbles the proud, according to the text of the *Magnificat*, but Hobbes assigns this task to the secular sovereign. And it is this concern with pride that provides the reason why Hobbes chose to call his book *Leviathan*, as he explains at the end of chapter 28:

> Hitherto I have set forth the nature of Man, (whose Pride and other Passions have compelled him to submit himselfe to Government;) together with the great power of his Governour, whom I compared to *Leviathan*, taking that comparison out of the two last verses of the one and fortieth of *Job*; where God having set forth the great power of *Leviathan*, calleth him King of the Proud. *There is nothing*, saith he, *on earth, to be compared with him. He is made so as not to be afraid. He seeth every high thing below him; and is King of all the children of Pride.*[101]

If this examination of Hobbes began by considering his continuities with Stoic and Neostoic thinking, it ends at the heart of what we might call the Augustinian Hobbes—or at any rate, a Hobbes who set about systematically secularising themes that were familiar from Augustinian theology and displacing theological voluntarism into the world of politics. Pride was central to his analysis, though no longer understood as an offence against God but as an offence against one's fellow human beings; and the Leviathan was characterised as nothing less than 'Mortall God' whose decree was law, and whose law was necessarily just.[102] In chapter five I consider the seventeenth-century reception of Hobbes, and in particular the question of how he was understood as being both a funny (and dangerous) kind of Stoic and later as a funny (and dangerous) kind of Epicurean. Before doing so, however, it is time to cross the Channel and consider the contemporary assault on Stoic moral psychology from the pens of the French Augustinians.

CHAPTER FOUR

The French Augustinians

THE INFLUENCE OF THE STOIC revival of the sixteenth century continued to be felt in a variety of spheres in seventeenth-century France. In addition to the dissemination and translation of Lipsius's works, the various works of Guillaume du Vair gave shape to a distinctively French version of contemporary Neostoicism. His *Traité de la constance*, which drew inspiration from Lipsius's work of the same name, purported to be the report of a conversation that had taken place during the Siege of Paris in 1590.[1] Like *De constantia*, this, too, was a very popular work, going through fifteen editions before 1641.[2] Du Vair also published a short handbook, *De la sainte philosophie*, translated as *The Moral Philosophie of the Stoicks*, which presented in summary form the main principles of his doctrine. In some ways, du Vair departed from the Lipsian template. He dropped, for example, Lipsius's scepticism about patriotic identification in favour of a very strong patriotic ideology, which he expressed in almost Ciceronian terms. 'For good cause wee owe of dutie more loue vnto our countrie, then vnto al other things contained in the world', he wrote. 'Out of the fountaine of this worthie affection, what a number of worthie and excellent deedes haue gushed foorth?'[3] In general, there was in du Vair's writing much greater use of the maxims of Epictetus's *Encheiridion*, which du Vair was one of the first to translate into French, than was to be found in Lipsius, who barely drew on Epictetus at all.[4] Lipsius's passage on Epictetus in the *Manuductio*, for example, dwelt more on his life than on his thought, which was summed up with the bland motto, *Contine et abstine*, and Lipsius did not cite Epictetus as a source for any Stoic doctrine throughout either the rest of the *Manuductio* or in his *Physiologiae Stoicorum*.[5]

Stoic texts remained popular in France, being frequently translated and re-edited, and were widely used in the Jesuit academies. In the case of Seneca, to take the most prominent example, there were several Latin editions of his works in circulation, including those edited by Erasmus and Lipsius, with new French editions appearing in 1595, 1604, and 1659, in addition to numerous editions and translations of individual texts.[6] Nannerl O. Keohane and Anthony Levi have documented the impact of Neostoicism in French debates on early seventeenth-century political thought and moral psychology.[7] J. H. M. Salmon, describing the aristocratic ideology of the first half of the seventeenth century, has written that the 'Stoic ideal contributed to the current vogue of the noble hero, which, far more than the views of the skeptics and the rationalists, dominated the ethos of the aristocracy' for much of the first half of the seventeenth century and 'provided a code of anarchic individualism which resisted the pressures of Richelieu's rule.'[8] Salmon was here referring to Paul Bénichou's 1948 *Morales du Grand Siècle*, one of the classic accounts that presents Pierre Corneille as an exponent of this code, his plays celebrating Stoic heroic self-sacrifice and aristocratic '*générosité*' in the face of the machinations of *raison d'état*.[9] As Katherine Ibbett has recently shown, however, the opposition between Corneille's 'French integrity' and Richelieu's 'Italian duplicity', which has 'proved surprisingly resilient in post-war criticism', is largely a construction of French patriotic and, later, republican ideology, with only an insecure grounding in Corneille's texts, which are far more heavily implicated in the techniques of Machiavellianism and *raison d'état* than Bénichou and others would have us believe.[10]

The impact of Stoicism on French intellectual culture gave rise to a variegated landscape. In his detailed surveys of the uses of Stoicism in the writings of French humanists and apologists in the first half of the seventeenth century, Julien-Eymard d'Angers distinguished six basic orientations towards the Stoics. There was Christian Stoicism (*un stoïcisme christianisant*), which he associated with Jean-Pierre Camus or, in England, Joseph Hall. He used the label 'Stoic Christianity' (*un Christianisme stoïcisant*) to characterise the works of Etienne Binet or Nicolas Caussin. François de Sales was a representative of what d'Angers called Christian humanism. There was also the new Cartesian humanism, which might accept the Epictetan distinction between what was and what was not in our power, but which attacked Stoic apathy using the categories of the new physics, which treated the body as a machine, and the new physiology, which presented a distinctive account of the separation of body and mind. Fifth, there was the 'double attitude' of the *libertins érudits*, for while they approved of the Stoics insofar as the Stoics challenged the monopoly the Christian apologists claimed to possess with respect to virtue, they disapproved of the Stoics' dogmatism.[11] Finally, there was the nascent anti-Stoicism of the 1640s, to be considered in what follows.[12] This took on its distinctive form in the pages of Jansen's *Augustinus*, but it quickly demonstrated that it was not by any means confined to narrow Jansenist circles.

CORNEILLE JANSEN

Corneille Jansen (in Latin, Cornelius Jansenius), the bishop of Yprès, died of the plague in 1638. The controversy that was to bear his name began with the posthumous publication of his *Augustinus*, first in Louvain in 1640 and then in Paris the following year.[13] Convinced that much Catholic teaching on the key questions of grace and free will had strayed too far from its Augustinian origins, and in particular that the free will teaching espoused by the Jesuits, who followed the doctrine of Luis Molina, was both false and dangerous, Jansen presented what he argued was the authentic and authoritative teaching of Augustine on these matters. Predestination was reasserted, and the role that divine grace played as a necessary cause of right action was emphasised—as was the apparently arbitrary distribution of this grace across the human species.[14] Jansen's strategy was to argue that the views he opposed were variants of the Pelagianism that Augustine had opposed in the last great theological controversy of his life, which began in 411 and lasted until his death in 430 and which the church had officially decreed as heretical in two condemnations of 416 and 417. Pelagius had taught that sin was in its essence voluntary, and relatedly, that Adam's disobedience could not have resulted in an inherited original sin that would afflict all of his descendants. In opposing this position Augustine defended the reality and heritability of original sin, arguing that (among other things) the practice of infant baptism would otherwise be unintelligible. From Augustine's point of view, Pelagianism raised the possibility of a life led by a person who consistently chose not to sin and for whom Christ's redeeming sacrifice was therefore in vain. If such a person then could not with justice be damned to hell, this in turn restricted the absolute sovereignty of God, yet it was axiomatic that God could not be beholden to any part of his creation, or, to borrow the title of Leszek Kolakowski's study of Pascal's Jansenism, that God owes us nothing.[15] Raising the spectre of Pelagianism in the way that he did was bound to provoke controversy. Jansen was not just insinuating that the Jesuit Molinists were heretics. In doing so he risked appearing to Catholics as one who was defending Calvinist positions against the orthodoxies of Rome.

It should not be altogether surprising that Jansen found a place for a critical treatment of Stoicism in his book. Since grace was the central site of theological controversy, any attack on Pelagianism from an Augustinian standpoint would have to give an account of the nature of the Fall—as *Augustinus* did, at some length—and we have seen that Augustine's own narrative of the Fall was intimately tied to his presentation and critical dissection of Stoic ethics. In an important respect, however, Jansen went beyond Augustine's own account, insofar as he was much more explicit about identifying Stoicism as a stage in the genealogy of Pelagianism than Augustine had been in his various anti-Pelagian writings, in which his comments on Stoic philosophy were few and far between.[16] The most significant references to the Stoics in *Augustinus* appear in the first volume, spread over the end of the fourth and the beginning of the fifth books.[17] The nineteenth chapter of the fourth book is devoted to the topic of *apatheia*, which Jansen defined as 'an incapacity for suffering the *perturbationes* or passions by which the human spirit is accustomed to being disturbed',[18] and he went on to argue that the Pelagians taught something equivalent, with their notion of the man without sin. A little later, in chapter 22, Jansen asserted a link between Pelagianism and the Stoic claim that the wise man is in relevant respects the equal of God, in support of which he cited passages from Seneca and Epictetus comparing the sage to the gods, as well as the verse from Genesis (3:5) in which the serpent offers the First Couple the chance to be like the gods (*sicut Dii*).[19] The fifth book of the first volume is given over to a treatment of three stages in the development of Pelagianism, which Nigel Abercrombie suggests was a division original to Jansen and which he glosses as roughly corresponding to Paganism (*Ethnicismus*), Semipaganism, and Judaism.[20] In the brief treatment of the first stage, or secular philosophy uninformed by grace, all of Jansen's citations were from Stoic sources, mostly from Seneca.

The criticism of Stoicism was an incidental rather than central component of Janesn's theological project, and nothing in the ensuing controversy between Jansen's party and the representatives of a more orthodox Catholicism that produced the official papal condemnations of Jansen's heterodox theology in 1653 (the encyclical *Cum occasione*) and 1713 (the bull *Unigenitus*) focused on his treatment of the Stoics. But three interrelated aspects of Jansen's treatment of the Stoics were important in shaping the way in which the Augustinian anti-Stoics who wrote in his wake developed their critique, whether they were Jansenists or not. First, the decision to bypass recent Catholic teaching in order to concentrate directly on Augustine's own texts helped encourage an engagement with the Stoics on something like Augustine's original terms. Second, the equation between Stoicism and Pelagianism that Jansen asserted gave contemporary Augustinianism a powerful ideological charge, yoking together French Neostoic intellectual culture and Jesuit theology as objects of a common, scathing attack. Third, while Jansen gave roughly equal attention to the Epicureans and the Stoics, it was the Stoics who were presented as the school of pagan philosophers to be reckoned with, because of their role in paving the way for the Pelagian heresy.

JEAN-FRANÇOIS SENAULT

Jansen's argument was quickly taken up by other Augustinian writers, in the first instance by the Oratorian Jean-François Senault (1601–72), who was from 1662 general of the order.[21] The anti-Stoicism of *Augustinus* had come in a formidably abstruse context, buried inside a dense, scarce, and controversial book. Senault, by contrast, presented his variation on Jansen's Augustinian theme in a much more accessible form. The three texts to be considered here were all published in the 1640s. *De l'usage des passions* was Senault's major work, an important contribution to the wide-ranging debates in French moral psychology about the nature of the passions and the book for which he is best known today;[22] it was also a popular book, with fourteen editions published in eight years.[23] Senault followed this book with a pair of works of Augustinian theology, *L'homme criminel* in 1644, and its companion volume, *L'homme chrestien* in 1648. These dealt, as their titles suggest, with the fall of man through original sin and the foundations of the Christian theology of grace, respectively.[24] None of these three books was principally an engagement with Stoicisms past or present. All three, however, contained attacks on the Stoics, above all in three passages: the preface to *De l'usage des passions*; its opening chapter, titled 'An apology for passion against the Stoics'; and, most comprehensively, the preface to *L'homme criminel*.[25]

In the preface to *De l'usage des passions*, a string of stock Christian objections to Stoicism is presented in polemical fashion and given structure by a series of stark Augustinian binaries: 'Man had freedom enough to undo himself, by his own proper motion', Senault proclaims, 'but he had not enough thereof to save himself by his own strength: his ruine came from his will, and his welfare could proceed from nothing but from Grace'. The Stoics 'thought virtue the only happiness', they 'fill the soul with arrogance', and they 'imitate the pride of Devils', whereas Christians 'allow of no felicity but Grace', 'acknowledg their weakness', and 'implore ayd from Grace'. The beliefs of the Stoics 'do infinitely differ from the belief of Christians', Senault observes, but this owed not to any errors of reasoning on the part of the Stoics, for they 'had a little more light then others'. Rather, the mistake that the Stoics made was that they did not realise the limits of philosophical reason itself. The root cause of this failure was their pride, the same pride that had preceded the Fall. Fallen man who lived without the intercession of grace was 'possesst with self-love' and 'could propose no other end to himself, but himself: He laboured either after Glory, or Pleasure', with the result that 'in all his actions [he] raised himself no higher than his own interests'. In the case of the Stoic philosophers, then, 'whatsoever names they gave unto their Vertues, one might easily finde, that they were animated onely by the desire of Honor or Voluptuousness'.[26]

In both the preface to this book and the preface to *L'homme criminal*, 'the Stoics' are treated generically. There is no significant effort to differentiate one Stoic philosopher from another, or to ground the argument in specific Stoic texts. Senault's Stoics are chiefly an ideological construction against which to juxtapose his Augustinian orthodoxy. Senault did draw very regularly on one Stoic author in particular. Anthony Levi reports that of 370 quotations from Latin authors to be found in *De l'usage des passions*, 151 are from Seneca's writings, and Seneca's account of the passions is, by and large, treated quite favourably.[27] But Seneca's argument is not regularly identified as Stoic in Senault's text, and while his doctrine might have been treated sympathetically, the man himself is the target of an ad hominem attack in *L'homme chrestien*. 'Reason without Grace hath hitherto brought up none but proud Scholars', Senault observes, before turning to consider the case of Seneca, identifying him explicitly with the Pelagian heresy:

> Whatever is rumored of the Letters and Conferences between *Seneca* and Saint *Paul*, I have always believed the conversion of that Stoick harder than that of the Covetous and most imprudent Lascivious. The Pride that animated his spirit, was so strong a bulwark against grace, that he had never stoopt to the Maximes of Christianity, if that Conqueress of hearts had not employed all her charms and all her forces to bring him under. . . . This Philosopher had he kept his opinions, had been the first Authour of *Pelagianisme* in the world; and his pride making him the capital enemy of grace, had obliged him to side with reason against her.[28]

Although both Augustine and Senault considered Stoicism as bound up with the Fall and the problematic of prideful self-love, their arguments addressed different moments in the Augustinian grand narrative. For Augustine, the arguments of the Stoics were best employed to understand the predicament of Adam in Paradise. Adam is presented as a kind of Stoic sage, the master of his passions who acts freely in everything he did but who ends up becoming 'pleased with himself', with the consequent fall from grace. Senault's account, by contrast, treated Stoicism in strictly postlapsarian terms, above all depicting it as a philosophy that implicitly denied humanity's fallen state. Those who subscribed to Stoicism did so by virtue of the delusions induced by their self-love, which made them think they could be sagelike, and therefore godlike, through their own efforts. Picking up on part of Augustine's analysis of the relationship between self-love and charity, and foreshadowing Pierre Nicole's more famous treatment of the same subject, Senault suggests there was a 'lost resemblance between Concupiscence and Charity'.[29]

> If the learned Tertullian, had reason to call the Devil Gods Ape; methinks I may stile Concupiscence the Ape of Charity, because she endeavours to copy her, therefore to obscure her, promising her slaves the same advantages Charity makes her subjects hope for: she takes the

same course, continues the same designs, and in her opposition is so perfect a Transcript of this Excellent Original, that the most part of Philosophers confound them together.[30]

According to Senault, the Stoic is armed with a set of false beliefs about both human and cosmic nature, such that the inevitable result of the encounter between the Stoic and the world is failure. The world did not cooperate with the Stoic's ambitions, nor indeed did the Stoic's own human nature, and the result was a misery that provokes ridicule:

> These reasons so eloquently expresst by the Stoicks, have as yet framed a wiseman onely in Idea. Their admirers have reaped nothing but confusion; after having courted so Proud and so Austere a vertue, they are become ridiculous to all ages. And the wisest amongst them have found, that whilst they would go about to make so many Gods, the Product hath been so many Idols.[31]

In the preface to *L'homme criminel*, the link between Stoicism and Pelagianism that Jansen had posited is made stark. The text opens with assertions about the centrality of pride to the lives of fallen men; the Stoics are introduced in the fourth paragraph as a group of philosophers who, 'enlivened by vain-glory', make the claim that 'if man were irregular, 'twas only because he *Would* be so'; and in the sentence that follows, Senault remarks that 'diverse ages before *Pelagius* his birth, *Zeno* and *Seneca* had tane upon them the Defence of *Corrupted Nature*'.[32] Whereas Jansen presented a developmental account in which Stoicism featured as one stage in a genealogy of Pelagianism, Senault by contrast keeps things simpler, asserting that the Stoics taught the same errors as the Pelagians, and even associating the disappearance of the Stoa with the appearance of the Pelagian heresy itself, for 'Their Sect was borne down when the *Pelagians* raised up their heresie upon its ruines'. Saint Augustine 'hath triumphed over this proud and learned heresie', but 'it hath out-lived that defeat'. Even today, Senault warns, 'we speak the *Language* of the *Pelagians*', attributing 'more to *Liberty* or *Free-will* then to *Grace*' as if 'we will be *Our Selves*, the *Authors* of our *Salvation*'.[33] The Stoics and the Pelagians are also lined up alongside one another in a passage from *L'homme chrestien* on those who are 'perswaded that Vertue is nothing else but a naturall inclination guided by reason . . . so that to live according to the Laws of Nature, was to live according to the Laws of Vertue'.

> This opinion is approved of by the Stoicks among Philosophers, and by the *Pelagians* among Heretiques; it infuseth blindness and arro-

gance into the spirit of those that side with it, and the esteem it puffs them up with of Nature makes them neglect the assistance of Grace. It seems they would retrieve the state of Innocence, that they have a design to perswade us that sin hath done no hurt to the will of man, that he is free under the captivity of Concupiscence, as under the dominion of Original righteousness; and that Nature having lost nothing of her primitive purity, may scrve for a guide to guilty man, as well as to man an innocent.[34]

Senault was an able propagandist rather than an incisive philosophical writer. Following Jansen, he constructed an argument that could be deployed against both contemporary Senecan Neostoicism and the suspected 'Pelagian' tendencies of much contemporary theology. Where Jansen had chiefly built his case on his rejection of the Stoic or Pelagian conception of a man without sin, however, Senault organised his sharp opposition of Stoicism to Christianity on the straightforwardly Augustinian terrain of the problematic of charity and self-love. In both renewing and drastically simplifying Augustine's critique of the Stoics, he helped both to elaborate and popularise Jansen's template for anti-Stoic criticism and to prepare the way for the considerably more original criticisms of Stoicism in the subsequent interventions of two other French Augustinians, Blaise Pascal and Nicolas Malebranche.

BLAISE PASCAL

In the document known as the 'Discussion with Monsieur de Sacy', an oral report of Blaise Pascal's visit to Port-Royal in January 1655, we find the most elegant statement of the Jansenists' suspicion of Stoicism.[35] In this text, Pascal stresses the virtues of the ethics of Epictetus. The focus on the centrality of God is salutary, he maintains, and Epictetus's account of our duties is unrivalled: he emphasises man's dignity, and he tells us what God would have us do with great clarity and power. Pascal continues, however, by outlining the dangers of this ethics:

> Our spirit cannot be forced to believe what is false, nor our will to love something which makes it unhappy. These two powers are, therefore, free, and it is through them that we can become perfect; man through these powers can know God perfectly, love, obey, and please him, cure him of all his vices, acquire virtue, and thereby become saintly and God's friend. These wickedly proud principles lead man into other errors, such as that the soul is part of the divine being, that pain and death are not evils, that we can commit suicide when we are so af-

flicted that we have to believe God is calling us, and there are still more.[36]

Epictetus is praised for his clear-sighted recognition of one half of human nature, the dignity of humankind, but this came at the cost of obscuring a clear view of its other half, our profound wretchedness and inability to function without God. Montaigne is the other philosopher discussed by Pascal in this conversation, a philosopher who understood the limitations of the human intellect very well and whose scepticism was a useful anti-dote against many errors, yet who in the end was unable to do much more than tolerate present practices and search for a comfortable life within them. If the Stoicism of Epictetus nurtured pride, Pascal suggests, the scepticism of Montaigne fostered laziness. Since Epictetus and Montaigne were the most eloquent spokesmen for these two opposing philosophical standpoints, Pascal concludes, these problems highlighted the inability of humankind to live by reason alone. Pascal does not argue that these Stoic errors could be corrected or mitigated by the addition of a Christian supplement. The gap between Stoicism and Christianity was more fundamental than that. Rather, Pascal presents Augustinian Christianity as the appropriate framework for a life that alone could comprehend the errors of the rationalist philosophers but that is in no simple sense merely a position midway between two erroneous extremes. Armed with a living Augustinianism, furthermore, the Christian is able to embark on a careful reading of both Epictetus and Montaigne for the sake of the instruction they are able to provide, while their errors would cancel each other out and do no real harm.[37]

A similar pattern of argument can be reconstructed from the fragments of the *Pensées*—and has to be reconstructed, given the radically unfinished nature of this work. Only a handful of Pascal's remarks were addressed to the Stoics, but it is possible to see reasonably clearly how the Stoics functioned within the economy of the text as a whole. The general tone is set early on, in an isolated *pensée* from the first *liasse* (or 'bundle' of several *pensées* organised under a common heading):

The stoics say: 'Go back into yourselves. There you will find peace'. And it is not true.

Others say: 'Go out, look for happiness in some distraction.' And that is not true. Illness is the result.

Happiness is neither outside us nor within us. It is in God, and both outside and within us.[38]

This pattern is then repeated, in diverse fragments. Some aspect of Stoicism is identified and it is then juxtaposed against a rival philosophical thesis, which is usually Epicurean (though not always, and not in the example given above). Pascal then employs one of two strategies. Either both theses are claimed to be instructively false and a contrasting Christian truth is articulated, or the competing philosophical claims are treated as in some sense both true but incompatible, and so a Christian dogma is deployed as a way of making sense of this paradox of human affairs.[39]

The most detailed commentary on Stoicism belongs in the *liasse* on the 'philosophers'. This section is almost wholly concerned with the Stoics and begins with this remark:

> Even if Epictetus saw the way perfectly well he said to us: 'You are following the wrong one.' He shows that there is another but does not lead us to it. It is wanting what God wants. Jesus Christ alone leads to it. *Via, veritas.*[40]

Although other philosophical 'sects' are alluded to in the remaining fragments in this section, the Stoics are the only ones mentioned by name, and a series of charges is elaborated against them concerning their inability to provide a pathway to God and the foolishness of their goal ('What the stoics propose is so difficult and worthless'), together with the criticism 'They conclude that you can always do what you can sometimes do', which had led Epictetus to infer that 'because there are resolute Christians, everyone can be one'.[41] The discussion begun in 'Philosophers' continues into the next *liasse*, on 'the sovereign good' (*le souverain bien*). But as it has come down to us, this section of Pascal's work contains only two fragments. The first is a short, bleak remark, directed against Seneca, who teaches his reader to be content with himself and 'end[s] up advising suicide'.[42] The second is a more elaborate, wide-ranging and obviously unfinished fragment in which the Platonists are singled out among the pagan philosophers as having come closest to the nature of the good, the decisive role played by God in any adequate account of the good is reiterated, and, as in the previous fragment, the Stoics' endorsement of suicide is again used to cast doubt on their lofty ideals.

> He alone [God] is our true good. From the time we have forsaken him, it is a curious thing that nothing in nature has been capable of taking his place: stars, sky, earth, elements, plants, cabbages, leeks, animals, insects, calves, snakes, fever, plague, war, famine, vice, adultery, incest. From the time he lost his true good, man can see it everywhere, even in his own destruction, though it is so contrary to God, reason, and nature, all at once.[43]

(The suggestion that the Egyptians had worshipped leeks had been made by Juvenal in his fifteenth *Satire* and was recycled by a number of seventeenth- and eighteenth-century authors, including Thomas Hobbes, Nicolas Malebranche, John Wesley, and David Hume.)[44]

Where Senault's technique was to set up dichotomies, sharply contrasting Stoic and Christian positions to the advantage of the latter, Pascal's more dialectical technique involves an acknowledgment of the partial truths that Stoicism expressed. This made him better attuned to the ideological appeal of the Stoics and the reasons why so many people found inspiration in the surviving Stoic literature. The errors of the Stoics were not simple errors but seductive and ultimately instructive errors. But any consideration of Pascal's thinking about the Stoics must remain tentative when the two key texts under examination are a report of his conversation and the incomplete manuscript of the *Pensées*. These certainly help us understand how Stoicism was being discussed in the Jansenist circle in the latter part of Pascal's life, but we need to be cautious before doing much more with them. For an example of an Augustinian philosopher's creative engagement with Stoicism in the second half of the seventeenth century in published work, we turn to Nicolas Malebranche.

Nicolas Malebranche

> We must speak to men as Jesus Christ did, and not as the
> Stoics, who knew neither the nature nor the malady of the
> human mind. Men must be told unceasingly that it is in
> a sense essential for them to hate and despise themselves,
> and that they must not search for settlement and happiness
> here below; that they must carry their cross.[45]

An Augustinian, though not a Jansenist, Malebranche spent his working life at the Oratory in Paris, serving his novitiate when Senault was its general. His major work, *The Search After Truth*, contains several passages that discuss the Stoics, from book 1, chapter 17, where he makes moves similar to those that Pascal had made with respect to mounting parallel criticisms of the Stoics and the Epicureans regarding the nature of the sovereign good,[46] through to book 5, chapter 4, in which he criticises the Stoics for their 'confused understanding of the disorders caused by Original Sin'.[47] This discussion will concentrate, however, on Malebranche's longest engagement with a Stoic author, from book 2, part 3, chapter 4, his discussion of 'the imagination of Seneca'.[48]

The subject of book 2 of *The Search After Truth* is the imagination; part 3 of this book addresses the subject of the contagious nature of the strong imagination. Malebranche begins his account by setting out the general problem of people who have strong imaginations:

> Strong imaginations are extremely contagious: they dominate weaker
> ones, gradually giving them their own orientation, and imprinting

their own characteristics on them. Therefore, since those who have a strong and vigorous imagination are completely unreasonable, there are few more general causes of men's errors than this dangerous communication of the imagination.[49]

The imagination is dangerous, but it is not entirely bad; indeed, as with everything fashioned by God, it serves a useful purpose—and one that speaks to the perennial Augustinian problematic of charity and self-love:

> To understand what this contagion is, and how it is transmitted from one person to another, it is necessary to know that men need one another, and that they were created that they might form several bodies, all of whose parts have a mutual correspondence. To maintain this union God has commanded us to have charity for one another. But because self-love can gradually destroy charity, and break the bond of civil society, it was appropriate for God to preserve it by also uniting men through natural ties, which subsisted without charity and appealed to self-love.[50]

Pierre Nicole had considered a version of the same problem: how does human society persist in a reasonably orderly fashion if human beings are as corrupt as the most authoritative theology teaches? In his essay on charity and self-love he had articulated and developed a line of argument rooted in Augustine's writings that suggested that by a trick of Providence, the operations of self-love came to imitate those of charity.[51] Malebranche, by contrast, took the same Augustinian elements—God, self-love, and imitation—and reassembled them in a different configuration. In his version, God created the world and our natures in such a way that our self-love leads us to imitate one another, and this works to bring about a certain kind of social uniformity:

> These natural ties . . . consist in a certain disposition of the brain all men have to imitate those with whom they converse, to form the same judgments they make, and to share the same passions by which they are moved. And this disposition normally ties men to one another much more closely than charity founded upon reason, because such charity is very rare.[52]

There were two chief causes of our disposition to imitate others. One was found in the soul and was closely related to what Hobbes and others had described under the heading of 'glory':

> The inclination all men have for grandeur and high position, and for obtaining an honourable place in others' minds. For this is the inclina-

tion that secretly excites us to speak, walk, dress, and comport ourselves with the air of people of quality. This is the source of new styles,
the instability of living languages, and even of certain general corrup-
tions of mores. In short, this is the principal source of all the extrava-
gant and bizarre novelties founded not upon reason, but only upon
men's fantasies.[53]

But it was the second that engaged his attention over the following chapters. This was 'a certain impression made by persons of strong imagination upon weak minds, and upon tender and delicate brains'.[54] A strong
imagination was 'that constitution of the brain which renders it capable
of having very deep vestiges and traces that so occupy the soul's capacity
that they prevent it from focusing its attention on things other than those
represented by these images',[55] and these came in two varieties. The first
were the insane, who 'receive these deep traces from an involuntary and
disordered impression of the animal spirits'.[56] The second 'receive them
from the disposition found in their brain substance'[57] and were of more
interest to Malebranche, for it was this kind of imagination that produced the contagion with which he was concerned. It was not a defect to
have a strong imagination, as long as 'the soul always remain[ed] the
master of the imagination'. It could be a very good thing indeed, and it
was the 'origin of subtlety and strength of mind'.[58]

> But when the imagination dominates the soul, and when without
> attention to the direction of will these traces are formed because of
> the disposition of the brain and by the action of objects and the ani-
> mal spirits, it is clear that this is a very bad quality and a sort of
> madness.[59]

People with strong imaginations of this kind, Malebranche claimed,
displayed above all two defects. In the first place, they were unable to
make 'sound judgements about difficult and intricate things'.[60] Second,
they were 'visionaries, though in a delicate way that is rather difficult to
recognise', and prone to exaggeration and distorted perceptions.

> They are vehement in their passions, biased in their opinions, and
> always conceited and very self-satisfied. . . . They do not walk, they
> bound. . . . They ordinarily stop at the surface of things, and are
> completely occupied with visible ceremonies and rituals of little
> importance.[61]

Furthermore—and this was something that might be an advantage to
them but could also be extremely dangerous—people like this could be

quite persuasive. Thus, in chapter 3, Malebranche turned to the trio of Tertullian, Seneca, and Montaigne, three writers who, in his view, suffered in different ways from an excess of imagination.

In contrast to Senault or Augustine, with their generic attacks on 'the Stoics', Malebranche concentrated on one Stoic philosopher in particular. As for Jansen, Seneca provided the most suitable target. While Malebranche agreed with Senault and the other Augustinians that it was the Stoic's pride that induced him to write in the way that he did, his account of what was going on was different. Senault's Stoics relied too much on their reason, 'not knowing that reason was blind', and disregarded both religion and their own experience of their corrupt human nature. In another part of his book, Malebranche presented Stoics who championed reason over experience, in these terms:

> I grant that reason teaches us that we ought to suffer exile without sadness, but this same reason teaches us that we should not feel pain when our arm is cut off. . . . But experience sufficiently shows us that things are not as reason says they should be, and it is ridiculous to philosophize against experience.[62]

Here, however, Malebranche's Seneca was a rhetorician who did not reason clearly enough. 'As long as he makes great strides, designed strides in a precise cadence', Malebranche wrote, 'he imagines he has made great progress, but in truth he is like a dancer who always ends up where he begins.'

> He convinces because he arouses the emotions and because he pleases, but I do not believe he can persuade those who can read him calmly, who are prepared against surprise, and who are accustomed to yield only to the clarity and evidence of arguments.[63]

Seneca's depiction of the wise man was 'magnificent and pompous', but also 'vain and imaginary'. Malebranche remarked that 'Cato had neither the hardness of a diamond unbreakable by iron nor the solidity of rocks immovable by floods, as Seneca pretends'.[64] It was in his comparison of Cato with Christ, Paul, and other early Christians that we could see how the errors of the Stoics played out in concrete ethical contexts.

> The virtue of the Stoics could not render them invulnerable, since true virtue does not prevent one from being miserable and worthy of compassion when one suffers some evil. St Paul and the first Christians had more virtue than Cato and the Stoics. They nevertheless admit that they were wretched because of the pain they endured, although they were made happy by the hope of eternal reward.[65]

Cato's celebrated patience, on the other hand, 'was only blindness and pride'.[66] Seneca tells us that he regarded his enemies as beasts, against whom it would be shameful to become angry, but this was not admirable at all.

> How dangerous it is, especially to Christians, to instruct themselves in morality from an author so injudicious as Seneca, whose imagination is so strong, so lively, and so imperious that it dazzles, distracts and carries away those with but little firmness of mind and much sensibility for all that flatters the concupiscence of pride?[67]

Christ, on the other hand, on being struck by an officer became neither angry nor vengeful. Instead, he pardoned his assailant, an action that presupposed an acceptance of the fact that he had been wronged.[68]

Following in Jansen's footsteps, Malebranche explicitly compared the Stoic pride that made men want to become God—or godlike, in the form of the sage—with the serpent tempting Adam and Eve by telling them they could become like God, for the serpent knew 'that the desire for independence was the weakness through which they had to be taken'.[69] The serpent, like Cato, tended to be believed, because 'when a bold liar lies with great assurance, he often causes the most unbelievable things to be believed, for the assurance with which he speaks is a proof that affects the senses, and consequently is exceedingly strong and quite persuasive to most men'.[70]

> All this shows that few errors are more dangerous, or more easily communicable, than those with which Seneca's books are filled. For these errors are refined, suited to man's nature and similar to that in which the demon engaged our first parents. They are clad in these books with pompous and splendid ornaments, which gain entry for them into most minds. They enter, grasp, stun, and blind them. But they blind them with a proud blindness. . . . not a humiliating blindness full of shadows that makes one aware that one is blind and force one to admit it to others. . . . Thus, nothing is more contagious than this blindness, because the vanity and sensibility of men, the corruption of their senses and passions, dispose them to search after it, to be struck by it, and excite them to impress others with it.[71]

Not all of Seneca was false and dangerous, Malebranche conceded. Echoing Pascal's argument about Epictetus and Montaigne, he could 'be read with profit by those who see things correctly and know the foundation of Christian morality'. (He suggested that the same was also true of the Qu'ran and the works of Nostradamus.) A keen awareness of our inescapable dependence on our body, parents, friends, prince, and country was sufficient 'to destroy the Stoic wisdom completely'.[72] Having dealt almost exclusively with Seneca up to this point, Malebranche closes his discussion with a critical observation against Epictetus and a restatement of the claim made earlier, not merely the Augustinian commonplace that we are dependent on God but that in accordance with God's command, we are dependent on every living thing in his Creation:

> Hence, this magnificent division of all things not dependent on us and upon which we ought to depend is a division that seems consistent with reason, but that is inconsistent with the disordered state to which sin has reduced us. We are united to all creatures by God's order, and we depend upon them absolutely because of the disorder of sin.[73]

In the 1684 *Treatise on Ethics*, Malebranche presented a condensed version of his fundamental criticism of the Stoics. 'We must love God', he insisted, 'not only more than the present life, but more than our own being. Order requires that it be so. . . . We cannot find our happiness and perfection outside ourselves. We can only find them in God, since only God is capable of acting in us and making us happy and perfect.'[74] He then turned his attention to the Stoics, in order to flesh out his charge that 'it is the ultimate of crimes to place our end in our selves':

> That was the folly of the Stoic's Sage, for whom happiness did not in the least depend upon God. Convinced of our powerlessness and of that of creatures, we must incline toward the Creator with all our strength. We must do everything for God. We must trace back all our actions to the One from whom alone we have the strength to do them. Otherwise we injure Order, we offend God, we commit injustice. This is incontestable. But we must search, in the invincible love which God gives us, for our happiness and for motives which could make us love Order. For, finally, God being just, we cannot be solidly happy if we are not submissive to Order, and *he hates his soul, who loves iniquity* [Psalms 10:5].[75]

The same text, finally, insisted on the crucial difference between the Christian's duty of acting in accordance with universal Reason and the divine Logos and the Stoic's insistence on 'following God or nature'. At 1.1.22, Malebranche set out an important part of his doctrine concerning God's 'general laws':

> When we resist the actions of men, we offend them. For since they act only by particular wills, we cannot resist their actions without also

resisting their designs. But when we resist God's actions, we do not in the least offend Him, and often we even promote His designs. For since God constantly follows the general laws which He has set for Himself, the combination of effects which are necessary consequences therefrom cannot always be conformed to Order or suited to the execution of the most excellent work.[76]

He then proceeded to attack the Stoics once more, undermining the central notion of Stoic ethics that we should somehow choose to 'follow nature', where nature was understood in term's of God's decree. On the one hand, 'It is not a question of duty, however, but of necessity for us to submit to His absolute power';[77] on the other hand, even if it were a matter of moral duty, unfailingly to 'follow God or nature' would be impossible, for the Stoics' ethics failed to acknowledge the unknowability and inscrutability of God's decree for the world:

> By contrast, we are able to know Order by way of our union with the Eternal Word, with universal Reason. Therefore it can be our law, and can lead us. But the Divine Decrees are absolutely unknown to us. Let us not in any way make them into rules for ourselves. Let us leave to the sages of Greece and to the Stoics that chimerical virtue of *following God or nature*. For us, let us consult Reason, let us love and follow Order in all things. To submit ourselves to the law God invincibly loves and which He inviolably follows is truly to follow him.[78]

In many ways, therefore, Malebranche's critique of the Stoics represented the culmination of the tradition of French Augustinian anti-Stoicism. More sophisticated than Senault's and far more attuned to contemporary philosophy than Jansen's, Malebranche's arguments against the Stoics were more systematic and sustained than those found in Pascal. Indeed, Malebranche's philosophy provided the most developed and sophisticated Catholic opposition to Stoicism in the seventeenth century.

FRANÇOIS, DUC DE LA ROCHEFOUCAULD

The fifth writer in this survey of seventeenth-century French Augustinian reactions to Stoicism is François, 6ᵉ duc de La Rochefoucauld (1613–80), whose *Réflexions ou sentences et maximes morales*, generally known as the *Maxims*, first appeared in 1665. There are various ways in which La Rochefoucauld stands apart from the four Augustinians considered hitherto. He was neither a Jansenist nor an Oratorian, for example, but an aristocrat, soldier, and politician, who campaigned in the wars of the 1630s and 1640s and fought against Cardinal Mazarin's ministry during the Fronde, being badly wounded at the battle of the Faubourg Saint-Antoine in July1652. In further contrast to Jansen, Senault, Pascal, and Malebranche, La Rochefoucauld's argument was more or less secular, with hardly any overtly theological concerns on display in his writing. Nevertheless, the tendency of the scholarship over the past fifty years or so has been to place the *Maxims* squarely in an Augustinian framework,[79] and it is certainly the case that the treatment of Stoic and Neostoic moral psychology in the *Maxims* is broadly continuous with the other criticism that has been considered in this chapter. The well-known epigraph to the *Maxims* sets the tone for the rest of the work—'our virtues are, most often only vices disguised'[80]—and this thought is given a distinctively Augustinian twist in a variation stated in no. 120: 'We are so accustomed to disguise ourselves from others that we end up disguising ourselves from ourselves.'[81] Those who claim to exemplify Stoic virtues delude themselves; it is rather their self-love (*amour-propre*) that makes them do what they do in the ways in which they do it.

There is only one explicit mention of any Stoic philosopher in the text of the *Maxims*: 'The philosophers, and Seneca above all, have not eliminated crimes with their precepts: they have only employed them for the building of pride.'[82] This maxim appeared only in the early editions and was subsequently withdrawn. Seneca did not need to be named, however, for the frontispiece engraving by Stéphane Picart that appeared in the first four editions of the *Maxims* made it clear that he was the target of the work a whole. The engraving depicted a cupid labelled 'L'Amour de la Verité' pointing and laughing at a bust of Seneca, having just removed both a mask and a laurel wreath.[83] (Aphra Behn's translation of the *Maxims* was published in 1685 as *Seneca Unmasqued*.)[84] In the early sections of the *Maxims*, fully in line with the action of the frontispiece, La Rochefoucauld's strategy was to unmask particular virtues characteristically associated with Senecan Stoicism. The Machiavellian observation that the clemency of princes is 'often only a policy for winning the affection of the people'[85] is followed by a more searching criticism of Seneca's signature virtue: 'This clemency of which virtue is made is sometimes practiced out of vanity, now and then out of laziness, often out of fear, and almost always out of all three together.'[86] La Rochefoucauld also paid attention to another characteristic Neostoic virtue: 'The constancy of the wise is only the art of containing the agitation in their hearts.'[87] This is followed by a reflection on constancy in the face of death:

> Those who are condemned to the rack sometimes affect a constancy and a contempt of death which is in fact only the fear of facing it; so that one could say that this constancy and contempt are to their spirit what a blindfold is to their eyes.[88]

La Rochefoucauld signalled the importance of this subject through his return to it in no. 504, right at the end of the book, in what is by far the longest entry in the collection and the only one it feels awkward to describe as a maxim rather than as an essay in its own right.

In this essay, La Rochefoucauld introduces his theme as 'this contempt for death which the pagans boast of deriving from their own strength, without the hope of a better life', and he draws a distinction between 'steadfastly enduring death and having contempt for it.'[89] The latter was the recommendation of Seneca, who urged his reader to overcome both his natural desire of life, the 'one chain which binds us to life', and his fear of death through the cultivation of a philosophical contempt of death, for 'he who has learned to die has unlearned slavery'.[90] Seneca's position was not uncomplicatedly Stoic. The view set out by Marcus Aurelius, for example, was that the Stoics accept death as part of nature and, for that reason it was neither an evil nor an appropriate object of contempt.[91] According to La Rochefoucauld, constancy in the face of death is 'quite ordinary', while contempt for death is 'never sincere'; and he rejects both of these Stoic views, for while much had been written against the idea that death is not an evil, 'I doubt that anybody with good sense ever believed it', and he remarks that 'One can have various objects of disgust in life, but one is never right to have contempt for death.'[92] Seneca had taught that 'He that is not prepared for death, shall be perpetually troubled',[93] and that 'The way never to fear it, is to be often thinking of it'.[94] For La Rochefoucauld, by contrast,

It is necessary to avoid imagining it in all of its particulars if one does not want to believe that it is the greatest of all evils. The most clever and the most brave are those who find more honest pretexts to prevent themselves from considering it. But any man who knows how to see it as it is finds that it is a dreadful thing.[95]

It was 'the necessity of dying' that had been the cause of 'all the constancy of philosophers':

They believed that one had to go willingly where one could not prevent oneself from going; and, unable to make their lives eternal, there was nothing they did not to make their reputations eternal, and to save from the ship-wreck what there is no guarantee of saving.[96]

To cope adequately with death, we should not 'tell ourselves all we think about it', and 'we flatter ourselves when we believe that death appears to be from close-up what we judged it to be from afar'. We also misunderstand our *amour-propre* if we think 'that it could help us consider as nothing that which must necessarily destroy it'. Far from 'inspiring us with the contempt for death', our reason 'helps us to discover what is frightful and terrible to it', and 'all reason can do for us is to advise us to turn our eyes away from death in order to have them rest upon other objects'. Cato and Brutus 'chose some illustrious ones'. Both 'great men and common people' have 'receive[d] death with the same face', though in neither case is a proper appreciation of Stoic philosophy the reason. When great men show contempt for death, 'it is the love of glory which takes their view away from it', while for the common people, 'it is only an effect of their meagre enlightenment which prevents them from knowing the magnitude of their affliction and allows them the liberty to think about something else'.[97]

An Acceptable Alternative? The Stoicism of Marcus Aurelius

French Senecan Neostoicism had flourished in the first half of the seventeenth century. The sustained barrage of Augustinian criticism considered in this chapter dates from the 1640s, by which time the genre of French Neostoic treatises on the passions was largely exhausted. But the criticism did not go entirely unanswered. The major reply from a French Senecan came from Antoine Le Grand, whose 1662 book, *Le Sage des Stoiques*, set out a restatement of a Neostoic theory of the passions.[98] The details of that theory are not especially interesting; more significant for current purposes is a passage at the end of the second discourse in his book that explicitly engages the developing Augustinian argument. With reference to Augustine's *City of God* 22.24, 'Of the blessings which the Creator has filled this life, even though it is subject to condemnation',[99] Le Grand identifies the peculiar way in which the Augustinians of his age were using an exaggerated binary of God–Nature, presenting the latter category in excessively negative terms, even from a strictly Augustinian perspective:

> And even St Austin, though an Enemy to the Vertues of the Heathen, attributing (with much heat) all to Grace, and seeming to grant Nature nothing, that all might be owed to the assistance of Jesus Christ, is astonished that Sin which brought all our Senses into a Cloud of Error, darkened our minds, depraved our Wills, and poured into our Souls the Seeds of all Vice, could not choak the inclination we have for that which is good. . . . Some of his Disciples doubted his Arguments, they could hardly comprehend how that which makes the fountain of our Crimes, should be the Original of our good Deeds, and that, against

those inclinations which he maintains, she often brings forth perfection instead of Monsters. . . . Methinks it is not very hard to clear all these Doubts, and without stumbling at the Difficulties they lay down, it may Suffice to propose them a Dilemma, to shew them the Truth by day light. For after Adam's fall it must be, either that God forsook his Works, or that he knew Nature potent enough to do well, without the aid of written Laws.[100]

Le Grand ends with a caution to anyone tempted by the rigour of the Augustinian critique:

If to augment the guilt of the first Man; or diminish the rigor of his punishment, you represent God infinitely offended; who justly denies his assistance to Adams Descendants, be careful that you do not equally question both his providence and his Mercy, and remember, that you cannot take from him the Care of his Creatures without offending his Bounty.[101]

Le Grand's Neostoicism ultimately failed to secure even his own philosophical allegiance, however, and he ended up renouncing Stoicism for Cartesianism, on behalf of which he wrote a long, unsophisticated defence.[102]

Among those writers anxious to defend the moral probity of Stoic ethics who were not attracted by the prospect of simply reiterating much criticised Senecan pieties, the characteristic move was to turn away from Seneca and in the direction of the *Meditations* of Marcus Aurelius. The story of the career of Marcus Aurelius in European letters from the time of his first modern editor, Wilhelm Holtzmann, better known as 'Xylander', down to the publication of the *Encyclopédie* has been narrated by Jill Kraye in an excellent article packed with interesting detail and at least one good joke.[103] But her account of how the *Meditations* became 'the best-known Stoic text in the second half of the seventeenth century' is largely a descriptive one;[104] what needs to be explained is why Marcus became quite so popular over the course of the seventeenth century. The simplest answer relates to the Augustinian attack on Neostoic moral psychology, which, as we have seen, tended to be largely derived from an appropriation and redeployment of Seneca. It was a comparatively simple move for those who wanted to continue to engage sympathetically with Stoicism to switch their attention away from Seneca and towards Marcus Aurelius, thereby bypassing much of the criticism, which could be considered specifically anti-Senecan rather than generically anti-Stoic. Seneca had drawn a lot of fire for his arrogance and pride; by contrast, Marcus appeared an acceptably humble alternative, the Roman emperor who was always reminding himself that he was but a small part of a much larger whole, and reiterating his willing submission to the divine intelligence. It is striking, in fact, that many of the seventeenth- and early eighteenth-century editions of the *Meditations* that were published in England and France begin with remarks in their various prefaces about why readers should prefer the Stoic emperor to the (then) far better-known Seneca.

If Isaac Casaubon had been the first modern scholar to understand the significance of the *Meditations* as an important source of Stoic philosophy in his commentary on Persius of 1605, his son Meric was the first editor to give the work its modern title, *Meditations concerning Himself*, publishing the first English translation in 1634 (dedicated to the royalist archbishop William Laud), and a Greek-Latin edition in 1643 (dedicated to the parliamentarian John Selden),[105] and in his preface he observed that 'Yet shall you not find in him [Marcus Aurelius] those blasphemies, in exaltation of this humane power and libertie, which you shall in Seneca, and other Stoics'.[106] Thomas Gataker's Greek-Latin edition of 1652 was a remarkable feat of scholarship—indeed, the history of the Cambridge University Press judges that it was 'the single major scholarly achievement of the press' during the period of the Civil War and interregnum.[107] Gataker's 'Praeloquio', translated as 'Preliminary Discourse', was widely recognised as one of the most authoritative treatments of Stoicism in English, and different portions of it were reprinted in a number of other places over the following century, being included in, for example, both Jeremy Collier's 1701 edition of Marcus Aurelius as well as the edition published in Glasgow in 1742 by the Foulis Press (which I consider at the end of chapter seven).[108]

Gataker discusses the three surviving Stoic authors—Marcus Aurelius, Epictetus, and Seneca—and opines that 'Of these three, Seneca is the first in Time, but in my Opinion, the least in Value, and Merit'.[109] Gataker concedes that Seneca has his strong points: 'He has a great many shining Sentences, his Precepts are admirable, his Manner noble, and his way of arguing very acute in many places'.[110] These were, however, outweighed by his vices, which were enumerated as flattery and hypocrisy with respect to the emperors and an inconsistency of attitude with respect to the Epicureans, and Gataker also registers his dislike of aspects of Seneca's philosophical style, anticipating, to my mind, Nietzsche's later description of Seneca as the 'toreador of virtue' (*der Toreador der Tugend*):[111]

And lastly, he is sometimes guilty of the same Trifling, which he finds fault with in Zeno and Chrysippus. He is Gay sometimes when he should be Solemn, and Flourishes when he should strike home.... He gives you sometimes a turn of Fancy, instead of Solid Proof....

[His notions] have generally a Point, but no Weight of Body for Execution.[112]

This verdict was echoed by a later editor, Jeremy Collier, who judged that Marcus Aurelius's style was preferable to Seneca's, who 'moves more by start and sally'.[113]

Writing in a context in which a question mark had been raised over the compatibility of Stoic ethics with Christian theology, these editors drew attention to those aspects of the emperor's thought that seemed most congruent with Christian morality. For Casaubon, 'The chiefest subject of the Book, is, the vanity of the world and all worldly things, as wealth, honour, life, &c. and the end and scope of it, to teach a man how to submit himself wholly to God's providence, and to live content and thankfull in what estate or calling soever.[114] But it was Gataker who presented the most elaborate account of the confluence of Marcus Aurelius's Stoicism and Christian teaching, arguing that 'it may be boldly asserted, there are no remaining monuments of the ancient strangers, which none nearer to the doctrine of CHRIST, than the writings and admonitions of these two; Epictetus and Antoninus'.

> 'Tis certain, whatever precepts our Lord himself has given, in those sermons and conversations of his . . . of abstaining from evil, even in thought, of suppressing vicious affections, of leaving off all idle conversation; of cultivating the heart with all diligence; and fashioning it after the image of God; of doing good to men from the most single disinterested view; of bearing injuries with contentment: of using moderation and strict caution, in our admonitions and reproofs: of counting all things whatever and even life itself, as nothing, when reason and the case demand them: and of undertaking and performing almost all the other duties of Piety. Affection, Equity and Humanity, with the greatest diligence and ardour: All these same precepts are to be found in Antoninus, just as if he had habitually read them; they are everywhere interspersed through this collection of his thoughts and meditations; and continually inculcated with a surprising strength and life, which pierces to the bottom of the heart, and leaves the dart deep fixed in the soul. This every attentive reader will perceive; every honest one confess.[115]

Asking why Christians should take instruction from this pagan author, Gataker answers that 'A careful perusal and serious reflection on these Meditations of Antoninus, are several ways useful', for what was 'summarily proposed' in the New Testament is 'more extensively applied' and 'more fully explained' by Marcus Aurelius. 'Further, in these following books, the good Providence and kindness of God shines forth; and He did not suffer his own image to be quite worn out and lost in man who had fallen off from him.'[116] Far from divine revelation supplementing philosophical reason, the positions are here swapped around.

Casaubon and Gataker did acknowledge a string of positions Marcus Aurelius held that are inassimilable to Christian teaching, but they pass over them quickly, and offer various reasons for excusing the emperor. For Casaubon, there are moments where Marcus Aurelius 'may give offence' for his views which are 'repugnant to our Christian faith, and impious, as when he seemeth to speak doubtfully of God, and his Providence, and to adscribe all things to Fatal necessitie, and the like'; but he urges the reader not to judge Marcus Aurelius only by reference to isolated passages. In his discussion of the emperor's treatment of Providence, he cites groups of passages that lend themselves to libertarian and determinist readings of the text, respectively, going on to argue in a somewhat Lipsian fashion that what Marcus Aurelius calls 'Fate, or Destiny' is 'no other than God's sovraign power and providence in ordering the matters of the world', and he ends his discussion by insisting that Marcus Aurelius uses the vocabulary of providence, fortune ,and chance in a manner 'allowed by the best Schoolmen'.[117] Gataker in turn passes swiftly over the Stoic emperor's less Christian opinions, such as 'his ambiguity on the immortality of the soul'.[118]

If the critique of Senecan Neostoicism was most fully elaborated in seventeenth-century France, we might not be surprised to find that the most systematic attempt to portray Marcus as a Stoic author immunised against that critique was presented in the major French edition of the *Meditations* to be published in the second half of the seventeenth century. This was the edition produced by the husband-and-wife team André and Anne Dacier, first published in Paris by Claude Barbin in 1690 and periodically republished thereafter (a fifth edition, for example, appeared in Amsterdam in 1732). Although they joined in the criticism of Seneca with their observation that he had 'combined the virtues of the earliest Stoics with all the pride of their disciples',[119] the more interesting aspect of the essay that introduces their translation is their attempt explicitly to meet, rather than merely to sidestep, the Augustinian objections to Stoic ethics. Against the kind of argument that we have seen presented by Malebranche, the Daciers asserted that the Stoics 'knew the weakness that is natural to humankind', and that they therefore sought to push 'their duties farther than nature is able to go', treating their readers in the manner of 'a bent tree, which one wants to straighten by pulling it in the opposite direction'.[120] But the full presentation of what we might call their anti-anti-Stoicism comes a few pages later, in the central section of their preface, which sets out six Augustinian objections to Stoic ethics that they propose to refute: first, that the Stoics do not teach that one is required to love God; second, that they do not ask of him the power to follow him; third, that they do not teach man to hate himself, as they ought; fourth, that they do not establish that man is both the most excellent and the most wretched of all creatures; fifth, that they do not teach humility; and sixth, that they do not point out that the tendency to place ourselves above everything else is a sin that comes naturally to us, and is one against which they provide no remedy.[121]

The Daciers then sought to demonstrate that all of these objections fail. In some cases, this was more or less straightforward—Marcus Aurelius repeatedly enjoined his reader to love and praise God, for example—but other attempts to fit the *Meditations* to an Augustinian template are more surprising:

> He shows in many places that man is the most excellent of all creatures because of his origins and because of the perfections that God has deigned to provide to him, and that at the same time he is the most miserable, because his vices make him lose all his advantages, and render him a slave, in separating him from God.[122]

The Stoics did not clearly teach the Christian virtue of humility, the Daciers conceded, and neither the Academy nor the Stoa had a word for it, but 'if this virtue consists of knowing one's insignificance before God, to believe that it is He alone who is the author of everything that is good, and of nothing that is evil', and to teach that everything bar God is 'vile, perishable, temporary, and subject to corruption', then the *Meditations* were exemplary. The Daciers ended their response to the Augustinian objections with some of their most striking claims. They sought to meet the Augustinian argument about self-love head-on, by insisting that Marcus Aurelius held that *amour-propre* was a 'revolt against God' in that it induced men to 'break their social bonds' (*rompre les liens de la société*), and they further maintained that the core ethical teaching of the Gospels was to be found in Marcus Aurelius, for whom 'the first and principle duty of man is to love his neighbour'.[123] They concluded, therefore, that the Augustinian critique failed, while the Stoic argument, by contrast, remained '*tres-solide, tres-vray*' and '*tres-conforme*' to St Paul's teaching in Philippians 4.13 that 'I can do all things in Him that strengtheneth me'.[124]

CHAPTER FIVE

From Hobbes to Shaftesbury

THE RECEPTION OF HOBBES

The Augustinian Catholic critics of Stoicism in seventeenth-century France tended to view it as a philosophy organised around the attribution of excessive power to the free human will. In Protestant Europe, by contrast, Stoicism was much more likely to be criticised as a philosophy of determinism, or as one that denied the freedom of the will. The Augustinians had attacked Stoicism as a philosophy of self-love that dissolved the bonds of society. But for others, Stoicism taught the natural sociability of humankind, and its texts could be exploited in the battle against new theories that seemed to deny this, such as that of Thomas Hobbes. This was done by portraying thinkers like Hobbes as restating Epicureanism, the great rival to Stoicism among the philosophical schools of the Hellenistic world.

Before Hobbes was stigmatised as a kind of Epicurean, however, he was interpreted for equally polemical purposes as being, in Jon Parkin's words, 'a sort of unusual stoic',[1] in particular in his celebrated controversy with John Bramhall, the Arminian bishop of Derry. Hobbes and Bramhall debated the question 'of liberty and necessity' in front of William Cavendish, the Marquess of Newcastle, when all three were living among the royalist exiles in Paris. (This William Cavendish was not the same William Cavendish whom we met in the third chapter, the second Earl of Devonshire, who died in 1628, but his cousin, the royalist general in the Civil War, who was successively from 1628 the Earl, from 1643 the Marquess, and from 1665 the Duke of Newcastle-upon-Tyne, and who died in 1676.) The exact date of the debate is not clear, but it must have taken place sometime between April 1645, when Cavendish arrived in Paris, and July of the same year, when Hobbes departed for Rouen.[2] The controversy entered print in 1654, apparently against the wishes of both parties, and the pirate publication provoked a sequence of increasingly polemical exchanges down to the time of Bramhall's death in 1663.[3] On one occasion, Bramhall characterised Hobbes's position as 'this rare piece of sublimated Stoicism',[4] and in the third section of his original contribution he presented four reasons as to why he found Hobbes's account of liberty and necessity to be false, the fourth being that

This necessity which TH hath devised, which is grounded upon the necessitations of a mans will without his will, is the worst of all others and is so far from lessening the difficulties and absurdities which flow from the fatal destiny of the Stoicks that it increaseth them, and rendereth them unanswerable.[5]

Bramhall considered Hobbes's position to be a deeply subversive one:

I hate this doctrine from my heart. . . . It destroys liberty, and dishonours the nature of man. It makes the second causes and outward objects to be the rackets, and men to be but the Tenis-balls of destiny. It makes the first cause, that is, God Almighty, to be the introducer of all evil, and sin into the world. . . . And if they being thus determined, did necessitate *Adam* inevitably, irresistibly, not by an accidental, but by an essential subordination of causes to whatsoever he did, then one of these two absurdities must needs follows, either that *Adam* did not sin, and that there is no such thing as sin in the World, because it proceeds naturally, necessarily, and essentially from God. Or that God is more guilty of it, and were the more the cause of evil than man, because man is extrinsically, inevitably determined, but so is not God. . . . It were better to be an Atheist . . . or be a Manichee . . . or with the Heathens . . . than thus to charge the true God to be the proper cause, and true Author of all the sins and evils which are in the world.[6]

'Notwithstanding any thing which is pleaded here', Bramhall proclaimed, 'this Stoical opinion doth stick hypocrisy and dissimulation close to God, who is truth it self'.[7] Bramhall warned of the dangers to piety if liberty were to be set aside,[8] and Jon Parkin has observed that Hobbes was sufficiently vulnerable to Bramhall's charge that on his account, Adam's sin was necessitated, and that this was the reason he was keen for the original exchange not to enter the public domain.[9]

In the numbered sections of the argument, part 18 is the setting for the most concentrated comments on the Stoics' fate, with Bramhall closely following Lipsius's presentation in *De constantia*. The 'Patrons of necessity', he wrote, 'have certain retreats of distinctions which they fly unto for refuge', and he identified and refuted three different ways of distinguishing between 'Stoical' and 'Christian' necessity:

First, say they, the Stoicks did subject Jupiter to destiny, but we subject destiny to God; I answer, that the Stoical and Christian destiny are one and the same *fatum quasi effatum Iovis*. . . .

Next, they say, that the Stoicks did hold an eternal flux and necessary connexion of causes; but they believe that God doth act, *praeter &*

contra naturam, besides and against nature. I answer, that it is not much material whether they attribute necessity to God or to the Stars, or to a connexion of causes, so as they establish necessity.

Lastly, they say, the Stoicks did take away liberty and contingence, but they admit it; I answer, what Liberty or contingence is it they admit, but a titular Liberty and an empty shadow of contingence who do profess stiffly that all actions and events which either are or shall be cannot but be nor can be otherwise, after any other manner, in any other place, time, number, order, measure, nor to any other end than they are, and that in respect of God, determining them to one; what a poor ridiculous liberty or contingence is this?[10]

In his reply, Hobbes denied that he had ever distinguished between Stoic and Christian necessity, which was correct, insofar as Lipsius was the target of Bramhall's charges on this point, and he insisted in his characteristic fashion that he had not 'drawn my answer to his arguments from the authority of any sect, but from the nature of the things themselves'.[11] Bramhall in reply then noted, again correctly, that the two disputants had different motives for their similar denials of this Lipsian distinction:

My reason is, because I acknowledge no such necessity. . . . But yet he likes not the names of Stoical and Christian destiny: I do not blame him, though he would not willingly be counted a Stoick. . . . If he had been as careful in reading other men's opinions, as he is confident in setting down his own, he might have found not onely the thing, but the name it self often used. But if the name of *fatum Christianum* do offend him, let him call it with Lipsius *fatum verum* who divides destiny into four kinds: Mathematical or Astrological destiny, Natural destiny, Stoical or violent destiny, and true destiny . . . and defines it just as TH doth his destiny; to be a series or order of causes depending upon the Divine Council. . . . TH saith, he had not sucked his answer from any sect; and I say, so much the worse; It is better to be the disciple of an old Sect, than the ringleader of a new.[12]

On this point, at least, both men understood one another well. When Hobbes came to write his 'Animadversion' on this part of the debate, he wrote that Bramhall's mistake was to suppose that he 'had taken my opinion from the Authority of the Stoick Philosophers, not from my own Meditation', with the result that he 'falleth into dispute against the Stoicks: whereof I might if I pleas'd, take no notice, but pass over to Number 19'. But Hobbes then admitted that he found the Stoics' doctrine accurate in its substance, but that their mistake 'consisteth not in the opinion of Fate, but in faigning of a false God'—that is, Jupiter; and in the same passage he further agreed that Lipsius was right to identify fate as 'a series or order of causes depending upon the Divine counsel'.[13] In his 'Castigations', in turn, Bramhall reiterated in sections 6 and 18 the ways in which the necessitarian position that Hobbes had adopted was in fact even more extreme than those staked out by Lipsius, on the one hand, and the Stoics on the other: Lipsius because 'He was no such friend of any sort of destiny, as to abandon the Liberty of the Will'; the Stoics because they

> together with their fate, did also maintain the Freedom of the Will. And as we find in many Authors, both theirs and ours, did not subject the Soul of man, nor the will of man to the rigid dominion of destiny. The Stoicks subtracted some causes, and subjected others to necessity. And among those which they would not have to be under necessity, they placed the will of man.[14]

Bramhall's attempt to pin some kind of Stoic label onto Hobbes, however, was not one that really caught on among Hobbes's many and varied opponents, and from around 1660 it became increasingly common to see him portrayed in the critical literature as being a modern follower of the Epicureans, an association that appears in both his English and German reception. Robert Sharrock's *Hypothesis ethike* made the connection in England in 1660, for example, and Jacob Thomasius did so in his 'De statu naturali adversus Hobbesium' in Germany in 1661.[15]

The elements of Hobbes's argument that were picked out as Epicurean by his German critics, such as the Aristotelian Hermann Conring in his 1662 *De civili prudentia*, included his emphasis on self-preservation, his account of the state of nature as a state of war, and his social contract theory.[16] The work of pressing Hobbes into such an Epicurean mould was to create a space for the restatement of a non-Hobbesian natural law theory that stood squarely in the Grotian tradition, which emphasised its foundation in sociability as much as in self-preservation—and the Germans were quick to latch on to the Stoic moment in Grotius's original presentation. In correspondence with Johann Christian von Boineburg, Samuel Pufendorf, and Johann Heinrich Böcler in 1663, Conring urged on Pufendorf that the treatise on natural law that he was preparing (and that would become the *De jure naturae*) should incorporate extensive references to ancient philosophers in order to avoid the 'geometric' method, which in this discussion was associated with Erhard Weigel.[17] Böcler similarly urged Pufendorf to pay more attention to the ancients so that he might better appreciate the extent to which Grotius's theory was a redeployment of ancient ideas,[18] and in the same year Böcler published a new edition of the first book of Grotius's *De Jure Belli ac Pacis* with notes to identify what he considered the very many unacknowledged references in that text to classical authorities: 'Many of these points stem from Cicero', Böcler wrote, 'and Cicero took them from the Stoics above all, although Aristotle and Plato were of a like mind'.[19] As T. J. Hochstrasser notes in his examination of this episode, 'Pufendorf clearly was not initially receptive to all these methodological recommendations; but they do seem to have become of decisive importance in the course of the composition of *De Jure Naturae et Gentium*'.[20] Just to take one crude set of quantitative measures, for example, Horst Denzer calculated there were 155 references to Cicero, 109 to Seneca, 12 to Marcus Aurelius, and 34 to Epictetus in the book, citations that are concentrated in those parts of the second book where Pufendorf most directly confronts Hobbes's argument from *De cive*.[21] Occasional quotation from Lucretius's *De rerum natura* in these sections helped sediment the association of Hobbes's political argument with the views of the Epicureans,[22] and in the third chapter Pufendorf summarises his central point against Hobbes with the remark that 'Self-love and Sociableness ought by no means to be made opposites'.[23]

THE BISHOPS: RICHARD CUMBERLAND AND SAMUEL PARKER

As in Germany, so in England, where a number of Hobbes's critics converged on characterising his theory as Epicurean, appealing again to the Stoic arguments as they were presented in Cicero's philosophical dialogues. *De natura deorum, De finibus*, and *De legibus* in particular were repeatedly plundered in search of ammunition to fire in Hobbes's direction.[24] As Jon Parkin has remarked, following an earlier observation by Noel Malcolm, 'This classical mode of argument also carried with it additional benefits for those who might be worried about Hobbes's proximity to their own discourse', for 'by redefining Hobbes as an Epicurean it was possible to put some clear classical water between *Leviathan* and one's own argument'.[25] For however much Hobbes's readers might have disliked the political theory he presented in *Leviathan*, it was impossible to ignore. The contributions of Hobbes and John Selden combined to focus the contemporary debate over natural law around questions of obligation, highlighting the weakness of Grotius's appeal to the *consensus omnium*, which was always vulnerable to the most elementary sceptical objection.[26] In contrast, Hobbes supplied the straightforward answer of the theological voluntarists. Law was the command of a superior, and it obligated when two conditions were met: first, that it was appropriately promulgated to those it was to bind; second, that it was backed up with sanctions against those who went on to break it. Hobbes argued, therefore, that the various natural laws, whose content he described in *Leviathan* and elsewhere, were not properly laws at all but rather were 'theorems of reason' or 'virtues'—for in the absence of positive law there were not the kind of sanctions against those who acted otherwise that would allow the natural laws to have a real purchase on human behaviour. The challenge facing those exponents of natural jurisprudence who wanted to retain voluntarism but who were anxious not to succumb to Hobbesian civil absolutism—such as Bishop Richard Cumberland of Peterborough or Bishop Samuel Parker of Oxford—was to show how to incorporate the right kind of sanctions into the natural law argument.

Much of the interest and importance of Cumberland's magnum opus, *De legibus naturae*, first published in 1672 and translated into English by John Maxwell in 1727, comes from his attempt to construct an alternative model of natural law to that of Hobbes from premises both philosophers could reasonably be thought to share, not only with one another but also with the Stoics and Epicureans. These premises were, first, the foundational ethical concern with self-preservation and, second, the empiricist commitment to the idea that knowledge about the world had to come through the senses. In common with Pufendorf, Cumberland thought that natural sociability could be grounded in an account of the calculations of self-interested agents, that the best way for individuals to promote their own good was by attending to the common good. But this was not just a prudential rule of thumb. It was also was a part of the divinely ordained natural law, which aimed at 'promoting the common Good of the whole System of rational Agents, [which] conduces . . . to the good of every Part, in which our own Happiness, as that of a Part, is contain'd'.[27] Where Hobbes had followed an 'Epicurean' strategy, arguing that social morality rested on a kind of contractual agreement among self-interested agents, Cumberland preferred to follow the argumentative pathway of the Stoic characters in Cicero's dialogues, who argued that the natural world was an emanation of the divine Logos. Cumberland's distinctive contention was that if the laws of nature could be considered the will of God, and if they could be accurately stated through the use of the methods of the modern experimental science, then they could be considered to have been properly promulgated to the human species.[28]

The laws of nature not only required a 'competent Author' and appropriate promulgation; they also had to be accompanied by 'a sufficient Sanction by Rewards and Punishments'.[29] In the fifth chapter of *De legibus naturae*, therefore, Cumberland presented his argument about how the laws of nature were accompanied by the right kind of sanctions. He acknowledged that he was here departing from the Stoics' analysis, for they were 'to be reprehended, who *affirm'd*, "nothing to be *Good*, but

Virtue; nothing *Evil*, but *Vice*"'. Virtue was good, he maintained, 'because it determines Human Actions to such effects as are principal parts of the Publick *Natural Good*; and, consequently, tends to improve in all Men, the Natural perfections, both of Mind and Body'—and these consequences were themselves good, not just virtue itself.[30] The rewards of virtue, furthermore, included a fuller knowledge of God and men, the conformity of our nature with the divine, and the dominion of one's reason over the passions (and Cumberland observed that this last reward could be considered the way in which 'the Opinion of the *Stoicks* and others, who would have *Virtue sought for its own sake*', could 'be reconcil'd to Truth').[31] Just as virtue had its natural rewards, the breaking of the natural laws incurred natural punishments.[32]

> Altho' *some wicked Actions* may escape *some kind of Punishment*, that is, such as is inflicted by *Man*, yet even these Crimes do not wholly go *unpunished*; and, therefore, there is not wanting an *Obligation* arising from the consideration of this Punishment, which *cannot be avoided*. For it is impossible to separate from the Crime all degrees of *Anxiety of Mind*, arising from the struggle between the sounder Dictates of Reason, which enforce our Duty, and those rash Follies which hurry Men on to Wickedness: There likewise ensue *Fears* (which cause present Grief) of *Vengeance*, both *Divine* and *Human*, and an *Inclination* to the *same Crimes*, or even *worse*; which, because it hurts the Faculties of the Mind, seems to me that it ought to be also reckon'd among Punishments: Even the very *Malice* and *Envy*, which are essential to every Invasion of another's Right, do necessarily and naturally *torture* every malevolent Mind; and so the wicked Man drinks deep of the poyson'd Draught of his own Mixture.[33]

As Parkin has remarked, Cumberland's 'was an unusual way of solving the problem of moral obligation'.[34]

Of all the philosophical sects, Cumberland suggested, it was only the Epicureans who denied that God looked after the universe, and it was time now, he thought, 'to dismiss *Epicurus* and his Herd, tho' lately increas'd'.[35] And although, as just noted, Cumberland did not entirely agree with the Stoics' position on virtue, shortly after this dismissal of the Epicurean view he praised 'the *Stoicks* and *Academicks*' for their opinion 'That the *Virtues* necessarily bring Happiness along with them, as essentially connected therewith'.[36] Nor was it just Cumberland who thought of his position as having something to do with Stoicism. In the preface to the 1688 edition of *De jure naturae*, Pufendorf endorsed Cumberland, who, he said, had 'destroyed' Hobbes's argument 'very effectively in England with his learned and able book *De legibus naturae*', and, as he had done so, 'he established the contrary thesis which approximated closely to the views of the Stoics, and which of the two was my view too'.[37]

In *A Demonstration of the Divine Authority of the Law of Nature and of the Christian Religion* (1681), Bishop Samuel Parker of Oxford, in contrast to Cumberland, argued that God backed up the natural laws not with natural sanctions in this world but with supernatural sanctions after death. It was the threat of punishment and the promise of reward in an afterlife, he thought, that provided us with the right kind of motivation to obey the natural law. Parker's critique of the Epicureans was familiar: they 'would take away all natural Obligations to Religion, Justice and Honesty' and they 'first endeavour to free the minds of men from all apprehensions of a Divine Providence'.[38] 'Without a Lawgiver there can be no Laws', he remarked in a classically voluntarist manner, using this observation to slide from the Epicureans, who were at least 'consistent with themselves and their Principles', over to a consideration of 'Master *Hobs*', who, 'that he may be constant to his own way of contradicting himself', has 'given us a Body of Natural Laws that were never enacted by the Authority of a Legislator'.[39] This kind of criticism of the Epicureans was not, however, balanced with any praise for the Stoics. Rather, 'having thus far and fairly casheird the Epicurean Principles' over thirty pages, Parker continued with a section on 'the vanity of the stoical Philosophy represented'. Here he could be 'so much the more brief', he judged, in part owing to the way in which 'they relie upon the same Principles' as the Epicureans, so that 'when reduced to practice [they] will resolve themselves into the same Actions'.[40]

The basic mistake of the Stoics, according to Parker, was their belief that 'every Man's Happiness' could be 'spun out of his own Bowels'.[41] 'This indeed were a great and glorious Account of things, were it supported by any wise and sober Principles', he wrote, 'but alas it is so far from having any real Foundation, that it is inconsistent with the first and fundamental Principle of humane Nature', which Parker described as 'the natural passion of Self-love' that led mankind 'to pursue what it supposes will advance its Content and Happiness, and shun whatever may impair or destroy it'.[42] The Stoics' vanity induced them to neglect the fact that 'their Bodies are one half of their Natures', with 'sensual Appetites too gross to be satiated by bare Thoughts and Reflections'; and their pedantry made them far too concerned with the 'power of Phrases' at the expense of 'the nature and reality of things'.[43] Addressing what he took to be the Stoics' position on happiness and virtue directly, Parker argued in each case that either Stoicism collapsed back into Epicureanism or else it had no power against his own 'hypothesis' or 'supposition', namely, the Christian argument for the existence of a future state after death involving punishments and rewards. Parker understood happiness in largely hedonistic terms, and this, as Terence Irwin notes, 'leads him to misunderstand the Stoic and the Aristotelian and Platonic position'.[44]

> Either then humane Nature is nothing but Body, or compounded of Body and Soul; if it be nothing but Body, then upon the Stoical Principles it is capable of no Happiness at all, seeing they pass nothing in their Account of Good and Evil but onely the Vertues of the Mind, and therefore if they are nothing but Body, all the qualities of their Mind are nothing. But if beside that we have a Soul, either it perishes with the Body or it survives it; if it perishes then it is no more than the sense of the Body it self, and it plainly casts us back upon the Epicurean Principle, that there is no Happiness but present Pleasure and Interest; if it survive, then that entitles it to an Happiness beside that of this Life, and so we are advanced to our own Hypothesis.[45]

With respect to virtue, Parker noted that 'the whole Sect place it in one Catholick Principle of living according to Nature':

> But then the difficulty is to discover what they mean by Nature, and there every Man is a Sect to himself, and we have as many different Accounts of it, as there are ruling Schoolmasters of the Porch. But what Interpretation soever we follow, unless founded upon our Supposition, we are still forced back to the School of *Epicurus*, for his Principle too was to live according to Nature, which was to enjoy the utmost Pleasure of this present Life; and if there be no other State, it is certain there can be no other way of living according to Nature.[46]

Stoic constancy, Parker claimed, 'would amount to no more than this, that every wise Man ought to consult how to live here with as much ease and pleasure as he can; for if there be no other State, he cannot be wisely constant in the pursuit of any better Design'.[47]

THE CAMBRIDGE PLATONISTS AND THE LATITUDINARIANS

The Augustinian critics in seventeenth-century France had sought to delegitimate Stoicism by highlighting the various ways in which it either failed to buttress or served to subvert their preferred interpretations of Christianity. In England, by contrast, the spectre of Hobbism—understood as unsociable, materialist, and, often enough, atheist—encouraged a movement in the opposite direction. Following the Restoration, one group that was prominent in this effort consisted of those known as the latitude-men or the latitudinarians in the Church of England. Isabel Rivers's survey of the ethical language of this period reports that the ancient authors cited most often by the latitude-men were Plato, Aristotle, Cicero, Seneca, Plutarch, Epictetus, Marcus Aurelius, Plotinus, and Hierocles—a set of authors including, but not limited to, the major Stoics of the Roman period. 'These names are invoked for a consistent purpose', she remarks, for 'the authors praised are those who define man as a free, rational, and social being, capable of imitating God.'[48]

Many of the older latitudinarians were Cambridge men, and since the nineteenth century some of these have become known as the Cambridge Platonists, a group that includes Benjamin Whichcote, Henry More, John Smith, and Ralph Cudworth. A constructive engagement with aspects of Stoicism was a regular feature of some of their works on ethical theory. Nathaniel Culverwell, for example, repeatedly referred to Stoic authors in his *Elegant and Learned Discourse of the Light of Nature*.[49] Henry More's *Enchiridion Ethicum* was a book that mined the *Meditations* of Marcus Aurelius extensively for remarks on the divine administration of the universe, or concerning our status as fellow citizens with God.[50] Most significant of all, perhaps, was Ralph Cudworth's use of Epictetus's notion of the *hegemonikon* in the theory of accountability he developed in his unpublished manuscript, the *Treatise on Free Will*. Cudworth argued there that the responsibility for an action lay with the originating intention, deploying the example of the clock-maker rather than the bell hammer being responsible for the clock striking the hour. Considering the ascription of responsibility for moral action, Cudworth turned to two parts of Epictetan argument: first, to the distinction between what is and what is not in our power; second, to the notion of the *hegemonikon*, or (to borrow Sarah Hutton's gloss), 'an internal principle . . . which performs the function of the will in directing the soul how to act'. Cudworth allocated to this *hegemonikon* both the function of directing the soul towards the good and the power of initiating actions with this end in view, with the consequence that persons were reasonably held responsible for their actions which flowed from such self-determination, both by their fellow persons and by God on the day of judgement.[51]

Like the natural lawyers Cumberland and Parker, the Cambridge Platonists who came after Culverwell were strongly opposed to Hobbes's theory. But their opposition had a different focus. Cumberland and Parker had defended voluntarism in ethics, and the problem posed to them by Hobbes was that he threatened to give voluntarism a bad name. The Platonists, by contrast, opposed voluntarism. They worried that voluntarism reduced morality to obedience, in particular that it instrumentalised morality, reducing it to prudential self-interest; and they worried that it turned God into a cosmic tyrant at the same time. For the anti-voluntarists, the Stoic philosophical texts had an appeal not only because they presented an account of a divinely inspired and rationally ordered nature that could be juxtaposed against the Epicurean philosophy they claimed to find in Hobbes but also because the Stoics, along with Plato, had argued that morality was something to do with the internal organisation of the mind, rather than with any kind of external conformity of behaviour to some standard.

ANTHONY ASHLEY COOPER, EARL OF SHAFTESBURY

Anthony Ashley Cooper, from 1699 the third Earl of Shaftesbury, was heir to this line of antivoluntarist argument. His credentials as an anti-Hobbist strongly sympathetic to the perspective of the latitude-men were secured with his first publication, an edition of Benjamin Whichcote's sermons, the introduction to which presented the sermons as an antidote to Hobbes, for whom there was 'only one Master-Passion, Fear, which has, in effect devour'd all the rest, and left room only for that infinite Passion towards Power after Power, Natural (as he affirms) to All Men, and never ceasing but in Death'.[52] Throughout his life, Shaftesbury's philosophical sympathies continued to follow the latitudinarians' preferences among the ancient philosophers. Indeed, he transformed these preferences into a general theory about the development of the history of ancient philosophy in a letter of 1 October 1706 to the Huguenot Pierre Coste. Much of the letter presents a discussion of Horace, beginning with Shaftesbury's description of his encounter with André Dacier's 1681 edition of Horace:

> I could not but look into Monsieur Dacier out of a kind of insulting malice, to see how he with his Court models of breeding and friendship would relish that place of Horace, which you commend so heartily. . . . But Mons. Dacier knew little of the simplicity of Horace or measure of his irony.[53]

Shaftesbury then advances his own interpretation of Horace's philosophical commitments, dividing his career into 'three principal states or periods', that of his 'free republican state', followed by his 'debauched, slavish, courtly state', followed in turn by his 'recovering, returning state', a pendulum movement from one kind of philosophy to another and back.[54] Indeed, Shaftesbury argues, there were only two kinds of 'real distinct philosophies, the one derived from Socrates', which he calls 'civil, social,

Theistic', which passed 'into the old Academic, the Peripatetic, and Stoic; the other derived in reality from Democritus, and passing into the Cyrenaic and Epicurean'.

> The first, therefore, of these two philosophies recommended action, concernment in civil affairs, religion. The second derided all, and advised inaction and retreat, and with good reason. For the first maintained that society, right, and wrong was founded in Nature, and that Nature had a meaning, and was herself, that is to say in her wits, well governed and administered by one simple and perfect intelligence. The second again derided this, and made Providence and Dame Nature not so sensible as a doting old woman.

The new Academy, according to Shaftesbury, could be ignored altogether: 'it had no certain precepts, and so was an exercise or sophistry rather than a philosophy'.[55]

Shaftesbury's own philosophy was clearly aligned in this 'civil, social, Theistic' tradition. Can we be more precise and call it Stoic? One might think that one obstacle to interpreting the *Characteristics* in substantially Stoic terms is that the book barely mentions the Stoic philosophers at all, and neither Marcus nor Epictetus appeared in the original index of *Characteristics*. But Shaftesbury did signal his interest in the Stoics there, albeit in a cryptic fashion: the emblematic illustration on the title page of the first volume of *Characteristics* depicted a calm harbour and a ray of light on a bowl of water, images that derived from Marcus Aurelius and Epictetus, respectively, and that were both referenced in a footnote in *Miscellany* 4:

> Apprehension [*hypolepsis*] is everything, and this is up to you. Therefore, remove the apprehension when you wish, and there is a great calm as though you were rounding the headland, and all is still and the bay is still: Marcus Aurelius, *Meditations* 12.22. The soul is like the basin of water. Fancies [*phantasiai*] are like the ray of light that strikes upon the water. Thus, when the water is disturbed, the ray seems too to be disturbed; but it is not. And so when anyone is agitated, it is not the arts and the virtues that are confounded but the spirit in which they exist. And when this steadies, they do as well: Epictetus, *Discourses* 3.3.20–2.[56]

Had he been too cryptic? Isabel Rivers has pointed out that for the second edition of the book, Shaftesbury 'added a cross reference to the relevant pages in the *Miscellaneous Reflections* at the foot of the emblem', to make things a bit more transparent.[57] Shaftesbury's contemporaries and near contemporaries were certainly aware of his interest in the Stoics, in any case, and the *General Dictionary*, which was one of the English versions or adaptations of Pierre Bayle's *Dictionnaire historique et critique*, had this to say:

> among the writings which he most admired, and carried always with him, were the moral works of Xenophon, Horace, the *Commentaries* and *Enchiridion* of Epictetus as published by Arrian, and Marcus Antoninus. These authors are now extant in his library, filled throughout with marginal notes, references and explanations, all written with his own hand.[58]

The depth of Shaftesbury's interest in the Stoics has become clearest in the twentieth century, however, with the publication of his private philosophical notebooks by Benjamin Rand in 1900. These two books, now in the Public Record Office, contain philosophical reflections, organised thematically and dated (though Rand stripped the dates out when he published them), that Shaftesbury began in Rotterdam in August 1698, after he had left the House of Commons (where he had sat as one of the Members for Poole in Dorset) and before he reentering public life as the third earl, following his father's death in 1699. Additional paragraphs were added in two further spells, in England in 1699–1700, and back again in Holland in 1703–4. The contents of the notebooks emboldened scholars to start declaring Shaftesbury a Stoic in fairly unequivocal terms. For Rand, he was 'the greatest Stoic of modern time', to be ranked alongside Epictetus and Marcus Aurelius: 'The Greek slave, the Roman emperor, and the English nobleman must abide the great exponents of stoical philosophy'.[59] In an article published in 1923, 'Shaftesbury as Stoic', Esther A. Tiffany argued that the unpublished Stoic notebooks could plausibly be read as the intellectual foundation for the published *Characteristics*, which had hitherto mostly been interpreted as inspired by the Platonism of the previous generation, and her view was endorsed by Alfred Owen Aldridge in his 1951 study of 'Shaftesbury and the Deist Manifesto'.[60]

That Shaftesbury's thinking draws on Stoic ideas at key moments in his overall argument is clear (and I shall have more to say on this later). But we probably don't need to go further than that, least of all into an argument, such as that rehearsed by Aldridge, over whether it is more appropriate to describe the body of his thought in general as either Stoic or Platonist. First, the positions we will come up with if we attempt to answer that question will vary according to what we take the relevant criteria to be, and it isn't obvious what set of criteria is the most suitable one to employ for this purpose. Second, in bundling the Stoic and the Platonist, or 'the old Academic', schools together in the letter to Coste, Shaftesbury himself appeared to indicate that what these schools had in common was, for him at least, more significant than what separated them. Third, and most important, too much concern with picking apart the ancient legacies in Shaftesbury's thought draws attention away from how he was working in a much more modern idiom, and thus impedes and understanding of just what Shaftesbury was trying to do.

One fruitful way of coming to grips with Shaftesbury's project is to read it as an extended response to the philosophy of the man who had directed his own education, John Locke. Locke never published a major work devoted to ethical theory, however much some of his friends, such as James Tyrrell, were keen that he do so.[61] But from the unpublished *Essays on the Law of Nature* through to the two published editions of the *Essay Concerning Human Understanding*, scholars have been able to reconstruct the development of his moral thinking, which headed increasingly towards a perspective on morality with certain resemblances to that of Samuel Parker, insofar as it combined a hedonistic conception of happiness with the thought that the existence of divine rewards and punishments in the hereafter was necessary to motivate obedience in this world to principles of morality. On Locke's mature view, there were neither innate moral principles nor a natural law that could be known by 'the general consent of men'. For motivation to be rational, it required reference to the agent's good, understood in hedonistic terms. For the natural law to bind, therefore, it had to be God's will, backed up with supernatural punishments for those who disobeyed.[62] For Lawrence E. Klein, 'Though he never called Locke an Epicurean, it should be clear that Locke was a signal instance for Shaftesbury of the infestation of the best thought of the era by Epicurean motives.'[63] And as Shaftesbury himself famously wrote in a letter to his young friend Michael Ainsworth, years after Locke died,

> It was Mr. Locke that struck the home blow: for Mr. Hobbes's character and base slavish principles in government took off the point of his philosophy. 'Twas Mr. Locke that struck at all fundamentals, threw all order and virtue out of the world, and made the very ideas of these (which are the same as those of God) *unnatural*, and without foundation in our minds.[64]

To develop a perspective on the good that stood in sharp contrast to Locke's hedonistic account, Shaftesbury began his argument in the *Inquiry concerning Virtue and Merit* with a depiction of nature as a teleologically ordered system, or, in Stephen Darwall's gloss, as 'an integrated system in which subsystems function together to realize a well-functioning whole'.[65]

> There being therefore in every creature a certain interest or good, there must be also a certain end to which everything in his constitution must naturally refer. . . .
>
> If therefore, in the structure of this or any other animal, there be anything which points beyond himself and by which he is plainly discovered to have relation to some other being or nature besides his own, then will this animal undoubtedly be esteemed a part of some other system. . . .
>
> Now, if the whole system of animals . . . be properly comprehended in one system of a globe or earth and if, again, this globe or earth itself appears to have a real dependence on something still beyond, as, for example, either on its sun, the galaxy or its fellow-planets, then is it in reality a part only of some other system.[66]

The case of nonhuman animals was straightforward. An animal's behaviour was determined by its affections, and '*a good creature is such a one as by the natural temper or bent of his affections is carried primarily and immediately, and not secondarily and accidentally, to good and against ill*',[67] the good in question being the good of the systems of which the animal forms a part.

The case of human beings, however, being rational, was a bit more complicated. A human being with the equivalent set of affections would be a good human being, but not necessarily a virtuous one.

> In a creature capable of forming general notions of things, not only the outward beings which offer themselves to the sense are the objects of the affection, but the very actions themselves and the affections of pity, kindness, gratitude and their contraries, being brought into the mind by reflection, become objects. So that by means of this reflected sense, there arises another kind of affection towards those very affections themselves, which have been already felt and have now become the subject of a new liking or dislike.[68]

Human beings can reflect on the set of affections that are governing their behaviour, and, if they approve of that set of affections as being the kind that promote the general interest, then, if that judgement is correct, they qualify as properly virtuous. The kind of self-reflection that Shaftesbury was describing is not, however, made up of a series of complex quasi-mathematical calculations about the likely real-world consequences of having a particular set of affections, in the way in which a later utilitarian might reason about the matter. Rather, Shaftesbury was presenting his account of what he called the 'natural moral sense', which functioned analogously to our aesthetic senses.[69] Just as we are naturally drawn to judge appearances as 'foul and fair' or sounds as 'a harmonious and a dissonant', we are naturally moved to judge our own affections, and just as the elementary distinction between the beautiful and the ugly is innate, not learned, there are, contra Locke, various innate moral ideas—'there may be implanted in the heart a real sense of right and wrong, a real good affection towards the species or society', and so on[70]—to help get ethical judgement off the ground.

> However false or corrupt it be within itself, it [= the heart] finds the difference, as to beauty and comeliness, between one heart and another, one turn of affection, one behaviour, one sentiment and another and, accordingly, in all disinterested cases, must approve what is dishonest and corrupt.[71]

Shaftesbury's theorisation of innate ideas was one decisively Stoic moment in his argument that stands at the heart of his reply to Locke. As Daniel Carey has argued, Shaftesbury was here 'indebted to a Stoic adaptation of what was originally an Epicurean concept—that of prolepsis, which can be translated as "preconception" or "anticipation"'. Prolepses were 'naturally formed concepts; they did not depend on or derive from instruction or from experience', and they both constituted a truth criterion, for disputed matters could be settled by an appeal to a prolepsis, and made empirical knowledge itself possible, enabling us 'to make sense of experience in the world, to recognise things because we were predisposed toward them'.[72] Epictetus spoke of prolepsis in his *Discourses*, and Shaftesbury used the Greek term as the title of one of the sections of his unpublished notebooks. In *The Moralists*, he spoke of 'presentations' and 'preconceptions' in terms that recall the Stoic prolepsis, and in the *Miscellaneous Reflections* he wrote of 'our natural Anticipation', with a footnote connecting this notion up to the 'presentations' and 'preconceptions' he had discussed earlier.[73] Prolepses were innate ideas (although Shaftesbury sometimes preferred the language of their being 'connatural'), but they could be deployed in ways that evaded Locke's particular criticisms from the *Essay*. 'The enormous advantage of the concept of prolepsis for Shaftesbury', Carey writes, 'was that it implied the possibility of knowledge without guaranteeing it—it was an anticipation rather than a fully formed idea or principle'.[74] Analogously to taste in matters of aesthetics, moral judgement had a natural foundation, but one that needed to be cultivated, and when that process of cultivation or education went wrong, the connatural prolepses ended up being misapplied. All humans might have the relevant prolepses, therefore, but the fact of observed radical diversity in the world did not in and of itself undermine Stoic claims about the moral uniformity of humankind.[75]

The other strikingly Stoic moment in the presentation of Shaftesbury's core moral philosophical argument—another Epictetan moment, in fact—is his brief reference to the 'principal or leading part'. (The notebooks also refer to the 'principal and commanding part'.)[76] As we saw above, the language of the *hegemonikon* was being used by the Cambridge Platonists; indeed, Stephen Darwall speculates that Shaftesbury might have had access to Cudworth's unpublished manuscripts on the will, which also draw heavily from Epictetus, when he visited Locke and Damaris Masham at Oates.[77] Shaftesbury's reference to the *hegemonikon* in the *Inquiry* comes in a passage in which he is clarifying the relevant differences between humans and animals. 'For though we may vulgarly call an ill horse vicious', he observes, 'yet we never say of a good one, nor of any mere beast, idiot or changeling, though ever so good-natured, that he is worthy or virtuous'.[78] In addition to being generous, compassionate, and so on, one had to be able to 'reflect on what he himself does or see others do' to have the potential to qualify as virtuous, and our affections had to be 'equal, sound and good'. And then Shaftesbury has this:

> Neither can any weakness or imperfection in the senses be the occasion of iniquity or wrong if the object of the mind itself be not at any time absurdly framed nor anyway improper, but suitable, just and worthy of the opinion and affection applied to it. For if we will suppose a man who, being sound and entire both in his reason and affection, has nevertheless so depraved a constitution or frame of body that the natural objects are, through his organs of sense, as through ill glasses, falsely conveyed and misrepresented, 'twill be soon observed, in such a person's case, that since his failure is not in his principal or leading part, he cannot in himself be esteemed iniquitous or unjust.[79]

The failures in the 'principal or leading part' that matter for virtue were not the factual errors we might make, which, 'being no cause or sign of ill affection, can be no cause of vice', but rather those errors we make concerning 'opinion, belief or speculation', especially those that cause 'a misconception or misapprehension of the worth or value of any object, so as to diminish a due or raise any undue, irregular or unsocial affection'. (It would be 'wrong and wicked in the believer', for example, to reckon it was better to save a cat than a parent, so that 'every action grounded on this belief, would be an iniquitous, wicked and vicious action'.)[80] The distinction between matters of fact and the reliability of our senses, on the one hand, and matters of 'opinion, belief or speculation' on the other is fairly close here to Epictetus's fundamental distinction between the matters that are and are not under our control, or 'up to us',[81] and Darwall certainly interprets this part of Shaftesbury's argument along Epictetan lines: 'One reason why a capacity for moral sense and second-order affection is necessary for genuine virtue or merit, then, is that we can properly attribute these to the agent "in himself" only if they result from a self-governing capacity, and moral sense is required for that'.[82]

The notion of the 'principal or leading part' may be Stoic, but the basic psychological theory that Shaftesbury deploys here is not. In his 1967 book *Shaftesbury's Philosophy of Religion and Ethics*, Stanley Grean criticises those scholars such as Tiffany and Aldridge who 'overemphasize the Stoic element' in Shaftesbury's thought[83] and suggests that it was Shaftesbury's positive valuation of some affections, especially the social affections, that made his position incompatible with the Stoa.[84] This does not seem to me to be quite right. The Stoics were comfortable with the idea of the benign sentiments, or *eupatheiai*, as Margaret Graver's recent book makes clear;[85] 'Stoic insensibility' might have been a popular criticism in the sixteenth and seventeenth centuries, but it was never an especially accurate one. But Grean also notes that Shaftesbury endorsed the criticism George Stanhope, the translator of Epictetus's *Manual*, also levelled against the Stoics for their failure to appreciate how the affections served as the 'Secret Springs that move and actuate us', and this seems closer to the mark.[86] Shaftesbury's theory of the affections, or passions, was basically Lockean, in that he considered our behaviour to be determined by the affections, and these have a variety of origins and objects.[87] What, then, might the role of our reasoning apparatus be in Shaftesbury's psychological theory? From the *Inquiry*:

> But when, either through superstition or ill custom, there come to be very gross mistakes in the assignment or application of the affections, when the mistakes are either in their nature so gross, or so complicated and frequent, that a creature cannot well live in a natural state nor with due affections compatible with human society and civil life, then is the character of virtue forfeited.
>
> And thus we find how far worth and virtue depend on a knowledge of right and wrong, and on a use of reason sufficient to secure a right application of the affections, that nothing horrid or unnatural, nothing unexemplary, nothing destructive of that natural affection by which the species or society is upheld, may on any account or through any principle or notion of honour or religion be at any time affected or prosecuted as a good and proper object of esteem.[88]

We might then distinguish two functions for reason in Shaftesburian moral psychology. First, guided by the promptings of the natural moral sense, reason regulates our affections, attempting to curate a particularly benign set, in order to generate the kind of behaviour that will further the general interest of the systems and subsystems of which we form a part. Second, because the natural moral sense itself is not infallible (except on a strikingly implausible reading of Shaftesbury's argument), reason attempts to correct the promptings of the natural moral sense on those occasions when it is apparent that, for whatever reason, it seems to be endorsing injustice or other varieties of vice.

With regard to both the prolepses and the *hegemonikon*, concepts derived from Stoic theory have been fitted by Shaftesbury into a substantially Lockean epistemological and psychological framework. This made for an attractive argumentative strategy. Considered as an attempted refutation of Locke's philosophy, Shaftesbury's theory was more likely to be persuasive to the extent that it shared its philosophical foundations with those of Locke's own enterprise rather than presenting itself as a fundamental alternative substantially derived from ancient models. In both those cases, furthermore, it was the Stoic element of the argument that did much of the work to drive the argument away from Locke's own conclusions. The prolepses underpinned Shaftesbury's argument for the natural moral unity of the human race, and, as with the earlier Cambridge Platonists, the argument that the distinction between virtue and vice was to be centered on the operation of the *hegemonikon* rather than on the content of our actual behaviour provided an alternative to Locke's voluntarist ethics, in which the moral life threatened to be reduced to external conformity to sanctions-backed laws. When Shaftesbury turned to the question of why we should seek to be virtuous, or, as he put it at the start of book 2 of the *Inquiry*, 'what obligation is there to virtue, or what reason to embrace it?',[89] his answer was eudaemonist: virtue promotes happiness, and it is therefore in the interests of the agent to work towards living a life of virtue. (As Darwall has written, 'although he is certainly no psychological egoist, Shaftesbury *is* a kind of rational egoist'.)[90] Shaftesbury's notion of happiness was complex. Roughly speaking, he considered that virtue generates and sustains the kind of psychic balance that makes it possible to live a life enriched by love and the other natural social affections, affections that provided deeper satisfactions than other kinds of goods.[91] This vision of the moral life as a kind of psychic harmony intimately related to personal happiness was a broadly Platonic one; the building blocks of the argument that sustained that vision, however, were recognisably versions of Stoic concepts.

According to Schneewind, Shaftesbury's theory can be regarded as one that provides 'the psychology for a classical republic'. Whereas James Harrington's republican political theory was open to the criticism that it offered 'no account of how the strong self-interest of his citizens comes to be tempered enough so that each is content with a fair share and is attached to the commonwealth that provides it',[92] Shaftesbury's argument precisely filled this gap. In Schneewind's words, again: 'Because the obligation or reason to embrace virtue is that we will be happiest if we do so, and the balance of motives approved by the moral sense is also that which contributes most to the well-being of others, there is no real conflict between private and public interest', and this means that—against the voluntarists, again—'no sanctions are needed to bring about this congruence'.[93] The contrast to Hobbes's political psychology, in which the external might of the sovereign is required to discipline citizens' unruly passions and render them governable, is stark. Shaftesbury's theory might have been republican, but it was emphatically not democratic. Shaftesbury considered moral judgement, like aesthetic taste, to be a fine art that required extensive cultivation in propitious circumstances; indeed, he explicitly linked philosophy to good breeding—which was a Shaftesburian key word:

> To philosophize, in a just signification, is but to carry good breeding a step higher. For the accomplishment of breeding is to learn whatever is decent in company, or beautiful in arts, and the sum of philosophy is to learn what is just in society and beautiful in nature, and the order of the world.[94]

In Shaftesbury's aristocratic republic, a well-bred sociable elite governed both itself and the wider population. Shaftesbury may have opposed Locke's philosophy insofar as it seemed to deny us the power of self-command, but Shaftesbury considered that the bulk of humanity did lack just that in practical terms, and although there is no reason to think that he believed that the dogmas of the Church of England were true, nevertheless, he thought that the established Church played an important role in upholding public morals. For this reason, Shaftesbury always sought to dissociate himself from those contemporary Deists—many of whom he knew well—who were critics of the Church, and who sought to undermine its privileged role in public life.

The discussion in the third chapter considered, among other things, the Jacobean critique of the Stoic politician. Full of high-minded language about virtue and the common good, the self-professed Stoic was alleged to be a seditious figure, whose self-deluding pride drew him into the politics of faction and conspiracy. The question of sedition loomed large for Shaftesbury, given his own lineage. His grandfather, the first earl, was the most controversial figure at the centre of the politics of what has come to be called the exclusion crisis, or the attempt by the opposition Whigs to get the Duke of York excluded from the line of succession to the throne in 1680–61 on the grounds of his adherence to the Roman Church. Arrested in July 1681 and sent to the Tower of London on suspicion of high treason, the first earl's application for a writ of habeas corpus culminated in the government's indictment being thrown out by a grand jury in November, and, the first earl having been released on bail, the prosecution was dropped in February 1682. That year was then taken up with various levels of involvement in a series of increasingly radical schemes—in the spring, to plan for a rebellion in the event of Charles's death to ensure a Protestant succession; in the summer, to organise simultaneous uprisings in various parts of the country while Charles was still alive; in the autumn, to plot an attempt on the life of the king and the Duke of York after they had attended the races at Newmarket—and still more rebellions. When other plotters decided in November to postpone their insurrection, the first earl decided it was time to flee to the Netherlands, where he died in Amsterdam in January 1683.[95] For John Dryden, in 'Absalom and Achitophel', widely regarded as the finest satire in the English language, the first earl (Achitophel) was 'For close designs, and crooked counsels fit; / Sagacious, bold, and turbulent of wit; / Restless, unfixed in principles and place; / In power unpleased, impatient of disgrace'.[96] In his essay, *Sensus communis*, the first earl's grandson, the third earl, presented a novel perspective on the politics of sedition.

Shaftesbury began his discussion of the matter by expressing surprise that anyone could subscribe to the Hobbesian view that society and government are both artificial. 'For my own part', he observed, 'this herding principle and associating inclination is seen so natural and strong in most men, that one might readily affirm it was even from the violence of this passion that so much disorder arose in the general society of mankind'.[97] The problems of faction and sedition arose from an excess of sociability, not from its deficiency. In smaller groups it was easier to discern the general good, but on a much larger scale, 'Universal good, or the interest of the world in general, is a kind of remote philosophical object', and it was not possible readily to apprehend 'a national interest, or that of a whole people, or body politic'. Men therefore congregated 'in less parties', where they 'may be intimately conversant and acquainted with one another' and could 'better taste society, and enjoy the common good and interest of a more contracted public'.[98] By contrast, it was very hard to pursue the common good of 'the body politic at large', for 'here perhaps the thousandth part of those whose interests are concerned, are scarce so much as known by sight'. In 'so wide a field', Shaftesbury maintained, 'close sympathy and conspiring virtue is apt to lose itself, for want of direction'. Hence this somewhat paradoxical reflection:

> Nor is the passion anywhere so strongly felt or vigorously exerted as in actual conspiracy or war in which the highest geniuses are often known the forwardest to employ themselves. For the most generous

spirits are the most combining. They delight most to move in concert and feel, if I may say, in the strongest manner the force of the confederating charm.

It is strange to imagine that war, which of all things appears the most savage, should be the passion of the most heroic spirits. But it is in war that the knot of fellowship is closest drawn. It is in war that mutual succour is most given, mutual danger run, and common affection most exerted and employed. For heroism and philanthropy are almost one and the same. Yet by a small misguidance of the affection, a lover of mankind becomes a ravager; a hero and deliverer becomes an oppressor and destroyer.[99]

Cabal and sedition were to domestic politics what warfare was to international politics, '[f]or sedition is a kind of cantonizing already begun within the state', and '[t]o cantonize is natural when the society grows vast and bulky'.[100] Large states governed by only a very few were those in which 'strong factions are aptest to engender', and, Shaftesbury observed, 'the associating genius of man is never better proved, than in those very societies, which are formed in opposition to the general one of mankind, and to the real interest of the state'.[101] Far from the seditious politician being the self-absorbed, proud man portrayed by the Jacobean anti-Stoics, for Shaftesbury, 'the very spirit of faction, for the greatest part, seems to be no other than the abuse or irregularity of that social love, and common affection, which is natural to mankind', so that it was 'of all characters, the thorough-selfish one is the least forward in taking party'.[102] We might even frame the general problem of Shaftesburian political conduct as that of how to cultivate the right kind of affections that tend to promote the common good, without becoming diverted into the wrong kind of partisan politics, in which the good of the faction is elevated above that of the political community as a whole.

From this perspective, it is plausible to think that one of the things Shaftesbury found in Marcus Aurelius and Epictetus was a set of tools that helped him navigate the tension that characteristically obtained between the twin demands of sociability and autonomy.[103] How might one be able to engage with the world of affairs without being corrupted by that world? Shaftesbury's philosophical notebooks, which he began to compile after his first sustained period of political engagement, have been read as a kind of spiritual diary or record of some of Shaftesbury's inner states and most personal thoughts; Klein has suggested, for example, that they reveal 'a gifted offspring of a gilded background, whose hypertrophied sensibility preyed on his inner conflicts to produce a late adolescent crisis'.[104] But the notebooks might alternatively be read principally through the same lens through which Pierre Hadot urges us to read the

Hellenistic philosophers themselves, as examples of what he calls spiritual exercises. So, although Marcus Aurelius's *Meditations*, for example, have frequently been read as evidence of the author's melancholic personality, or as expressions of his pessimism, or even in terms of the effects of a supposed gastric ulcer and an addiction to opium, Hadot argues that it is far more plausible to read them as a series of technical philosophical exercises, each of which aims to reinforce the emperor's adherence to a particular piece of Stoic dogma.[105] The reflection that his 'purple-edged toga is some sheep's hairs dipped in the blood of shellfish; as for sex, it is the rubbing together of pieces of gut, followed by the spasmodic secretion of a little bit of slime' isn't any kind of evidence of the emperor's disgust with the world but rather the practice of a specific Stoic exercise that calls for things to be described just as they appear to us, shorn of the meanings that humans characteristically project onto them.[106] The various exercises can be grouped under three headings, set out by Epictetus, relating to desire and aversion, inclinations and action, and assent. All three disciplines, furthermore, relate to the key Stoic distinction between that which is and that which is not under our own power, so that the goal of the discipline of desire, for example, is the renunciation of all desires that do not depend on our own power, that is to say, all desires that do not relate to moral virtue.[107]

Shaftesbury himself more or less invites us to interpret his notebooks along these lines. His own title for the notebooks was ἈΣΚΗΜΑΤΑ or 'Exercises' (which is also the title Laurent Jaffro has given to his French translation),[108] and the first quotation transcribed in the first volume was a passage from Epictetus 3.12 that explicitly references the discipline of desire:

> All the methods which are applied to the body by the persons who are giving it exercise, might also themselves be conducive to training, if in some such way as this they tend toward desire (ὄρεξιν) and aversion (ἔκκλισιν); but if they tend toward display, they are characteristic of a man who has turned toward the outside world, and is hunting for something other than the thing itself which he is doing.[109]

Many of the reflections in Shaftesbury's notebooks can be interpreted along similar lines, as a series of reflections aimed at improving the art of judgement, rather than as any kind of report of inner mental states.

This concern with making correct judgements in the troublesome conditions of the world was not confined to the private notebooks but also appears in Shaftesbury's published writings as what he called the 'Discipline of the Fancys',[110] or what Epictetus called the discipline of assent. 'Thus I contend with fancy and opinion, and search the mint and foundery of imagination', he wrote in *Soliloquy, or Advice to an Author*, 'For here the appetites and desires are fabricated; hence they derive their privilege and currency. If I can stop the mischief here and prevent false coinage, I am safe'. One of the techniques for so stopping the mischief was the Stoic exercise described a moment ago: 'Describe the flattering object but without flattery, plain, as the thing is, without addition, without sparing or reserve.'[111] And 'if the fancy or opinion of good be joined to what is not durable nor in my power either to acquire or to retain', Shaftesbury wrote in the final volume of *Characteristics*, 'the more such an opinion prevails, the more I must be subject to disappointment and distress.'[112] The two kinds of fancy that Shaftesbury explicitly criticised in this passage were the imagining of death as an 'apprehension of evil and calamity' and the 'imagination of something beautiful, great and becoming in things' such as 'plate, jewels, apartments, coronets, patents of honour, titles or precedencies'.[113] This second kind of fancy lay at the centre of Shaftesbury's refashioning of the Stoic critique of luxury; indeed, part of the problem with luxury was specifically that it got in the way of the practices of the spiritual exercises:

> In luxury and intemperance we easily apprehend how far thought is oppressed, and the mind debarred from just reflection, and from the free examination and censure of its own opinions or maxims, on which the conduct of a life is formed.[114]

For Shaftesbury, as Istvan Hont has written, luxury was 'the harbinger of horrid artificiality insofar as it created the wholly unnatural condition of insatiability, the precondition of all further moral degradation.'[115]

THE DEISTS AND THEIR CRITICS

Following the latitudinarians and the Cambridge Platonists, Shaftesbury was consistently hostile to those who emphasised divine rewards and punishments as the key motivation for adhering to religion.[116] This was not, however, part of a general attack on the idea that religious belief brought practical benefits. It was significantly easier for those who believed in God to be virtuous, for a belief that the universe together with its various systems and subsystems were the product of a designing intelligence had the practical tendency to strengthen belief in the tight connection between virtue and happiness.[117] Shaftesbury's God was not, in Darwall's words, 'the God of orthodox Christianity Who transcends nature and consigns mortals to a supernatural heaven or hell but an organizing presence immanent in nature.'[118] While Shaftesbury was familiar with the language of Deism, it was not a language he much used, and certainly not to describe his own position, which he considered straightforwardly theist.[119]

In the literature of the Deists, Stoic themes make their appearance from time to time. Jonathan Israel has drawn attention to Anthony Collins's insistence in his *Philosophical Inquiry Concerning Human Liberty* of 1717 that the latter's argument be understood as descending from the Stoics rather than from the Epicureans, for (he maintained) not only were the Epicureans on the side of the libertarians in this controversy but their 'absurd principles' could not be used to ground anything at all.[120] The key issue in this section of his argument turned on the question of religiosity: Collins was distancing himself from the '*Epicurean Atheists*, who were the most popular and most numerous sect of the *Atheists* of antiquity', as well as being 'the great asserters of *Liberty*', to identify his argument with that of 'the *Stoicks*, who were the most popular and most numerous sect among the religionaries of antiquity' and 'the greater asserters of fate and necessity'.[121] In the Latin liturgy that John Toland presented in his *Pantheisticon* of 1720, he imagines his pantheists chanting Stoic slogans. 'To lead a happy Life Virtue alone is sufficient / And is to itself an ample Reward', they declaim; and when the president follows up with 'What's Honest is the sole Good', the response comes, 'Neither is there any Thing useful but what is laudable.'[122]

When Samuel Clarke gave the Boyle Lectures in 1705, against the Deists and in defence of Christian orthodoxy, he argued that 'whoever denies a Future State of Rewards and Punishments, must of necessity by a chain of unavoidable Consequences be forced to recur to downright Atheism.' The only possible 'middle Opinion', he judged, was 'that Assertion of the *Stoicks*' that 'in all Cases and under all Circumstances' virtue was 'absolutely *Self-sufficient* to its own Happiness'.

> Whereas on the contrary, because it is manifestly *not Self-sufficient*, and yet undoubtedly the Cause of Virtue is not to be given up; therefore they ought from thence to have concluded the *Certainty* of a Future State.[123]

It was true that virtue was worthy to be chosen for its own sake, 'without any respect to any recompense or reward'.

> But it does not from hence follow, that He who *Dies* for the sake of Virtue, is really any more *Happy*, than he that dies for any fond Opinion or any unreasonable Humour or Obstinacy whatsoever.[124]

There have been 'some very few extraordinary men', such as Regulus, who lived up to the teachings of 'some of the Philosophers . . . upon this subject', but

> the general Practise of Virtue in the World, can never be supported on this Foot; It being indeed neither possible nor truly reasonable, that Men by adhering to Virtue should part with their Lives, if thereby they eternally deprived themselves of all possibility of receiving any Advantage from that adherence.[125]

Clarke was not the only writer of his time to call the identity of Stoicism as a variety of theism into question—and it is time now to back up a bit and to explore the wider and largely Continental story of how the Stoics became atheists.

CHAPTER SIX

How the Stoics Became Atheists

STOICISM IN BAYLE'S DICTIONARY

There is no article on 'Stoicism' or 'The Stoics' in Pierre Bayle's great *Dictionary* of 1697; on the other hand, there are no entries for Plato or Descartes either, in Bayle's notoriously idiosyncratic selection of articles.[1] In some places where we might expect to find discussions of Stoicism, furthermore, we find none: in the article 'Lipsius', for example, the only opinion about the Hellenistic philosophers that is reported is Conradus Schlusselburgius's, that Lipsius had been an Epicurean.[2] Yet Stoicism is by no means absent from the *Dictionary*. The article on Chrysippus has Bayle's major critical discussion of Stoic philosophy, and he makes important observations on Stoicism in 'Arcesilaus', 'Heracleotes', 'Hipparchia', 'Ovid', and 'Jupiter'; in the famous articles 'The Paulicians' and 'Spinoza'; and elsewhere.

With a background in Augustinian Calvinism, Bayle was heir to both Catholic and Protestant traditions of anti-Stoic criticism. In general, in the *Dictionary*, Bayle leans more to the Protestant side, insofar as he is more interested in the cosmological, metaphysical, theological, and epistemological arguments of the Stoics than in their treatments of ethics and human psychology, the chief concerns of the French Augustinians. Moreover, his discussions of Stoicism barely mention Seneca or Epictetus, who were the most important authors for the French critics. Yet there are also places where Bayle draws directly on the French tradition, repeating, for example, the chief complaint of the Augustinians in his most extended comment on the figure of the Stoic sage when he remarks that the 'capital error' of the Stoics was their 'supposing that it was in the power of man to root out every vicious passion', a mistake that demonstrated their 'ignorance with regard to the state and condition of man'.[3] Beyond this commonplace, however, there is a deeper and more interesting debt to the Augustinian anti-Stoic tradition. For these writers were distinctive in their refusal to treat Stoicism as mere doxography as they attempted to diagnose its spirit or identify an inner principle or fundamental motivation. Bayle followed this tradition by presenting Stoicism in the *Diction-*

ary as a distinctive worldview, a set of philosophical doctrines and arguments inseparable from a particular philosophical style, one that possessed its own characteristic intellectual vices. The false doctrines of the Stoics were generated, so Bayle seems to claim, by an erroneous approach to philosophical disputation. Form and content, philosophical substance and method, were closely intertwined.

It is this double concern, with both the content of several Stoic arguments and a certain philosophical style, that overdetermined the centrality of Chrysippus in Bayle's engagement with the Stoics. In the first place, Chrysippus was the most significant Stoic thinker on the set of philosophical topics that most interested Bayle, including fate and free will and the basis of perceptual knowledge. In the second place, however, Bayle also inherited and recast a tradition, both ancient and modern, of denigrating the character of Chrysippus to an intense degree. The ancient criticisms of Chrysippus are familiar enough: Plutarch in particular took great delight in finding flawed arguments in the works of Chrysippus in his text *On Stoic self-contradictions*. But the seventeenth-century critics of Chrysippus had a distinct motivation. These were writers who wanted to defend Stoic or Neostoic ethics against some of the contemporary criticisms of Stoic philosophy, and, exploiting the murky state of knowledge about the earliest development of Stoic philosophical doctrine, they ascribed what they found admirable in Stoic ethics to Zeno of Citium, and the least defensible arguments—or the arguments they, at least, were unwilling to defend—to a kind of rogue Stoicism elaborated by Chrysippus. On this view, Zeno's pure doctrine came to be corrupted by the pedantic, systematising spirit of Chrysippus. In the prologue to this book I referred to Lipsius's remark that Chrysippus had 'first corrupted that grave sect of philosophers with crabbed subtleties of questions'. Kaspar Scioppius offered a similar opinion in his 1606 *Elementa Philosophiae Stoicae Moralis*,[4] and André and Anne Dacier later took a similar line, explicitly pursuing this strategy to try to rebut Jansenist criticism of Stoicism. Their Chrysippus was one who wholly misunderstood the spirit of Stoicism: the Daciers write that while Zeno taught that 'all sins are equal' as a way of making the points that small transgressions as well as great crimes still mattered morally, this teaching was transformed in the hands of Chrysippus into the odious doctrine that there was no difference between acts of sacrilege and the theft of a cabbage.[5]

In the article 'Chrysippus' and elsewhere, Bayle criticises Chrysippus for a multitude of sins. Chrysippus is attacked, for example, for his 'unintelligible Jargon', the 'ill use' he made of his wit, for his 'hunting after idle subtleties', and for his inconsistency—he did not stick to his principles 'but altered them daily'. Bayle also criticises Chrysippus for his inability to see what constituted a worthwhile philosophical problem when Chrysippus wondered about the location of the rational soul,[6] and on occasion he is condemned without argument for particular opinions he held, including his notorious defence of incest and cannibalism, and of Diogenes the Cynic 'self-polluting the marketplace'.[7] Yet Bayle departed from the earlier tradition in a significant respect. Where Scioppius and the Daciers and, later, Jean Barbeyrac, in his 'Historical and critical account of the science of morality', presented Chrysippus as a heterodox deviant from the Stoic mainstream in order to celebrate the contributions of other Stoic philosophers,[8] Bayle's near silence about Zeno, Epictetus, and the others focuses the reader's attention on the deficiencies of Stoicism and of its chief representative in the pages of the *Dictionary*, Chrysippus. (There is an entry for Zeno in the *Dictionary*, but it refers to Zeno of Elea rather than to the founder of the Stoic school, Zeno of Citium, and when Bayle cites Diogenes Laertius's life of Zeno the Stoic he is not interested in Zeno himself but rather in the doxography of Stoicism presented there.) Thus, when Bayle makes remarks about 'the Stoics', they are almost always highly critical. The Stoics are called 'the Pharisees of Paganism', for example, for their unfair campaign of vilification against Epicurus. 'The Stoics professed a great severity in their morals', Bayle wrote, so that 'to contend with these people was almost as dangerous as it is at this day to be at variance with Bigots'.[9]

Why was it important for Bayle to criticise the Stoics? Stoicism mattered for Bayle because he took it to be the archetypal philosophy of constructive rationalism, one that not only sought to establish rational grounds for perceptual knowledge through its epistemology but also claimed through its physics to elucidate the structure of the universe and describe the nature of God. Yet for Bayle, philosophical reasoning was always a critical rather than a constructive tool. E. D. James has drawn attention to Bayle's simile in 'Acosta' comparing philosophy to 'to those caustics which clear up sores, but which would go on to destroy sound flesh and bones if allowed to do so', so that while its 'value lies in correcting errors', its corresponding 'danger lies in the fact that if it be not limited to the correction of errors it attacks truths themselves'.[10] On Bayle's view—to some extent anticipating Kant's strategy in the 'transcendental dialectic' of the *Critique of Pure Reason*—the mistake the Stoics made was to attempt to deploy philosophical reason well outside the boundaries of safety.

Bayle agreed with Scioppius that the root cause of Chrysippus's defective philosophy was his desire for victory rather than truth in philosophical argument, and he therefore continued to agree with the Augustinian critics who located a moment of pride at the heart of the problem with Stoicism.[11] Bayle drew on Plutarch to describe and condemn Chrysippus's methods:

Let us explore here the falsity of Chrysippus's maxims. He pretended, that they who undertake to teach only truth, must speak very sparingly of the arguments that might be alledged on the other side of the question, and ought to imitate the Lawyers. This was the reigning opinion amongst the Dogmaticks. . . . Now I assert, that the method of the Domaticks was very bad, and not much differ from the deceitful art of the Sophistical Rhetoricians, which rendered them so odious, and which was, to make the best cause of that which was the worst.[12]

In part, the trouble was that in his desire for victory, Chrysippus unwittingly aided his sceptical opponents. His vanity led him to collect 'so many arguments in favour of the Sceptical Hypothesis', in order to refute them all together, but 'he could not afterwards confute them himself' and 'thus furnished Carneades with weapons against them'.[13] He also employed whatever weapons were to hand in attacking sceptical arguments, with the result that he was frequently led into the self-contradictions celebrated by Plutarch, who is quoted repeatedly in the pages of the *Dictionary*.

The deeper problem that Bayle associates with the 'Dogmatick' style, however, is summed up in the tag *'nimium altercando veritas amittitur'*— 'truth is lost by too much argument'. (The line is attributed to the poet Publilius Syrus as recorded by Aulus Gellius in *Attic Nights* 17.14, and repeated by Scioppius, whom Bayle quotes.) The pedantry encouraged by strenuous argument on one side of a proposition had quite the reverse effect to what was intended: 'the disputes between Philosophers produce quite another effect; they make both the spectators of the battle and the champions lose the truth; no body does nor can seize upon it in the sequestration in which it is put, while the suit is depending.'[14] Bayle returns to the theme in a handful of additional footnotes scattered through the *Dictionary*, recruiting Seneca, Augustine, Montaigne, and other authorities to support his claim about the pernicious results of there being too much heated philosophical debate.[15] His criticisms of the dogmatic style prompted more general reflections on philosophical method:

Observe that there were amongst the Ancients two sorts of Philosophers; some were like the Pleading counsellors, and the others, like a Recorder or Judge, who sums up the evidence on both sides. . . . The latter were the Scepticks or the Academicks.[16]

While the sceptic's role of 'Recorder' or 'Judge' or, elsewhere, 'Umpire' is the appropriate one for philosophers to adopt, Bayle insisted that it was a different matter for the theologians, for 'Religion does not suffer that academical or sceptical humour: it requires that we absolutely deny or affirm'. In theological discussions, one who acts the sceptic, presenting arguments on both sides of the case on questions of theology, 'becomes odious and suspected, and is in danger of being treated like an infamous prevaricator who betrays his own party'.[17]

Bayle's implicit suggestion is that the Stoic style of philosophy generated certain patterns of disreputable behaviour on the part of its practitioners. The faults Bayle criticises in Lipsius, for example, closely parallel his condemnations of Chrysippus. Lipsius behaved badly in philosophical confrontations—so that rather than tell us what Lipsius argued in his debate with Koornhert on the subject of toleration, Bayle reports on how Lipsius tried to get Koornhert's pamphlets suppressed.[18] Both are also criticised for their silences: Chrysippus when confronted by the problem of the sorites,[19] Lipsius when challenged by the accusations in the anonymous tract *Idolum Hallense*.[20] Both the ancient and the modern Stoic, furthermore, are accused of producing bogus philosophical solutions to classic problems: Bayle reports that Carneades found a sorites paradox embedded in Chrysippus's attempted solution to the problem,[21] and Lipsius's attempt to solve the problem of evil by drawing a distinction between two kinds of souls displaced rather than resolved the problem of theodicy.[22]

When Bayle turns to the epistemological debates between the Stoics and the Sceptics, he emphasises precisely those sceptical objections that could be brought to bear against the modern Cartesians. In 'Arcesilaus', for example, Bayle observes that it was reported that the question was put to Zeno:

> [W]hat will be the case if the wise man should not be able to know any thing clearly, and if he must admit of any thing for true which is not clear and evident? and that Zeno answered, He will clearly comprehend some things, and therefore will admit of nothing which is obscure. He should afterwards have laid down a rule whereby to judge what things are clearly comprehended. That which Zeno gave was opposed by Arcesilaus, who urged to him, that falsehood may appear under the shape of truth, as that therefore one would be at a loss to distinguish the one for the other. Zeno granted that nothing could be comprehended, if that which does not exist can appear in the same form as that which does exist; but he denied that there could be that conformity of ideas betwixt that which is and that which is not. Arcesilaus on the other hand insisted upon this conformity.[23]

The mistake the Stoics made was to insist that there was necessarily a phenomenological distinction between what was true and what was false; this sceptical objection also lay at the heart of Bayle's anti-Cartesian epistemology, too, for the 'clear and distinct idea' could not be the basis of indubitable knowledge, insofar as it did not carry any kind of guarantee of its own veracity. One implication of this was that the proof of God's existence presented by Descartes in the third of his *Meditations* could not be granted.

In the article on Heracleotes, the Stoic philosopher better known as Diogenes of Heraclea, Bayle extends his attack on the philosophical theologians. Since Heracleotes professed Stoicism, and then professed something else, Bayle asserts, he

> ought to believe that falsehood presents itself to our minds, and impresses itself there under the same characteristic or image under which truth exhibits itself; and consequently that this distinguishing characteristic of truth and falsehood, which you trust to in affirming or denying, is deceitful and illusive.

Bayle goes on to comment:

> This objection may puzzle such modern Protestants, as assert that the truths of the Gospel do not enter the mind by way of evidence [*évidence*], but by that of sense [*sentiment*]. What will they say should they be shewed some Christians, who change their religion, and who in imitation of our Heracleotes, a long time espouse with incredible zeal and ardor, the very tenets which they afterwards reject with equal ardor? Does not the sensation of falsehood, will it be asked, impress or stamp itself on the mind, with all the same characteristics as the sense of truth?[24]

If Arcesilaus's objection to Zeno was sound, then, while qualities of clearness and distinctness might make something *évident*, they still do not make it true. Here in 'Heracleotes' Bayle extends this objection to cover Protestant accounts of the truth of religious belief: to claim that one's *sentiment* or feeling of inner conviction carry a guarantee of truth is equally fraught with difficulty. Instead, Bayle implies that there could be no criterion to determine the truth of religious belief, and that the philosophers' search for such a criterion was misplaced.

When Bayle turns his attention to Stoic fate, as defended by Lipsius,[25] he repeats Bramhall's objection that if it were true, God would be responsible for sin. Lipsius, he argues, 'only winds and turns himself about':

> He says that there are some minds, which having been well framed from the beginning, go without any hurt thro' the storm, which falls upon them from fate; and that there are others, which are so ill-framed,

that if fate hits them ever so little, or even not at all, they fall into sin by a voluntary motion. This is owing to a natural imperfection, which is in the cause. . . . In order to clear his Chrysippus [Lipsius] supposes, that the Stoicks ascribed the defects of the soul of man not to God, but to a real and unconquerable imperfection of matter. . . . But hark you, Chrysippus, if this constitution and deviation be from Nature, how can you avoid making God the author of evil? How is it possible that the Author of Nature, who is nature herself, should not have produced evil, and bad men, if he made them as they are?[26]

The Stoics' attempt to carve out a space for human freedom failed to address the problem of evil adequately, and Bayle insists that one who uses Stoic arguments would not be able to hold on to both the claim that God is good and that He controls His parts.[27]

The problem with the Stoics' theism goes beyond this problem of evil, however. For when Bayle considers 'the doctrine of the soul of the world', which made up 'a principal part of the system of the Stoics', he declares that such a conflation of God and nature was a 'real Atheism'[28]. What, then, lurks behind such a judgement? The briefest answer to this question is 'Spinoza'. But it is worth going back a little further and tracing a new passage through the seventeenth century once again, to see just what was going on.

FROM LIPSIUS TO CUDWORTH

The Neostoicisms of the late sixteenth and early seventeenth century had been explicitly intended as supplements to mainstream varieties of Christianity. Although Lipsius was notorious for switching confessional allegiance over the course of his life—from Catholicism to Lutheranism to Calvinism and back to Catholicism again—he remained consistent with his argument, presented most straightforwardly in *De constantia*, that Stoicism, with respect to both its ethics and its physics, provided an appropriate philosophical framework for a well-lived Christian life. Some of his contemporaries agreed, with Thomas James, fellow of New College, Oxford, and later Bodley's Librarian, writing in 1598, 'Let it not seem strange unto us that Philosophie should be a meanes to help Divinitie, or that Christians may profit by the Stoicks.'[29]

Given that the ancient Stoics had taught, among many other things, the materiality of God, indeed, the identification of God with nature, a strict physical determinism, and a doctrine of eternal recurrence, it might seem surprising that the Neostoics were able to recycle Stoic arguments in the service of the Christianities they professed. But there were ways in which this could be done. Lipsius, for example, had an effective monopoly over the interpretation of Stoic physics owing to his authorship of the standard textbook on the subject, the *Physiologiae Stoicorum* of 1604. This book presented a series of arguments that had something recognisably to do with the Stoics, and it provided a series of references to relevant Greek and Latin texts that had not previously been analysed or edited in any systematic way; but it also managed to falsify the arguments of the Stoics to a considerable extent: Lipsius denied, for example, that the Stoics taught a pantheistic materialism when he claimed that they had argued that 'God is contained in things but not infused with them'.[30] An alternative and more common approach was to avoid the matter of Stoic physics altogether. Guillaume du Vair (1556–1621), whose preferred Stoic text was Epictetus's *Encheiridion*, found himself in his *Moral philosophie of the Stoicks* able to exalt the piety and the monotheism of the Stoics, presenting the God of the Stoics as identical to the God of the Christians, for the maxims of this short compilation stuck to moral exhortation and avoided the reefs of theological controversy.

Problems were therefore bound to arise for these syncretist understandings of Stoicism when the conditions that made these Neostoic interpretations plausible no longer obtained—and the Neostoics themselves inadvertently contributed to undermining their own arguments. On the one hand, Lipsius encouraged scholarly attention to the physics of the Stoics through his publication of the *Physiologiae Stoicorum*, yet a more assiduous investigation of the sources for those physics would prove troublesome for his argument about the symbiotic relationship that could obtain between Stoicism and Christianity. On the other hand, du Vair did much to popularise the philosophy of Epictetus in early seventeenth-century France, but a broader understanding of the systematic nature of his Stoicism and, in particular, sustained attention to the arguments of Epictetus's longer *Diatribai* (or *Discourses*) rather than the shorter *Encheiridion* (or *Handbook*), would subvert his claims about the compatibility of this Stoicism with conventional religion. In the long run, Neostoic syncretism was unsustainable. But even in the middle of the seventeenth century, the best scholarship on the Stoics could still be placed in the service of Christian Stoicism, as Thomas Gataker's edition of Marcus Aurelius demonstrates.

The extensive notes in Thomas Gataker's 1652 edition of the *Meditations* covered a far wider range of sources in technical Stoic philosophy than Lipsius had examined in his Stoic textbooks. But despite Gataker's more sophisticated understanding of Stoic physics and a much deeper interest in Epictetus than that possessed by the Neostoics of the previous century, he nevertheless remained anxious to present his Stoics as fairly conventional theists, and certainly as thinkers in whom contemporary

Christians could find inspiration. He expounded their core theological position in these ringing terms in the 'Preliminary Discourse':

> God Almighty governs the Universe; that his Providence is not only General, but Particular, and reaches to Persons and Things. That he presides over Humane Affairs; that he assists Men not only in the greatest Concerns, in the Exercise of Virtue, but also supplies them with the Conveniences of Life. And therefore that God ought to be Worshipp'd above all Things, and applied to upon all Occasions; that we should have him always in our Thoughts, acknowledge his Power, resign to his Wisdom and adore his Goodness for all the satisfactions of our being. To submit to his Providence without Reserve. To be pleased with his Administration; and fully persuaded that the Scheme of the World could not have been mended, nor the Subordination of Things more suitably adjusted, nor all Event have been better timed for the common advantage; and therefore that 'tis the duty of all Mankind, to obey the Signal and follow the Intimations of Heaven, with all the Alacrity imaginable: that the Post assign'd us by Providence must be maintained with Resolution; and that we ought to die a thousand times over, rather than desert it.[31]

As had been the case for du Vair with respect to Epictetus, Gataker was interested in Marcus Aurelius chiefly as a source of moral inspiration, which he argued was almost entirely compatible with Christian ethics.[32]

It is not in Gataker's pages, however, but in those of his contemporary, the Cambridge Platonist Ralph Cudworth, who was writing on the physics rather than the ethics of the Stoics, that we begin to see how the concerns about Stoic theology were to be articulated, for the discussion of Stoicism in the second volume of Cudworth's massive 1678 *True Intellectual System of the Universe* represents the most sustained discussion in the seventeenth-century English tradition of the question as to whether the Stoics' physics should permit their philosophy to be interpreted as a form of theism. Cudworth ultimately followed Gataker, Lipsius, and du Vair in arguing that the Stoics were theists: according to the central classificatory scheme of his book, theirs was presented as a teaching of '*divine* fate, morall and naturall'. They might have been, in Cudworth's fine phrase, 'sottish corporealists',[33] but they were not themselves atheists; though, as he remarked casually in the third volume, they were 'imperfect, mongrel and spurious theists'.[34] In Cudworth's account, the decisive issue was that of Creation:

> [A]s to that controversy so much agitated amongst the ancients, whether the world were made by chance, or by the necessity of mate-

rial motions, or by mind, reason and understanding; they [the Stoics] avowedly maintained that it was neither by chance nor by material necessity, but *divina mente*, 'by a divine and eternal mind' every way perfect.[35]

Furthermore, Cudworth had some praise for the way in which Cicero set out the Stoics' arguments for the existence of God under three headings in his *De natura deorum*, using an argument from design, an argument from 'universal harmony', and an argument from the 'scale of nature', reasons that, he said, were not 'at all contemptible, or much inferior to those which have been used in these latter days'.[36] While Cudworth acknowledged and copiously documented evidence of the Stoics' polytheism, he concluded these passages of exposition with a stress on Epictetus's and Cleanthes' invocations of a single deity, 'because many are so extremely unwilling to believe that the Pagans ever made any religious address to the supreme God as such', and he reprinted the famous hymn of Cleanthes both in the original Greek and in a Latin translation by 'my learned friend Dr. Duport'.[37]

Cudworth's general verdict was that the Stoic school taught a form of theism. But as Jonathan Israel has noted, Cudworth drew a distinction between this orthodox Stoicism and the position of some of the later Stoics, who were properly categorised as atheists.[38] The earlier Stoics held both that 'there was an animalish, sentient and intellectual nature, or a conscious soul and mind, that presided over the whole world, though lodged immediately in the fiery matter of it' and that 'this sentient and intellectual nature, or corporeal soul and mind of the universe, did contain also under it, or within it, as the inferior part of it, a certain plastic nature, or spermatic principle which was properly the fate of all things'.[39] But later Stoics such as Boethus and Seneca, Cudworth argued, 'divided these two things from one another, and taking only the latter of them, made the plastic or spermatic nature, devoid of all animality or conscious intellectuality, to be the highest principle in the universe.'[40] Boethus 'did plainly deny the world to be an animal' but considered it 'a body governed by a plastic or vegetative nature, as trees, plants and herbs', and 'Seneca himself was not without a doubtful tincture of this atheism'.[41] This variety of atheism, 'which supposes one plastic or spermatic nature, one plantal or vegetative life in the whole world, as the highest principle', Cudworth labelled as 'cosmoplastic', 'Pseudo-Stoical' or 'Stoical', atheism.

Direct evidence is hard to come by, but the most plausible explanation for this critical scrutiny of Stoic arguments about the nature of God concerns the circulation of Spinoza's arguments, which generated, in Jonathan Israel's words, 'an urgent need for a rigorous re-evaluation of Stoic fatalism'.[42] Spinoza's most detailed examination of the nature of God was presented in the first part of his *Ethics*, first published as a part of the *Opera postuma* in 1677. But the notorious argument against the possibility of miracles in chapter 6 of the *Tractatus theologico-politicus*, which ignited the controversy in 1670, deployed an account of the nature of things that touched on Stoic cosmology in significant ways, with Spinoza's argument against the possibility of miracles premised, in the first instance, on the identification of the laws of nature with the decrees of God. More particularly, however, the violence that Spinoza's account of God in the *Tractatus* performed on traditional Christian notions of Providence conjured up all of the anxieties and objections that had been expressed against Lipsius's arguments about Stoic fate and divine providence in *De constantia*. For Spinoza to assert that 'God's decree, command, edict and word are nothing other than the action and order of Nature' was to proclaim the truth about Stoic determinism that Lipsius had endeavoured to deny, or at least to shuffle under the carpet.[43] And the controversy surrounding Spinoza's philosophy gave those who might have been unsure just how to categorise the Stoics an incentive to adjust the criteria as to what was to count as theism, until they could be presented as not just atheists but as Spinozist atheists. In particular, the matter of divine punishment and reward after death, which Spinoza denied, became increasingly significant in discussions and definitions of atheism.[44]

Jacob Thomasius (1622–84), the father of the more eminent philosopher Christian and the tutor of Leibniz, may have been the first scholar to publish an attempted refutation of the argument of the *Tractatus*: Spinoza's book was first published in Amsterdam in January 1670 (although the title page said Hamburg), and Thomasius had his own *Adversus anonymum, de libertate philosophandi* published in Leipzig in May of the same year.[45] In 1676 he followed this up with a neo-Aristotelian attack on Lipsius's syncretist ambition to reconcile Christian theology and Stoic physics, *Exercitatio de stoica mundi exustione*, in which he claimed, 'Nothing has more disgracefully corrupted the history of philosophy than the attempt to reconcile the Christian faith, now with Plato, now with Aristotle, now with the Stoics or other pagan groups'.[46] Thomasius's attack on Lipsius was organized on three main fronts: first, he criticized Lipsius's interpretation of the inseparability of the two principles (active and passive) which the Stoics had argued structured the universe; second, he identified and criticised the Stoics' conflation of God and the world, the key claim of their pantheism and one that Lipsius had specifically attempted to deny; and third, he insisted that Lipsius's attempt to deny that God was responsible for evil, given his Stoic premises, had to fail.[47]

This, then, is part of the philosophical context in which the *True Intellectual System* was assembled—and J. A. Passmore in his classic study of

Cudworth suggests that it was the lengthy critique of 'hylozoic atheism' that was intended as a refutation of Spinoza. This kind of atheism, in Cudworth's words,

> being too modest and shamefaced to fetch all things from the fortu-
> itous motion of atoms, would therefore allow to the several parts of
> matter a certain kind of natural (though not animal) perception, such
> as is devoid of reflexive consciousness, together with a plastic power,
> whereby they may be able artificially and methodically to form and
> frame themselves to the best advantage of their respective capabilities;
> something like to Aristotle's nature, but that it hath no dependence at
> all upon any higher Mind or Deity. And these Atheists may be also
> called hylozoic (as the other atomic,) because they derive all things in
> the whole universe, not only sensitive, but also rational souls, together
> with the artificial frame of animals, from the life of matter.[48]

Hylozoistic atheism was a doctrine, Cudworth noted, that began with the Peripatetic scholarch Strato of Lampsacus, then 'slept in perfect silence and oblivion', but that had 'of late [been] awakened and revived by some'. Spinoza's work, Passmore judged, Cudworth 'knew only imperfectly but interpreted as reviving a tradition which was worth opposing in detail'.[49] 'Cosmoplastic' or 'Pseudo-Stoical' atheism was clearly a variation on this hylozoic theme.

There are many strong parallels between Stoicism and Spinoza's philo-sophical system, set out above all in the *Ethics*. There is a systematic philosophical vision that integrates cosmology and ethics. There is strict determinism, with Providence just another name for the course of nature, and an identification of God with the totality of the universe (in Spinoza's phrase, *Deus sive natura*). There is a distinction between active and pas-sive nature (*natura naturans* and *natura naturata*), and a claim that the universe is pervaded by reason (*logos*), the active principle that infuses nature. All animal behaviour is determined by the *conatus*, or the striving to conserve oneself—Spinoza's version of the Stoics' *oikeiosis*. Human passions are equated with false judgements. And the ethical theory is a version of eudaimonism, in which to be virtuous is to be happy; happi-ness depends not on external things but on our attitude towards those things—but that only the wise man is capable of such happiness.[50] In her article 'Spinoza the Stoic', furthermore, Susan James has not only empha-sised some of these parallels but also strengthened the association be-tween Spinoza and Stoicism by arguing that in his presentation, 'Spinoza displays an awareness of the objections to which the Stoic account of virtue was habitually subjected, and that in responding to them he draws still further on the resources of Stoic philosophy'.[51] The exploration of

Spinoza's philosophy in light of its points of contact with Stoic thought is a project that is continuing in the present day: Firmin de Brabander's book, *Spinoza and the Stoics*, is one significant contribution; Justin Jacobs's recently completed study on the *conatus* in Hobbes and Spinoza is another; and Jon Miller's work in progress will doubtless be a third.[52]

It is not my intention here to explore the question of Spinoza's Stoicism in any depth. (That is a matter for the Spinoza specialists, of which I am not one.) Rather, I want to draw attention to the way in which this opinion, that Spinoza was in important respects a sophisticated kind of modern Stoic, was not one confined to the present and very recent past. During the Spinozist controversy itself, both Pierre Bayle and J. F. Buddeus found the Stoic label an appropriate one to use when considering the content and structure of Spinoza's arguments, and Giambattista Vico was also clear that there were significant continuities, referring at one point in his *New Science* to the Stoics, 'in this respect the Spinozists of their day'.[53]

J. F. Buddeus and the Historiography of Philosophy

Bayle might have branded the Stoics atheists on account of their pantheism, but the writer who devoted the most time and attention to an investigation, elaboration, and denunciation of the connections that were claimed to hold between Stoicism, Spinozism, and atheism was Johann Franz Buddeus (1667–1729), professor at Halle and Jena, who devoted a series of studies over the length of his career to different aspects of the matter. The first, on the errors of the Stoics,[54] was followed by 'Spinozism before Spinoza',[55] a widely read treatise, *Atheism and Superstition*,[56] a scholarly edition of Marcus Aurelius with a detailed introductory essay,[57] and important works on the history of philosophy,[58] which are the focus of attention in what follows.

In the middle of the seventeenth century, the standard approach to the historiography of philosophy, which at this time almost universally meant writing the history of ancient philosophy, was still closely modelled on Diogenes Laertius's *Lives of Eminent Philosophers*. A typical work would be organized by sect, each section being subdivided by author, with a doxography of the sect's distinctive arguments presented in the section devoted to its founder—in the case of the Stoics, Zeno of Citium.[59] Passages on later philosophers adhering to the particular school would follow the treatment of the founder, in broadly chronological order. While mention would be made of particular specialisms or idiosyncracies that appeared in the work of these later adherents, there would be no detailed treatment of what scholars would today recognise as the basic stuff of the history of philosophy, the presentation of how the course of philosophical argument over time led to modifications in the doctrines maintained by the philosophers and the schools. Those who wrote on the history of philosophy could discuss whether theses were true or false in light of the best philosophical accounts of their own age or of revealed religion, but they provided no serious account of how progress in philosophy might be made, of how within a certain philosophical tradition arguments might be found wanting and replaced, where possible, with better ones.

The leading English work in this vein was the compendious *History of Philosophy* by Thomas Stanley (1625–78), first published in 1655, when the author was twenty-eight.[60] Following this template, Stanley treated the Stoics in isolation from other philosophical schools and presented a life of Zeno together with a comprehensive doxography of Stoic doctrine, much of it taken straight out of Diogenes Laertius. He had little specific to say about the Stoics after Zeno, and nothing at all to say about the Stoics of the Roman period.[61] There were two pages on Cleanthes,[62] five pages on Chrysippus, largely given over to the lengthy catalogue of his works,[63] and fewer than two pages in total on Zeno of Tarsus, Diogenes of Seleucia, Antipater of Sidon, Panaetius, and Posidonius, the other Stoics treated in his part 8. When it came to the theism of the Stoics, which he discussed in part 8, chapter 17, Stanley noted that the historical record reported a variety of opinions about the Stoics' God.

> The substance of God, Zeno affirms to be the whole World and Heaven; so also Chrysippus in the 11th of the Gods, and Posidonius in the first of the Gods. But Antipater in his Seventh of the World, affirms his substance to be aerial. Boethius in his Book of Nature, saith, the substance of God is the Sphere of fixed Stars. Sometimes they call him a nature containing the World, sometimes a nature producing all upon Earth.[64]

Here, the problem of treating the Stoics as simple monotheists is clearly in view, given the way in which Stanley tacks back and forth between references to the 'God' and the 'Gods' of the Stoics in his reports of the teachings found in the various ancient authorities (in this section, Plutarch, Diogenes Laertius, and Cicero). The closest he came to resolving this tension was to suggest that 'God is a Spirit, diffused through the whole World, having several denominations, according to the several parts of the matter through which he spreadeth, and the several effects of his power shewn therein', before rattling off a variety of these names (Dia, Minerva, Neptune, etc.).[65]

In the latter part of the seventeenth century, however, a revolution in the historiography of philosophy pioneered by Pufendorf and Christian

Thomasius (1655–1728), associated with a new understanding of 'eclecticism' in philosophy, paved the way both for a coherent notion of philosophical progress and for the large, multivolume histories of philosophy written in the eighteenth century.[66] Instead of providing accounts of the teachings of the different schools or sects in isolation from one another, the historiography of philosophy became, as we might say, problem-driven, examining particular philosophical questions, the arguments to which these had historically given rise, and, crucially, those moments in which the participants in those arguments appeared to agree that the state of the question had changed, or that the argument had moved on. In considering the topics that were debated between the partisans of the different schools, furthermore, the new historians of philosophy had the highest praise for those they considered to be 'eclectic' philosophers, those who were not beholden to the dogmas of a particular school but who enjoyed the freedom to draw as they saw fit from among the various authorities and arguments that were available to them. But there was also another development in the technique of writing the history of philosophy, pioneered in the early eighteenth century and associated in particular with Buddeus, that has been less remarked on in the recent literature on the historiography of philosophy in this period. Rather than examining each of the ancient philosophical schools by listing their opinions on various topics, Buddeus sought to identify the nuclear or constitutive principles of those philosophical schools, the key teachings from which other doctrines were considered to flow. This was a way of distinguishing the core from the peripheral arguments of the various schools, which could help scholars cope with the fact—quite an obvious fact, in the case of the Stoics—that a number of the source materials for the study of the Hellenistic schools made contradictory claims.

Given Buddeus's triple preoccupation with atheism, Stoicism, and Spinoza, it is perhaps not surprising that his methodological innovation in the historiography of philosophy had a specific application to precisely this polemic. Indeed, this distinctive method seems to have been developed out of Buddeus's extensive reflections on Stoicism, after his observation that the moral precepts of Seneca and Marcus Aurelius, which appeared attractive and assimilable to Christian truth, were in fact generated by deeper arguments deeply antithetical to religious orthodoxy—indeed, were generated by arguments familiar to the contemporary world above all through the philosophy of Spinoza.[67] According to Buddeus's presentation, the single most important dogma of the Stoics was their identification of God with the world, and the various other principles that they maintained were held ultimately to follow from this.[68] In the realm of Stoic moral philosophy, the contradiction between the admirable individual maxims of the Stoics and the impious premises by which they were generated found its expression in the hypocrisy of individual Stoic philosophers, a subject in which Buddeus was quite interested.[69]

In the work on atheism, Buddeus distinguished between two varieties of atheists:

> In the first category, I put those who shamelessly and straightforwardly deny the existence of God, or those who—owing to their bad faith— can only deny or ignore the atheism that necessarily flows from their principles. In the second category, I put those who set up principles from which one can validly infer conclusions which are either prejudicial or injurious to the Providence and the liberty of God.[70]

Buddeus assigned the Epicureans to the first category and the Stoics and Aristotle to the second, but he then distinguished between the latter two, in order to make an argument as to why the former were closer to Spinoza than the latter:

> While Aristotle remained content to assert that God was always present in the world, the Stoics maintained that he was immanent in the world itself, as was clearly demonstrated by JAC THOMAS *de Exustione Mundi Stoica Dissert.* 15. Their system, therefore, is closer to that of Spinoza than is Aristotle's.[71]

Early in this study, Buddeus noted that many readers had found in the Stoics 'their fine sentences concerning religion, virtue, etc.', and he commented, characteristically, 'But these only serve to show that one can infer valid conclusions from false principles, or that the Stoics at least did not always reason logically'.[72] A little later he observed that he did not intend to say anything specific about Epictetus or Marcus Aurelius but noted that while no one objected to *their* atheism, their cases were covered by his earlier more general treatment of the Stoics, so that they could clearly be treated as such.[73]

Buddeus is relatively obscure today. If he is remembered at all, it is for his attacks on Christian Wolff in the 'War of the Philosophers' from 1723.[74] He remains an important figure, however, for understanding the academic presentation of Stoicism in the early eighteenth century. In particular, there are three sites where we can discern the impact of his arguments about the Stoics for eighteenth-century authors. First, there was an attempt to sidestep the implications of Buddeus's arguments about Stoicism, exemplified above all by Jean Barbeyrac in his 'Historical and critical account of the science of morality'. Second, Buddeus's own followers continued to make recognisable versions of his arguments about the Stoics, and in this context I examine J. L. Mosheim's commentary on Cud-worth's *The True Intellectual System*. Third, the Buddean argument could also be redeployed in the service of quite un-Buddean goals, and this, I suggest, is what happened when Diderot appropriated J. J. Brucker's pre-sentation of the Stoics when assembling the article on Stoicism for the *Encyclopédie*.

Although Buddeus developed his arguments about the proper methods for understanding ancient philosophers over his entire academic career—he died in 1729, and his final work, the *Compendium historiae philoso-phiae observationibus illustratum*, was edited and published by his son-in-law in Halle in 1731—his core argument equating the philosophical systems of Spinoza and the Stoics was available from 1701, in his treatise *De Spinozismo ante Spinozam* (Spinozism before Spinoza). But this argu-ment could be sidestepped by means of an approach to the Stoics that deemphasised their physics or cosmology or that denied that the ethics and the physics had much to do with one another. The tendency of the new historiography of philosophy associated with Pufendorf was to ex-amine ancient philosophy by subject area rather than by school, and it is to one of the most important texts for the development of philosophical eclecticism itself that I now turn. 'An historical and critical account of the science of morality' by Jean Barbeyrac (1674–1744) was published as a preface to his celebrated edition of Pufendorf's treatise *On Natural Law* in 1706. This essay presented an account of the history of moral philoso-phy that was organized around a central thread of argument and linked together ancient and modern ethics, culminating in his account of the natural law system of Pufendorf as the one uniquely able to come to grips with the problems bequeathed by the Grotian system, which itself had, in Barbeyrac's famous phrase, 'broken the ice' of the scholastics' moral thought. In chapter 27 of this work, Barbeyrac discussed the Greek Stoics.[75]

In contrast to many of the Stoic and anti-Stoic writings of the seven-teenth century, Barbeyrac's style was analytical rather than either apolo-getical or polemical. His points were backed up with precise references to both ancient texts and modern scholarship, and he generally followed the best authorities: Bayle, Jacob Thomasius, and Buddeus all feature in his apparatus. He was also careful to make sure his observations were rele-vant to the philosophical subject matter under discussion. When he re-ferred to the accusations of hypocrisy and vice that attended the lives of various Stoics, for example, he commented that 'these are personal faults, and extend not to their doctrines', and while he mentioned what were generally taken to be the least acceptable opinions of the Stoics—canni-balism, incest, the doctrine that all sins are equal, and the fact that 'What the Stoics said about the love of Beautiful boys is, at least, liable to very odd constructions'[76]—his rejection of these positions was peripheral to his main enquiry, for he understood the interest and importance of Stoic ethics to lie elsewhere.

Barbeyrac's distinctive move was explicitly to separate Stoic physics from its ethics. With regard to the former, he wrote, 'These principles, I must own, are monstrous; and the several philosophers of that Sect have, each in particular, added thereto some new Absurdities'.[77] With regard to the latter, his opinion was quite different, and fully in the tradition of Thomas Gataker: 'However, except a few things, nothing can be more beautiful than their Morality, very near approaching that of the Gospel, which alone is entirely conformable to the Dictates of right Reason'. In contrast, therefore, to Buddeus's argument, which sought to yoke the Stoics' ethics to their physics in order to condemn the seemingly attractive ethics by highlighting its basis in the defective physics, Barbeyrac's strategy was to break the Stoics' system apart, and to examine their ethics with respect to the rest of the history of moral philosophy. Considering the basis of Stoic ethics, therefore, Barbeyrac was careful to give one of its central claims, the notion of a life according to nature (*kata ton physin*), a rather vague reading, which had the effect of relaxing the notorious rigour of the Stoics' system:

> By this Nature, some of them meant directly the Constitution of the Human Nature; or that light of Reason by the help of which we discern what is truly suitable to our state, and condition; others meant universal Reason or the will of God . . . and others again meant both these things.[78]

The ethics of Marcus Aurelius were presented (following Gataker, to some extent, whom he cited as a 'learned Englishman') as an example of how far natural reason could lead a sincere inquirer after truth, an account that presupposed that Marcus Aurelius was engaged in the kind of moral theory that might contribute to a 'science of morality'. Barbeyrac, who was himself attempting to contribute to that science of morality, drew these (fairly conventional) conclusions concerning the Stoics: that for all its fine content, Stoic virtue could not be a complete account of the matter, for the Stoics did not present any hope of another life; the Stoics did not properly acknowledge the immortality of the soul; and they failed to appreciate that 'rigid and over-strained maxims are not at all proper to inspire virtue', or that there ought to be no place for the use of paradoxes in moral philosophy.[79]

The ancient ethical writer for whom Barbeyrac professed most admiration was Cicero, and he praised *De officiis* in particular—'that excellent work, so well known to the world . . . without Dispute, the best Treatise of Morality, that all Antiquity has produc'd; the most regular, the most methodical, and what comes the nearest to a full & exact system'—presenting its author as himself a kind of eclectic who borrowed as he saw fit from the various doctrines of the sects.[80] On the face of it, this might seem to mark a retreat to a kind of Renaissance Ciceronianism, with Barbeyrac holding up Cicero's Stoic-like moral doctrine as the one to be preferred while disdaining interest in the Stoics' philosophy of nature, but it is important to see that it is not. Barbeyrac's broader argument was that it was the modern natural rights tradition in general and the system of Pufendorf in particular that provided the right account of the proper justification of the content of ethics. From this standpoint, the Ciceronianism of the Renaissance represented the last appearance of the ancient doctrines, before they were swept away by the Grotian revolution in the postsceptical 'science of morality'. And this was the revolution that gave rise to the modern natural law theory whose exponents were able to fashion an adequate reply to the sceptical criticisms of Cicero's ethics that had been formulated, above all, by Montaigne.[81]

On one level, therefore, Barbeyrac agreed with Buddeus: Stoic physics was full of error, and when the Stoic system was fully understood, it had to be rejected. But the contrasts in their respective styles and approaches were dramatic. Buddeus's historiography was one in which Stoicism as a system appeared in both ancient and modern contexts, substantially unaltered, whether in the theory of Chrysippus or Spinoza; Barbeyrac's presentation, by contrast, had no time for this kind of transhistorical argument: the true scientists of morality learned from one another's mistakes, neither simply replicating nor anathematising the Stoics' ethics. By breaking up the unity of the Stoics' system, furthermore, Stoicism became a series of philosophical resources or arguments that could be drawn on selectively, indeed eclectically. In moving to insulate the Stoics' ethics from their physics, finally, Barbeyrac made an important move, and one that Montesquieu and others would reiterate later in the century.[82]

The second place to trace out the influence of Buddeus's anti-Stoic polemic is in academic writing on the problem of understanding Stoic philosophy, and one place where we can see the implications of this new approach to the history of philosophy being followed through is in the extensive commentaries prepared by another German Enlightenment academic, J. L. Mosheim (1694–1755), for his edition of Cudworth's *True Intellectual System*, published in 1733.[83] Methodologically, Mosheim aligned himself with Buddeus's approach when he wrote that

> The discipline of this sect is not to be learned from the magnificent phrases of this or that Stoic, but the whole of it ought to be placed before our view as a system, and afterwards a judgment formed as to the utility and excellence of the several dogmas. . . . Wherefore, if the dogmas or sayings of this or that Stoic be considered in themselves, we

shall never be at a loss for arguments to justify and uphold the cause of this sect. For my part, I consider that the goodness and badness of any doctrine should be judged of from its fundamental principles, and from its general tenor and context, and that we should take into especial consideration, not what some have said or written, but what they ought to have said or written consistently with the rest of their opinions.[84]

Taken as a whole, Cudworth's text and Mosheim's notes constitute an interesting dialogue between two erudite representatives of seventeenth- and eighteenth-century scholarship that ranged across the interpretation of philosophical authors both ancient and modern and discussed at length a number of topics in metaphysics and theology.[85]

On the face of it, Mosheim and Cudworth might not seem to be very far apart in their interpretations of Stoic theology. Cudworth had labelled the Stoics 'spurious theists', but refused to categorise them alongside other ancient atheists; Mosheim, too, was reluctant to employ the atheist label. But the different reasons each author leant on when drawing their similar conclusion were decisive in indicating their general attitude to Stoic theology. Cudworth's interest in Creation, intelligent design and monotheism ultimately inclined him to a more generous judgement concerning Stoic theology. Mosheim's concerns, by contrast, were those dictated by the Buddean anti-Spinozist polemic, and invited a harsher verdict. So, for example, while he held back from labelling the Stoics atheists ('That the Stoics professed a certain God or fiery nature, eternal, wise and provident, admits of no controversy'),[86] the two particular features of Stoic theology to which he drew attention in the ensuing exposition were precisely those canvassed by Buddeus when he was expounding the distinction between the two different kinds of atheists. The first of these was the question of God's freedom of action, for the Stoics 'openly acknowledged, that this God was unable to accomplish all that he wished, and that he did not possess the power of free agency, being bound down by the fate inherent in the very nature of matter',[87] and the second was the matter of 'external justice', or the divine justice of punishing and rewarding, which the Stoics denied, '[B]y doing which they extinguish in mankind all motive for the practice of virtue and destroy the very foundations of divine worship'.[88] Mosheim and Buddeus may not have agreed on the label, but they certainly were of one mind when it came to the substance of the Stoics' argument.

The third place to look for the influence of Buddeus's presentation of the Stoics is in the works of his most illustrious student, Johann Jakob Brucker (1696–1770), whose colossal *Historia critica philosophiae* became the standard work of reference on the history of philosophy before the followers of Kant and of Hegel got to work rewriting that history to place in the foreground the achievements of these latter-day masters.[89] Brucker is a far more significant figure than Buddeus, considered in terms of both his own historiographical achievement and his influence upon academic posterity, but when it came to writing about the Stoics, Brucker was largely content to follow in the footsteps of his predecessor,[90] most characteristically when Brucker observed that one should not judge the Stoics from words and sentiments 'detached from the general system' but that one should 'consider them as they stand related to the whole train of premises and conclusions'.[91]

Following Buddeus again, Brucker's judgement on Stoicism was resolutely hostile, and despite his 'critical' method, his discussion was couched in familiar terms: the Stoics wasted much time and threw away much ingenuity 'upon questions of no importance',[92] and they 'largely contributed towards the confusion, instead of the improvement, of science, by substituting vague and ill defined terms in the room of accurate conceptions'.[93] With respect to their moral philosophy, Brucker found it to be 'an ostentatious display of words, in which little regard was paid to nature and reason',[94] and while it aimed at raising 'human nature to a degree of perfection before unknown', in fact it served 'merely to amuse the ear' with 'fictions which can never be realised'. He concluded that 'a system of philosophy, which attempts to raise men above their nature, must commonly produce, either wretched fanatics, or artful hypocrites'.[95] Turning from the ethics to the physics, he resisted the move of those apologists for the Roman Stoics, who tried to equate Stoic fate with divine providence:

This doctrine, according to Zeno and Chrysippus (who herein meant to combat Epicurus's doctrine of the fortuitous concourse of atoms) implies an eternal and immutable series of causes and effects, within which all events are included, and to which the Deity himself is subject: whereas, the later Stoics, changing the term Fate into The Providence of God, discoursed with great plausibility on this subject, but still in reality retained the antient doctrine of universal fate.[96]

In his discussion of the modern authorities who had written on the Stoics, Brucker consistently criticized the syncretist ambitions of Lipsius, Heinsius, Schioppius, and Gataker, appealing to the scholarship of Thomasius and Buddeus to support his opinions. Concerning Gataker, for example, Brucker wrote,

I think it is clear enough from the above that this very erudite man was deceived by the study of the Stoa, and did not attend to the real hypotheses of the Stoics accurately enough and without prejudice, but certainly granted much to emotion and hatred, through which he persecuted the philosophy of Epicurus, and even tacitly attacked Gassendi himself, who was fighting on behalf of the most learned Epicurus; so there is no need to add more here.[97]

Brucker drew heavily on Buddeus when writing his account of Stoicism, and Brucker in turn became the chief source for Denis Diderot (1713–84) when he was compiling the articles on the history of philosophy for the *Encyclopédie*. Indeed, many articles on this subject essentially consist of lengthy passages from Brucker's work, translated into French and only very lightly edited, and the article on Stoicism is a very good example of this.[98] In this way, therefore, Buddeus's anti-Spinozist views on the nature of Stoicism ended up being presented substantially intact before a significant new reading public in the pages of the *Encyclopédie*. Presenting in outline form the basic principles of the Stoics, Diderot worked closely with Brucker's text and agreed with Buddeus when he wrote that 'it is not difficult to conclude from these principles that the Stoics were materialists, fatalists and, strictly speaking, atheists'.

The decisive difference this time around, of course, was that in Diderot's view of the matter, to be a materialist, fatalist atheist was no bad thing at all.

CHAPTER SEVEN

From Fénelon to Hume

RECENT SCHOLARSHIP ON THE ENLIGHTENMENT has been interested in the idea that the late seventeenth century witnessed a kind of confluence of the traditions of Augustinian criticism and the neo-Epicureanism deriving from Pierre Gassendi. Jean Lafond first developed the theme, and it has been taken up by both John Robertson in his study of intellectual life in Naples and Scotland and Pierre Force in his book on the idea of self-interest before Adam Smith.[1] Augustinian and Epicurean perspectives had hitherto stood sharply opposed to one another. *The City of God* offered an overarching account of God's providence at work in human history, but the Epicureans denied providence and argued that the gods took no interest in human affairs. Nor was there anything analogous in Epicurus's philosophy to the drama of original sin, central to the Augustinian vision of the human predicament. A number of developments in the seventeenth century, however, prepared the way for this coming together of the rival traditions. One significant factor was the way in which they shared a common antagonist in the various Stoic-inflected moral psychologies that had been so popular since the time of Justus Lipsius and Guillaume du Vair, which suggested that virtue could be sufficient for happiness and associated that virtue with public-spirited action. More directly relevant, however, were the specific contributions of writers like La Rochefoucauld, Blaise Pascal, Pierre Nicole, Nicolas Malebranche, Jacques Abbadie, and Pierre Bayle.

La Rochefoucauld had argued that even the most seemingly altruistic behaviour could be understood in terms of self-interest, or *amour-propre*.[2] Pascal's *Pensées* showed how vanity led people to spend much time in various distractions (*divertissement*)—'gambling, hunting, visits, theatre-going, false perpetuation of one's name'—which combined to make them sociable and to make life far more tolerable than it might otherwise be.[3] In his essay 'Of Charity, and Self-Love', the Jansenist Nicole argued not only that we can never be confident even through conscientious self-inspection that our behaviour is motivated by Christian charity rather than by sinful self-love but also that we can make no reliable inferences about our motivations based on the consequences of our actions. Divine providence ensures both that this cannot be done and that, regardless of our motivations, such consequences are generally tolerable from the point of view of the necessity of our living together peacefully, and prosperously, too, in the commercial society constituted by our mutual self-interested intercourse.[4] For the Oratorian Malebranche, pleasure was a good, and the Epicureans' error was to locate the source of pleasure in external objects, when only God 'can fill us with all the pleasures of which we are capable'.[5] The exiled Huguenot and anti-Jansenist Jacques Abbadie sought to fashion an Epicurean moral theory that was not dependent on Epicurean materialist physics in his 1692 treatise, *L'art de se connoître soi-même*.[6] Pierre Bayle, finally, interpreted the Epicurean account of human nature as one that was powerfully consonant with the traditional Augustinian account of humanity in its postlapsarian condition.[7] As John Robertson has summarised the Augustinian engagement with themes from Epicurean philosophy, 'it was from this encounter that there developed the realization that a society of purely self-interested men, driven by their passions rather than their reason, could nevertheless survive and meet its needs, with little or even no external assistance from Divine Providence and only limited intervention by government'.[8]

The opposition of 'Stoic' and 'Epicurean' was widely deployed in the early eighteenth century in relation to a number of contemporary questions. Most frequently it appeared in discussions of sociability, with the label 'Stoic' attachable to stronger and 'Epicurean' to weaker or nonexistent conceptions of the natural sociability of humankind or, in particular, to those who grounded sociability in utility. There were other, to some extent related, binaries that might also have been in play during this period with respect to the language of Stoics and Epicureans. 'Stoics' could be associated with republicanism in politics in a way that Epicureans were not; 'Stoics' were critics of luxury, while 'Epicureans' were not; and, touching on one of the central religious anxieties of the age, 'Stoics' subscribed to some conception of divine providence, which 'Epicureans' denied. And one way of viewing a sequence of philosophical exchanges in Britain in the first half of the eighteenth century, between Shaftesbury and Hume, is in terms of a pendulum swinging back and forth between plausibly Stoic and Epicurean concerns and arguments. Shaftesbury's system had quite a lot of points of contact with Stoicism; Bernard Mandeville's critique of Shaftesbury straightforwardly flowed from the major concerns of this new Epicurean Augustinianism or Augustinian Epicureanism. Joseph Butler and Francis Hutcheson each inserted distinctively Stoic elements into their moral philosophies, which they directed against Mandeville and in defence of Shaftesbury; and finally, recent scholarship has helped to construct a persuasive interpretation of David Hume as a somewhat Epicurean and certainly anti-Stoic moral theorist. Before turning to Mandeville, however, we need to take a brief look back across the

Channel at Fénelon, who was the major opponent from within French Catholicism of the Augustinian tendency towards Epicureanism, as well as the target of much of Mandeville's polemic.

FRANÇOIS DE SALIGNAC DE LA MOTHE-FÉNELON

François de Salignac de la Mothe-Fénelon, archbishop of Cambrai and the dauphin's tutor, was one of those French Catholics engaged in anti-Jansenist polemic who became alert to the increasing number of Epicurean strands to be found in the arguments of their Augustinian opponents.[9] In particular, he denounced the view that the way in which God's grace moves the soul was by presenting the prospect of infinitely more pleasure than that which might be procured through sin. 'Epicurus believed that every man must follow his greatest pleasure, because pleasure is the end of human life and happiness', he wrote in the twenty-third letter of his *Instruction pastorale en forme de dialogues.* 'Don't your theologians say that *pleasure is the only spring moving the hearts* of all men?'[10] *Amour-propre*, for Fénelon, was something to be overcome, renounced, or transcended, and the Jansenists' Epicureanizing tendency was to be deplored because it pushed in just the opposite direction. Against the Jansenists' brand of ultra-Augustinianism Fénelon presented an alternative vision, one based on a notion of pure or disinterested love, a love that should in particular characterise our orientation towards God, for Fénelon contended that we ought to love God without any regard for our personal salvation or damnation. This opinion, associated with the so-called Quietism of Jeanne-Marie Bouvier de la Motte-Guyon, better known as Madame Guyon, lay at the root of Fénelon's epic dispute with Bishop Bossuet, a dispute that was to end in 1699 when Innocent XII denounced twenty-three propositions from Fénelon's *Maxims of the Saints* and Fénelon formally submitted to papal authority. This kind of love was also the leitmotif of Fénelon's political theory. The 'idea of pure disinterested love', he wrote, somewhat implausibly 'dominates the political theories of all ancient legislators'.[11] Plato was the ancient philosopher from whom Fénelon drew the most inspiration (in Patrick Riley's words, he 'loved the *Symposium* and the *Phaedrus* with non-concupiscent passion'),[12] but it may be significant that his Scottish disciple, the Chevalier Ramsay, described the Stoics as followers of Plato in his *Essay on Civil Government* 'according to the principles of the late Archbishop of Cambray', in which he also defended the natural sociability of humankind in Stoic terms, quoting Cicero on how we are all 'Citizens of one and the same City', with the universe 'one great Common-wealth', and Marcus Aurelius on how 'If Reason is common to all, the Law is also common', so that 'we therefore live under one and the same Government, and the whole World is consequently but as one City'.[13]

Fénelon's major political work, *Telemachus,* describes his hero's journeys around the Mediterranean while searching for his father, Ulysses, and the political education he receives along the way from his tutor, Mentor, who is actually the goddess Minerva in disguise. While Telemachus is off fighting elsewhere in southern Italy, Mentor reorganises the city of Salente, which had been founded by Idomeneus, the exiled king of Crete, but had become corrupted by luxury and embroiled in war. Through his description of the reformed post-luxury Salente, Fénelon presents his vision of a populous agrarian society, with commerce encouraged but strictly regulated and the economic surplus channelled not into the consumption of luxuries but into the manufacture of armaments to deter foreign aggression.[14] One of Mentor's main concerns is to drive out luxury, for, as he tells Telemachus, 'As arbitrary power is the bane of kings, so luxury poisons a whole nation';[15] and as this analogy might suggest, Fénelon's book taken as a whole offered a sharp attack on the policies associated with Louis XIV and his minister of finance, Jean-Baptiste Colbert. Its unauthorised publication in 1699 ensured that Fénelon, who had already been banished to his diocese at Cambrai in 1697, would never again appear at court.

To describe a regime populated by virtuous farmers is not to present a distinctively Stoic society but to indulge in a celebration of more generically Roman values. For the late seventeenth century, however, as Christopher J. Berry has indicated, Stoicism offered the richest philosophical resources for a critique of luxury. When we ask what it means to live according to nature, as the Stoics recommended, we find that '[t]here is a proper limit to meeting the body's requirements', that '[h]umans have bodily needs, but Nature herself fixes a boundary to their satisfaction'.[16] The Stoics therefore taught a certain frugality. This did not require a Stoic or a would-be Stoic to live in accordance with the Cynic lifestyle of Diogenes of Sinope—living in a barrel, masturbating in public—for that would lack *decorum*, and would be inappropriate when it came to the various social roles we are called on to play. But the Stoic demand was that we work on our desires, trimming them back within their proper, natural limits; and, in particular, to be suspicious of those of our desires related to bodily pleasures.[17] From this point of view, to engage in the pursuit of luxury goods is to lose the kind of self-control we need to live the good life. Fénelon took over this Stoic view: there is no reason to think he dissented from the description of luxuries put into the mouths of the primitive, egalitarian inhabitants of Bétique, for example, who say they are 'superfluities' that 'enervate, intoxicate, and torment those who possess them, while they tempt those that are destitute of them to have recourse to violence and injustice to acquire them', and who ask whether 'a superfluity that serves only to make a man vicious' can 'be deemed a source of happiness'. Those people of Bétique are themselves described in Stoic terms in *Telemachus* by the Phoenician Adoam, who calls them 'these sages, who are indebted to simple nature alone for their wisdom'.[18]

BERNARD MANDEVILLE

Bernard Mandeville's *Fable of the Bees* took shape over the course of a quarter century. His poem 'The Grumbling Hive: or, Knaves Turn'd Honest', first appeared in 1705. In 1714 he published *The Fable of the Bees, or, private vices, publick benefits*, a volume in which the poem was reprinted, together with an essay, 'An Enquiry into the Origin of Moral Virtue', and a commentary on the poem consisting of twenty 'Remarks'. A second edition appeared in 1723, with additions to the 'Remarks' and two new essays, one on charity schools, the other called 'A Search into the Nature of Society', which initiated Mandeville's critical dialogue with Shaftesbury's *Characteristics*. In addition to minor changes that were made to new editions published over the course of the 1720s, Mandeville also began to include at the end of the work his short 'Vindication of the Book', chiefly written in response to the denunciation of the *Fable* by the Middlesex Grand Jury. In 1728 Mandeville published part 2 of the *Fable*, consisting of a preface and six dialogues, in which 'Cleomenes', who is broadly sympathetic to the argument of part 1 of the *Fable*, discusses various matters with the Shaftesburian 'Horatio', who is not. In 1733 the two parts were published together in a two-volume edition for the first time, and this is how the *Fable* has been republished down to the present.[19]

Although the final text of the *Fable* reads as an extended attack on Shaftesbury, this was not how it was first presented in 1714. Rather, as Istvan Hont has argued, the original target of Mandeville's satire was Fénelon, and the *Fable* was written to counteract the influence of his political and economic ideas in England.[20] As it happens, while serving as tutor to the Duc de Bourgogne, the dauphin's eldest son, Fénelon had himself composed a short fable of the bees, which recommended that modern society model itself along the lines of a beehive. 'Laziness and Inactivity were banish'd that State', Fénelon had written, 'every thing was in motion, but without any kind of Confusion or Disorder'. This is probably just a marvellous coincidence: there is no reason to think that Mandeville knew this text, as Fénelon's *Fables* were published only posthumously, appearing in French in 1718 and in an English translation in 1722.[21] Fénelon's political ideas, on the other hand, were well known in England. *The adventures of Telemachus* had begun to appear in English from 1699, a fifth edition had appeared before Mandeville published his 'Grumbling Hive', and by the time the *Fable* appeared for the first time in 1714, the original English-language version had reached its eighth edition, and an English-language verse edition of book 1 had been published in 1712.[22]

Although Fénelon's political economy had taken shape in the specific context of his criticism of Colbert's policy under Louis XIV, it had an obvious application to Britain, where the complex new financial architecture regulating the public finances was enabling the government to borrow heavily in order to finance its wars with France. For the critics of the ministry this was a recipe for corruption, in particular because of the way in which a significant proportion of the political class would have its own personal fortunes bound up with the perpetuation of the public debt. From a Fénelonian perspective, one could endorse all this and go further. The problem lay deeper than the institutions that governed the system of debt finance, for Fénelon argued that a commercial economy engaged in the production of luxury goods was one that both made war inevitable and weakened the ability of the state to wage it. As Mentor warns Idomeneus, 'If you had taken care at first to avoid jealousy of your neighbours, your new city would have flourished in a happy peace'.[23] For Mandeville and other supporters of the Orange and, later, Hanoverian ministries, the prospect of Fénelonian politics was appalling. They supported the war with France, deemed essential for pinning back the ambitions of a would-be universal monarch and defending the interests of key Protestant populations on the continent, such as Mandeville's native Holland. The implementation of Fénelonian reforms, furthermore, would require rolling back the political gains of the seventeenth century, for it was clear that the powers of an absolute monarch would be required for anything like the restructuring of political and economic life that Mentor had directed at Salente. Fénelonian politics were also Jacobite politics. Fénelon had hosted the Old Pretender at Cambrai after the battle of Malplaquet in 1709,[24] and when the *Fable* was first published in 1714, the Chevalier Ramsay was living in Cambrai, where Fénelon had received him into the Catholic Church. Fénelon's *Telemachus* had been written to set out the conditions under which there might be a stable balance of power in Europe; were a Fénelonian Britain to live in peace with its continental neighbour, it would not be as part of such a balance of power but rather as a Jacobite satellite.

Far from generating and sustaining peace and virtue, Mandeville charged that the practical consequences of a Fénelonian reform programme would be poverty and military defeat, with virtuous frugality unable to generate the kind of tax base that would allow the government to wage war successfully in the modern world. Following both Hobbes and the Augustinians, pride lay at the heart of Mandeville's analysis of human behaviour. He adapted Pierre Nicole's argument about the morally rotten foundations of social stability and gave it a secularizing twist. For Nicole, the intercourse of self-interested agents mutually pleasuring one another might be deplorable from the moral point of view, but the various ties of reciprocal self-interest to which this gave rise supported rather than undermined a general social cohesion. Mandeville restated a version of this argument about the integrative and beneficial social consequences of vice against Fénelon. Our vanity impelled us to work to improve our appearance in the eyes of others; this fuelled demand for the goods of fashion and other objects of luxurious consumption; and the resultant economic activity generated both work for the labouring poor and revenue for the government with which to fight its wars. Nor would luxury generate any military difficulties. Even if it were true that 'the Ease and Pleasures the Grandees and the rich People of every great Nation live in, render them unfit to endure Hardships, and undergo the Toils of War', there would not be a problem, for the 'Hardships and Fatigues of War that are personally suffer'd, fall upon them that bear the Brunt of every Thing, the meanest Indigent Part of the Nation, the working slaving People'.[25]

Mandeville's basically anti-Stoic orientation was signalled in the original poem, 'The Grumbling Hive', with its flat rejection of the equation of what was *honestum* with what was *utile*: 'Fools only strive / To make a Great an honest Hive'.[26] There was also a sharp dissent from the Stoic and Fénelonian critique of luxury, which Mandeville defined as including 'every thing . . . that is not immediately necessary to make Man subsist', including the most trivial improvement that savages might make to 'the Preparation of their Eatables'. Mandeville conceded that 'every body will say' his definition was 'too rigorous', but he stuck to it on the ground that 'if we are to abate one Inch of this Severity, I am afraid we shan't know where to stop'.[27]

> [I]f once we depart from calling every thing Luxury that is not absolutely necessary to keep a Man alive, that then there is no Luxury at all; for if the wants of Men are innumerable, then what ought to supply them has no bounds; what is call'd superfluous to some degree of People, will be thought requisite to those of higher Quality.[28]

There were also open disagreements with significant elements of Stoic moral theory. In the original edition of 1714, Mandeville discussed 'most of the ancient Philosophers and grave Moralists, especially the Stoicks', who 'would not allow any Thing to be a real Good that was liable to be taken from them by others'.

They wisely consider'd the Instability of Fortune, and the Favour of Princes; the Vanity of Honour, and popular Applause; the Precariousness of Riches, and all earthly Possessions; and therefore placed true Happiness in the calm Serenity of a contented Mind free from Guilt and Ambition; a Mind, that, having subdued every sensual Appetite, despises the Smiles as well as Frowns of Fortune, and taking no Delight but in Contemplation, desires nothing but what every Body is able to give to himself: A Mind, that arm'd with Fortitude and Resolution has learn'd to sustain the greatest Losses without Concern, to endure Pain without Affliction, and to bear Injuries without Resentment.[29]

'Many have own'd themselves arriv'd to this height of Self-denial', Mandeville continued; the question was whether anybody should believe them. Although proponents of this opinion 'among the Ancients have always bore the greatest Sway', Mandeville sided with those 'others that were no Fools neither', who 'have exploded those Precepts as impracticable' and 'endeavour'd to prove that what these Stoicks asserted of themselves exceeded all human Force and Possibility', so that 'the Virtues they boasted of could be nothing but haughty Pretence, full of Arrogance and Hypocrisy'. Mandeville continued in this vein of straightforwardly Augustinian criticism, with his reference to the 'generality of Wise Men that have liv'd' who 'agree with the Stoicks' that

there can be no true Felicity in what depends on Things perishable; that Peace within is the greatest Blessing, and no Conquest like that of our Passions; that Knowledge, Temperance, Fortitude, Humility, and other Embellishments of the Mind are the most valuable Acquisitions; that no Man can be happy but he that is good; and that the Virtuous are only capable of enjoying real Pleasures.[30]

But in place of a characteristically Augustinian claim that such goods might only be achievable through the intercession of divine grace and in a world to come, Mandeville here took a different, more Epicurean tack. Why had he 'call'd those Pleasures real that are directly opposite to those which I own the wise Men of all Ages have extoll'd as the most valuable'?

My Answer is, because I don't call things Pleasures which Men say are best, but such as they seem to be most pleased with; how can I believe that a Man's chief Delight is in the Embellishments of the Mind, when I see him ever employ'd about and daily pursue the Pleasures that are contrary to them?[31]

Mandeville then turned his attention to Seneca:

I could swagger about Fortitude and the Contempt of Riches as much as Seneca himself, and would undertake to write twice as much in behalf of Poverty as ever he did, for the tenth Part of his Estate: I could teach the way to his Summum bonum as exactly as I know my way home: I could tell People that to extricate themselves from all worldly Engagements, and to purify the Mind, they must divest themselves of their Passions, as Men take out the Furniture when they would clean a Room thoroughly; and I am clearly of the Opinion, that the Malice and most severe Strokes of Fortune can do no more Injury to a Mind thus stript of all Fears, Wishes and Inclinations, than a blind Horse can do in an empty Barn. In the Theory of all this I am very perfect, but the Practice is very difficult; and if you went about picking my Pocket, offer'd to take the Victuals from before me when I am hungry, or made but the least Motion of spitting in my Face, I dare not promise how Philosophically I should behave my self. But that I am forced to submit to every Caprice of my unruly Nature, you'll say, is no Argument that others are as little Masters of theirs, and therefore I am willing to pay Adoration to Virtue wherever I can meet with it, with a Proviso that I shall not be obliged to admit any as such, where I can see no Self-denial, or to judge of Mens Sentiments from their Words, where I have their Lives before me.[32]

As Mandeville expanded *The Fable of the Bees* in the 1720s, his polemical target shifted from Fénelon to Shaftesbury, with economic and foreign policy concerns giving way to an engagement with what Lawrence Klein has called the 'culture of politeness'.[33] The antagonism towards Shaftesbury was new: Mandeville's editor, F. B. Kaye, has observed that even as late as 1720 in his *Free Thoughts on Religion, the Church and National Happiness*, the only references to Shaftesbury's writings were favourable.[34] The anti-Stoic argumentative framework that Mandeville had built for the purposes of his attack on Fénelon was, however, very easily redirected against Shaftesbury's more ostentatiously Stoic edifice. Shaftesbury's 'Notions I confess are generous and refin'd: They are a high Compliment to Human-kind', Mandeville wrote in his 1723 essay, 'A Search into the Nature of Society', 'What Pity it is that they are not true'.[35] The 'imaginary Notions that Men may be Virtuous without Self-denial', he declared, were 'a vast Inlet to Hypocrisy', a phrase he liked so much that he repeated it in part 2 of the *Fable*.[36] Such hypocrisy acquired the force of habit, whereupon, with echoes of La Rochefoucauld, 'we must not only deceive others, but likewise become altogether unknown to our selves'.[37] Elaborating on the proviso offered above, Mandeville's spokesman 'Cleomenes' paired Cicero and Shaftesbury under a common, French Augustinian critique in the second dialogue in part 2 of the *Fable*:

> The true Object of Pride or Vain-glory is the Opinion of others; and the most superlative Wish, which a Man possess'd, and entirely fill'd with it can make, is, that he may be well thought of, applauded, and admired by the whole World, not only in the present, but all future Ages. This Passion is generally exploded, but it is incredible, how many strange and widely different Miracles are and may be perform'd by the force of it; as Persons differ in Circumstances and Inclinations. In the first place, there is no Danger so great, but by the help of his Pride a Man may slight and confront it; nor any manner of Death so terrible, but with the same Assistance, he may court, and if he has a firm Constitution, undergo it with Alacrity. In the second, there are no good Offices or Duties, either to others or ourselves, that Cicero has spoke of, nor any Instances of Benevolence, Humanity, or other Social Virtue, that Lord Shaftsbury has hinted at, but a Man of good Sense and Knowledge may learn to practise them from no better Principle than Vain-glory, if it be strong enough to subdue and keep under all other Passions, that may thwart and interfere with his Design.[38]

From being one of the chief causes of war in the Hobbesian state of nature, vainglory is here repositioned as one of the mechanisms that manufactures sociable behaviour out of unsociable human nature in Mandevillean commercial society.

When it came to the question of how to judge men's sentiments, 'where I have their Lives before me', finally, Mandeville offered his own interpretation of the life and death of a famous Stoic in 'A Search into the Nature of Society'. Cato's name was familiar to Mandeville's own time both as the eponymous hero and super-patriot of Joseph Addison's 1712 play— 'What a pity it is / That we can die but once to serve our country'—and also as the pseudonymous author of the *Letters* which appeared from November 1720 until July 1723, first in the *London Journal* and then, after the government took it over, in Trenchard and Gordon's own *British Journal*.[39] Malebranche had earlier wondered whether Cato's celebrated patience was merely blindness and pride; now Mandeville elaborated on the theme, in a manner reminiscent of Bayle's treatment of Lucretia in his *Dictionary*. 'How strict and severe was the Morality of rigid Cato', Mandeville began, 'how steady and unaffected the Virtue of that grand Asserter of Roman Liberty!' But 'for all the Self-denial and Austerity he practised', his final hour disclosed the truth about the man:

by his Suicide it plainly appeared that he was governed by a Tyrannical Power superior to the Love of his Country, and that the implacable Hatred and superlative Envy he bore to the Glory, the real Greatness and Personal Merit of Cæsar, had for a long time sway'd all his Actions under the most noble Pretences.

Had Cato been a prudent man, 'he might not only have saved himself, but likewise most of his Friends that were ruined by the Loss of him, and would in all probability, if he could have stooped to it, been the Second Man in Rome'.

But he knew the boundless Mind and unlimited Generosity of the Victor: it was his Clemency he feared, and therefore chose Death because it was less terrible to his Pride than the Thought of giving his mortal Foe so tempting an Opportunity of shewing the Magnanimity of his Soul, as Cæsar would have found in forgiving such an inveterate Enemy as Cato, and offering him his Friendship; and which, it is thought by the Judicious, that Penetrating as well as Ambitious Conqueror would not have slipt, if the other had dared to live.[40]

MANDEVILLE'S CRITICS: FRANCIS HUTCHESON AND JOSEPH BUTLER

In the same way that Hobbes, although only arguably Epicurean himself, became *the* Epicurean demon figure for the seventeenth century, so too Mandeville—the 'man-devil'—came to play this role for the eighteenth, and *The Fable of the Bees* became the focus of contemporary polemic. Just as Mandeville had drawn on the Epicureanizing currents of recent Augustinian theory in fashioning the argument of the *Fable*, which was explicitly directed in the 1720s against Shaftesbury's moral philosophy, so too, in their different ways, both Francis Hutcheson and Joseph Butler drew on strands of Stoic philosophy when framing their own critiques of Mandeville, even as their arguments pulled in different directions, Hutcheson towards a fully sentimentalist moral theory, Butler remaining far closer to the rationalist elements of Shaftesbury's position.

Francis Hutcheson

In the letter to Pierre Coste, Shaftesbury had divided the history of philosophy into two streams—the one 'civil, social, Theistic', the other not so much—and Hutcheson broadly followed suit. The subtitle to the first

1725 edition of his *Inquiry into the Original of our Ideas of Beauty and Virtue* announced that this was a work '*In which the principles of the late Earl of Shaftesbury are explain'd and defended, against the author of the Fable of the Bees: and the ideas of moral good and evil are establish'd, according to the sentiments of the antient moralists*', and this indicated the core elements of the basic dichotomy: on the one hand, Bernard Mandeville, the author of *The Fable of the Bees*; on the other, Shaftesbury, Hutcheson himself, and the various 'antient moralists'.[41] The key question separating the two kinds of moralists was that of natural sociability. When he took up the chair in moral philosophy at Glasgow in 1730, Hutcheson announced the topic of his inaugural lecture as 'to inquire whether the seeds of perhaps all the virtues, or at least inducements to every kind of virtue, are found in our nature';[42] he concentrated his attention on 'those parts of the human mind which make us sociable'; and he addressed himself to a 'question about which there is substantial controversy . . . in what sense is this social life natural to man?'

> Is it the case that all our benevolence toward the mass of mankind, that desires to protect whole peoples and do all that can be done for them, has its origin in each man's want, weakness, and indigence? Is it so that there may be others from whom each man may obtain what he wants for himself, so that by doing and receiving favors, he may get from another what he cannot get by himself? Or on the other hand, does benevolence arise from nature, and are we disposed to beneficence by nature, and not because we expect a favor in return or calculate the advantage our benevolence will obtain for us?[43]

Hutcheson associated the former position with the Epicureans, for whom 'self-love (*philautia*) alone, or the desire of each man for his own private pleasure or advantage, is the spring of all actions' and for whom 'social life is natural to man' only insofar as 'we need the help of others to avoid almost all the human evils and to obtain almost all the external pleasures or advantages which human life affords'.[44] When, elsewhere, Hutcheson criticised both Hobbes and the Epicureans for their reduction of all desires to self-love, he also showed his awareness of the confluence of the Epicurean and Augustinian currents in recent thought by placing these philosophers together with 'Our *Christian Moralists*' who 'introduce other sorts of Happiness to be desires, but still "'tis the *Prospect of private Happiness*, which, with some of them, is the sole *Motive of Election*"'.[45] And Mandeville's theory, he wrote in the first of his 'Letters to Hibernicus', published in 1726 in the *Dublin Weekly Journal*, was even less attractive than those of the Epicureans, for while they might have 'denied any affection distinct from self-love', the 'better sort' of Epicurean 'yet taught the same way to private happiness' as that advocated by the other sects, i.e., through 'love, gratitude, and submission to the deity, and in kind affections towards our fellows, and study of their greatest good'.[46]

Although Pufendorf and Cumberland had both positioned themselves as 'Stoic' critics of Hobbes's 'Epicureanism', Hutcheson in the inaugural lecture filed Pufendorf along with the Epicureans. He conceded that Pufendorf's philosophy 'ascends a little higher' than theirs, for his argument that 'knowledge of the great and good God and of the duty which he requires of us is easy for man' and that 'clear indications of this are given by the very constitution of our nature as creatures who desire happiness which can only be obtained in social life'.[47] But Hutcheson thought that Pufendorf was nevertheless fundamentally mistaken, in that his argument still supposed that 'men were driven into society merely by external advantage and dread of external evils, contrary to the nature of their hearts, contrary to all their natural desires and affections'. Such a view neglected the manner in which 'there are many desires directly implanted by nature which do not seek either pleasure or physical advantage but things more sublime which themselves depend upon the company of others', such as 'the pleasures of praise and honor' or the way in which 'by some wonderful provision of nature it happens that, though there is no small joy in the mere investigation of truth, yet that joy is immensely increased when there is another to whom one may communicate one's findings'.[48] It further failed to see how human nature went beyond an orientation towards one's own pleasure, but was rather 'in itself immediately and primarily kind, unselfish, and sociable without regard to its advantage or pleasure', so that 'when images of other men and their fortune come to our attention, they excite public and unselfish feelings, even though there is no prospect of private advantage'.[49] Cumberland occupied a slightly more ambiguous position in Hutcheson's thinking, for while he was presented as one who agreed with Pufendorf concerning sociability,[50] he was elsewhere listed as one of those who had effectively criticised Hobbes,[51] and in the company of Shaftesbury as one who had described just how pleasurable the social pleasures really were.[52]

As we might expect by now, Hutcheson's 'antient moralists' were, above all others, the Stoics. At the start of the inaugural lecture, he explained that 'the best of the ancients' were those 'who described virtue as the best and most perfect life in accordance with nature',[53] which precisely picked out the Stoics, and although the lecture was delivered in Latin, he retained technical terms from Stoic philosophy in the original Greek, describing the moral sense as the Epictetan ruling principle, or *hegemonikon*,[54] and talking of divine providence as *pronoia*.[55] From the Latin authors, furthermore, he took the Stoic pairing of *decorum* and *honestum* to describe what 'is natural to man'.[56] Hutcheson did, however, remain somewhat cagey about his affinities to the Stoics in these texts, and he rarely endorsed their views explicitly, something that may very well reflect a strategy of prudence with respect to his overwhelmingly Presbyterian environment. One occasion on which he did directly and sympathetically invoke the Stoics was his reply to Mandeville's arguments about luxury in the second of his 'Letters to Hibernicus'. There he made the point that while 'All sects, as well as the Stoics, recommended the correction of our opinions and imaginations about the pleasures above necessity', they still permitted them to be enjoyed, 'when it is not inconsistent with the offices of life', for 'in such circumstances they were always looked upon as preferable to their contraries'.[57] But it may be significant in this context that this is a pseudonymous text.

If Hutcheson was cautious about announcing his affinities with the Stoics, he was also cautious with respect to some of his philosophical disagreements with Shaftesbury and the 'antient moralists', too. In the *Essay on the Nature and Conduct of the Passions*, Hutcheson sounds like one of the seventeenth-century anti-Senecan writers when he attacks 'the Vanity of some of the lower rate of Philosophers of the *Stoick Sect*' when they boasted 'of an undisturbed Happiness and Serenity'. This was, Hutcheson judged, 'wholly inconsistent with the *Order* of Nature, as well as with the Principles of some of their great Leaders'.

> That must be a very fantastick Scheme of Virtue, which represents it as a *private sublimely selfish Discipline*, to preserve our selves wholly unconcerned, not only in the Changes of Fortune as to our *Wealth* or *Poverty*, *Liberty* or *Slavery*, *Ease* or *Pain*, but even in all *external Events* whatsoever, in the Fortunes of our dearest *Friends* or *Country*, solacing ourselves that we are easy and undisturbed.[58]

But although Hutcheson appeared here to be endorsing these other, unnamed Stoics—Marcus Aurelius, presumably, among them—it is clear from the way in which this discussion continued that he did in fact have major disagreements with the structure and content of Stoic ethical theory, and with Shaftesbury's theory, too, but these were disagreements to which he was not especially keen to draw attention.

For Hutcheson, true virtue was '*affectionate Temper*' rather than '*undisturbed Selfishness*', a view that he associated with the philosophy of benevolence from the Stoicism he found in Marcus Aurelius.[59] It was appropriate for us to feel pleasure when we reflected on our own 'kind *disinterested Affections* towards our Fellows', Hutcheson thought, but since these affections were themselves directed 'toward an uncertain Object' they must sometimes 'occasion Pain', and, when they did so, they would 'directly produce one sort of Misery to the virtuous in this Life', unless, he went on to reflect,

> we suppose, *what* no Experience can confirm, that Men may have strong Desires, the Disappointment of which will give no *Uneasiness*, or that Uneasiness is no Evil. Let the *Philosopher* regulate his own Notions as he pleases about Happiness or Misery; whoever imagines himself unhappy, is so in reality; and whoever has *kind Affections* or Virtue, must be uneasy to see others really unhappy.[60]

This thought generated Hutcheson's major modification to Stoic moral psychology: the Stoics were wrong to hold that the virtuous agent or the wise man would never have occasion to feel any kind of distress. When Hutcheson presented his table of the passions in the *Essay*, therefore, he took its basic structure from Cicero's Stoic typology presented in the *Tusculan Disputations*, but he added sorrow (*aegritudo*), or present distress at present evil, to his list of the 'calm' and 'natural' affections, which were, in Stoic terms, the *constantiae* or *eupatheiae*.[61] If virtue resided in your natural affections, furthermore, even when they did not in fact bring any kind of benefit to yourself or to others, then there was a break with the structure of Stoic ethics as well as with the content of Stoic passion theory. Hutcheson in fact held to a straightforwardly hedonistic conception of happiness and denied that the prospect of one's own happiness or welfare was any kind of foundation for moral motivation. The distinctive obligation to virtue lay elsewhere, in the workings of Hutcheson's moral sense, which responded approvingly to its perceptions of benevolence. Stoic, and, as it happened, Shaftesburian eudaimonism had been abandoned.

As we saw in the fifth chapter, Shaftesbury's ethics were not fully sentimentalist, with reason still having a function within the moral theory of regulating the affections and potentially correcting the moral sense when it misfired. Hutcheson squeezed the place of reason in his account of ethics still further, conceiving of practical reason as a Lockean calculating faculty whose 'only function', in Irwin's words, 'is to find means to ends that are independently fixed by non-rational desires'.[62] It is perhaps for this reason that Hutcheson's attempt to assimilate the moral sense to the Stoics' *hegemonikon*, or the rational, ruling principle, seems most misplaced.[63] But here Hutcheson's modifications to Shaftesbury's position may have helped him towards an orientation more democratic than that of the third earl. Shaftesbury's 'natural moral sense' had required extensive education, cultivation, and refinement if it were always to function effectively, such that his conception of a well-ordered republic was of necessity a fairly aristocratic affair. Hutcheson's moral sense, by contrast, was designed and implanted by God and worked effectively in all human beings. The moral judgements of ordinary people could therefore be considered more robust; and, far from virtue being reserved to heroes, someone like 'an honest Trader' could be virtuous, Hutcheson thought, through his ability to contribute towards the common good by way of the various 'Offices which his Station in the World gave him an Opportunity of performing', whether as 'the kind Friend, the faithful prudent Adviser, the charitable and hospitable Neighbour, the tender Husband and affectionate Parent, the sedate yet chearful Companion, the generous Assistant of Merit, the cautious Allayer of Contention and Debate' or even 'the Promoter of Love and good Understanding among Acquaintances'.[64]

There has been a disagreement in the recent scholarly literature about the relationship of Hutcheson to the Stoic tradition. James Moore has argued for the plausibility of interpreting Hutcheson as a kind of Stoic,[65] while David Fate Norton is sceptical, pointing out some of the various ways in which Hutcheson doesn't actually agree with the Stoics.[66] In general, I think it is fair to say that Moore has had the better of the argument, and his replies to many of Norton's objections are persuasive.[67] From the interpretation presented here, however, it becomes easier to see why this particular disagreement has arisen. It is Hutcheson himself who has constructed a philosophical tradition going back at least as far the Stoics and who has placed himself squarely in it. In the course of developing his more fine-grained arguments, however, he has moved away from some of the most distinctively Stoic commitments. If we just look at the content of the final position that he defends, there is much that is not classically Stoic about it, and to that extent, Norton is right. But we should not lose sight of the reasons why Hutcheson associated his project with that of the Stoics. A commitment to the natural sociability of humankind was a central component of his philosophical vision, as we have seen, but neither should we underestimate the providentialist strand in Hutcheson's thinking, which again aligned him with the Stoics and against the Epicureans. On Hutcheson's view, human beings had been designed in such a way that they got a great deal of pleasure not only from participating in sociable activities but also from reflecting on their own naturally benign affections.[68] The practice of virtue as benevolence did not aim at the agent's own happiness, to be sure, but the providential ordering of the world meant that, nevertheless, the 'surest Happiness of the Agent' was the unintended by-product.[69] Strip the more Stoic and providentialist elements out of Hutcheson's philosophy and it comes to look a lot more like the secular theory that would later come to be known as utilitarianism. As Hutcheson had written in the *Inquiry*, after all, 'That Action is best, which procures the greatest Happiness for the greatest Numbers'.[70]

Joseph Butler

Joseph Butler also drew on the resources of Stoic moral theory in his *Fifteen Sermons Preached at the Rolls Chapel* when he fashioned his response to what he called the 'strange affectation in many people of explaining away all particular affections, and representing the whole of life as nothing but one continued exercise of self-love'. He specifically mentioned the Epicureans, Hobbes, and La Rochefoucauld ('the author of *Reflexions, Sentences, et Maximes Morales*'); in 1726, Bernard Mandeville's name was an absent presence on any such list.[71] Butler announced the goal of his enquiry in Stoic terms, 'to explain what is meant by the nature of man, when it is said that virtue consists in following, and vice in deviating from it; and by explaining to show that the assertion is true', and he invoked and endorsed the 'ancient moralists', who held 'that man is born to virtue, that it consists in following nature, and that vice is more contrary to this nature than tortures or death'. We saw earlier how a writer like Barbeyrac had offered a rather vague interpretation of the idea of the life according to nature in his exposition of Stoic ethics. Butler alluded to William Wollaston's similar criticism in his recent *Religion of Nature Delineated* that 'at best this talk is loose', and through his own interrogation of the idea, the generally Stoic character of his project becomes quite clear.[72]

To consider something as a work of nature was to consider it in terms of its 'system, oeconomy, or constitution', and as something conducive to 'one or more ends'. Butler's well-known example was that of a watch: we have the correct idea of a watch only when we understand how the various parts are organised in a particular way that makes it possible to tell the time. Human beings were analogous:

> 'Tis from considering the relations which the several appetites and passions in the inward frame have to each other, and above all the supremacy of reflection or conscience, that we get the idea of the system or constitution of humane nature. And from the idea itself 'twill as fully appear, that this our nature, *i.e.* constitution is adapted to virtue, as from the idea of a watch it appears, that its nature, *i.e.* constitution or system is adapted to measure time.[73]

The relevant difference between a human being and a watch was that a 'machine is inanimate and passive: but we are agents', such that 'Our constitution is put in our own power. We are charged with it: and therefore are accountable for any disorder or violation of it.'[74] The claim that our constitution was adapted to virtue, furthermore, was a straightforward rejection of Mandeville's account of virtue, which he understood in terms of self-denial. If this were right, then 'nothing can possibly be more contrary to nature than vice':

> Poverty and disgrace, tortures and death are not so contrary to it. Misery and injustice are indeed equally contrary to some different parts of our nature taken singly: but injustice is moreover contrary to the whole constitution of the nature.[75]

Butler's 'ancient moralists' or 'philosophers'

> had a perception that injustice was contrary to their nature, and that pain was so also. They observed these two perceptions totally different, not in degree, but in kind: and the reflecting upon each of them as they thus stood in their nature, wrought a full intuitive conviction, that more was due and of right belonged to one of these inward perceptions, than to the other; that it demanded in all cases to govern such a creature as man.[76]

This was, Butler concluded, 'a fair and true account of what was the ground of their conviction' when they say that virtue consisted in following nature, 'a manner of speaking, not loose and undeterminate, but clear and distinct, strictly just and true'.[77]

While Butler agreed with the Stoics that virtue consisted in following nature, he maintained, with Hutcheson, a hedonistic conception of happiness, and he therefore denied the Stoics' claim that the virtuous life was ipso facto the happy life.[78] His account of the content of human nature, however, echoed that of the Stoics in two important respects. First, his claim that there was in human nature both a principle of self-love and a principle of benevolence, and that the two ends of private and public good 'do indeed perfectly coincide' such that 'they mutually promote each other', was close to the Stoics' account of developed *oikeiosis*, in both its personal and social dimensions.[79] It seems probable that Cicero's *De officiis* was the main Stoic text that Butler was working with while assembling these parts of his argument. With reference to the account of the relationship between virtue and nature, Irwin has noted close parallels between Butler's exposition and *De officiis* 3. 21 and 3.26, for example,[80] and concerning these principles of human nature, Long has pointed to strong parallels between Butler and *De officiis* 1.11–15.[81] '[I]t is as manifest that *we were made for society*', Butler wrote, '*and to promote the happiness of it, as that we were intended to take care of our own life, and health, and private good*', but they may as well have been Cicero's words, in one of his more Stoical moods.[82]

Second, Butler described 'a principle of reflection in men, by which they distinguish between, approve and disapprove their own actions', for 'We are plainly constituted such sort of creatures as to reflect upon our own nature', and he called this principle conscience.[83] Butlerian conscience lay at the heart of his moral theory, indeed, of his theory of human nature. Stephen Darwall has written that, for Butler, conscience is 'a condition of the very possibility of an agent's having reasons to act at all, since only a being who has the capacity for maintaining a self-regulated *constitutional* order can have reasons for acting, and this capacity depends on the agent's taking her conscience to be authoritative'.[84] The theorisation of conscience as a principle of reflection also marked Butler's most important disagreement with his predecessor Shaftesbury, and also with his contemporary Hutcheson, on whose accounts conscience could furnish just one motive among many for action, and was effective only to the extent that it happened to be more strongly felt than the others.[85] But this was to mischaracterise the nature of conscience, Butler thought, which, regardless of its felt strength, 'plainly bears upon it marks of authority' over the other principles of action, such that it 'claims the absolute direction of them all, to allow or forbid their gratification'.[86] It is clear from a remark in the second dissertation, 'Of the Nature of Virtue', appended to the *Analogy of Religion*, that Butler again had Stoic moral theory in mind in setting out this account of the nature of conscience. In that text, when he introduced conscience as 'this moral approving and disapproving faculty', a note adds, 'This way of speaking is taken from *Epictetus* (Arr. Epict. L I. c. I.), and is made use of as seeming the most full, and least liable to cavil'.[87]

MARCUS AURELIUS AND EPICTETUS

Hutcheson and Butler may have agreed on the importance of defending the reality of natural benevolence in somewhat Stoic terms in the face of Mandeville's challenge; in other respects, their commitments were different. Within the Church of Scotland, Hutcheson's work helped to lay the foundation for what became known as the Moderate movement, which was in some respects similar to the latitudinarian tendency inside the Church of England from the previous century insofar as it shifted attention away from the major themes of Reformed theology in favour of a concern with personal ethics.[88] Butler, by contrast, had started life as a nonconformist, subscribed to the Thirty Nine Articles only in adulthood, and defended these against the latitudinarians of the eighteenth century. With this contrast in mind, we can compare what may be the two most important mid-century editions of Stoic authors that were published in Britain: the 1742 Foulis Press edition of Marcus Aurelius that was prepared by Hutcheson and his collaborator, the classicist James Moor, and the first complete English-language edition of Epictetus that appeared in

1758, translated by the Bluestocking Elizabeth Carter. Butler died in 1752, but his close friend and theological ally Thomas Secker had played a significant role in the production of *All the Works of Epictetus*, and Carter's introduction presented a critical overview of Epictetan Stoicism fully consonant with Butler's ethics and theology.

Hutcheson and Moor's Marcus Aurelius

Robert Foulis set up his printing and bookselling operation in Glasgow in 1741, and in 1743 he was appointed printer to the university. Over the years to come, the Foulis Press published a large number of classical and modern editions; there were, for example, twenty-four editions of Cicero and twenty-eight of Hutcheson.[89] One early and popular edition was an English translation of the *Meditations* of Marcus Aurelius, which appeared in 1742, and was reissued in 1749, 1752, and 1764. Although anonymously presented, this edition was largely Hutcheson's work, together with that of a colleague, James Moor, who became the university's librarian in 1742 and professor of Greek in 1746. There has been some uncertainty about the exact division of labour in the edition, but the editors of the recent Liberty Fund edition present persuasive evidence to assign the handling of books 9 and 10 to Moor and the rest to Hutcheson: in particular, the annotation of these two books concentrates on linguistic points and make cross references to the Gospels, whereas elsewhere the notes address philosophical topics.[90]

The editors' introduction praised Marcus in his *Meditations* in significantly Hutchesonian terms, as offering 'some of the plainest, and yet most striking considerations, to affect the hearts of those who have any sense of goodness', to 'warm them with . . . good-will and compassion toward our fellows, superior to all the force of anger or envy, or our little interfering worldly interests.[91] The *Meditations*, they declared, present to 'every judicious reader' a 'great soul; adorned with the soundest understanding, the most amiable sweetness and kindness of affections, the most invincible meekness, steddy justice, humility, and simplicity, and the most entire resignation to GOD'.[92] The emperor's seventeenth-century editors had emphasised his humility in order to fend off the stock accusations of Stoic pride, and Hutcheson and Moor followed in their footsteps:

> 'Tis one of the most ancient maxims or precepts, 'Reverence or stand in awe of thyself' which is the most remote from any encouraging of pride or vanity. It means, that men, conscious of the dignity of their nature, and of that temper of soul, and course of action which they must approve, should continually endeavour to behave suitably to their dignity, in preserving that temper, and practising such actions,

with a sincere simple view to answer the end for which God created them, with such dignity and such endowments; and be ashamed to act unsuitably to them. Now, to be influenced by views of glory from men, is what Antoninus here reckons among the dishonours or affronts done to ourselves.[93]

They were also concerned to smooth over relations between Marcus's Stoicism and Pauline Christianity:

> It may be remembered here once for all, the life according to nature, in Antoninus, is taken in a very high sense: 'Tis living up to that standard of purity and perfection, which every good man feels in his own breast: 'Tis conforming our selves to the law of God written in the heart: 'Tis endeavouring a compleat victory over the passions, and a total conformity to the image of God. A man must read Antoninus with little attention, who confounds this with the natural man's life, condemned by St. Paul.[94]

Hutcheson and Moor did not, however, follow the Daciers and argue that Marcus's Stoicism was compatible with more Augustinian varieties of Christianity, and Hutcheson's emphasis on natural benevolence, both in his own philosophy and in his notes to the translation, presented an account of human nature at odds with Augustinian tradition. 'The Stoics always maintained, that by the very constitution of our nature, all men are recommended to the affectionate good-will of all', he wrote, 'which would always appear, were it not for the interfering of falsely imagined interests'.[95] His elucidation of the idea of the life according to nature linked it both to divine providence and to the 'individual or proper nature' of each person, with no suggestion that that nature might have been corrupted by the Fall.

> All vice is such a separation, as the Stoics define virtue to be an agreement or harmony with 'nature' in our affections and actions. They tell us this nature is two-fold, the common nature presiding in the universe, or the deity, and the individual or proper nature in each one. We conform to the common nature, by acquiescence in all events of providence, and by acting the part which the structure of our proper nature requires and recommends, especially the governing part of it, we at once conform to both the common nature and the proper; since our constitution was framed by God, the common nature.[96]

Elsewhere, Hutcheson would label Marcus's account of providence an 'amiable notion', that has brought about 'those circumstances, which infinite wisdom foresaw were fittest for [man's] solid improvement in virtue, according to that original disposition of nature which God had given him'—all of which was a long way from the Reformed Church of Scotland's Westminster Confession.

At the end of their introduction, Hutcheson and Moor considered the persecution of the Christians that took place during Marcus Aurelius's reign. In the absence of evidence that he himself had ordered the persecutions, they could 'only charge him with the omission of his duty, in not making a strict inquiry into the cause of the Christians'. This was a 'great fault', but it was 'less than that of the apostle Paul, who himself persecuted with great fury; and yet could afterwards truly say, he had served God with all good conscience; that is, sincerely, according to what he then thought his duty.'[97] Even if Marcus had persecuted the Christians, we should 'consider, that any persecution is the more odious, the smaller the difference is, between the religious tenets of the persecutor, and those of the persecuted; as it shews a greater insolence of pride and ill-nature, to be so much provoked for such small differences', and the differences between the 'devout heathen' and Christianity were large. 'Let none make this objection to Antoninus', Hutcheson and Moor proclaimed,

> but those, who, from their hearts, abhor all Christian persecutions, who cannot hate their neighbours, or deem them excluded from the divine favour, either for neglecting certain ceremonies, and pieces of outward pageantry, or for exceeding in them; for different opinions, or forms of words, about some metaphysical attributes or modes of existence, which all sides own to be quite incomprehensible by us; for the different opinions about human liberty; about which the best men who ever lived have had opposite sentiments: for different opinions about the manner in which the Deity may think fit to exercise his mercy to a guilty world, either in pardoning of their sins, or renewing them in piety and virtue.[98]

And a little later, warming to their theme:

> Christians may be ashamed to censure our author on this account; considering how rashly, arrogantly, and presumptuously, they are cursing one another in their synodical anathemas; and in their creeds, pronouncing eternal damnation on all who are not within the pale, or hold not the same mysterious tenets or forms of words.[99]

Indeed, Moore and Silverthorne plausibly speculate that it may well have been the ferocity of these passages that made Hutcheson and Moor judge it prudent to withhold their own names from the title page of their edition, Hutcheson already having been publicly accused of 'teaching many dangerous Errors' only a few years before.[100] But even if his name did not appear on his translation, the association between Hutcheson and Marcus Aurelius was clear to his critics. John Witherspoon, later president of the college at Princeton and a signatory to the Declaration of Independence, wrote of the 'moderate men' in his 1753 satire, the *Ecclesiastical Characteristicks*, that 'there is no controversy about Arian, Arminian, Pelagian, or Socinian tenets, but only whether this good-of-the-whole scheme holds'; and he concluded with the 'Athenian Creed':

> In fine, I believe in the divinity of L[ord] S[haftesbury], the saintship of Marcus Antoninus . . . , and the perpetual duration of Mr H[utcheso]n's works, notwithstanding their present tendency to oblivion. Amen.

Elizabeth Carter's Epictetus

The most remarkable Stoic publication of the British eighteenth century was Elizabeth Carter's translation, *All the Works of Epictetus*.[101] The short *Encheiridion* had appeared in English on several occasions, and the *Discourses* had been translated into French by Desmarets de Saint Sorlin a hundred years earlier, but there had been no comparable English edition before the middle of the eighteenth century.[102] Carter had been asked by her Greekless friend, Catherine Talbot, if she could prepare translations of Epictetus, and she worked on the project from 1749 until 1755. One who encouraged Carter to publish her work was Thomas Secker, in whose household Talbot lived. Secker corresponded with Carter throughout this period, offering advice on the translation; he spent a month correcting the final text while laid up with gout,[103] and it is through Secker that we can forge a connection between Carter's *Epictetus* and Joseph Butler. Butler and Secker had first met at Samuel Jones's college for dissenters at Tewkesbury, where, to keep the young Butler's correspondence with the Anglican Samuel Clarke concerning his *Demonstration of the Being and Attributes of God* a secret, the young Secker had served as postman, ferrying correspondence back and forth from the post office at Gloucester. Both men later conformed, Butler prior to matriculating at Oriel College, Oxford, and Secker a few years later,[104] and the two remained friends and allies as they rose through the ranks of the Church of England, with Butler becoming bishop of Bristol in 1738 and of Durham in 1750 and Secker bishop of Bristol in 1735 and of Oxford in 1737, dean of St Paul's in 1750, and archbishop of Canterbury in 1758, the year Carter's *Epictetus* appeared in print. He died in 1768.

Carter had been urged by Catherine Talbot to write 'some kind of prefatory discourse' to her edition, to give an account of 'the plan of the Stoic philosophy' in which 'to mark out those points in which it is false, wild, or defective; and to draw comparisons between that and the only true philosophy, the Christian',[105] and Talbot later added that, 'It is terrifying to think what effects a book so mixed up of excellence and error might have in this infidel age, if it not be sufficiently guarded with proper notes and animadversions.'[106] Carter initially resisted, wondering whether any infidel 'will find any great comfort in the study of Epictetus, unless he is perverse enough to take comfort in finding himself obliged to practise the morality of the Gospel without its encouragements and supports.'[107] Her resistance prompted Talbot to weigh in once again on Secker's behalf:

> Many persons will study your book who scorn to look into the Bible. . . . You do not believe that any but good persons will read this book. Fine gentlemen will read it because it is new; fine ladies because it is yours; critics because it is a translation out of Greek; and Shaftes-burian Heathens because Epictetus was an honour to heathenism, and an idolator of the beauty of virtue.[108]

Carter gave in, and her published introduction was more or less of the kind that Secker had wanted her to write.

That introduction began by juxtaposing the Stoics and the Epicureans, in a manner reminiscent of Pascal in the 'Discussion with Monsieur de Sacy'. Philosophers of both sects agreed that the 'End of Man' was 'to live conformably to Nature', but they disagreed on what this meant in practice. Neither sect 'seem to have understood Man in his mixed Capacity', with the result that the Epicureans 'debased him to a mere Animal' and placed the human good in pleasure, while the Stoics 'exalted him to a pure Intelligence'.

> The Stoical Excess was more useful to the Public, as it often produced great and noble Efforts towards that Perfection to which it was supposed possible for human Nature to arrive. Yet, at the same time, by flattering Man with false and presumptuous Ideas of his own Power and Excellence, it tempted even the Best to Pride: a Vice not only dreadfully mischievous in human Society, but, perhaps of all others, the most insuperable Bar to real inward Improvement.[109]

Having begun with criticism, Carter moved on to an outline of Epictetus's technical vocabulary, covering the '*Desires* and *Aversions*' (*orexeis* and *ekkliseis*), the '*Pursuits* and *Avoidances*' (*hormai* and *aphormai*), and the '*Assents* of the Understanding'.[110] 'That Judgment, which is formed by the Mind concerning the *Appearances* (*phantasiai*), the Stoics termed

Principles (*dogmata*): and these Principles give a Determination to the Choice (*prohairesis*).'[111] The 'Office of Reason' was to adapt the '*Preconceptions*' (*prolepseis*) to 'particular Cases';[112] and Carter explained that she translated Epictetus's *euroia* as '*Prosperity*', by which 'the Stoics understood the internal State of the Mind, when the Affections and active Powers were so regulated, that it considered all Events as happy: and, consequently, must enjoy an uninterrupted Flow of Success; since nothing could fall out contrary to its Wishes'.[113]

There followed a paragraph on Stoic logic ('very tedious and perplexed')[114] and several sections on Stoic theology ('strangely perplexed and absurd').[115] Carter surveyed the disagreements among the various Stoics as to what happened to the soul after death—'*Cleanthes* taught, that all Souls lasted till that Time [of the great conflagration]: *Chrysippus*, only those of the Good. *Seneca* is perpetually wavering'[116]—and this topic permitted a return to the case for the prosecution against Stoic moral philosophy by way of the question of future punishments and rewards. Carter declared her preference for the Socratic opinion that reconciled 'the present Appearances of Things' with 'our Ideas of the Justice, Wisdom, and Goodness of God' by means of 'the Doctrine of a *future* State', against the opinion maintained by the Stoics, which contradicted both sense and reason.[117] The section that followed showed Carter writing fully in the spirit of Butler, as she sought to break the link between moral virtue and earthly happiness:

> That there is an intrinsic Beauty and Excellency in moral Goodness; that it is the Ornament and Perfection of all rational Beings; and that, till Conscience is stifled by repeated Guilt, we feel an Obligation to prefer and follow, so far as we perceive it, in all Cases; and find an inward Satisfaction, and generally receive outward Advantages from so doing, are Positions, which no thinking Person can contradict: but it doth not follow from hence, that in such a Mixture, as Mankind, it is its own sufficient Reward.[118]

This mistake, together with the related rejection of 'the Doctrine of Recompences in another Life', led the Stoics to further errors, in particular, 'That a good Man stretched on a Rack, or reposing on a Bed of Roses, should enjoy himself equally',[119] and their 'Permission of Suicide'.[120] Carter branded the notion 'that human Souls are literally Parts of the Deity' as 'shocking, and hurtful',[121] and, in contrast to the Stoic promise of the possibility of this-worldly happiness, which 'insults human Nature', Carter preferred 'the Christian System', which 'represents Mankind, not as a Part of the Essence, but a Work of the Hand of God: as created in a State of improveable Virtue and Happiness: Fallen, by an Abuse of Free Will, into Sin, Misery, and Weakness; but redeemed from them by an Almighty Saviour'.[122]

Although its principles might have generated 'Pride, Hard-heartedness, and the last dreadful Extremity of human Guilt, Self-murder',[123] Stoicism was not all bad. In antiquity, the Stoics' 'zealous Defence of a particular Providence' provided 'a valuable Antidote to the atheistical Scheme of *Epicurus*'[124] and 'the Lives of several among them' helped preserve 'the Subjects of arbitrary Government, from a wretched and contemptible Pusilanimity'.[125] Concluding with further echoes of Pascal and Malebranche, Carter decided that if Stoic teachings could be subordinated to Christian teachings, they would provide 'excellent Rules of self-Government, and of social Behaviour; of a noble Reliance of the Aid and Protection of Heaven, and of a perfect Resignation and Submission to the divine Will.'[126] As she had intimated in her correspondence, furthermore, Christianity with an Epictetan supplement trumped Epictetan Stoicism on its own, for those who reject 'the Doctrines of the New Testament' will find themselves 'laid under moral Restraints, almost equal to those of the Gospel, while they are deprived of its Encouragements and Supports.'[127]

All in all, Carter's strategy was unlike that of Hutcheson and Moor in their Marcus Aurelius. Where Hutcheson sought to present the Stoicism of Marcus Aurelius, his preferred version of Christianity, and the best account of moral philosophy as all more or less continuous with one another, Carter continued to insist on the gap between pagan error and Christian truth, and—fully in the spirit of Butler and Secker's theology—on the continuing importance of traditional religious dogma. But for all their differences, the two editions both belong to the tradition of the appropriation and transformation of themes from Stoic philosophy that Shaftesbury had set in motion and that was extended throughout the 1720s as the critical response to Mandevillle took determinate shape. The main source of resistance to these developments in eighteenth-century British intellectual culture was David Hume, and it is to aspects of his own philosophical project that we now turn.

David Hume

Hutcheson published his *Inquiry* in 1725, and Joseph Butler his *Sermons* in 1726, which was also the year when the young David Hume acquired a copy of Shaftesbury's *Characteristics*. We don't know what he did with it, but we do have a document from 1734, known as the 'Letter to a Physician', in which Hume describes how the five years 1729–34 were a period of frustration, as he was beset by various ailments that prevented him from engaging in sustained intellectual work.[128] In the letter—although we do not know to whom it was addressed, or even whether it was ever sent—Hume reported that 'when I was about 18 Years of Age, there seem'd to be open'd up to me a new Scene of Thought',[129] which is generally reckoned to refer to the beginning of the train of ideas that ultimately led to the publication of the *Treatise of Human Nature* a decade later. The letter also affords us a tantalising glimpse of the young Hume's relationship with ideas drawn from the Stoics. Hume's crisis began in September 1729, he writes, when 'all my Ardor seem'd in a moment to be extinguisht, & I cou'd no longer raise my Mind to that Pitch, which formerly gave me such excessive Pleasure'.[130]

> There was another particular, which contributed more than any thing, to waste my Spirits & bring on me this Distemper, which was, that having read many Books of Morality, such as Cicero, Seneca & Plutarch, & being smit with their beautiful Representations of Virtue and Philosophy, I undertook the Improvement of my Temper & Will, along with my Reason & Understanding. I was continually fortifying myself with Reflections against Death, & Poverty, & Shame, & Pain, & all the other Calamities of Life. These no doubt are exceeding useful, when join'd with an active Life; because the Occasion being presented along with the Reflection, works it into the Soul, & makes it take a deep Impression, but in Solitude they serve to little other Purpose, than to waste the Spirits, the Force of the Mind meeting with no Resistance, but wasting itself in the Air, like our Arm when it misses its Aim.[131]

Towards the end of the letter, Hume describes a second period of Stoic self-exhortation. When he 'began to despair of ever recovering',

> To keep myself from being Melancholy on so dismal a Prospect, my only Security was in peevish Reflections on the Vanity of the World & of all humane Glory; which, however just Sentiments they may be esteem'd, I have found can never be sincere, except in those who are possest of them.[132]

In a passage from the middle part of the letter, Hume sets out his future intellectual trajectory:

> Having now Time & Leizure to cool my inflam'd Imaginations, I began to consider seriously, how I shou'd proceed in my Philosophical Enquiries. I found that the moral Philosophy transmitted to us by Antiquity, labor'd under the same Inconvenience that has been found in their natural Philosophy, of being entirely Hypothetical, & depending

more upon Invention than Experience. Every one consulted his Fancy in erecting Schemes of Virtue & of Happiness, without regarding human Nature, upon which every moral Conclusion must depend. This therefore I resolved to make my principal Study.[133]

It is not clear what Hume means when he describes the ancient philosophies as 'Hypothetical', or as neglecting human nature. The various ancient traditions had developed distinctive accounts of human nature, and the philosophers argued with one another about the relationship of their ethical theories to those various accounts.[134] Whatever his objections to their methods, Hume seemed satisfied with at least some of their more Stoic conclusions; in a letter to Hutcheson of 1739, for example, he writes that, 'Upon the whole, I desire to take my Catalogue of Virtues from *Cicero's Offices*, not from the *Whole Duty of Man*'.[135] What is clear from the letter, though, is that Hume felt himself to be turning away from the Stoic therapies that he had tried and found inadequate; and it seems likely that it is in the subtitle of *Treatise of Human Nature*, '*Being an attempt to introduce the experimental method of reasoning into moral subjects*', that we are presented with the proper contrast to these 'hypothetical' methods of the ancients.[136]

Hume listed Butler in the introduction to the *Treatise*, along with Locke, Shaftesbury, Mandeville and Hutcheson, as having 'begun to put the science of man on a new footing'. He did not work, however, with anything like the framework of Butler's ethics. When he considered the question of whether the distinction between virtue and vice is a natural one, in that same section in the *Treatise* that introduced the moral sense, he contrasted 'natural' with what was miraculous, 'rare and unusual' and 'artificial', and concluded that 'nothing can be more unphilosophical than those systems, which assert with the Stoics, that virtue is the same with what is natural, and vice with what is unnatural'.[137] Irwin has remarked of this discussion that Hume does not in fact engage with the particular sense in which Butler uses the term, which refers to that which is required by the whole constitution or system of an organism rather than by any particular part.[138] Hume's scepticism towards the stability of personal identity, however, would seem to commit him to rejecting Butler's position. If what we are is no more than a series of mental episodes, lacking any kind of essence that persists through time, as Hume thought, then the project of describing a human being in terms of the kind of constitution or system that Butler's theory requires cannot get off the ground, for without such a description we are unable to undertake an enquiry into the principles that promote the good of that system.[139] Given its Stoic affinities, in fact, we might plausibly think that Butler's approach is an example of the kind of 'hypothetical' moral philosophy Hume was anxious to reject: if the human being can be understood in terms of this kind of constitution or system, then Butler's moral philosophy might apply; but it can't, so it doesn't.

Hume agreed with Hutcheson's sentimentalist approach, against Butler. But Hume criticised the details of Hutcheson's account of the moral sense. On Hume's view, the moral sense didn't just respond positively to its perceptions of benevolence—in this respect (if only in this respect, perhaps) Hume's moral sense was more like Shaftesbury's 'natural moral sense' than Hutcheson's. Indeed, Hume's remark about taking his 'Catalogue of Virtues from *Cicero's Offices*' came in the context of his reply to Hutcheson's criticism that he had included characteristics like intelligence, strength, and good humour among the virtues, and he reiterated his insistence that benevolence was not 'the only Virtue'.[140] One reason why Hutcheson had thought that moral philosophy could be organised around an account of a moral sense that only responded to perceptions of benevolence (and its absence or opposite) was that he linked his account of justice very closely to his account of benevolence. To be perfectly just, on Hutcheson's view, was to be motivated to act in accordance with universal benevolence. Hume, however, denied that justice could be considered straightforwardly as an outgrowth of benevolence:

> When I relieve persons in distress, my natural humanity is my motive; and so far as my succour extends, so far have I promoted the happiness of my fellow-creatures. But if we examine all the questions that come before any tribunal of justice, we shall find that, considering each case apart, it would as often be an instance of humanity to decide contrary to the laws of justice as conformable to them. Judges take from a poor man to give to a rich; they bestow on the dissolute the labour of the industrious; and they put into the hands of the vicious the means of harming both themselves and others. The whole scheme, however, of law and justice is advantageous to the society; and 'twas with a view to this advantage, that men, by their voluntary conventions, establish'd it. After it is once establish'd by these conventions, it is *naturally* attended with a strong sentiment of morals; which can proceed from nothing but our sympathy with the interests of society.[141]

The virtue of justice was quite distinct from that of benevolence; and was an example of what Hume called an artificial virtue, insofar as it 'produce[d] pleasure and approbation by means of an artifice or contrivance, which arises from the circumstances and necessities of mankind'.[142] With the Epicureans, and against the Stoics, Hume located the origins of justice in a social convention for mutual advantage. And when Hutcheson objected to Hume calling justice an artificial virtue, Hume denied that it was unnatural, just that it was artificial, and he quoted Horace's Epicurean opinion that utility was the mother of justice—the same tag that Grotius had deployed, first approvingly, in *De Jure Praedae*, and later disapprovingly, in *De Jure Belli ac Pacis*.[143]

This general hostility to Stoicism found expression in a number of other writings. The second, 1742 edition of the *Essays* contained four character sketches, 'The Epicurean', 'The Stoic', 'The Platonist' and 'The Sceptic', with the Stoic—subtitled 'the man of action and virtue'—presented as wallowing in smugness, which is punctured in the following essay by the Platonist, who charges that 'Thou surely art conscious of the hollowness of thy pretended probity'[144] and that 'Thou art thyself thy own idol'.[145] Hume also added to that edition—though subsequently withdrew—another essay, 'Of Moral Prejudices', in which he observed that 'The *Stoics* were remarkable' for the 'Folly among the Antients' of 'the great philosophic Endeavour after Perfection, which, under the Pretext of reforming Prejudices and Errors, strikes at all the most endearing Sentiments of the Heart, and all the most useful Byasses and Instincts, which can govern a human Creature.'[146] In the first *Enquiry* (1748), Hume declared that the philosophy of 'Epictetus and other *Stoics*' was 'only a more refined system of selfishness'. This was not a restatement of the familiar Augustinian criticism, for Hume already reversed the traditional valuation of pride in the second book of the *Treatise*, arguing that it was a good thing, because fundamentally a pleasurable sensation, while humility wasn't, because it wasn't. Rather, Hume offered a reflection that drew on his own experiences as reported in the 'Letter to a Physician':

> While we study with attention the vanity of human life, and turn all our thoughts towards the empty and transitory nature of riches and honours, we are, perhaps, all the while flattering our natural indolence, which, hating the bustle of the word, and drudgery of business, seeks a pretence of reason to give itself a full and uncontrolled indulgence.[147]

The fourth appendix to the second *Enquiry* (1751), 'Of some verbal disputes', remarked that, 'Epictetus has scarcely ever mentioned the sentiment of humanity and compassion, but in order to put his disciples on their guard against it.'

Christopher J. Berry has argued that the 1752 essay 'Of Luxury' (retitled 'Of Refinement in the Arts' in some subsequent editions) continues this engagement with Epictetus.[148] As is well known, Hume there criticised the 'men of severe morals' who declaimed against luxury and praised virtuous austerity, and argued that 'In a nation, where there is no

demand for such superfluities, men sink into indolence, lose all enjoyment of life, and are useless to the public, which cannot maintain or support its fleets and armies, from the industry of such slothful members'.[149]
Epictetus is himself not specifically named in this essay, but Berry's persuasive suggestion is that it is his conception of value that is Hume's
specific target in this essay. Epictetus in the *Encheiridion* is reported as
saying that (in Elizabeth Carter's translation):

> The Body is to every one the Measure of the Possessions proper for it;
> as the Foot is of the Shoe. If, therefore, you stop at this, you will keep
> the Measure: but, if you move beyond it, you must necessarily be car-
> ried forward, as down a Precipice: as in the Case of a Shoe, if you go
> beyond its Fitness to the Foot, it comes first to be gilded, then purple,
> and then studded with Jewels. For to that which once exceeds a due
> Measure, there is no Bound.[150]

As Berry notes, the 'clear message is that these are superfluous refinements that should be eschewed', and that it follows 'that there is no poverty in possessing "merely" an unadorned sandal; indeed, the converse is
true'.[151] Hume in this essay rejects this view entirely: there is nothing
virtuous about material poverty; commerce is a good thing, in that it
helps to raise people out of such destitution; and a commercial society is
one in which people will value luxury goods, such as a pair of fancy slippers, in precisely the way in which Epictetus thinks they should not.[152]

Hume also engaged with arguments about the Stoics' God. The essay
titled *The Natural History of Religion* (1757) sided with those who
sought to deny the Stoics 'the honourable appellation of theism', with a
specific mention of Marcus Aurelius, for

> if the mythology of the heathens resemble the ancient EUROPEAN
> system of spiritual beings, excluding God and angels, and leaving only
> fairies and sprights; the creed of these philosophers may justly be said
> to exclude a deity, and to leave only angels and fairies.[153]

In a magnificent passage, Hume heaps ridicule on the Stoics' susceptibil-
ity to superstition:

> The STOICS bestowed many magnificent and even impious epithets
> on their sage; that he alone was rich, free, a king, and equal to the im-
> mortal gods. They forgot to add, that he was not inferior in prudence
> and understanding to an old woman. For surely nothing can be more
> pitiful than the sentiments, which that sect entertain with regard to
> religious matters; while they seriously agree with the common augurs,

that, when a raven croaks from the left, it is a good omen; but a bad one, when a rook makes a noise from the same quarter. PANAETIUS was the only STOIC, among the GREEKS, who so much as doubted with regard to auguries and divination. MARCUS ANTONINUS tells us, that he himself had received many admonitions from the gods in his sleep. It is true, EPICTETUS forbids us to regard the language of rooks and ravens; but it is not, that they do not speak truth: It is only, because they can fortel nothing but the breaking of our neck or the forfeiture of our estate; which are circumstances, says he, that nowise concern us. Thus the STOICS join a philosophical enthusiasm to a religious superstition. The force of their mind, being all turned to the side of morals, unbent itself in that of religion.[154]

Finally, there are the *Dialogues on Natural Religion*, which Hume worked on from around 1750 until his death in 1776, and which were first published in 1779. In Cicero's *De natura deorum*, on which Hume's *Dialogues* were closely modelled, the Stoic position was defended by 'Balbus', and in the work's final line his arguments are judged to have 'approximated more nearly to a semblance of the truth'.[155] In Hume's *Dialogues*, the argument from design that had been so important for Shaftesbury and others was presented and defended in Stoic terms by a character with a Stoic name, 'Cleanthes':

> Look around the world: Contemplate the whole and every part of it: You will find it to be nothing but one great machine, subdivided into an infinite number of lesser machines . . . adjusted to each other with an accuracy, which ravishes into admiration all men, who have ever contemplated them.

As in Cicero, the narrator of the *Dialogues* also concludes by judging that it is the Stoic's principles that 'approach still nearer to the truth' than those of his interlocutors. But this is Hume making mischief, and most readers of parts 2 to 8 of the *Dialogues* down to the present day have always considered this to be the work in which the argument from design was subjected to the most thoroughgoing critical scrutiny at the hands of the more sceptical 'Philo', found severely wanting, and left on the philosophical scrapheap.

CHAPTER EIGHT

Jean-Jacques Rousseau

ADAM SMITH OFFERED HIS OWN NARRATIVE of the history of modern philosophy in his anonymous 'Letter to the Authors of the *Edinburgh Review*', which was published in 1756. With reference to 'natural philosophy' as well as 'morals, metaphysics, and part of the abstract sciences', he wrote that until recently, and with the exception of Descartes, 'Whatever attempts have been made in modern times towards improvement in this contentious and unprosperous philosophy, beyond what the antients have left us, have been made in England'.[1] He cited in evidence the names of Hobbes, Locke, Mandeville, Shaftesbury, Butler, Clarke, and Hutcheson, all of whom, 'according to their different and inconsistent systems, endeavoured at least to be, in some measure, original; and to add something to that stock of observations with which the world had been furnished before them'. But, Smith continued, 'This branch of the English philosophy, which seems now to be intirely neglected by the English themselves, has of late been transported into France'.[2] Traces of it were observable in the *Encyclopédie* of Diderot and d'Alembert, he thought, and also in Louis Jean Levesque de Pouilly's recent *Théorie des sentiments agréables*, but 'above all, in the late Discourse upon the origin and foundation of the inequality amongst mankind by Mr. Rousseau of Geneva'.

> Whoever reads this last work with attention, will observe, that the second volume of the Fable of the Bees has given occasion to the system of Mr. Rousseau, in whom however the principles of the English author are softened, improved, and embellished, and stript of all that tendency to corruption and licentiousness which has disgraced them in their original author.[3]

Smith went on to explain why he associated Rousseau with Mandeville by picking out three characteristically Epicurean themes in their respective works—although he did not label them as such. Both writers denied natural sociability—in Smith's words, echoing a formulation of Mandeville's from 'A Search into the Nature of Society', 'there is in man no powerful instinct which necessarily determines him to seek society for its own sake'.[4] Both 'suppose the same slow progress and gradual development of all the talents, habits, and arts which fit men to live together in society, and they both describe this progress pretty much in the same manner'. Both, finally, considered the 'laws of justice, which maintain the present inequality amongst mankind', to be 'originally the inventions of the cunning and the powerful, in order to maintain or to acquire an unnatural and unjust superiority over the rest of their fellow–creatures'.[5]

There was yet another reason for associating the *Discourse on the Origin of Inequality* with the second volume of *The Fable of the Bees* that Smith did not mention. For the distinction that Mandeville set out there between 'self-love' and 'self-liking' closely foreshadowed Rousseau's own—and subsequently much better-known—distinction between two varieties of self-love, which he called *amour de soi-même* and *amour-propre*. In the first part of *The Fable of the Bees*, the idea of 'self-love' had been employed in a manner broadly continuous with Pierre Nicole's essay on the subject: it was pride, and it issued in pleasure-seeking behaviour. A more refined account of the psychology of self-love was presented in the third dialogue of the second part of *The Fable*, where Mandeville's spokesperson, 'Cleomenes', explained the new position:

> That Self-love was given to all Animals, at least, the most perfect, for Self-Preservation, is not disputed; but as no Creature can love what it dislikes, it is necessary, moreover, that every one should have a real liking to its own Being, superior to what they have to any other.[6]

Self-love and self-liking were both common to humans and to other animals. Self-liking, this 'instinct, by which every Individual values itself above its real worth', and which Horatio and Cleomenes agreed was 'evidently pride', was apparent when, for example, a cat washed her face, and adorned herself as much as it was in her power.[7] What human beings had in addition to this self-liking was the 'Diffidence, arising from a Consciousness, or at least an Apprehension, that we do over-value ourselves',[8] and it was this that gave them their fondness for the approbation of others, because it provided psychologically reassuring support for the good opinion that they had of themselves.

Mandeville then took the discussion onto the terrain of the political philosophers' state of nature. On the one hand, he offered a simple illustration of the different kinds of behaviour to which self-love and self-liking gave rise.

> Self-love would first make it ['a Creature endued with Understanding, Speech, and', interestingly, 'Risibility'] scrape together every thing it wanted for Sustenance, provide against the Injuries of the Air, and do

every thing to make itself and young Ones secure. Self-liking would make it seek for Opportunities, by Gestures, Looks, and Sounds, to display the Value it has for itself, superiour to what it has for others.[9]

On the other hand, Mandeville also observed that the extent to which self-liking determined human behaviour was a function of the development of society. In 'a savage State, feeding on Nuts and Acorns', there would be 'infinitely less Temptation, as well as Opportunity' for self-liking to display itself, as compared with 'civiliz'd' life.

[Y]et if a hundred Males of the first, all equally free, were together, within less than half an Hour, this Liking in question, though their Bellies were full, would appear in the Desire of Superiority, that would be shewn among them; and the most vigorous, either in Strength or Understanding, or both, would be the first, that would display it: If, as suppos'd, they were all untaught, this would breed Contention, and there would certainly be War before there could be any Agreement among them; unless one of them had some one or more visible Excellencies above the rest.[10]

As in Hobbes's earlier account, the equality that obtained in the state of nature contributed to its being a state of war, and material scarcity was not required in order to generate conflicts between men, which could easily turn on these matters of recognition.

Both volumes of Mandeville's *Fable* appeared in Jean Bertrand's French translation in 1740, where the distinction between self-love and self-liking was rendered as that between '*vanité*' and '*estime de soi-même*'.[11] Rousseau preferred to use different terminology, that of the abbé Jean-Baptiste Dubos, who contrasted *amour de soi-même* and *amour-propre* in his 1719 *Réflexions critiques sur la poésie et de la peinture*.[12] But the substance of Rousseau's distinction closely paralleled Mandeville's. The nucleus of *amour de soi-même* was that it was 'a natural sentiment which inclines every animal to watch over its own preservation', while *amour-propre* was 'only a relative sentiment, artificial and born in Society, which inclines each individual to have a greater esteem for himself than for anyone else'.[13] Rousseau appeared to mark a difference with Mandeville's account of self-liking when he went on to assert that 'in the genuine state of nature, *amour-propre* does not exist', but if there is a difference, it does not seem to me to be an especially significant one. The reason Rousseau gave for his view was that in this state, 'each particular man regarding himself as the sole Spectator to observe him...it is not possible that a sentiment having its source in comparisons he is not capable of making could spring up in his soul'. But we might reflect that there is no strong reason why Mandeville might not have agreed that self-liking would not manifest itself if humans were ever in fact to be in such circumstances. (Indeed, we might note in this context that elsewhere in the *Discourse* Rousseau suggested that the origins of pride might even predate the earliest human societies, since humans became aware of their 'superiority over the other animals' after discovering their ability to trap them and to trick them 'in a thousand ways'.)[14]

Rousseau's narrative of social development, presented in the second part of the *Second Discourse*, continued to track Epicurean sources closely, especially the account found in Lucretius's poem *De rerum natura*, book 5, beginning at line 925. The parallels have been well set out in two works of twentieth-century scholarship, Arthur O. Lovejoy and George Boas's 1935 study of primitivism and the mildly Straussian book by James H. Nichols, Jr., on Epicurean political philosophy, and we can juxtapose passages from these authors get a clear view of what the major similarities have been thought to be.[15] In the pure state of nature, 'primeval man was but a solitary, roving, stupid and unmoral beast',[16] 'originally independent, self-sufficient, with desires limited to natural pleasures'.[17] For both Lucretius and for Rousseau, 'the happiest state of mankind was not the earliest, but that of *la société naissante*, the intermediate between the primitive and the civilized ... , a state which was reached only after the development of language and the family and the discovery of a number of simple arts'.[18] And both Rousseau and Lucretius present a strikingly similar account of what we might call the psychodynamics of the 'fall' of natural humankind:

> [M]an's ... strangely factitious desires, his tendency to crave things, not because they of themselves gave him pleasure or serve his real needs, but because under the corrupting influence of social suggestion, they seem to him necessary for the gratification of self-esteem.[19]

The development of living together with other men, the discovery of new things that seem to improve life, arts, and greater foresight—all these serve to destroy man's former self-sufficiency and to present limitless new objects of desire. The crucial interrelated elements in all this, for both Rousseau and Lucretius, are vanity or pride, a concern for and a dependency on the opinions of other men, an ambitious desire for superiority over others in wealth, power, and esteem, and in consequence the unlimited desire for things that are not by nature good but are merely goods in the (misguided) opinions of others.[20]

The most interesting bit of Lucretius for present purposes is lines 1131–34:

proinde sine incassum defessi sanguine sudent,
angustum per iter luctantes ambitionis,
quandoquidem sapiunt alieno ex ore petuntque
res ex auditis potius quam sensibus ipsis
nec magis id nunc est neque erit mox quam fuit ante.

A typical translation into English is something like the following:

Leave them then to be weary to no purpose, and to sweat blood in struggling along the narrow path of ambition; since their wisdom comes from the lips of others, and they pursue things on hearsay rather than from their own feelings. And this folly does not succeed at the present, and will not succeed in the future, any more than it has succeeded in the past.[21]

But Lovejoy and Boas suggested that 'sapiunt' might mean something significantly different here, so that the third and fourth lines should read, 'since for them things *have savor* only through the mouths of other men and they pursue objects only because of what they have heard others say, rather than from their own feelings,' and this is a more intriguingly Rousseauvian rendition.[22] Rousseau and Lucretius agreed on the artificial nature of political institutions, and finally, both criticised actually existing politics in similar ways, both arguing that 'political society is the realm of false opinions, unnatural passions, and aggravated fears, all of which are incompatible with genuine happiness, with natural satisfaction, with unspoiled pleasure.'[23] In summing up their overall case, Lovejoy and Boas wrote that 'The themes which Rousseau sounds in unison with Lucretius are enriched and elaborated by him, and he has, of course, others foreign to the Roman poet; but, with respect to the issues pertinent to the controversy over primitivism, Lucretius may on the whole be said to stand nearer to Rousseau's position than any other classical writer'.[24]

In his 'Letter', Smith also noted various matters on which Mandeville and Rousseau had disagreed. 'Dr. Mandeville represents the primitive state of mankind as the most wretched and miserable that can be imagined', for example, while 'Mr. Rousseau, on the contrary, paints it as the happiest and most suitable to his nature'.[25] But the philosophical difference to which Smith gave the most prominence in his letter—and which therefore might plausibly be considered to be the reason why he took Rousseau's *Discourse* to contain a real contribution to the 'English philosophy'—was his observation that, on Rousseau's view, it was 'pity, the only amiable principle which the English author allows to be natural to man', that was 'capable of producing all those virtues, whose reality Dr.

Mandeville denies'. For Mandeville, as we have seen, virtue only resided in self-denial, and he did not think there was much of that around; but he did think that there were natural feelings of pity. In his *Essay on Charity, and Charity-Schools*, Mandeville had explained how charity, 'that Virtue by which part of that sincere Love we have for our selves is transferr'd pure and unmix'd to others', was 'often counterfeited by a Passion of ours, call'd Pity or Compassion, which consists in a Fellow-feeling and Condolence for the Misfortunes and Calamities of others'. In order to persuade his readers that there was such a passion, he offered what would later come to be called a thought-experiment.

> Should any of us be lock'd up in a Ground-Room, where in a Yard joining to it there was a thriving good-humour'd Child at play, of two or three Years old, so near us that through the Grates of the Window we could almost touch it with our Hand; and if while we took delight in the harmless Diversion, and imperfect Prittle-Prattle of the innocent Babe, a nasty over-grown Sow should come in upon the Child, set it a screaming, and frighten it out of its Wits; it is natural to think, that this would make us uneasy.[26]

Were the 'half-starv'd Creature' then to 'lay hold of the helpless Infant, destroy and devour it'—Mandeville went on to describe the scene in extravagantly lurid prose—'to hear and see all this, What Tortures would it give the Soul beyond Expression!'[27] For Rousseau, however, 'One sees with pleasure the author of the *Fable of the Bees*, forced to recognize man as a compassionate and sensitive Being' and to acknowledge the naturalness of feelings of pity.[28] On the account that Rousseau went on to develop, furthermore, pity was far more than simply a feeling of repugnance that we experience on witnessing another's distress.

> Mandeville sensed very well that even with all their morality men would never have been anything but monsters if Nature had not given them pity in support of reason; but he did not see that from this quality alone flow all the social virtues he wants to question in men. In fact, what are generosity, Clemency, Humanity, if not Pity applied to the weak, to the guilty, or to the human species in general? Benevolence and even friendship are, rightly understood, the products of a constant pity fixed on a particular object: for is desiring that someone not suffer anything but desiring that he be happy?[29]

According to Pierre Force, who has discussed these passages in some detail, Rousseau was here engaged in a 'reconstruction of Mandeville's anthropology based on pity, not self-love', a reconstruction that 'presents itself as a neo-Stoic critique of the Epicurean/Augustinian critique of virtues'.[30] The main reason why Force thinks this is that he is employing what David Hume had memorably called 'the selfish hypothesis' as his main criterion for separating rival philosophical traditions in the late seventeenth and eighteenth centuries. Those who subscribed to this hypothesis, and who thus believed that self-interest was 'the engine of human behavior', could be considered as belonging to the 'Epicurean/Augustinian tradition', he writes; whereas the 'neo-Stoic tradition', by contrast, 'uses self-interest as one among other principles'.[31] (There are other issues in play in his account, but this is by far the most important one.) This criterion is, however, flawed, and Force would have done better to have invented his own jargon than to employ terms that were themselves deployed in the eighteenth century in different ways. ('Beckerites' and 'anti-Beckerites' might have been suitable, for example, since the disagreements about the foundations of contemporary economic science that have involved Gary Becker in the twentieth century seem to be important to his enquiry.)[32] The easiest way to see how Force's jargon terms can be misleading is to consider the case of David Hume. Hume mentions the 'selfish hypothesis' only to criticise it in the second appendix to the second *Enquiry*, and in the *Treatise*, he argues that there were a number of 'natural virtues' that had a 'tendency to the good of society', such as 'Meekness, beneficence, charity, generosity, clemency, moderation, equity'.[33] According to Force's schema, this must be evidence of Hume's fundamental disagreement with Epicureanism and maybe even of his sympathy with Stoicism or with a Neostoic tradition that uses more than one 'principle' to explain behaviour—and it is true that Hume does offer remarks against the Epicureans. Yet given the extent to which Hume's philosophy is built on a rejection of Stoicism, as we saw at the end of the previous chapter, and the extent to which his thinking is continuous with aspects of Epicurean philosophy, as other scholars have demonstrated,[34] it is sensible to be severely sceptical of the validity of Force's fundamental binary rather than to employ it as a way of excluding Hume from a modern Epicurean tradition altogether—whether or not we then take the implausible further step of arguing that Hume is, in some important sense, a Stoic or Neostoic (as at least one scholar has done).[35] Insofar as Rousseau was here engaged in a project that paralleled Hume's, that of showing how one might reject Mandeville's account of virtue as self-denial while in other respects sticking very close to Mandeville's neo-Epicurean anthropology, we should be similarly sceptical that it is this aspect of his argument that shows any useful evidence of a distinctive 'Stoicism' or 'Neostoicism'.

Smith was not the only one of Rousseau's contemporaries to recognise the substantially Epicurean character of the argument of the *Second Dis-*

course. Jean de Castillon was another, writing in his reply to Rousseau that 'It is almost a year since he revived the Epicureans' delusions concerning our origins; that he reduced our earliest ancestors to the ranks of the stupidest beasts; that he accused us of being the most wicked and ferocious of all animals'.[36] But despite its generally Epicurean orientation and argument, there were nevertheless some moments in Rousseau's *Discourse* where he appeared to be thinking about or along the same lines as the Stoics. First, there was his description of how the savage in the pure state of nature enjoyed the 'perfect quietude of the Stoic' (*l'ataraxie même du Stoïcien*).[37] Rousseau's terminology was a bit wobbly here—*ataraxia* was the goal of the Epicureans, analogous to *apatheia* for the Stoics—but it was reasonably clear why he might have been thinking here of the Stoics: the desires of the savage he described matched his powers, which implied a life that was lived, however unwittingly, in observance of the fundamental Epictetan distinction between what was and what was not in one's power. Second, when Rousseau wrote that 'Man's first sentiment was that of his existence, his first care that of his preservation',[38] he apparently was following the Stoics' *oikeiosis* argument, for the *sentiment de l'existence* was something Chrysippus had called *syneidesis*, which Cicero had translated into Latin as *sensus sui*. Third, there was the famous Note XV on self-love. As I have just indicated, the account Rousseau offered generally followed Mandeville's distinction from the second part of *The Fable of the Bees*, but he also wrote there that *amour de soi-même*, 'directed in man by reason and modified by pity, produces humanity and virtue',[39] and a story about how the virtues derived from self-love would chime quite harmoniously with the Stoics' account of *oikieosis*. We should be clear, however, that such a story would stand in some tension with the main text of the *Discourse*, in which humanity is presented as something that 'flow[ed]' not from *amour de soi-même* but rather from pity, or, in an alternative formulation, as a simple application of pity to 'the human species in general'.[40]

The most straightforward way to resolve such a tension between the main text of the *Discourse* and material from the notes would be if we were able to present pity itself as essentially derivative from *amour de soi-même*. That was not a move, however, that Rousseau made anywhere in the *Discourse*. In the preface, for example, pity was presented, along with *amour de soi-même*, as one of 'two principles' in the human soul 'anterior to reason', with no suggestion that one of them might be derivative from the other.[41] But this was a move that Rousseau went on to make in his later book, *Emile*, where he presented a much more systematic and a much more thoroughgoing Stoic account of his basic moral psychology of self-love. It seems to me plausible to think, in fact, that there was something of a progression in his thinking, from the largely Epicurean text of the *Second Discourse* as it was submitted to the Academy in 1754, to the published version that appeared of the following year, which contained this suggestively Stoicizing moment in the notes, to the much more Stoic account in *Emile*, assembled a few years later and published in 1762. (Such a transition might also help to illuminate the significance both of Denis Diderot's remark that the *Second Discourse* was his favourite text by Rousseau and of Rousseau's own verdict that *Emile* was the 'best of my writings, as well as the most important'.)[42] If this is right, we might further consider, with reference to the earlier discussion of Pierre Force's thesis, that he has in fact got things back to front. According to Force, as we have seen, an account of human motivation that involved 'more than one principle' is regarded as being evidence of a writer belonging to a Stoic or Neostoic tradition, whereas those who argue for the existence of just 'one principle of self-interest' are correspondingly Epicurean. But on the view presented here, it is when Rousseau reduces his account of human nature from a multi-principle account, in which *amour de soi-même*, *amour-propre*, and pity are all treated as distinct and separable principles of human nature, to one in which one, complex principle, *amour de soi-même*, is doing the key work that he is being most decisively Stoic in his thinking.

In *Emile*, Rousseau signals his interest in Stoicism right from the start of the book with an epigraph taken from Seneca: 'We are sick with evils that can be cured; and nature, having brought us forth sound, itself helps us if we wish to be improved.'[43] At the start of book 1, Rousseau explains the centrality of nature in his project of educating a man to be 'in agreement with himself' such that he might live 'consistently'—itself a Stoic key word. Education came from three sources. First, there was the 'education of nature', or the 'internal development of our faculties and our organs'. Second, there was the 'education of men', or 'the use that we are taught to make of this development'. Third, there was the 'education of things', which was 'what we acquire from our own experience about the objects which affect us'.[44] 'Since the conjunction of the three educations is necessary to their perfection', Rousseau writes, 'the two others must be directed toward the one over which we have no power'.[45] The Epictetan distinction is thus invoked from the beginning to indicate the primacy of the education of nature.

The Stoic theme sounds repeatedly throughout the early parts of *Emile*, even—or especially—when Rousseau appears to be distancing himself from what are often held to be Stoic attitudes. Early in book 2, for example, Rousseau makes it clear that he does not believe that 'human wisdom' consists in 'diminishing our desires'. This might sound like a rejection of the Hellenistic project that Martha Nussbaum has called the 'therapy of desire', but Rousseau immediately goes on to make two points that resonate with the Stoic tradition: first, what human wisdom does consist in is 'putting power and will in perfect equality' so that 'with all the powers in action, the soul will nevertheless remain peaceful and that man will be well ordered',[46] another allusion to the classic Epictetan distinction that opened both the *Discourses* and the *Encheiridion*; second, that the danger of the active or 'awakened' imagination is that this is the vehicle through which our desires come to outstrip our powers, so that 'one exhausts oneself without getting to the end, and the more one gains in enjoyment, the further happiness gets from us'. 'The real world has its limits; the imaginary world is infinite', Rousseau writes. 'Unable to enlarge the one, let us restrict the other, for it is from the difference between the two alone that are born all the pains which make us truly unhappy'.[47] It is also in these pages at the start of book 2 that we get one of the clearest statements of what we might call Rousseau's modified Stoic project, that of exploring the conditions under which not only individuals but also whole populations might live together in freedom, understood as a certain kind of autonomy, self-mastery, or lack of dependence on the wills of others:

> There are two sorts of dependence: dependence on things, which is from nature; dependence on men, which is from society. Dependence on things, since it has no morality, is in no way detrimental to freedom and engenders no vices. Dependence on men, since it is without order, engenders all the vices, and by it, master and slave are mutually corrupted. If there is any means of remedying this ill in society, it is to substitute law for man and to arm the general wills with a real strength superior to the action of every particular will. If the laws of nations could, like those of nature, have an inflexibility that no human force could ever conquer, dependence on men would then become dependence on things again; and in the republic all of the advantages of the natural state would be united with those of the civil state, and freedom which keeps man exempt from vices would be joined to morality, which raises him to virtue.[48]

A declaration like this in turn is followed almost immediately by a Stoic insistence on the boundedness of our 'true' or 'natural' needs, which 'must be carefully distinguished from the need which stems from nascent whim or from the need which comes only from the superabundance of life', so that 'one should distrust' what children 'desire but are unable to do for themselves'.[49]

The narrative of *Emile*, which charts the development of the child's mind and character over time, sits very easily with both of the main Latin texts that have come down to us expounding the Stoic doctrine of *oikeio-*

sis, whether Cicero's account, which he puts into the mouth of 'Cato', from book 3 of *De finibus*, or Seneca's exposition from his 121st *Letter*. Cicero's exposition, which I considered at some length in the discussion of the foundations of Grotius's natural law theory in the chapter three, also concentrates on a narrative of childhood development. What Seneca added to Cicero is the idea that the developing organism has a series of distinct 'constitutions'. 'There is a constitution for every stage of life, one for a baby, another for a boy', and 'another for an old man', he wrote, and 'although everyone has one different constitution after another, the attachment to one's own constitution is the same', for 'nature does not commend me to the boy or the youth or the old man, but to myself'.[50] The structure of *Emile* flowed from this Senecan thought, with the five books of *Emile* presenting an analysis of five quite different stages of life—of Emile as a baby (I), in two quite distinct phases of childhood (II and III), as an adolescent (IV), and finally as a young man on the threshold of marriage and citizenship (V). (The Senecanism of *Emile* was apparent to its contemporary readers, though the author of *Les plagiats de M. J-J Rousseau de Genève sur l'éducation* judged that it was the 94th *Letter* and the treatise *De beata vita* that were the main objects of Rousseau's unscrupulous literary attention.)[51]

One of these critical moments of transition comes at puberty, when Emile's childhood constitution makes way for something else, and he has to learn how to relate to his new constitution in the right kinds of ways. (Perhaps it would be better to say that it is Emile's tutor who now has to develop new strategies through which his pupil can end up relating to his new constitution in the right kinds of ways.) It is in the opening pages of book 4, then, that Rousseau sets out his most extensive examination of the psychology of self-love, which is treated there in a far more systematic manner than it had been in the early *Discourse on Inequality*. As he did in the earlier book 2, Rousseau begins what is to be a heavily Stoic-inflected exposition by making clear which aspect of Stoic psychology it is that he is not endorsing. 'Our passions are the principal instruments of our preservation', he wrote.

> It is, therefore, an enterprise as vain as it is ridiculous to want to destroy them—it is to control nature, it is to reform the work of God. If God were to tell men to annihilate the passions which He gives him, God would will and not will; He would contradict Himself. Never did he give this senseless order. Nothing of the kind is written in the human heart.

Someone who 'wanted to prevent the birth of the passions' is 'almost as mad as someone who wanted to annihilate them', Rousseau declares, 'and those who believed that this was my project up to now would surely have understood me very badly'.[52] Having disclaimed the Stoics' goal of extirpating the passions, however, Rousseau begins his positive account of the psychology of passions on a different Stoic note. It may be 'man's nature to have passions', he suggests, but not all of the passions that we do in fact have are natural ones.

> Our natural passions are very limited. They are the instruments of our freedom; they tend to preserve us. All those which subject and destroy us come from elsewhere. Nature does not give them to us. We appropriate them to the detriment of nature [*la nature ne nous les donne pas, nous nous les approprions à son prejudice*].[53]

We might note in this passage the appearance of the language of *oikeiosis*, often described with a vocabulary of appropriation, with Rousseau here calling attention to those unnecessary, indeed pernicious, varieties of appropriation that go beyond the call of nature.

Rousseau proceeds to make the claim that is at the heart of this interpretation of his thinking as a modern redeployment of the *oikeiosis* doctrine. In the *Second Discourse*, there had been 'two principles', 'anterior to reason', which Rousseau placed at the foundation of his account of human nature. In *Emile*, there is now just one: 'The source of our passions, the origin and principle of all the others, the only one born with man and which never leaves him so long as he lives is self-love [*amour de soi-même*]'.[54] This is described as 'a primitive, innate passion, which is anterior to every other, and of which all the others are in a sense only modifications'. There are, however, two kinds of modifications. There are the ones that derived naturally from *amour de soi-même* itself and continue to promote its fundamental goals, and then there are the other passions, modifications with 'alien causes', which 'alter the primary goal and are at odds with their own principle'. When our lives are driven by passions of this second kind, 'It is then that man finds himself outside of nature and sets himself in contradiction with himself'. In contrast, Rousseau observes of *amour de soi-même*, employing *Malebranchiste* jargon but articulating what is also a Stoic thought, that it 'is always good and always in conformity with order'.[55]

Rousseau then launches into the kind of narrative of early childhood development familiar from 'Cato's' exposition of *oikeiosis* in the third book of *De finibus*. We not only 'love ourselves to preserve ourselves', we also 'love what preserves us', with the result that 'Every child is attached to his nurse'. At first this love is a pre-rational or 'mechanical' attachment or a 'blind instinct', but as the baby begins to discern the intention to help or to harm behind human behaviour, 'instinct' is transformed into 'sentiment', 'attachment into love, aversion into hate'.

> At first the attachment he has for his nurse and his governess is only a habit. He seeks them because he needs them and is well off in having them; it is recognition rather than benevolence. He needs much time to understand that not only are they useful to him but they want to be; and it is then that he begins to love them.[56]

The child is therefore 'naturally inclined to benevolence'.

It is in this part of the discussion that Rousseau introduces the theme of *amour-propre*. As the child 'extends his relations, his needs, and his active or passive dependencies', the sentiment of 'duties and preferences' is produced by 'the sentiment of his connections with others'. This serves to make him 'imperious, jealous, deceitful, and vindictive', and this in turn allows Rousseau to state his famous contrast of *amour de soi-même* and *amour-propre*.

> Self-love [*amour de soi-même*], which regards only ourselves, is contented when our true needs are satisfied. But *amour-propre*, which makes comparisons, is never content and never could be, because this sentiment, preferring ourselves to others, also demands others to prefer us to themselves, which is impossible. This is how the gentle and affectionate passions are born of self-love [*amour de soi-même*], and how the hateful and irascible passions are born of *amour-propre*.[57]

The declaration here is harmonious with the earlier thought that there are two kinds of modifications to *amour de soi-même*, so that now the first kind of modifications, identified straightforwardly with *amour de soi-même* itself, are described in terms of the 'gentle and affectionate passions', whereas the other kind of modifications are now described in terms of *amour-propre* and relate to the 'hateful and irascible passions'. It is harmonious, in particular, because both distinctions were explained with respect to the question of the satisfaction of natural needs: the first kind of modification of *amour de soi-même* concerned those limited, natural needs, while the second kind did not, referring instead to the 'countless alien streams' that have 'swollen' the passions, and that do not contribute to self-preservation and the life according to nature. In this passage, *amour de soi-même* speaks to 'our true needs', which can be satisfied, while *amour-propre* 'is never content and never could be'. But it is important to be clear that this is not Rousseau's final word on the matter, for we will go on to learn, for example, that the passions inspired by *amour-propre* can be 'humane and gentle' as well as 'cruel and malignant',[58] and that the cruder contrast suggested here does not capture the complexity or the depth of Rousseau's developed position.

'The study suitable for man is that of his relations', Rousseau proposes. 'So long as he knows himself only in his physical being, he ought to study himself in his relations with things.' With the transition to adolescence, however, he begins 'to sense his moral being', and therefore, he ought to study himself in his relations with men'.[59] If the *amour-propre* of pre-adolescent children is aroused, this is because its 'germ' was placed in their hearts by others, from outside. 'But this is no longer the case with the young man's heart', and 'whatever we may do, these passions will be born in spite of us', so that 'It is therefore time to change the method' of educating young Emile.[60] There's an echo here of Seneca's 121st *Letter*— as our constitution changes, so we change the way in which we relate to our constitution—but we might also observe how Rousseau's discussion to some extent parallels Butler's Stoic project. For both Butler and Rousseau, there is a natural organisation of our constitution, understood as a kind of system, and we live in accordance with nature by doing what we can to try to maintain that natural ordering. With a further emphasis familiar not so much from Butler's modern Stoicism as from Shaftesbury's, keeping the imagination under control is, for Rousseau, a key part of that project:

> Do you wish to put order and regularity in the nascent passions? Extend the period during which they develop in order that they have the time to be arranged as they are born. Then it is not man who orders them; it is nature itself. Your care is only to let it arrange its work. If your pupil were alone, you would have nothing to do. But everything surrounding him influences his imagination. The torrent of prejudices carries him away. To restrain him, he must be pushed in the opposite direction. Sentiment must enchain imagination, and reason silence the opinion of men. The source of all the passions is sensibility; imagination determines their bent. . . . It is the errors of imagination which transform into vices the passions of all limited beings—even those of angels, if they have any, for they would have to know the nature of all beings in order to know what relations best suit their nature.[61]

Rousseau then announces the 'summary of the whole of human wisdom in the use of the passions' in somewhat Stoic terms: '(1) To have a sense of the true relations of man, with respect to the species as well as the individual. (2) To order all the affections of the soul according to these relations.' But he then presents his basic shift in emphasis with respect to the

Stoics' own training programme: 'the issue here is less what a man can do for himself than what we can do for our pupil by the choice of circumstances in which we put him'.[62]

Rousseau then moves on to explain how both pity and *amour-propre* are developments out of *amour de soi-même* itself, and how the virtues could derive from these passions. With respect to pity, a child who is 'raised in a happy simplicity' would be 'drawn by the first movements of nature toward the tender and affectionate passions', and his 'compassionate heart is moved by the sufferings of his fellows'.[63] Rousseau states the basic Pufendorffian position on sociability: 'It is man's weakness which makes him sociable'. But that position is immediately clarified in such a way that pushes the argument in a different direction: 'it is our common miseries which turn our hearts to humanity; we would owe humanity nothing if we were not men'.

> It follows from this that we are attached to our fellows less by the sentiment of their pleasures than by the sentiment of their pains, for we see far better in the latter the identity of our natures with theirs and the guarantees of their attachment to us. . . . If our common needs unite us by interest, our common miseries unite us by affection.[64]

Owing to the disadvantages to which it so often can give rise, Rousseau had earlier maintained the importance of keeping the imagination under control. Imagination had its uses as well as its disadvantages, however, especially insofar as we could only experience pity through acts of the imagination. This is, in fact, another example of how Rousseau's thinking had moved on considerably since writing the *Second Discourse*.[65] The implication of the earlier text was that pity is strongest in humans in the condition of the pure state of nature and is gradually silenced by the accretions of social development, whereas here in *Emile*, Rousseau can write that if the savage 'had remained stupid and barbaric', he would not have 'these new movements within him'.[66] The task for Emile's tutor, then, is to learn how to fire his young pupil's imagination in the right way, so that a humanitarian sensibility can be nurtured and cultivated.

> To excite and nourish this nascent sensibility, to guide it or follow it in its natural inclination, what is there to do other than offer the young man objects on which the expansive force of his heart can act, objects which swell the heart, which extend it to other beings, which make it find itself everywhere outside of itself—and carefully to keep away those which contract and concentrate the heart and tighten the spring of the human *I*?[67]

Just as in the Stoics' account of *oikeiosis*, the developing child continues to live in accordance with nature through an expansion of the self's zone of concern, so that the project of taking care of oneself becomes one of taking care of others, and *amour de soi-même* now finds an outlet as 'goodness, humanity, [and] beneficence'.[68] The Stoics' account concerned the development of a reasoning faculty, whereas Rousseau describes a sentimental education—though, as he writes towards the end of book 3, the task of this part of Emile's education is 'to perfect reason by sentiment'.[69] The Stoics, furthermore, would have found this kind of argument about pity bizarre, for their sharply rationalist ethics denied that pity was a virtue; indeed, they identified it as a distinctive vice, because pity made people unhappy when they reflected on things, such as the misery of others, that were not under their control. (Nietzsche announced from time to time, finally, that he was '*against* Rousseau',[70] and the recent scholarship notes that it is precisely when he attacks Rousseau's ethics of pity that he is drawing most heavily from Stoic moral philosophy.)[71] Yet while the content of Rousseau's exposition frequently contrasts with that presented by the Stoics, the concerns and the structure of the argument, focusing on the question of how we derive social dispositions out of the natural development of self-interest, is broadly the same. Or, as he states in a footnote right at the end of his examination of pity, 'Love of men derived from love of self is the principle of human justice'.[72]

After considering the origins and extension of pity, Rousseau turns to consider the other major 'relative sentiment' in human nature, *amour-propre*. In an earlier contribution I argued that Rousseau's distinctive 'splitting' of the notion of self-love into two parts, *amour de soi-même* and *amour-propre*, could be viewed as an attempt to recuperate the Stoics' concept of *oikeiosis* and to keep it in a foundational role for ethics while simultaneously enabling him to signal a great deal of agreement with the Augustinians about the iniquities of self-love.[73] These, however, were placed firmly on the *amour-propre* side of this new binary, in a place where they were insulated from *amour de soi-même*, and therefore unable to call this benign kind of self-love radically into question—as, for example, Blaise Pascal had done in the haunting fragment in which he wrote, 'Thus we are born unjust, for each inclines towards himself'.[74] But that earlier account is misleading because it is based on the old, discredited view that *amour-propre* is intrinsically suspect, and it failed to take into account the work of scholars such as Nicholas Dent and Timothy O'Hagan, who have presented a much more compelling interpretation of Rousseau's *amour-propre* and its significance.[75]

Dent and his followers—who include, most recently, Frederick Neuhouser—have challenged the familiar, relentlessly negative view of *amour-*

propre on the grounds that this 'does not describe what is intrinsic to it'. On their view, what is intrinsic to *amour-propre* is that it 'directs us to secure for ourselves recognition from others', and that to enjoy such recognition is 'one of our proper goods', to the extent that '*amour-propre* is simply the form that *amour de soi* (which directs us to the enjoyment of our proper good) takes when the personal good sought is one that we need in our dealings with others'.[76] Indeed, once human beings are outside the original state of nature and living in some kind of society with one another, we can no longer distinguish between our purely 'natural' and our 'social' needs. As Neuhouser puts it, 'This blurring of the distinction between physical and psychological needs is due to the fact that for beings in whom *amour-propre* has begun to operate—and that includes all *human* beings—no aspect of one's existence remains untouched by the concern for one's standing among others'.[77] Proponents of this interpretation of *amour-propre* point to two passages in particular in book 4 of *Emile*. The first is one that I flagged above, which appears right at the start of the discussion of *amour-propre* and makes the point that *amour-propre* can give rise to good passions as well as bad ones:

> Since my Emile has until now looked only at himself, the first glance he casts on his fellows leads him to compare himself with them. And the first sentiment aroused in him by this comparison is the desire to be in the first position. This is the point where love of self [*amour de soi*] turns into *amour-propre* and where begin to arise all the passions which depend on this one. But to decide whether among these passions the dominant ones in his character will be humane and gentle or cruel and malignant, whether they will be passions of beneficence and commiseration or of envy and covetousness, we must know what position he will feel he has among men, and what kinds of obstacles he may believe he has to overcome to reach the position he wants to occupy.[78]

The second passage comes a little later, when Rousseau writes, 'Let us extend *amour-propre* to other beings. We shall transform it into a virtue, and there is no man's heart in which this virtue does not have its root.'[79] (Such remarks have proved troubling to some commentators, to the extent that they have explained that while he says '*amour-propre*' here, he means '*amour de soi*'.)[80] On Dent's interpretation, there are two ways in which we might unpack this passage. Either the point is that the individual recognises who his or her own *amour-propre* expects moral recognition from others, and when we 'extend' this 'expectation for ourselves to others, we are recognizing and acknowledging that they have, should have, these same requirements for themselves as well'. Alternatively, 'I extend my *amour-propre* to others by taking *their* need for human standing "on board" as *my own* concern, and thus strive for them to enjoy this just as much as I strive to have it for myself'.[81]

Such an interpretation of the nature of noninflamed *amour-propre* fits quite well with the view advanced here that Rousseau's extended account of self-love is structured around a reworking of the Stoics' *oikeiosis*. The developmental story the Stoics offered concerning *oikeiosis* was a story about the progression of reason. Even in his brief remarks on *amour-propre* in the notes to the *Second Discourse*, Rousseau offered the thought that 'reason engenders *amour propre* and reflection fortifies it'.[82] The Stoics also used *oikeiosis* in order to try to explain how natural self-love might be extended to encompass the interests of others—alternatively, of how 'personal' *oikeiosis* ends up becoming something like 'social' *oikeiosis*—and a narrative of this kind is what we have here in Rousseau, too, with a more rationalistic, and to that extent more Stoic, orientation than we had in the earlier argument about how pity lies at the origin of virtues such as benevolence and justice. Indeed, Neuhouser has gone so far as to argue that developed *amour-propre* is a precondition of being able to occupy what he calls the standpoint of reason at all.[83] *Amour-propre* is here helping to discharge one of the functions of developed Stoic *oikeiosis* in particular, with respect for other persons and respect for their legitimately held property bound up one with another. And the story Rousseau tells in *Emile* is one about how the development of noninflamed *amour-propre* generates the distinctive passions associated with, for example, the romantic love of Emile and Sophie, together with the other benign civic sentiments, and the distinction between the passions of 'petulant' *amour-propre* and these more benign sentiments can plausibly be mapped in turn back onto the Stoics' classic distinction between the passions or *pathe*, which are bad, and the sentiments or *eupatheiai*, which aren't.[84]

The final place to look for evidence of Rousseau's adaptation of the Stoic doctrine of *oikeiosis* comes towards the end of the passage known as the 'Profession of faith of the Savoyard vicar', in particular when the vicar presents his thoughts about the nature of conscience. Conscience, he says, is 'an innate principle of justice and virtue according to which, in spite of our own maxims, we judge our actions and those of others as good or bad'.[85] 'Although all our ideas come to us from outside', the vicar argues, 'the sentiments evaluating them are within us, and it is by them alone that we know the compatibility or incompatibility between us and the things we ought to seek or flee.'[86] The vicar reports the conventional view that virtue is the love of order, and asks whether this love 'can and should . . . win out in me over that of my own well-being'. Order itself is not decisive, he considers, for 'I say that vice is the love of order, taken in a different sense'.

There is some moral order wherever there is sentiment and intelligence. The difference is that the good man orders himself in relation to the whole, and the wicked one orders the whole in relation to himself. The latter makes himself the center of all things; he is ordered in relation to the common center, which is God, and in relation to all the concentric circles, which are the creatures. If the divinity does not exist, it is only the wicked man who reasons, and the good man is nothing but a fool.[87]

Just as Butler's conscience was a necessary element in his Stoic conception of human nature organised as a constitution or system that was adapted to virtue, here too Rousseau's vicar presents the voice of conscience as, in Dent's words, 'an expression, an awareness, of the demands of this proper inner order of man, which constitutes his true need and good and directs him to act well in accord with God's overall providential design for all human beings'.[88] The process described by the Stoics' *oikeiosis* began with the infant's instinctive drive for self-preservation and culminated in the figure of the Stoic sage, whose commitment to the good of the whole generated an equal concern for the welfare of each individual. So too Rousseau's account of human nature in *Emile* is built around his account of *amour de soi-même* as the fundamental principle of human nature, a principle that begins with basic concerns about self-preservation but that ultimately can generate the altruistic and, if necessary, self-sacrificing moral agent, whose *amour de soi-même* is now concentrated on living in accordance with the promptings of conscience and whose conduct is thereby oriented towards 'the whole', which includes a conception of God's role as the intelligence that designed and presides over the entire universe.[89]

There is obviously much more that could be said about Rousseau's later writings and its relationship with Stoicism. Rousseau was himself the first to reflect on the limits of the education described in *Emile*, in that book's unfinished and posthumously published sequel, *Emile et Sophie, ou les Solitaires*, in which things go horribly wrong for the unhappy couple. In a letter to his tutor written years later, Emile summarises his education in sharply Stoic terms: 'I learned that the primary wisdom is to want what is, and to regulate one's heart based on its destiny. That is all that depends on us, you told me; all the rest is from necessity.'[90] What Emile goes on to describe, however, suggests that his Stoic education failed to enable him to flourish in the absence of his tutor. In Paris, Emile's life with Sophie falls apart after she becomes pregnant with another man's child, and Emile's subsequent wanderings result in him being captured by Moorish pirates. Emile's education might not have prepared him adequately for the dilemmas of modern urban living, but it fitted him very well indeed for life as a slave in Algiers.

> [T]he sentiment that still occupied me in its entire force made me say inside with a sort of satisfaction: "Of what will this event deprive me? The power of doing something stupid. I am more free than before." "Emile a slave!" I resumed, "Ah! In what sense? Have I lost any of my primitive freedom? Was I not born a slave of necessity? What new yoke can men impose on me?"...Yes, my father, I can say it; the time of my servitude was that of my reign, and never did I have so much authority over myself as when I bore the chains of the people of Barbary.[91]

Rousseau continued thinking about the Stoics right to the end. His final text, the unfinished and posthumously published *Reveries of the Solitary Walker*, gives us a complex, fascinating, and utterly distinctive blending of Stoic and Epicurean themes, describing the search for happiness in old age through new strategies of self-sufficiency and an attempt to escape from dependence on or frustration with the wills of others. In the story Rousseau tells of being bowled over and knocked out after a collision with a large dog, for example, we have a vivid redeployment of one of the Stoics' own spiritual exercises.[92] The full story of Rousseau's engagements with the Hellenistic philosophies in his post-*Emile* writings—including the other autobiographical texts, the *Confessions* and the *Dialogues*—would be well worth the telling. But that story will not be pursued here, as this study is long enough already, and it is time to begin to draw it to a close.

In general, in these pages, I have tracked the changing fortunes of a fundamental opposition between more Stoic and more Augustinian perspectives on human life, and we have seen that as the seventeenth century gave way to the eighteenth, the patterns of Augustinian anti-Stoicism often found expression in a more secular, Epicurean register. What Rousseau attempts, more strenuously than any other thinker of the period, is an extraordinary synthesis of Epicurean, Augustinian, and Stoic argumentative currents. In common with the modern Epicureans, Rousseau uses claims about self-love to illuminate all areas of human behaviour in modern times. But by presenting that self-love as inflamed *amour-propre*, Rousseau tilts sharply towards the more critical Augustinians than towards those Epicurean writers who were making their apology for commercial society. For Rousseau and for the Augustinians, there is something pathological about human behaviour in the world with which we're familiar. We are obsessed with our standing relative to others, and this leads us to engage in courses of action that just aren't ever going to make us happy, courses of action that have a pernicious, self-reinforcing dynamic.

But even as Rousseau endorses a great deal of the Augustinians' emphasis on understanding a corrupted kind of self-love in explaining actually existing human affairs, human unhappiness, and human unfreedom, he refuses to agree with the Augustinians on the foundations of their argument. Indeed, it was Rousseau's flat denial of original sin, his insistence that there could not have been any 'original perversity in the human heart', that got his book into trouble with the ecclesiastical authorities and sent him fleeing into exile. As Neuhouser has argued in his recent book, Rousseau presents a secular theodicy, an attempt to acknowledge the manifold bad things that human beings introduce into their lives, while still pointing to the natural goodness of humankind and expressing a hope, if not an expectation, that we might find better ways of living in this world—a possibility the Augustinian tradition has generally denied. And as I have tried to describe in this chapter, the project Rousseau was engaged in after the *Second Discourse*, as he worked to create distance between himself and the other *philosophes* with whom he had earlier been so closely associated, was that of restructuring his argument to move away from modern Epicureanism and towards a reformulated modern Stoicism, outlined, above all, in the pages of *Emile* I've considered here, with Rousseau's most detailed depiction of what the life according to nature outside the pure state of nature might consist.

Rousseau takes a great deal from Stoic moral psychology. But there is one respect in particular where he departs from the Stoics, with important consequences for his political theory. For Rousseau, when human beings begin to maintain social relations, one with another, their *amour-propre* awakens, and they come to need recognition from one another. The classical Stoics had a certain interest in glory, but they would never have made an argument about such recognition being a genuine human need; rather, it was something outside our power, and therefore not something over which we should concern ourselves. It is reasonable to act in a manner that does good things for your reputation—which can be considered a 'preferred indifferent'—but we make a mistake if we think that it is a human need; what other people think of us just doesn't matter. For Rousseau, recognition really is a human need, at least when human beings quit the pure state of nature, as the consequence of not receiving the right kind of recognition is the inflammation of *amour-propre* in a way that wrecks the possibilities of good living, our own and other people's. Human institutions could always threaten to fall out of the picture altogether in ancient Stoicism, preoccupied as it was with the relationship between the individual and the cosmos. Rousseau's modified Stoicism displaces our attention precisely onto the nature of those institutions through his claim that if we are to live in accordance with nature, but together in society, then we need certain kinds of social organisation to obtain.

Stoic politics were generally elite politics. Epictetus analogised the defiance of Helvidius Priscus before the emperor Vespasian to the purple hem of the *toga praetexta*, that 'small and brilliant portion which causes the rest to appear comely and beautiful'.[93] The Senecan mirror-for-princes genre of political writing had always defended monarchical politics, and Justus Lipsius sought to fashion a new Stoic monarchism at the close of the sixteenth century. A hundred years later, Shaftesbury offered a Stoic argument for an aristocratic republic—an argument that met resistance from the more popularly minded Hutcheson. But it is above all in Rousseau's political thought that we get a rigorously theorised Stoic framework for a modern citizen republic. We shouldn't overstate either its democratic or its egalitarian credentials. Gender inequality runs deep in Rousseau's political imagination, for example, and it is reasonably clear that Rousseau did not envisage that all the inhabitants of the city he describes and defends in the *Social Contract* should have citizenship rights, or even that citizenship itself should be a uniform legal and political status. But we do get a pretty good picture from his various writings on politics of what the political society ought to look like: organised to prevent domination, to facilitate living in accordance with natural *amour de soi-même*, and to foster the natural sentiments to which *amour-propre* can give rise, in place of the petulant, inflamed passions that bedevil actually existing commercial societies. The city of the *Social Contract* is by no means the Stoics' *cosmopolis*, to be sure. The citizens' general will is the functional substitute for the Stoics' cosmic reason, ordering the parts towards the interests of the whole, but it runs out at the boundaries of the political community. Rousseau might have suggested in the earlier *Discourse on Political Economy* that there could be a 'general will of the human race', but he had changed his mind on this point by the time he came to compose the so-called 'Geneva Manuscript', an early draft of the *Social Contract*, and that text also contains an explicit repudiation of the cosmopolitan, who was said to love mankind so that he didn't have to extend his love to any actually existing member of the species. But Rousseau's vision of undominated republican citizens living together in freedom seems to me to be more than generically Roman in inspiration; it is specifically Stoic.

Epilogue

IN AN ESSAY PUBLISHED to mark the thirtieth anniversary of Karl Marx's death in 1913, Vladimir Ilych Lenin wrote of the 'three sources and component parts of Marxism'. 'The Marxist doctrine is omnipotent because it is true', he asserted; it was, furthermore, 'the legitimate successor to the best that man produced in the nineteenth century, as represented by German philosophy, English political economy and French socialism'.[1] The account that Lenin went on to elaborate is a little more complicated than this summary might suggest: eighteenth-century French materialism plays a significant role, for example, in the story that he tells about Marxism's intellectual origins, and we can quibble over the details—surely the political economy in question was as much Scottish as it was ever English. But a version of Lenin's core thought remains both powerful and plausible: that what eventually crystallized under the banner of Marxism was in an important sense a putting together, as well as a radical transformation, of major elements of German idealist philosophy, especially Hegel; of the classical political economy that reaches back to Adam Smith; and of the radical French politics that unfolded over the course of the Revolutionary decade of the 1790s.

When scholars refer to 'the Young Karl Marx', they are often using the phrase to pick out the period 1844–48, often reckoned to be the critical phase in his intellectual development, from the time of the 'Economic and Philosophical Manuscripts' down to the publication of the *Communist Manifesto*, an extraordinarily fertile time that also saw *The Holy Family*, *The German Ideology*, the 'Theses on Feuerbach', and *The Poverty of Philosophy*. If we look just a little earlier, however—at the Very Young Karl Marx, as we might call him—we find someone whose formal academic studies came to concentrate on Epicureanism and culminated in a doctoral thesis titled 'The Difference Between the Democritean and Epicurean Philosophy of Nature', submitted in 1841 to the University of Jena.[2] After a brief career as a journalist ended in March 1843 when the Prussian authorities closed down his newspaper, the *Rheinische Zeitung*, he began sustained intellectual work on just the three areas of inquiry picked out by Lenin's article. Over the summer he wrote a lengthy and destructive commentary on a significant portion of the final chapter of

Hegel's *Philosophy of Right*.[3] The following winter he turned his attention to a project, which he never completed, to write a study of the French Revolutionary Convention, in preparation for which he read and took notes on Rousseau's *Social Contract*.[4] In the spring of 1844 he embarked on the studies in political economy that he would continue for the rest of his life, beginning with a set of notes on James Mill.[5] The thought I want to press here, in these closing pages, is that these 'sources and component parts', the three intellectual streams that fed into what was eventually to become Marxism, themselves not only took shape as partial appropriations and transformations of Rousseau's ideas but also each embodied a continuing engagement with Stoicism.

However brilliant many of its component parts might have been, it is difficult to argue that Rousseau's theoretical and political project was not a failure. He was never able to complete his book on political institutions, a work meant to supplant Montesquieu's *Spirit of the Laws* as the eighteenth century's bible of political science;[6] his *Social Contract* openly presented itself as but a fragment of this much larger work.[7] None of the polities he specifically addressed in his writings—whether Poland, Corsica, or Geneva—ever adopted his practical recommendations.[8] He almost despaired of finding 'a form of government that might place the law above man'.[9] His thinking about international politics reached an impasse: there could be no end to war until the monarchies of Europe had been ushered off the stage of history, and those monarchies were, he correctly predicted, on the threshold of an era of wars and revolutions that threatened their survival. But he was apprehensive about the inevitable loss of innocent life rather than exhilarated by the potential such revolutions might hold out for the political transformation of the continent.[10] One consequence of Rousseau's failure, perhaps, was the way in which so much of the most enduring thought of the second half of the eighteenth century was marked by a sustained grappling with his ideas, but only rarely by more than a highly selective appropriation of them.

Immanuel Kant, standing at the head of the tradition of German idealism, admired Rousseau intensely. As a young philosopher, he thought that the 'thirst for knowledge' alone constituted the 'honor of mankind', but 'Rousseau set me right', from whom he learned not to despise 'the rabble who knows nothing' and 'to respect human nature',[11] and the only picture that hung in Kant's house, over his writing desk, was a portrait of Rousseau.[12] The thread that connects their respective systems of thought, furthermore, is a Stoic thread. In the *Social Contract*, Rousseau describes moral freedom as autonomy, to live under a self-imposed law;[13] the Stoics held that freedom was the power to live as you will, that only the wise were free, and that the wise were those who lived in accordance with the rational law of nature;[14] and a notion of freedom as rational autonomy forms the innermost core of Kant's practical philosophy, outlined notably in his *Groundwork of the Metaphysics of Morals*.[15]

What the German idealists found in Rousseau, above all, was an argument about how freedom had to have both a subjective and an objective aspect. One had to feel free, and the reasons one felt free had to relate to a plausible account of what it actually was to be free. For Rousseau's citizens, in Joshua Cohen's words, 'having a general will . . . is not a means to autonomy', it is 'what autonomy consists in'.[16] On Frederick Neuhouser's reconstruction of Rousseau's position, furthermore, two conditions have to be met for citizens to have that general will: first, 'the laws that govern citizens must be objectively liberating—they must effectively mitigate the freedom-endangering consequences of dependence on other individuals', and second, the citizens must also subjectively affirm those laws as their own.[17] J. G. Fichte, who held the chair in philosophy at Jena in the 1790s, was a serious student of the writings of both Rousseau and Kant—and of Kant's reading of Rousseau—and his ideas, set out principally in two major works of political philosophy, the *Foundations of Natural Right* and *The Closed Commercial State*, could look very Stoic indeed. Fichte argued that autonomy was specifically realised in this twofold sense, subjective and objective, through the work that individuals did, which established a certain relationship of the will with nature. Perceptive readers of Fichte made the connection to the Stoics: writing in *Le Catholique* in 1827, the Baron d'Eckstein called Fichte's argument a piece of 'transcendental industrialism', arguing that his closed commercial state was really a 'republic of beavers' and that he sought to transform every citizen into the Stoics' sage.[18] And as Neuhouser has argued persuasively in his study, *Foundations of Hegel's Social Theory*, these two conditions for autonomy are carried over from Rousseau's thought and firmly embedded in the account of political freedom that G.W.F. Hegel, another Jena philosopher, offered in his 1821 *Philosophy of Right*.

Turning from German idealism to consider British political economy, Adam Smith remained gripped by Rousseau's arguments. As the letter to the *Edinburgh Review* suggests, in the 1750s they had a shared interest in fashioning a response to Mandeville's social theory by employing Mandeville's own neo-Epicurean premises. But where Rousseau's train of thought took him in an increasingly Stoicizing direction, Smith remained committed to David Hume's more Epicurean optimism about the possibilities of commercial society—not if the present policies were pursued by Europe's rulers, to be sure, but in a different but by no means utopian alternative future. The core of his response to Rousseau's *Discourse on Inequality* came in the 'invisible hand' passage in book 4 of *The Theory of Moral Sentiments*, which echoed the language of the translations he himself had once made from Rousseau's French and which concluded with the anti-Rousseauist verdict, 'When Providence divided the earth among a few *lordly masters*, it neither forgot nor abandoned those who seemed to have been left out in the partition', for 'These last too enjoy their share of all that it produces'.[19] The introduction of property might have led to inequality, but not necessarily to the kind of oppression and misery that Rousseau so vividly described. But whether Smith had a fully adequate response to Rousseau's indictment of commercial society is much less clear; and the question of how Smith's reply to Rousseau 'should be understood', John Robertson has written, 'is now central to Smith scholarship'. He points in particular to a passage that Smith added to the final edition of *The Theory of Moral Sentiments*, published posthumously, as the final, pessimistic result of his lifelong scratching of the Rousseau itch.[20] This is the new chapter on the 'corruption of the moral sentiments', whose 'great and most universal cause' Smith judged to be the 'disposition to admire, and almost to worship, the rich and the powerful, and to despise, or, at least, to neglect persons of poor and mean condition' so characteristically induced by commercial society.

Adam Smith has often been reckoned to be a kind of modern Stoic, certainly since the publication of D. D. Raphael and Alec Macfie's 'Glasgow' edition of *The Theory of Moral Sentiments* in 1976.[21] In their introductory essay to that edition, Raphael and Macfie declare that 'Stoic philosophy is the primary influence on Smith's ethical thought';[22] that the Smithian virtue of self-command, from which 'all the other virtues seem to derive their principal lustre', is 'distinctively Stoic';[23] and that 'a Stoic idea of nature and the natural forms a major part of the philosophical foundations' of both the *Theory of Moral Sentiments* and the *Wealth of Nations*. 'The Stoic doctrine went along with a view of nature as a cosmic harmony', they write, and they draw attention to the various turns of phrase in Smith's writings that intimated such a view: 'the great Conductor', the 'immense machine of the universe', the 'all-wise Architect' of 'one immense and connected system', and, of course, the 'invisible hand'.[24] Raphael and Macfie's introduction became an influential contribution to Smith studies, and over the next three decades a number of scholars, among them Norbet Waszek, Athol Fitzgibbons, Stewart Justman, and Pierre Force, followed their lead and devoted considerable attention to documenting the extent of Smith's 'Stoicism'.[25]

Nevertheless, as Smith himself wrote, 'The plan and system which Nature has sketched out for our conduct, seems to be altogether different from that of the Stoical philosophy',[26] and the most thorough recent historical studies of Smith have been generally sceptical of the alignment such scholars have proposed of Smith and the Stoics. John Robertson's remarks towards the end of his *The Case for the Enlightenment* that situate Smith in a tradition of modern Epicureanism that includes Mande-ville and Hume are persuasive.[27] In a detailed examination of Smith's use of classical sources, Gloria Vivenza denies that the Stoic influence on Smith was nearly as strong as Raphael and Macfie has contended; con-cerning the passage on self-command, she argues that 'the section evinces a closer connection with Aristotle than with the Stoics'.[28] And in her study of Smith and Condorcet, *Economic Sentiments*, Emma Rothschild scrutinises Smith's rhetoric of providential nature, rejects the more Stoic interpretations of his system, and provocatively concludes that his invo-cation of the 'invisible hand' was little more than a 'mildly ironic joke'.[29]

The third source and component part of Lenin's Marxism emerged out of the radical politics of the Revolutionary decade in France. Rousseau himself had been terrified of the prospect of revolution and was commit-ted to the view that republican politics could not possibly flourish in a large-scale inegalitarian society such as modern France. Nevertheless, many of the Revolutionaries looked to his political writings for inspira-tion, none more so than the Jacobin leader and architect of the Terror, Maximilien Robespierre, with his obsessive discourse of virtue, and in 1794 Rousseau's remains were exhumed and reburied in the Pantheon in Paris, alongside those of his nemesis, Voltaire. And if the political argu-ments of the period were so often conducted in Rousseauist vocabulary, the Revolution had its strikingly Stoic dimension, too.

On 29 Prairial, An III—or 17 June 1795, according to the once and future Gregorian calendar—Gilbert Romme, who was himself the author of the Republican calendar, together with five of his fellow Montagnard deputies and various others, was sentenced to death by a military tribunal that had been appointed to restore order to Paris after the popular upris-ings of 12 Germinal and 1 Prairial. Shortly after the sentence was handed down, the six deputies attempted to kill themselves with two concealed knives and a pair of scissors, and four of them succeeded. Their language was Stoic: Romme had told the court that although 'mon corps est à la loi, mon âme reste indépendante et ne peut être flétrie';[30] his colleagues Pierre Amable Soubrany, Jean-Marie Goujon, and Pierre Bourbotte simi-larly used the rhetoric of Epictetus and Seneca and invoked the example of Cato the Younger.[31] The dramas of the French Revolution, Karl Marx memorably noted, were often played out 'in Roman costume and with Roman phrases',[32] and these Montagnards' suicides were exemplary in this regard; Thomas Carlyle called them the '*ultimi Romanorum*'.[33] As Dorinda Outram has remarked in her discussion of these and other 'he-roic suicides', 'It was far better to die thus, in front of a chosen audience of one's equals, than in the derisorily brief theatre and before the unpre-dictable, heterogeneous spectators at the guillotine.' But as she also goes on to observe, 'If Stoicism had functions, it also had effects', one of which was that it 'undoubtedly made the Terror easier to operate against the political élite'.[34]

The political Stoicism of the French Revolution was an undoubtedly masculine affair.[35] But if, finally, we step outside the scaffolding provided by Lenin's argument and cross over to the other side of the English Channel, we can find Stoic philosophy being creatively appropriated by women for their own political projects in the era of the Revolution. Catharine Macaulay had used Elizabeth Carter's edition of Epictetus extensively when she was writing her *Treatise on the Immutability of Moral Truth*, published in 1783, which offered an explicit defence of Stoicism against the arguments of Hobbes and Hume.[36] When Mary Wollstonecraft reviewed Macaulay's 1790 *Letters on Education*, she specifically commended the sympathetic exposition of Stoic principles: 'the doctrines of the Stoics are clearly stated by Mrs. M. and some unjust aspersions wiped off, which bigotry and ignorance have industriously propagated, to render doctrines ridiculous or odious, which deserve respect'.[37] This favourable orientation to Stoicism is also visible in the argument of Wollstonecraft's 1792 *Vindication of the Rights of Woman*. There we find relentless appeals to reason and nature as trumps over mere social convention, however widespread; we find the Stoic denigration of emotion deployed to rescue women from their identification as passionate creatures, thereby to restore them to rationality, and therefore to equality with men; and we find the critique of appearance and reputation, which draws on Stoic elements discernible in Rousseau.[38] And if this book opened with Ernst Cassirer's opinion that Thomas Jefferson was 'speaking the language of Stoic philosophy' when he drafted the Declaration of Independence, it can appropriately close with perhaps the finest example of Mary Wollstonecraft doing the same:

> Would men but generously snap our chains, and be content with rational fellowship instead of slavish obedience, they would find us more observant daughters, more affectionate sisters, more faithful wives, more reasonable mothers—in a word, better citizens. We should then love them with true affection, because we should learn to respect ourselves.[39].

Notes

PREFACE

1. Ernst Cassirer, *The Myth of the State* (New Haven, CT: Yale University Press, 1961), pp. 166–70.

2. But see, e.g., Gérard Verbeke, *The Presence of Stoicism in Medieval Thought* (Washington, DC: Catholic University of America Press, 1983).

3. Gerhard Oestreich, *Neostoicism and the Early Modern State* (Cambridge: Cambridge University Press, 1982), p. 70.

4. William J. Bouwsma, 'The Two Faces of Humanism: Stoicism and Augustinianism in Renaissance Thought', in Heiko A. Oberman and Thomas A. Brady, Jr., eds., *Itinerarium Italicum: The Profile of the Italian Renaissance in the Mirror of Its European Transformation* (Leiden: E. J. Brill, 1975), p. 20.

5. Ibid. p. 22.

6. Thomas Hobbes, *Leviathan*, Richard Tuck, ed. (Cambridge: Cambridge University Press, 1991), chap. 28, p. 221, quoting Job 41:34.

7. Christopher J. Berry, 'Smith under Strain', *European Journal of Political Theory*, vol. 3, no. 4 (October 2004), p. 457.

8. Diogenes Laertius, *Lives of Eminent Philosophers*, R. D. Hicks, trans. (Cambridge, MA: Harvard University Press, 1975), 7.38ff.

9. Justus Lipsius, *On Constancy*, John Stradling, trans., John Sellars, ed. (Exeter: Bristol Phoenix Press, 2006), 1.18, p. 65.

10. Cicero, *On Moral Ends*, Julia Annas, ed. (Cambridge: Cambridge University Press, 2001), 3.74, pp. 87–88.

11. T. J. Hochstrasser, *Natural Law Theories in the Early Enlightenment* (Cambridge: Cambridge University Press, 2000), p. 1; also John Dunn, 'The Identity of the History of Ideas', in *Political Obligation in Historical Context* (Cambridge: Cambridge University Press, 1980), pp. 13–28.

12. Cf. T. S. Eliot, 'Shakespeare and the Stoicism of Seneca' (1927), in *Selected Essays* (London: Faber & Faber, 1951), pp. 126–40.

13. Hochstrasser, *Natural Law Theories*, pp. 1, 38. Samuel Pufendorf, *De origine et progressu disciplinae juris naturalis*, reprinted in Pufendorf, *Eris Scandica und andere polemische Schriften über das Naturrecht,* Fiammetta Palladini, ed. (Berlin: Akademie Verlag, 2002), pp. 124–28.

Prologue

1. In the references to Augustine's *The City of God against the Pagans* that follow, I have used the Latin text in the seven-volume Loeb Classical Library edition (Cambridge, MA: Harvard University Press, 1957–72) and the English trans-

lation by R. W. Dyson (Cambridge: Cambridge University Press, 1998), to which the page numbers refer.

2. '[F]ecerunt itaque ciuitates duas amores duo'. *City of God* 14.28, p. 632.

3. Augustine, *On Christian Doctrine*, D. W. Robertson, trans. (New York: Liberal Arts Press, 1958), 1.27. Oliver O'Donovan, *The Problem of Self-Love in Augustine* (New Haven, CT: Yale University Press, 1980).

4. Augustine, 'Second Discourse on Psalm 31', in *St. Augustine on the Psalms*, Scholastica Hebgin and Felicitas Corrigan, trans. (Westminster, MD: Newman Press, 1960), vol. 2, p. 69.

5. *City of God* 5, esp. chaps. 8–10, pp. 197–206. Marcia L. Colish, *The Stoic Tradition from Antiquity to the Early Middle Ages* (Leiden: E. J. Brill, 1985), vol. 2, pp. 229–32.

6. Cicero, *On Moral Ends*, Julia Annas, ed. (Cambridge: Cambridge University Press, 2001), 5.22.

7. Cf. Colish, *The Stoic Tradition*, vol. 2, pp. 208–9. Also on Augustine on Stoic ethics, see Richard Sorabji, *Emotion and Peace of Mind: From Stoic Agitation to Christian Temptation* (Oxford: Oxford University Press, 2000), pp. 375–80. Lactantius, *Divine Institutes*, Anthony Bowen and Peter Garnsey, trans. (Liverpool: Liverpool University Press, 2003), passim.

8. Cf. *City of God* 18.1, p. 821.

9. Ibid., 13.24, p. 580.

10. Ibid., 14.26, p. 629; 14.20, p. 619.

11. Ibid., 14.1, p. 581.

12. Ibid., 14.2, p. 582.

13. Ibid., 14.2, p. 583, quoting Galatians 5:19.

14. Ibid., 14.2, pp. 583–84.

15. *City of God* 14.3, p. 585, where Augustine quotes from Virgil, *Aeneid* 6.730ff.

16. *City of God* 14.3, p. 585, where the reference is given to Cicero, *Tusculan Disputations* 3.11.24 and 4.6.11f.

17. *City of God* 14.3, p. 585.

18. Ibid.

19. Ibid., 14.3, p. 586.

20. Ibid., 14.5, p. 589.

21. Ibid., 14.6, p. 590.

22. Sorabji, *Emotion and Peace of Mind*, esp. chaps. 2 and 21. For Epictetus on the *prohairesis*, see A. A. Long, *Epictetus: A Stoic and Socratic Guide to Life* (Oxford: Oxford University Press, 2002), chap. 8.

23. Sorabji, *Emotion and Peace of Mind*, pp. 244–46.

24. *City of God* 14.8, p. 595.

25. 1 Corinthians 7:8ff; *City of God* 14.8, p. 596.

26. *City of God* 14.8, p. 596.

27. Ibid., 14.9, p. 597.

28. Ibid., 14.9, p. 599.

29. Mark 3:5, John 11:15, 11:35, Luke 22:15, Matthew 26:38. *City of God* 14.9, p. 599.

30. Romans 1:31; Cicero, *Tusculan Disputations* 3.6.12; *City of God* 14.9, pp. 599–600.

31. *City of God* 14.9, p. 600.

32. Ibid., 14.9, p. 600.

33. Ibid., 14.9, p. 600.

34. Ibid., 14. 9, p. 601.

35. Ibid., 14.9, p. 602. Emphases added.

36. Ibid., 14.10, pp. 602–3.

37. Ibid., 14.10, p. 603.

38. Colish, *The Stoic Tradition*, vol. 2, p. 225.

39. *City of God* 14.10, p. 603.

40. Ibid., 14.10, p. 603.

41. Ibid., 14.11, p. 604.

42. Ibid., 14.11, p. 605.

43. Ibid., 14.11, p. 606.

44. 'Porro, male voluntatis initium quae potuit esse nisi superbia?'

45. *City of God* 14.13, p. 608.

46. Ibid., 14.13, p. 610.

47. E.g., ibid., 22.30, pp. 1178–82.

48. Ibid., 13.15, pp. 556–57.

49. Augustine, *Confessions*, William Watts, trans. (Cambridge, MA: Harvard University Press, 1989), 2.4.

Chapter One
Justus Lipsius and the Post-Machiavellian Prince

1. Mark Morford, *Stoics and Neostoics: Rubens and the Circle of Lipsius* (Princeton, NJ: Princeton University Press, 1991).

2. Press release issued in Brussels by the Council of the European Union, 18 December 2003, 'Signature of the deed of transfer of the Justus Lipsius Building, seat of the Council of the European Union'.

3. For a longer summary biography, see Justus Lipsius, ed., *Politica: Six Books of Politics or Political Instruction*, Jan Waszink, ed. (Assen: Van Gorcum, 2004), pp. 15–24.

4. Anthony Levi, SJ, *French Moralists: The Theory of the Passions 1585–1649* (Oxford: Clarendon Press, 1964), p. 5.

5. See, e.g., Larry Frohman, 'Neo-Stoicism and the Transition to Modernity in Wilhelm Dilthey's Philosophy of History', *Journal of the History of Ideas*, vol. 56, no. 2 (1995), p. 263.

6. Fortunat Strowski, *Pascal et son temps*, vol. 1, *De Montaigne à Pascal* (Paris: Plon-Nourrit, 1907), chap. 2.

7. Léontine Zanta, *La renaissance du stoïcisme au XVIᵉ siècle* (Paris: H. Champion, 1914). For a sketch of Zanta's life, see Robert Garric's introduction to Pierre Teilhard de Chardin, *Letters to Leontine Zanta*, Bernard Wall, trans. (London: Collins, 1969); Henri Maleprade, *Léontine Zanta: Vertueuse aventurière du feminisme* (Paris: Rive droit, 1997). Also Toril Moi, *Simone de Beau-*

voir: The Making of an Intellectual Woman (Oxford: Blackwell, 1994), pp. 50–51.

8. J. W. Allen, *A History of Political Thought in the Sixteenth Century* (London: Methuen, 1977).

9. Jason Lewis Saunders, *Justus Lipsius: The Philosophy of Renaissance Stoicism* (New York: Liberal Arts Press, 1955).

10. Michel de Montaigne, 'De l'institution des enfans', *Essais*, 1.26, in *Oeuvres complètes*, Albert Thibaudet and Maurice Rat, eds. (Paris: Gallimard, 1962), p. 147.

11. Gerhard Oestreich, *Neostoicism and the Early Modern State* (Cambridge: Cambridge University Press, 1982).

12. Ibid., p. 70.

13. Ibid., pp. 58–62.

14. Ibid., p. 45.

15. Ibid., p. 48.

16. Ibid., pp. 52–54.

17. Ibid., p. 71

18. Ibid., p. 77.

19. Ibid., p. 8.

20. Max Weber, *The Protestant Ethic and the Spirit of Capitalism*, trans. Talcott Parsons (London: George Allen & Unwin, 1930).

21. Felix Gilbert, ed., *The Historical Essays of Otto Hintze* (New York: Oxford University Press, 1975), pp. 88–154, cited in Oestreich, *Neostoicism*, p. 69.

22. Oestreich, *Neostoicism*, pp. 68ff.

23. Charles Taylor, *A Secular Age* (Cambridge, MA: Belknap Press of Harvard University Press, 2007), p. 789.

24. Lipsius, *Politica*, p. 13.

25. The italicised quotations come from Cicero, *Pro caelio* and *De natura deorum*, respectively.

26. Lipsius, *Politica*, p. 13.

27. Philip S. Gorski, *The Disciplinary Revolution: Calvinism and the Rise of the State in Early Modern Europe* (Chicago: University of Chicago Press, 2003), pp. 74–75; see also pp. 29, 31.

28. Peter N. Miller, 'Nazis and Neostoics: Otto Brunner and Gerhard Oestreich before and after the Second World War', *Past & Present*, vol. 176 (2002), pp. 144–86.

29. Ibid., p. 171.

30. Ibid., p. 185.

31. Ibid., p. 177.

32. Ibid., p. 174, translating Lipsius, *De constantia* 1.3: 'victor aliquis pugnando evasit, nemo fugiendo'.

33. Ibid., p. 175.

34. Ibid., p. 163.

35. Lipsius, *Politica*, pp. 100–101.

36. Oestreich, *Neostoicism*, p. 73.

37. Martin van Gelderen, 'The Machiavellian Moment and the Dutch Revolt: The Rise of Neostoicism and Dutch Republicanism', in Gisela Bock, Quentin

Skinner, and Maurizio Viroli, eds., *Machiavelli and Republicanism* (Cambridge: Cambridge University Press, 1990).

38. Richard Tuck, *Philosophy and Government, 1572–1651* (Cambridge: Cambridge University Press, 1993), pp. 57–58.

39. Robert Bireley, SJ, *The Counter-Reformation Prince: Anti-Machiavellianism or Catholic Statecraft in Early Modern Europe* (Chapel Hill: University of North Carolina Press, 1990), chap. 4.

40. Lipsius, *Politica*, pp. 98–102.

41. Jan Papy, 'Justus Lipsius', *Stanford Encyclopedia of Philosophy*, http://plato.stanford.edu/entries/justus-lipsius/.

42. Bireley, *Counter-Reformation Prince*, p. 73.

43. Ibid., p. 77.

44. Ibid., p. 81.

45. Ibid., p. 81.

46. Ibid., p. 85. Emphasis added.

47. Lipsius, *Politica*, pp. 120–21.

48. Ibid., p. 173.

49. Ibid., p. 175.

50. Bireley, *Counter-Reformation Prince*, p. 80.

51. Lipsius, *Politica*, p. 186.

52. Ibid., p. 713.

53. Ibid., p. 180.

54. Ibid., pp. 230–31.

55. Ibid., p. 184.

56. Papy, 'Justus Lipsius'.

57. Quentin Skinner, *The Foundations of Modern Political Thought* (Cambridge: Cambridge University Press, 1978), vol. 1, p. 129.

58. Ibid., p. 135.

59. Lipsius, *Politica*, p. 99.

60. Peter Stacey, *Roman Monarchy and the Renaissance Prince* (Cambridge: Cambridge University Press, 2007), passim.

61. Tuck, *Philosophy and Government*, p. 20.

62. Stacey, *Roman Monarchy*, p. 44.

63. Ibid., p. 46.

64. Ibid., p. 30.

65. Ibid., p. 31.

66. Ibid., p. 31.

67. Ibid., p. 48.

68. Ibid., p. 33, quoting Seneca, *De clementia* 2.6.3.

69. Stacey, *Roman Monarchy*, p. 61.

70. Ibid., p. 65.

71. Ibid., p. 66.

72. Ibid., p. 67.

73. Ibid., p. 68.

74. Ibid., p. 69.

75. Ibid., p. 70.

76. Ibid., p. 72.

77. Ibid., pp. 208–9.

78. Niccolò Machiavelli, *The Prince*, Harvey C. Mansfield, trans. (Chicago: University of Chicago Press, 1998), p. 5; Stacey, *Roman Monarchy*, p. 260.

79. Stacey, *Roman Monarchy*, p. 286.

80. Machiavelli, *The Prince*, p. 98; Stacey, *Roman Monarchy*, p. 287.

81. Stacey, *Roman Monarchy*, p. 283.

82. Ibid., pp. 282–83, 290.

83. Ibid., p. 290.

84. Ibid., p. 273.

85. Lipsius, *Politica* 1.4, p. 271, quoting (in italics) Livy 25.6.7.

86. Ibid., 2.10, p. 319 ('the sun'); 2.12, p. 325 ('the moon').

87. Ibid., preface, p. 227. See also 2.9, p. 317.

88. Ibid., p. 81.

89. Ibid.

90. Justus Lipsius, *Iusti Lipsi Epistolae*, A. Gerlo, M. A. Nauwelaerts, and H.D.L. Vervliet, eds. (Brussels: Koninklijke Academie voor Wetenschappen, Letteren, en Schone Kunsten van Belgie,1978–), vol. 1, 83 07 12: 'Namquam ille magnus erit, cui Ramus est magnus', cited in Lipsius, *Politica*, p. 53, n. 14.

91. In Victoria Kahn's words, in the *The Prince*, 'prudence has become what its critics always feared it would: a technical skill divorced from ethical considerations'. Kahn, *Rhetoric, Prudence and Skepticism* (Ithaca, NY: Cornell University Press, 1985), p. 186.

92. Lipsius, *Politica* 1.1, p. 261.

93. Ibid., 1.7, p. 283.

94. Ibid., 3.1, p. 349, quoting (in italics) Aristotle, *Politics* 1277b25.

95. Machiavelli, *The Prince*, p. 98.

96. Lipsius, *Politica* 1.4, p. 271.

97. Ibid.

98. Waszink discusses these objections and Lipsius's response in Lipsius, *Politica*, p. 180.

99. Ibid., p. 275.

100. Ibid., Epistle Dedicatory, p. 227.

101. Ibid., 2.2, p. 299. The italicised words are from Tacitus, *Annals* 1.12: 'unum imperii corpus, unius animo regendum'.

102. Lipsius, *Politica*, p. 13.

103. Seneca, *De clementia* 1.18.1. Justus Lipsius, *Six bookes of politickes or ciuil doctrine*, William Jones, trans. (London: Richard Field, 1594), p. 23.

104. Lipsius, *Politica* 2.4, p. 305.

105. Ibid., 2.4, p. 307, quoting (in italics) Tacitus, *Histories* 1.30.

106. Lipsius, *Politica* 2.6, p. 309; 'quae non aliud, quam subditorum commodum, securitas, salus'.

107. '[B]eata civium vita proposita est'; Cicero, *De re publica* 5.8 and *Epistulae ad Atticum* 8.11.1.

108. Lipsius, *Politica* 4.14, p. 531, quoting (in italics) Seneca the Elder, *Controversiae* 9.4.5.

109. Tuck, *Philosophy and Government*, pp. 57–58.

110. Ibid., pp. 50, 51.

111. Ibid., p. 54.

112. Justus Lipsius, *On Constancy*, John Stradling, trans., John Sellars, ed. (Exeter: Bristol Phoenix Press, 2006), 1.7, p. 42.

113. A. H. T. Levi, 'The Relationship of Stoicism and Scepticism: Justus Lipsius', in Jill Kraye and M. W. F. Stone, eds., *Humanism and Early Modern Philosophy* (London: Routledge, 2000), p. 94.

114. Lipsius, *Politica*, 'The rationale and form of this work', p. 231.

115. Ibid., 3.5, pp. 358–60.

116. Ibid., 4.9, p. 427.

117. Ibid., 4.9, pp. 429–31.

118. Ibid., 1.7, p. 283.

119. Machiavelli, *The Prince*, p. 91.

120. Justus Lipsius, *C. Cornelii Taciti Opera quae exstant* (Louvain: Plantin, 1588), sig. *4, cited in Tuck, *Philosophy and Government*, p. 46.

121. See table 1 in Lipsius, *Politica*, p. 163, for further information about these citations.

122. Lipsius, *Politica* 4.1, p. 383.

123. Ibid., 4.1, p. 385.

124. Machiavelli, *The Prince*, pp. 12–15.

125. Ibid., p. 95.

126. Ibid., p. 99.

127. Ibid., p. 100.

128. Ibid., p. 101.

129. Lipsius, *Politica* 5.5, p. 551.

130. Lipsius, *Politica* 5.5, pp. 551, 553, 555, quoting Sallust, *Jugurthan War*, 83.1, Augustine, *The City of God against the Pagans*, 19, and Pliny, *Panegyricus* 16.2, respectively.

131. Machiavelli, *The Prince*, pp. 13–14.

132. Ibid., p. 80.

133. Niccolò Machiavelli, *Discourses on Livy*, Harvey C. Mansfield and Nathan Tarcov, trans. (Chicago: University of Chicago Press, 1996), 1.27, p. 62.

134. Machiavelli, *The Prince*, p. 98.

135. Lipsius, *Politica* 1.7, p. 285; Lipsius, *Sixe bookes of politickes*, p. 12.

136. Michel Foucault, *Security, Territory, Population: Lectures at the Collège de France, 1977–1978*, Michael Senellart, ed. (Basingstoke: Palgrave Macmillan, 2007), p. 89.

137. Michel Foucault, *Discipline and Punish: The Birth of the Prison*, Alan Sheridan, trans. (New York: Pantheon Books, 1979), pp. 135–38, 170.

138. Foucault, *Security, Territory, Population*, p. 88.

139. Ibid., p. 89.

140. Ibid., p. 91.

141. Ibid., p. 92.

142. Ibid., pp. 94–95.

143. Ibid., p. 99.

144. Lipsius, *Politica* 2.1, p. 295.

145. Foucault, *Security, Territory, Population*, pp. 98–99.

146. Lipsius, *Politica* 2.6, p. 309.

147. See note 116, above.

148. Gorski, *The Disciplinary Revolution*, p. 24.

Chapter Two
Grotius, Stoicism, and *Oikeiosis*

1. These works include *Natural Rights Theories: Their Origin and Development* (Cambridge: Cambridge University Press, 1979); 'Grotius, Carneades and Hobbes', *Grotiana*, vol. 4 (1983), pp. 43–62; 'The "Modern" Theory of Natural Law', in Anthony Pagden, ed., *The Languages of Political Theory in Early-Modern Europe* (Cambridge: Cambridge University Press, 1987), pp. 99–119; 'Grotius and Selden', in J. H. Burns and Mark Goldie, eds., *The Cambridge History of Political Thought, 1450–1700* (Cambridge: Cambridge University Press, 1991), pp. 499–529; *Philosophy and Government, 1572–1651* (Cambridge: Cambridge University Press, 1993); *The Rights of War and Peace: Political Thought and the International Order from Grotius to Kant* (Oxford: Oxford University Press, 1999); and, more recently, the introduction to his and Jean Barbeyrac's new edition of Grotius, *The Rights of War and Peace* (Indianapolis, IN: Liberty Fund, 2005), 3 vols.

2. See, e.g., Knud Haakonssen, *Natural Law and Moral Philosophy: From Grotius to the Scottish Enlightenment* (Cambridge: Cambridge University Press, 1996); Istvan Hont, *Jealousy of Trade: International Competition and the Nation-State in Historical Perspective* (Cambridge, MA: Harvard University Press, 2005); Ross Harrison, *Hobbes, Locke, and Confusion's Masterpiece: An Examination of Seventeenth-Century Political Philosophy* (Cambridge: Cambridge University Press, 2003); and J. B. Schneewind, *The Invention of Autonomy* (Cambridge: Cambridge University Press, 1998).

3. Perez Zagorin, 'Hobbes without Grotius', *History of Political Thought*, vol. 21, no. 1 (2000), pp. 16–40; Thomas Mautner, 'Grotius and the Skeptics', *Journal of the History of Ideas*, vol. 66, no. 4 (2005), pp. 577–601.

4. Robert Shaver, 'Grotius on Scepticism and Self-Interest', *Archiv für Geschichte der Philosophie*, vol. 78, no. 1 (1996), p. 28.

5. Brian Tierney, *The Idea of Natural Rights: Studies on Natural Rights, Natural Law and Church Law, 1150–1625* (Atlanta, GA: Scholars Press, 1997), p. 323.

6. Grotius, *The Rights of War and Peace*, vol. 1, pp. 79–81.

7. E.g., Tuck, *Philosophy and Government*, pp. 45–64, chap. 5.

8. Tuck, *The Rights of War and Peace*, p. 37 n. 54.

9. Diogenes Laertius, *Lives of Eminent Philosophers*, R. D. Hicks, trans. (Cambridge, MA: Harvard University Press, 1975), 7.85–86; Cicero, in Julia Annas, ed., *On Moral Ends* (Cambridge: Cambridge University Press, 2001), 3.16, p. 70.

10. Tuck, *The Rights of War and Peace*, p. 89.

11. Ibid., p. 95.

12. Ibid., p. 96.

13. Ibid., p. 99.

14. Thomas Mautner, 'Not a Likely Story', *British Journal for the History of Philosophy*, vol. 11, no. 2 (2003); also Mautner, 'Grotius and the Skeptics'.

15. Schneewind, *The Invention of Autonomy*, p. 175.

16. Annabel Brett, 'Natural Right and Civil Community: The Civil Philosophy of Hugo Grotius', *Historical Journal*, vol. 45, no. 1 (2002), pp. 31–51.

17. Max Pohlenz, *Die Stoa: Geschichte einer geistigen Bewegung* (Göttingen: Vandenhoeck & Ruprecht, 1978), vol. 1, p. 471; vol. 2, p. 229. See Laurens C. Winkel, 'Les origines antiques de *l'appetitus societatis* de Grotius', *Tijdschrift voor Rechtsgeschiedenis*, vol. 68 (2000), pp. 394–95.

18. Matija Berljak, *Il diritto naturale e il suo rapporto con la divinità in Ugo Grozio* (Rome: Università Gregoriana Editrice, 1978).

19. Jon Miller, 'Innate Ideas in Stoicism and Grotius', in Hans W. Blom and Laurens C. Winkel, eds., *Grotius and the Stoa* (Assen: Van Gorcum, 2004), p. 162.

20. Ibid., p. 164.

21. Reinhard Brandt, 'Self-Consciousness and Self-Care: On the Tradition of *Oikeiosis* in the Modern Age', in Blom and Winkel, *Grotius and the Stoa,* pp. 73–91.

22. Cicero, *On Moral Ends* 3.18, p. 70; Seneca, *Epistula ad Lucilium* 9.17. For these sources, see Winkel, 'Les origines antiques de *l'appetitus societatis* de Grotius', p. 400. Cf. Benjamin Straumann, who suggests that Vázquez may have been Grotius's much more immediate source. Straumann, '*Oikeiosis* and *appetitus societatis*: Hugo Grotius' Ciceronian Argument for Natural Law and Just War', *Grotiana*, vol. 24–25 (2003–4), p. 45 n. 12.

23. Jon Miller, 'Stoics, Grotius and Spinoza on Moral Deliberation', in Jon Miller and Brad Inwood, eds., *Hellenistic and Early Modern Philosophy* (Cambridge: Cambridge University Press, 2003), p. 137 n. 28.

24. Straumann, '*Oikeiosis* and *appetitus societatis*', p. 66. See also his *Hugo Grotius und die Antike: Römisches Recht und römische Ethik im frühneuzeitlichen Naturrecht* (Baden-Baden: Nomos Verlagsgesellschaft, 2007), esp. pp. 143–57.

25. The three most important single texts for our knowledge of the ethics of the early Stoa are *De finibus* 3, Diogenes Laertius 7.84–131, and Arius Didymus's epitome of Stoic ethics, as preserved in Stobaeus 2.7.

26. Julia Annas, *The Morality of Happiness* (Oxford: Oxford University Press, 1993).

27. The passage that fills most of p. 264 of her *Morality of Happiness* is the same passage that Grotius both directly quotes from and otherwise paraphrases in *DJBP* 1.2.1.1–2. See below.

28. John Cooper, 'Eudaimonism and the Appeal to Nature in the Morality of Happiness: Comments on Julia Annas, *The Morality of Happiness*', *Philosophy and Phenomenological Research*, vol. 55, no. 3 (September 1995), pp. 587–98; Annas, 'Reply to Cooper', ibid., pp. 599–610. For a later reflection by Annas, see her 'Ethics in Stoic Philosophy', *Phronesis*, vol. 52, no. 1 (2007), esp. p. 85 n. 56.

29. E.g., Annas, *The Morality of Happiness*, p. 275.

30. This is not a universally shared view: cf. Arius Didymus, whose presentation of Stoic ethics ignores it altogether.

31. Annas, *The Morality of Happiness*, p. 262; A. A. Long and D. N. Sedley, *The Hellenistic Philosophers* (Cambridge: Cambridge University Press, 1987), vol. 1, p. 351.

32. Annas, *The Morality of Happiness*, pp. 262–63.

33. Diogenes Laertius, *Lives of Eminent Philosophers*, R. D. Hicks, trans., 2 vols. (Cambridge, MA: Harvard University Press, 1975),7.85–86; Cicero, *On Moral Ends* 3.16–17, pp. 69–70.

34. See note 23 above.

35. Cicero, *On Moral Ends* 3.23, p. 72.

36. Annas, *The Morality of Happiness*, p. 263.

37. Plutarch, 'On Stoic Self-Contradictions' 1038b, in *Moralia*, vol. 13, pt. 2, Harold Cherniss, trans. (Cambridge, MA: Harvard University Press, 1976).

38. Annas, *The Morality of Happiness*, p. 265.

39. Ibid., p. 265.

40. This passage is preserved in Stobaeus 4.671–73 and reproduced in Long and Sedley, *The Hellenistic Philosophers*, 57G.

41. Annas, *The Morality of Happiness*, pp. 267ff.

42. See Miller, 'Stoics, Grotius and Spinoza', pp. 117–20.

43. Tad Brennan, *The Stoic Life: Emotions, Duties, and Fate* (Oxford: Clarendon Press, 2005), p. 206.

44. Cicero, *On Duties*, M. T. Griffin and E. M. Atkins, eds. (Cambridge: Cambridge University Press), 3.42.

45. Brennan, *The Stoic Life*, p. 211.

46. Ibid., pp. 192–94.

47. Robert Nozick, *Anarchy, State, and Utopia* (New York: Basic Books, 1974).

48. Cicero, *On Duties* 2.73.

49. Long and Sedley, *The Hellenistic Philosophers*, vol. 1, p. 351, again.

50. A. A. Long, 'Stoic Philosophers on Persons, Property-Ownership, and Community', in his *From Epicurus to Epictetus: Studies in Hellenistic and Roman Philosophy* (Oxford: Oxford University Press, 2006), p. 345.

51. Ibid., p. 352.

52. Ibid., p. 357.

53. Ibid., p. 348.

54. Hugo Grotius, *De Iure Belli ac Pacis Libri Tres* (Amsterdam: Johannes & Cornelius Blaeu, 1642).

55. The bracketed material was added to the 1631 edition: Hugo Grotius, *De Iure Belli ac Pacis Libri Tres* (Amsterdam: Willem Jansz Blaeu, 1631). Grotius credits Aulus Gellius 12.5 as the source of the Greek original of Cicero's *prima naturae*.

56. Grotius, *The Rights of War and Peace*, vol. 1, pp. 180–81.

57. Hugo Grotius, *De Iure Belli ac Pacis Libri Tres* (Paris: Nicholas Buon, 1625), pp. 16–17. Emphasis and brackets added.

58. Grotius, *The Rights of War and Peace* 1.2.1.3, vol. 1, p. 183.

59. Ibid., vol. 1, p. 184.

60. Cicero, *On Moral Ends* 3.70, p. 87.

61. Grotius, *The Rights of War and Peace*, vol. 1, p. 184.

62. E.g., Martha C. Nussbaum, 'Patriotism and Cosmopolitanism', in Joshua Cohen, ed., *For Love of Country: Debating the Limits of Patriotism* (Boston: Beacon Press, 1996), pp. 6–9.

63. E.g., the extracts reproduced in Long and Sedley, *The Hellenistic Philosophers*, 57C–D.

64. The 'concentric circles' passage is reproduced in Long and Sedley, *The Hellenistic Philosophers*, 57G.

65. Jon Miller, 'Grotius and Stobaeus', *Grotiana*, vols. 26–28 (2005–7), pp. 104–26.

66. Gloria Vivenza, *Adam Smith and the Classics* (Oxford: Oxford University Press, 2001), pp. 204–5.

67. Grotius, *The Rights of War and Peace*, vol. 3, p. 1747.

68. See, e.g., Diogenes Laertius, *Lives of Eminent Philosophers*, where a discussion of *oikeiosis* as it pertains to all animal (and also plant) life is found at 7.85–86, before Zeno's treatise *Peri anthropou* is mentioned at the start of 7.87, and the discussion of the *oikeiosis* specific to human beings follows; or see Cicero, *On Moral Ends*, again, where the examination of *oikeiosis* begins with remarks about animal life in general (3.16, pp. 69–70), proceeds to a consideration of infants in general (it's not clear that the infants discussed at 3.16 are specifically human), and has examples drawn from human children (at the end of 3.17, p. 70), human adult males (the discussion of beards and male nipples at 3.18, p. 70), and animal life (the dove's plumage, also at 3.18) before becoming a discussion solely and specifically concerning human beings at the start of 3.21, p. 71.

69. Grotius, *The Rights of War and Peace*, vol. 1, p. 83 n. 3.

70. Ibid., vol. 3, pp. 1747–48.

71. Ibid., vol. 3, p. 1749.

72. Ibid., vol. 1, pp. 83–84.

73. Istvan Hont writes that the first edition of the *Prolegomena* 'suggests that man is born self-interested in order to become social; the second that man is by nature social and thus can correct his self-interested behavior'. Hont, *Jealousy of Trade*, p. 19 n. 33. Similarly, Jon Miller writes that 'As evidence that humans are naturally social, Grotius asserts in § 7 that "In children, even before their training has begun, some disposition to do good to others appears."' Miller, 'Innate Ideas', p. 164. Both claims seem to me to be troublesome: Grotius is arguing that children's apparently altruistic behaviour is to be explained the same way as it would be in animals, as motivated by an 'extrinsic principle' rather than being internally generated from the creature's own constitution.

74. Grotius, *The Rights of War and Peace*, vol. 1, pp. 84–85.

75. Cicero, *On Moral Ends* 3.20, p. 71.

76. Straumann, '*Oikeiosis* and *appetitus societatis*', p. 44.

77. Miller, 'Stoics, Grotius and Spinoza', pp. 118, 119.

78. Stephen Buckle, *Natural Law and the Theory of Property: Grotius to Hume* (Oxford: Clarendon Press, 1991), p. 20.

79. Ibid., esp. pp. 29–32.

Chapter Three
From Lipsius to Hobbes

1. Jacqueline Lagrée, 'Constancy and Coherence', in Steven K. Strange and Jack Zupko, eds., *Stoicism: Traditions and Transformations* (Cambridge: Cambridge University Press, 2004), p. 151.

2. Justus Lipsius, *On Constancy*, John Stradling, trans., John Sellars, ed. (Exeter: Bristol Phoenix Press, 2006), 1.1, p. 31.

3. Ibid., 1.1, p. 32.

4. Ibid., 1.4, p. 37. The Latin is from Lipsius, *De constantia libri duo* (London: George Bishop, 1586), p. 6.

5. Lipsius, *On Constancy*, 1.4, p. 37.

6. Ibid., 1.4, p. 37.

7. Ibid.

8. Ibid., 1.4, pp. 37–38.

9. Charles Taylor, *A Secular Age* (Cambridge, MA: Belknap Press of Harvard University Press, 2007), p. 115.

10. Ibid. Lipsius, *On Constancy*, 1.12, pp. 52–53, for the discussion of 'pity' (to be rejected) and 'mercy' (which is a good thing).

11. Taylor, *A Secular Age*, p. 115.

12. Cited in Geoffrey Miles, *Shakespeare and the Constant Romans* (Oxford: Clarendon Press, 1996), p. 80.

13. Simon Goulart, 'Ample discours sur la doctrine des Stoïques', in *Oeuvres morales et mêlées* (Geneva, 1606), vol. 3, p. 317, cited in Lagrée, 'Constancy and Coherence', p. 165.

14. Joseph Hall, *Heaven upon Earth, and Characters of Vertues and Vices*, Rudolf Kirk, ed. (New Brunswick, NJ: Rutgers University Press, 1939), p. 88, cited in Miles, *Shakespeare*, p. 81.

15. For a full discussion of constancy in Montaigne on which these remarks draw, see Miles, *Shakespeare*, chap. 5, pp. 83–109.

16. Montaigne, 'On Constancy', in *The Complete Essays*, M. A. Screech, trans. (Harmondsworth: Penguin, 1993), 1.12, p. 47.

17. Montaigne, 'On Drunkenness', ibid., 2.2, p. 381.

18. Ibid., 2.2, p. 390.

19. Ibid., 2.2, p. 389.

20. Ibid., 2.2, pp. 389–90. See also Miles, *Shakespeare*, pp. 91–93.

21. Miles, *Shakespeare*, chap. 8, pp. 149–68.

22. Ibid., p. 118. For more on Shakespeare's use of Plutarch, see also Christopher Pelling, 'The Shaping of *Coriolanus*: Dionysius, Plutarch and Shakespeare', in his *Plutarch and History* (Swansea: Duckworth, 2002), pp. 387–411.

23. Plutarch, *The lives of the noble Grecians and Romanes compared together*, Thomas North, trans. (London: Thomas Vautroullier and John Wight, 1579), p. 237.

24. Ibid., p. 248. Miles, *Shakespeare*, pp. 117–20.

25. Miles, *Shakespeare*, p. 120.

26. Niccolò Machiavelli, *Discourses on Livy*, Harvey C. Mansfield and Nathan Tarcov, eds. (Chicago: University of Chicago Press, 1996), p. 24. Livy, 2.33–40; see also R. M. Ogilvie, *A Commentary on Livy, Books 1–5* (Oxford: Clarendon Press, 1965), pp. 314ff.

27. William Shakespeare, *Coriolanus*, 4.7.41–45, cited in Miles, *Shakespeare*, pp. 121, 152.

28. Shakespeare, *Coriolanus*, 4.7.49–50.

29. Quentin Skinner, *The Foundations of Modern Political Thought* (Cambridge: Cambridge University Press, 1978), vol. 2, p. 278.

30. Ibid., vol. 2, p. 279.

31. Ibid., vol. 2, p. 281.

32. Lipsius, *Manuductionis ad Stoicam philosophiam libri tres*, 1.19, in his *Opera Omnia* (Wesel: Andreas van Hoogenhuysen, 1675), vol. 4, pp. 681–82, quoting Aulus Gellius, *Attic Nights*, 17.19 (in Greek: *anechou kai apechou*).

33. Miriam Griffin, 'The Flavians', in Alan K. Bowman, Peter Garnsey, and Dominic Rathbone, eds., *The Cambridge Ancient History*, 2nd ed., vol. 11, *The High Empire, AD 70–192* (Cambridge: Cambridge University Press), pp. 42–43. See also Griffin, *Nero: The End of a Dynasty* (London: Batsford, 1984).

34. Tacitus, *The Annals*, A. J. Woodman, trans. (Indianapolis, IN: Hackett, 2004), 14.12.1, p. 280.

35. For a discussion of this subject on which my own remarks draw, see Marcia L. Colish, *The Stoic Tradition from Antiquity to the Early Middle Ages* (Leiden: E. J. Brill, 1985), vol. 1, pp. 310–13 (though Colish conflates P. Clodius Thrasea Paetus with L. Caesennius Paetus on pp. 311–12, which introduces confusion).

36. '[O]stentanda uirtute', Tacitus, *Agricola* 9.4, in *Agricola and Germany*, Anthony R. Birley, trans. (Oxford: Oxford University Press, 1999), p. 8.

37. Ibid., 42.3–4, p. 31.

38. The final couplet here: 'nolo uirum facili redimit qui sanguine famam / hunc volo, laudari qui sine morte potest'. Martial, *Epigrams* 1.8; see also Peter Brunt, 'Stoicism and the Principate', *Papers of the British School at Rome*, vol. 43 (1975), pp. 7–35.

39. Tacitus, *Annals*, Woodman trans., 14.49.3, p. 297. Cf. George Gilbert Ramsay's remark on this passage in his translation of *The Annals of Tacitus* (London: John Murray, 1909), vol. 2, p. 225. On Seneca, Tacitus, *gloria*, and the like, see Thomas Habinek, 'Seneca's Renown: *Gloria*, *Claritudo*, and the Replication of the Roman Elite', *Classical Antiquity*, vol. 19, no. 2 (2000), pp. 264–303.

40. '[Q]uando etiam sapientibus cupido gloriae novissima exuitur'. Tacitus, *Histories*, 4.6, quoted in Colish, *The Stoic Tradition*, vol. 1, p. 311.

41. John Milton, 'Lycidas', ll. 70–72. The suggestion is made by, e.g., Ramsay, in Tacitus, *Annals*, vol. 2, p. 299.

42. Tacitus, *Annals*, Woodman trans., 14.57.3, p. 301. '[A]dsumpta etiam Stoicorum adrogantia sectaque, quae turbidos et negotiorum adpetentis faciat', quoted in Colish, *The Stoic Tradition*, vol. 1, p. 310.

43. Tacitus, *Annals*, Woodman trans., 15.60.2, p. 334 (Seneca); 15.70.1, p. 338 (Lucan).

44. Colish, *The Stoic Tradition*, vol. 1, p. 311.

45. Tacitus, *Annals*, Woodman trans., 16.21.1, p. 350.

46. Ibid., 16.34.1–35.2, p. 355. Miriam Griffin, 'Philosophy, Cato, and Roman Suicide: I', *Greece & Rome*, 2nd ser., vol. 33, no. 1 (April 1986), pp. 65–66.

47. Tacitus, *Annals*, Woodman trans., 16.22.4, p. 351.

48. Ibid., 16.25.1–2, p. 352.

49. '[A]uctoritatem Stoicae sectae praeferebat, habita et re ad exprimendam imaginem honesti: exercitus, ceterum animo perfidiosus, subdolus, avaritiam ac libidinem occultans.' Ibid., 16.32.3, pp. 354–55 (and quoted in Colish, *The Stoic Tradition*, vol. 1, p. 310).

50. Tacitus, *Annals*, Woodman trans., 16.32.3, p. 355.

51. Trajano Boccalini, *Advertisements from Parnassus* (London: Richard Smith, 1704), 1.23, vol. 1, p. 52.

52. Ibid., 1.23, vol. 1, p. 53.

53. Ibid., 1.23, vol. 1, pp. 53–54, although I have departed from the English translation here, which is loose.

54. 'Insegna molto bene Cornelio Tacito il modo di vivere e governarsi prudentemente, così come insegna a tiranni I modi do fondare la tirannide.' From the eighteenth maxim of Francesco Guicciardini's *Ricordi*, as quoted in Peter Burke, 'Tacitism', in T. A. Dorey, ed., *Tacitus* (London: Routledge & Kegan Paul, 1969), p. 163.

55. Giuseppe Toffanin, *Machiavelli e il tacitismo* (Padova: A. Draghi, 1921), and discussed in Burke, 'Tacitism', pp. 162–63.

56. E.g., Richard Tuck, *Philosophy and Government* (Cambridge: Cambridge University Press, 1993), who discusses Tacitism in Spain and Spanish Italy (pp. 65–82), in France (pp. 82–94), in Venice (pp. 94–104), and in England (pp. 104–19).

57. Mark Morford, 'Tacitean *Prudentia* and Lipsius', in T. J. Luce and A. J. Woodman, eds., *Tacitus and the Tacitean Tradition* (Princeton, NJ: Princeton University Press, 1993), p. 143.

58. Lipsius, *Politica*, 6.5, p. 695, quoting (in italics) Cicero, *On Duties*, 1.112.

59. Lipsius, *Politica*, 6.5, p. 695, quoting (in italics) Livy, 3.53.8.

60. Lipsius, *On Constancy*, 2.25, p. 126.

61. Epictetus, *The Discourses as reported by Arrian, the Manual, and fragments*, W. A. Oldfather, trans., 2 vols. (Cambridge, MA: Harvard University Press, 1985–89), 1.2.19–24. Guillaume du Vair, *The Moral Philosophie of the Stoicks*, Thomas James, trans. (London: F. Kingston, 1598). Barnabe Barnes, *Foure bookes of offices enabling privat persons for the speciall seruice of all good princes and policies* (London: G. Bishop, J. Adams & C. Burbie, 1606), p. 37.

62. J. H. M. Salmon, 'Stoicism and Roman Example: Seneca and Tacitus in Jacobean England', *Journal of the History of Ideas*, vol. 50, no. 2 (1989), p. 202.

63. Lipsius, *De recta pronuntatione Latinae linguae dialogus* (Antwerp, 1586). Salmon, 'Stoicism and Roman Example', p. 205; Adriana McCrea, *Constant Minds: Political Virtue and the Lipsian Paradigm, 1584–1650* (Toronto, ON: University of Toronto Press, 1997), p. 34.

64. Salmon, 'Stoicism and Roman Example', pp. 205–6.

65. Ibid., p. 207.

66. Francis Bacon, *Of the advancement and proficience of learning*, Gilbert Watts, trans. (Oxford: Leonard Lichfield, 1640), p. 307. On this, see Reid Barbour, *English Epicures and Stoics: Ancient Legacies in Early Stuart Culture* (Amherst: University of Massachusetts Press, 1998), pp. 216–18.

67. Salmon, 'Stoicism and Roman Example', pp. 207–8. McCrea, *Constant Minds*, p. 76.

68. King James, *Basilikon Doron* (Edinburgh: Robert Waldegrave, 1599), p. 117.

69. King James, *Basilikon Doron* (London: Richard Field, 1603), p. 97 (and quoted in Salmon, 'Stoicism and Roman Example', p. 223).

70. Andrew Shifflett, *Stoicism, Politics and Literature in the Age of Milton:*

War and Peace Reconciled (Cambridge: Cambridge University Press, 1998), pp. 23–24.

71. Ibid., p. 24.

72. Lipsius, *War and peace reconciled, or, A discourse of constancy in inconstant times*, Nathaniel Wanley, trans. (London: Royston, 1672). Thomas Hobbes, *Philosophicall rudiments concerning government and society* (London: Royston, 1651).

73. Tuck, *Philosophy and Government*, esp. p. xiv.

74. For a representative example of this genre, see David Burchell, 'The Disciplined Citizen: Thomas Hobbes, Neostoicism and the Critique of Classical Citizenship', *Australian Journal of Politics & History*, vol. 45, no. 4 (December 1999), pp. 506–24.

75. Richard Tuck, 'The Utopianism of *Leviathan*', in Tom Sorell and Luc Foisneau, eds., *Leviathan after 350 Years* (Oxford: Clarendon Press, 2004), p. 132.

76. J. B. Schneewind, *The Invention of Autonomy* (Cambridge: Cambridge University Press, 1998), p. 298, presents Hobbes's theory of the passions as 'an alternative' to a 'Socratic or neo-Stoic view'.

77. Noel Malcolm, *De Dominis, 1560–1624: Venetian, Anglican, Ecumenist, and Relapsed Heretic* (London: Strickland & Scott Academic Publications, 1984), pp. 49–50. Fulgenzio Micanzio, *Lettere a William Cavendish*, Roberto Ferrini, ed. (Rome: Istituto storico O. S. M, 1987).

78. Malcolm reviews the existing evidence concerning this translation in *De Dominis*, p. 51.

79. Ibid., p. 50.

80. Tuck, *Philosophy and Government*, p. 281.

81. John Aubrey, 'Brief life' of Hobbes, reprinted in Hobbes, *Human Nature and De Corpore Politico*, J. C. A. Gaskin, ed. (Oxford: Oxford University Press, 1999), p. 234.

82. *Horae subseciuae: Observations and discourses* (London: Edward Blount, 1620).

83. Leo Strauss, *The Political Philosophy of Hobbes* (Chicago: University of Chicago Press, 1952), p. xii n. 1.

84. Thomas Hobbes: *Three Discourses*, Noel B. Reynolds and Arlene W. Saxonhouse, eds. (Chicago: University of Chicago Press, 1995). For discussion, see Richard Tuck, 'Hobbes and Tacitus', in *Hobbes and History*, G. A. J. Rogers and Tom Sorell, eds. (London: Routledge, 2000), pp. 99–111. See also Jürgen Overhoff, *Hobbes's Theory of the Will: Ideological Reasons and Historical Circumstances* (Lanham, MD: Rowman & Littlefield, 2000), pp. 91–95.

85. Noel Malcolm, *Reason of State, Propaganda, and the Thirty Years' War: An Unknown Translation by Thomas Hobbes* (Oxford: Clarendon Press, 2007), introduction, p. 7.

86. Overhoff, *Hobbes's Theory of the Will*, p. 95.

87. Ibid., p. 96.

88. Ibid., p. 97.

89. Morford also considers this moment in his 'Tacitean *Prudentia* and Lip-

sius', pp. 143–44, though his interpretation of its significance differs somewhat from that offered here.

90. Lipsius, *Politica*, 6.4, p. 683, quoting (in italics) Tacitus. Overhoff quotes from this passage in *Hobbes's Theory of the Will*, pp. 96–97.

91. '[U]t imperium evertant, Libertatem praeferunt; si everterint, ipsam aggredientur'. See note 47 above.

92. Thomas Hobbes, *The Elements of Law*, pt. 1, chap. 9, in *Human Nature and De Corpore Politico*, p. 50.

93. Ibid., pt. 1, chap. 8, p. 48.

94. Thomas Hobbes, *On the Citizen*, Richard Tuck and Michael Silverthorne, eds. (Cambridge: Cambridge University Press, 1998), 1.2, p. 23.

95. Gabriella Slomp, *Thomas Hobbes and the Political Philosophy of Glory* (Basingstoke: Palgrave Macmillan, 2000) is good on charting the differences across the three accounts.

96. Thomas Hobbes, *Leviathan*, Richard Tuck, ed. (Cambridge: Cambridge University Press, 1991), p. 42.

97. Ibid., p. 72.

98. Ibid., p. 206.

99. Ibid., p. 54.

100. Ibid., p. 107.

101. Ibid., chap. 28, pp. 220–21 (emphasis in original).

102. Ibid., chap. 17, p. 120.

Chapter Four
The French Augustinians

1. Guillaume du Vair, *Traité de la constance et consolation ès calamitez publiques* (Paris: Librarie de la Société du Recueil Sirey, 1915).

2. Ira O. Wade, *The Intellectual Origins of the French Enlightenment* (Princeton, NJ: Princeton University Press, 1971), p. 147.

3. Guillaume du Vair, *The Moral Philosophie of the Stoicks*, Thomas James, trans. (London: F. Kingston, 1598), pp. 166–67. Maurizio Viroli, *For Love of Country* (Oxford: Clarendon Press, 1995), p. 49.

4. Du Vair, *Le manuel d'Epictète* (Paris: Langelier, 1591).

5. Lipsius, *Manuductionis ad Stoicam philosophiam libri tres*, 1.19, in his *Opera omnia* (Wesel: Andreas van Hoogenhuysen, 1675), vol. 4, pp. 681–82.

6. Julien-Eymard d'Angers, *Récherches sur le stoicisme aux XVIe et XVIIe siècles* (New York: G. Olms, 1976), pp. 4–8, 507–15.

7. Nannerl O. Keohane, *Philosophy and the State in France: The Renaissance to the Enlightenment* (Princeton, NJ: Princeton University Press, 1980); Anthony Levi, SJ, *French Moralists: The Theory of the Passions, 1585–1649* (Oxford: Clarendon Press, 1964).

8. J. H. M. Salmon, *Cardinal de Retz: The Anatomy of a Conspirator* (London: Weidenfeld & Nicolson, 1969), pp. 24–25.

9. Paul Bénichou, *Morales du Grand Siècle* (Paris: Gallimard, 1948). (Salmon was referring to p. 53.)

10. Katherine Ibbett, *The Style of the State in French Theater, 1630–1660:*

Neoclassicism and Government (Farnham: Ashgate, 2009), introduction, esp. pp. 16–17.

11. Julien-Eymard d'Angers, *Récherches sur le stoicisme*, p. 29.

12. Ibid., pp. 22–23.

13. Corneille Jansen, *Augustinus* (Paris: Guillemot, 1641).

14. On the metaphysics of Jansen's doctrine of the will, see Robert Sleigh, Jr., Vere Chappell, and Michael Della Rocca, 'Determinism and Human Freedom', in Daniel Garber and Michael Ayers, eds., *The Cambridge History of Seventeenth-Century Philosophy* (Cambridge: Cambridge University Press, 1998), pp. 1205–6.

15. Leszek Kolakowski, *God Owes Us Nothing* (Chicago: University of Chicago Press, 1995).

16. But see Augustine's anti-Pelagian *Letter* 104 on the Stoic claim that all sins are equal, in *Letters*, Sister Wilfrid Parsons, trans. (Washington, DC: Catholic University of America Press, 1964–89), vol. 2, pp. 191–95; as well as Augustine, *Against Julian*, Matthew A. Schumacher, trans. (Washington DC: Catholic University of America Press, 1977), 3.3.8 (on baptism), 4.12.58 (on Cicero's arguments in *De natura deorum*), 4.15.76 (on the sects' conceptions of the *summum bonum*), 4.14.72 (more on *De natura deorum*), 6.20.64 (on the wicked), and 6.12.59 (on citing from the philosophers).

17. There is a handful of other references. Book 1.7.8 has a passage on the 'Astrologers and the Stoics' that draws on book 5 of *The City of God*. In the second volume there is a string of references to the Stoics across pp. 599–614, in the section *De statu naturae lapsae*. See also *De statu purae naturae* 2.8, pp. 819–24.

18. Jansen, *Augustinus*, vol. 1, p. 225.

19. For the Seneca and Epictetus references, see Jansen, *Augustinus*, p. 232. The Genesis reference is on p. 233.

20. Nigel Abercrombie, *The Origins of Jansenism* (Oxford: Clarendon Press, 1936), p. 128.

21. Levi, *French Moralists*, pp. 215, 215–16 n. 5.

22. Jean-François Senault, *De l'usage des passions* (Paris: Journel, 1641). The English translation is Senault, *The Use of Passions*, trans. Henry Carey, Earl of Monmouth (London: J. L. & Humphrey Moseley, 1649).

23. Levi, reporting Miloyevitch's findings, *French Moralists*, p. 214.

24. Jean-François Senault, *L'homme criminel* (Paris: Camusat, 1644); idem, *L'homme Chrestien* (Paris: Camusat, 1648). The English translations are Senault, *Man become guilty, or, The corruption of nature by sinne, according to St. Augustines sense*, Henry Carey, Earl of Monmouth, trans. (London: William Leake, 1650), and Senault, *The Christian man: or, The reparation of nature by grace* (London: M. M. G. Bedell, 1650).

25. Cf. 'Réfutation et utilisation augustiniennes de Sénèque et du Stoicisme dans *L'homme criminel* (1644) and *L'homme chrétien* (1648) de l'oratorien J-F Senault', in d'Angers, *Récherches sur le stoicisme*.

26. All references in this paragraph are to the preface to Senault, *The Use of Passions*, sig. c2v–sig. c3v.

27. Levi, *French Moralists*, p. 214.

28. Senault, *The Christian man*, p. 209.

29. Senault, *L'homme Chrestien*, pp. 172–73. Cf. Levi, *French Moralists*, pp. 225–27, Pierre Nicole, 'Of Charity, and Self-Love', in *Moral Essayes* (London: Samuel Manship, 1696), vol. 3, pp. 78–112, and John M. Parrish, *Paradoxes of Political Ethics: From Dirty Hands to the Invisible Hand* (Cambridge: Cambridge University Press, 2007), chaps. 2 and 5, esp. pp. 186–203.

30. Senault, *L'homme chrestien*, pp. 233–34.

31. Senault, *The Use of Passions*, pp. 4–5.

32. Senault, *Man become guilty*, preface, sig. B2v.

33. Ibid., preface, sig. B2.

34. Senault, *The Christian man*, p. 208.

35. Blaise Pascal, 'Discussion with Monsieur de Sacy', in *Pensées and Other Writings*, Honor Levi, trans. (Oxford: Oxford University Press, 1995), pp. 182–92.

36. Ibid., p. 183.

37. Ibid., pp. 191–92. Cf. Immanuel Kant, *Immanuel Kant's Critique of Pure Reason*, Norman Kemp Smith, ed. (London: Macmillan, 1964), pp. 601–5.

38. Blaise Pascal, *Pensées*, no. 26, in *Pensées and Other Writings*, Honor Levi, trans. (Oxford: Oxford University Press, 1995), p. 9.

39. This section draws on Anthony R. Pugh, *The Composition of Pascal's Apologia* (Toronto, ON: University of Toronto Press, 1984), esp. pp. 122–35.

40. Pascal, *Pensées*, no. 172, pp. 49–50.

41. Ibid., nos. 177, 179, pp. 50–51. The allusion is to Epictetus, *Discourses*, 4.7.6. See Pugh, *The Composition of Pascal's Apologia*, pp. 122–27, for a treatment of other, unclassified fragments that might plausibly be considered in this section.

42. Pascal, *Pensées*, p. 51.

43. Ibid., no. 181, p. 52.

44. Juvenal, Satire 15, l. 9. Thomas Hobbes, *Leviathan*, Richard Tuck, ed. (Cambridge: Cambridge University Press, 1991), chap. 44, p. 423; Nicolas Malebranche, *The Search After Truth*, Thomas M. Lennon and Paul J. Olscamp, eds. (Cambridge: Cambridge University Press, 1997), p. 447; John Wesley, Sermon 102, in *The Works of the Rev. John Wesley* (New York: J. & J. Harper, 1826), vol. 7, p. 181; David Hume, *The Natural History of Religion*, in *Principal Writings on Religion*, J. C. A. Gaskin, ed. (Oxford: Oxford University Press, 1993), p. 168.

45. Malebranche, *The Search After Truth*, p. 310.

46. Ibid., p. 77.

47. Ibid., p. 361.

48. On Malebranche's attack on Seneca, see Geneviève Rodis-Lewis, 'L'anti-stoïcisme de Malebranche', in *7ᵉ Congres de l'Association Guillaume Budé, Aix-en-Provence, 1963* (1964), or Joseph Moreau, 'Sénèque et Malebranche', *Crisis*, vol. 12 (1965), pp. 345–52. Cf. Thomas M. Lennon, 'The Contagious Communication of Strong Imaginations: History, Modernity, and Scepticism in the Philosophy of Malebranche', in Tom Sorell, ed., *The Rise of Modern Philosophy* (Oxford: Clarendon Press, 1993), pp. 197–212.

49. Malebranche, *The Search After Truth*, p. 161.

50. Ibid.

51. Parrish, *Paradoxes of Political Ethics*, pp. 188–203; E. D. James, *Pierre Nicole, Jansenist and Humanist: A Study of His Thought* (The Hague: Martinus Nijhoff, 1973), pt. 5, chap. 2; and Nicole, 'Of Charity and Self-Love', in *Moral Essayes*, vol. 3, pp. 78–112.

52. Malebranche, *The Search After Truth*, pp. 161–62.

53. Ibid., p. 162.

54. Ibid., p. 162.

55. Ibid., p. 162.

56. Ibid., pp. 162–63.

57. Ibid., p. 163.

58. Ibid., p. 163.

59. Ibid., p. 163.

60. Ibid., p. 164.

61. Ibid., p. 165.

62. Ibid., p. 342.

63. Ibid., p. 176.

64. Ibid., p. 176.

65. Ibid., p. 178.

66. Ibid., p. 179.

67. Ibid., p. 179.

68. Ibid., p. 179.

69. Ibid., p. 180.

70. Ibid., p. 180.

71. Ibid., p. 181.

72. Ibid., p. 182.

73. Ibid., p. 183.

74. Nicolas Malebranche, *Treatise on Ethics (1684)*, Craig Walton, trans. (Dordrecht: Kluwer Academic, 1993), 1.8.16, pp. 105–6.

75. Ibid., 1.8.16, pp. 105–6.

76. Ibid., 1.1.22.

77. Ibid., 1.1.22.

78. Ibid., 1.1.22.

79. E.g., Jean Lafond, *La Rochefoucauld, Augustinisme et littérature* (Paris: Klincksieck, 1977). Jean Starobinski, introduction to his edition of La Rochefoucauld, *Maximes et mémoires* (Paris: Union Générale d'Éditions, 1964).

80. 'Nos vertus ne sont, le plus souvent, que des vices deguisés'. La Rochefoucauld, *Maxims*, Stéphane Douard and Stuart D. Warner, eds. (South Bend, IN: St Augustine's Press, 2001), p. 3.

81. 'Nous sommes si accoutumés à nous déguiser aux autres qu'enfin nous nous déguisons à nous-mêmes.' La Rochefoucauld, *Maxims*, no. 119, p. 24.

82. 'Les philosophes, et Sénèque surtout, n'ont point ôté les crimes par leurs preceptes: ils n'ont fait que les employer au bâtiment de l'orgeuil.' La Rochefoucauld, *Maxims*, withdrawn maxim no. 21, p. 109.

83. Isabelle Chariatte, 'Le frontispice des *Réflexions ou sentences et maximes morales* de La Rochefoucauld: Une clé de lecture à plusieurs niveaux', *Revue d'Histoire Littéraire de la France*, vol. 102 (2002), pp. 637–43.

84. Aphra Behn, ed., *Miscellany, being a collection of poems by several hands;*

together with Reflections on morality, or, Seneca unmasqued (London: J. Hindmarsh, 1685), pp. 301–82.

85. 'La clémence des princes n'est souvent qu'une politique pour gagner l'affection des peuples.' La Rochefoucauld, *Maxims*, no. 15, p. 6.

86. 'Cette clémence dont on fait une vertu se pratique tantôt par vanité, quelquefois par paresse, souvent par crainte, et presque toujours par tous les trios ensemble.' (I have replaced Douard and Warner's 'leniency' with my own 'clemency'.) Ibid., no. 16, p. 6.

87. 'La constance des sages nest que l'art de renfermer leur agitation dans leur coeur.' Ibid., no. 20.

88. 'Ceux qu'on condamne au supplice affectent quelquefois une constance et une mépris de la mort qui n'est en effet que la crainte de l'envisage. De sorte qu'on peut dire que cette constance et ce mépris sont à leur esprit ce que le bandeay est à leurs yeux.' Ibid., no. 21.

89. 'Il y a différence entre souffrir la mort constamment, et la mépriser.'

90. Seneca, *Letter 26*, in *Epistles*, Richard M. Gummere, trans. (Cambridge, MA: Harvard University Press, 2002).

91. E.g., 'Don't despise death; but receive it well-pleas'd; as it is one of the things which nature wills.' Marcus Aurelius, *The Meditations of the Emperor Marcus Aurelius Antoninus*, Francis Hutcheson and James Moor, trans., James Moore and Michael Silverthorne, eds. (Indianapolis, IN: Liberty Fund, 2008), 9.3, p. 108.

92. La Rochefoucauld, *Maxims,* no. 504, p. 93.

93. Seneca, *De vita beata*, p. 190 in the L'Estrange edition.

94. Ibid., p. 193.

95. La Rochefoucauld, *Maxims*, no. 504, pp. 93–94.

96. Ibid., no. 504, p. 94.

97. Ibid., no. 504, pp. 94–95.

98. Antoine Le Grand, *Le Sage des Stoiques* (The Hague: Sam Browne & Jean L'Escluse, 1662). The English translation is Anthony Le Grand, *Man Without Passion* (London: C. Harper and J. Amery, 1675).

99. Augustine, *The City of God against the Pagans*, R. W. Dyson, trans. (Cambridge: Cambridge University Press, 1998), 22.24, pp. 1159–66.

100. Le Grand, *Man without Passion*, pp. 17–18.

101. Ibid., pp. 18–19.

102. Antoine Le Grand, *The Entire Body of Philosophy* (London: Samuel Roycroft, 1694), esp. chap. 13, p. 367.

103. In Xylander's Latin translation, one of the emperor's characteristic reflections on the brevity of human life, 'Yesterday, a drop of mucus; tomorrow, a mummy's ashes', was rendered as 'Yesterday a fish; tomorrow, salted cod'. Jill Kraye, '"Ethnicorum omnium sanctissimus": Marcus Aurelius and His *Meditations* from Xylander to Diderot,' in Jill Kraye and M.W.F. Stone, eds., *Humanism and Modern Philosophy* (London: Routledge, 2000), p. 118.

104. Ibid., p. 107.

105. Ibid., pp. 110–1. Marcus Aurelius, *His Meditations concerning Himself*, Meric Casaubon, trans., 3rd ed. (London: James Flesher, 1663).

106. Ibid., pp. 27–28.

107. Kraye, "'Ethnicorum omnium sanctissimus'", p. 114, quoting D. McKitterick, *A History of Cambridge University Press* (Cambridge: Cambridge University Press, 1992–2004), vol. 1, p. 309. Marcus Aurelius, *Marci Antonini Imperatoris De Rebus Suis*, 2nd ed., Thomas Gataker, trans. (London: Edward Millington, 1697).

108. Marcus Aurelius, *The Emperor Marcus Antoninus his Conversation with Himself*, Jeremy Collier, ed. (London: Richard Sare, 1701); Moore and Silverthorne, *The Meditations of the Emperor Marcus Aurelius Antoninus*. The text of the 'Preliminary Discourse' also formed the basis of an advertisement for a new edition of Epictetus, never published, that was placed in the August 1730 edition of *The Present State of the Republic of Letters*, a London journal.

109. Gataker, in Collier, ed., *The Emperor Marcus Antoninus his Conversation with Himself*, p. 33.

110. Ibid., p. 35.

111. Friedrich Nietzsche, *Twilight of the Idols*, in *The Anti-Christ, Ecce Homo, Twilight of the Idols and Other Writings*, Aaron Ridley and Judith Norman, eds. (Cambridge: Cambridge University Press, 2005), p. 191.

112. Gataker, in Collier, *The Emperor Marcus Antoninus his Conversation with Himself*, p. 35.

113. Ibid., sig. A3v.

114. Marcus Aurelius Antoninus, *His Mediations concerning Himself*, Casaubon ed., p. 5.

115. Gataker, in Moore and Silverthorne, *The Meditations of the Emperor Marcus Aurelius Antoninus*, pp. 161–62.

116. Ibid., p. 163.

117. Marcus Aurelius Antoninus, *His Meditations concerning Himself*, Casaubon ed., pp. 25–27.

118. Kraye, "'Ethnicorum omnium sanctissimus'", p. 118.

119. Marcus Aurelius, *Réflexions morales avec des remarques de Mr. & de Mad. Dacier*, 2nd ed. (Amsterdam: Abraham Wolfgang, 1691), sig. *A7v.

120. Ibid., sig. *A3v–A4.

121. Ibid., sig. *A5–A5v.

122. Ibid., sig. *A6.

123. Ibid., sig. *A6v.

124. Ibid., sig. *A7.

Chapter Five
From Hobbes to Shaftesbury

1. Jon Parkin, *Taming the Leviathan: The Reception of the Political and Religious Ideas of Thomas Hobbes in England, 1640–1700* (Cambridge: Cambridge University Press, 2007), p. 260.

2. Parkin, *Taming the Leviathan*, p. 38.

3. The main texts are Thomas Hobbes, *Of libertie and necessitie a treatise: wherein all controversie concerning predestination, election, free-will, grace, merits, reprobation, &c. is fully decided and cleared in answer to a treatise written by the Bishop of London-derry, on the same subject* (London: F. Eaglesfield, 1654);

John Bramhall, *A Defence of True Liberty from Antecedent and Extrinsecall Necessity, being an answer to a late book of Mr. Thomas Hobbs of Malmsbury, intituled, A Treatise of Liberty and Necessity* (London: John Crook, 1655); Hobbes, *The questions concerning liberty, necessity, and chance: clearly stated and debated between Dr. Bramhall, Bishop of Derry, and Thomas Hobbes of Malmesbury* (London: Andrew Crook, 1656); Bramhall, *Castigations of Mr. Hobbes, his last animadversions, in the case concerning liberty and universal necessity* (London: John Crook, 1658); and Hobbes, *An answer to a book published by Dr. Bramhall, late bishop of Derry; called the Catching of the leviathan. Together with an historical narration concerning heresie, and the punishment thereof* (London: W. Crooke, 1682). For background and discussion of the theological content of the exchange, see Jürgen Overhoff, *Hobbes's Theory of the Will: Ideological Reasons and Historical Circumstances* (Lanham, MD: Rowman & Littlefield, 2000), pp. 133–42.

4. John Bramhall, *Works* (Dublin: His Majesty's Printing-house, 1676), vol. 3, p. 648.

5. Ibid., vol. 3, p. 653.

6. Ibid., vol. 3, pp. 667–68. See John Webster, *The Duchess of Malfi* [1623], Leah S. Marcus, ed. (London: Arden Shakespeare, 2009), 5.4.3: 'We are merely the stars' tennis-balls, struck and bandied / Which way please them'.

7. Bramhall, *Works*, vol. 3, p. 669.

8. Ibid., p. 686.

9. Parkin, *Taming the Leviathan*, p. 47.

10. Bramhall, *Works*, vol. 3, pp. 692–93.

11. Ibid., p. 693.

12. Ibid., p. 693–94.

13. For these various remarks, see Hobbes, *The questions concerning liberty, necessity, and chance*, p. 197.

14. Bramhall, *Works*, vol. 3, pp. 767–68, 798.

15. Robert Sharrock, *Hypothesis ethike: de officiis secundum naturae jus* (Oxford: Lichfield, 1660). For discussion, see Hans W. Blom, *Morality and Causality in Politics: The Rise of Naturalism in Dutch Seventeenth-Century Political Thought* (Utrecht: Universitaet Utrecht, 1995), pp. 131–39; and Parkin, *Taming the Leviathan*, pp. 212–14. Jacob Thomasius, 'De statu naturali adversus Hobbesium. Programma XIX, 16. January 1661', in *Dissertationes LXIII varii argumenti magnam partem ad historiam philosophicam et ecclesiasticam pertinentes* (Halle, 1693), touched on in Horst Dreitzel, 'The Reception of Hobbes in the Political Philosophy of the Early Enlightenment', *History of European Ideas*, vol. 29, no. 3 (September 2003), p. 264.

16. Hermann Conring, *De civili prudentia* (Helmstedt, 1662), chap. 2, n. 11, discussed in Dreitzel, 'Reception of Hobbes', pp. 259–60.

17. T. J. Hochstrasser, *Natural Law Theories in the Early Enlightenment* (Cambridge: Cambridge University Press, 2000), p. 50.

18. Letter from Johann Heinrich Böcler to Johann Christian von Boineburg, 26 January 1663, discussed in Hochstrasser, *Natural Law Theories*, p. 55.

19. Hochstrasser, *Natural Law Theories*, p. 58: the quotation is from Böcler,

In Hugonis Grotii Jus belli et pacis, ad illustrissimum baronem Boineburgium commentatio (Giessen: Caspar Wächtler, 1687), p. 47.

20. Hochstrasser, *Natural Law Theories*, p. 58.

21. Horst Denzer, *Moralphilosophie und Naturrecht bei Samuel Pufendorf* (Munich: Beck, 1972), p. 260, cited in Hochstrasser, *Natural Law Theories*, p. 62.

22. E.g. Samuel Pufendorf, *The Law of Nature and of Nations*, Jean Barbeyrac, ed., Basil Kennet, trans. (London: J. & J. Bonwicke, 1749), 2.2.2, pp. 99–100; 2.3.10, p. 127.

23. Ibid., 2.3.16, p. 137, quoted in Hochstrasser, *Natural Law Theories*, p. 63. For more detailed discussion of Pufendorf's distinctive theorisation of sociability, see Istvan Hont, *Jealousy of Trade: International Competition and the Nation-State in Historical Perspective* (Cambridge, MA: Harvard University Press, 2005), pp. 38–47, 159–85.

24. Jon Parkin, *Science, Religion and Politics in Restoration England: Richard Cumberland's* De Legibus Naturae (Woodbridge: Boydell Press, 1999), p. 93.

25. Parkin, *Taming the Leviathan*, p. 135. Parkin credits Malcolm's unpublished PhD dissertation, p. 7, for a similar point. Parkin, *Science, Religion and Politics*, p. 6.

26. See Parkin, *Science, Religion and Politics*, p. 60.

27. Richard Cumberland, *A Treatise of the Laws of Nature*, Jon Parkin, ed., James Maxwell, trans. (Indianapolis, IN: Liberty Fund, 2005), introduction, § IX, p. 256, quoted in Terence Irwin, *The Development of Ethics: A Historical and Critical Study*, vol. 2, *From Suarez to Rousseau* (Oxford: Oxford University Press, 2008), p. 221.

28. Parkin, *Science, Religion and Politics*, pp. 9, 95–96.

29. Cumberland, *Treatise*, introduction, § XIII, p. 260.

30. Cumberland, *Treatise*, p. 500. Also Irwin, *The Development of Ethics*, vol. 2, p. 224, who notes that Cumberland here follows Cicero's criticism of the Stoics in *On Moral Ends*, Julia Annas, ed. (Cambridge: Cambridge University Press, 2001), 4.31–33, pp. 100–101.

31. Cumberland, *Treatise*, p. 573.

32. E.g., Cumberland, *Treatise*, p. 542.

33. Ibid., p. 576.

34. Parkin, *Science, Religion and Politics*, p. 106.

35. Cumberland, *Treatise*, pp. 594, 596.

36. Ibid., p. 598.

37. Pufendorf, preface to *De jure naturae et gentium* (Amsterdam: Andreas van Hoogenhuysen, 1688), quoted in Hochstrasser, *Natural Law Theories*, p. 70.

38. Samuel Parker, *A Demonstration of the Divine Authority of the Law of Nature and of the Christian Religion in two parts* (London: M. Flesher, 1681), p. 2.

39. Ibid., p. 2.

40. Ibid., pp. 131–32.

41. Ibid., p. 132.

42. Ibid., p. 133.

43. Ibid., p. 133.

44. Irwin, *The Development of Ethics*, vol. 2, p. 277.

45. Parker, *Demonstration*, pp. 137–38.

46. Ibid., p. 138.

47. Ibid., p. 138.

48. Isabel Rivers, *Reason, Grace, and Sentiment: A Study of the Language of Religion and Ethics in England, 1660–1780*, vol. 1, *Whichcote to Wesley* (Cambridge: Cambridge University Press, 1991), p. 35.

49. Nathaniel Culverwell, *An Elegant and Learned Discourse of the Light of Nature* (Indianapolis, IN: Liberty Fund, 2001). For discussion, see Reid Barbour, *English Epicures and Stoics: Ancient Legacies in Early Stuart Culture* (Amherst: University of Massachusetts Press, 1998), p. 200, 203; also Stephen Darwall, *The British Moralists and the Internal 'Ought': 1640–1740* (Cambridge: Cambridge University Press, 1995), chap. 2.

50. Henry More, *Enchiridion Ethicum* (London: James Flesher, 1668). An English version was published as *An Account of Virtue* (London: Benjamin Tooke, 1690).

51. Sarah Hutton, 'Liberty and Self-determination: Ethics, Power and Action in Ralph Cudworth', in Luisa Simonutti, ed., *Dal necessario al possibile: Determinismo e libertà nel pensiero anglo-olandese del XVII secolo* (Milan: Franco Angeli, 2001), p. 91.

52. Benjamin Whichcote, *Select Sermons of Dr. Whichcot* (London: Printed for Awnsham and John Churchill, 1698), preface, A5.

53. Shaftesbury, letter of 1 October 1706 to Pierre Coste, in *The Life, Unpublished Letters and Philosophical Regimen of Anthony, Earl of Shaftesbury*, Benjamin Rand, ed. (London: Swan Sonnenschein, 1900), pp. 356–57. Lawrence E. Klein, *Shaftesbury and the Culture of Politeness: Moral Discourse and Cultural Politics in Early 18th-Century England* (Cambridge: Cambridge University Press, 1994), p. 60, has a closer transcript from the MS.

54. Shaftesbury, letter of 1 October 1706 to Coste, in *Life, Unpublished Letters . . .* , pp. 358, 360, 361.

55. Ibid., p 359. See also the discussion in Isabel Rivers, *Reason, Grace, and Sentiment*, vol. 2, *Shaftesbury to Hume* (Cambridge: Cambridge University Press, 2000), p. 92.

56. Anthony Ashley Cooper, Third Earl of Shaftesbury, *Miscellany* 4, in *Characteristics of Men, Manners, Opinions, Times*, Lawrence E. Klein, ed. (Cambridge: Cambridge University Press, 1999), p. 423.

57. Rivers, *Reason, Grace, and Sentiment*, vol. 2, p. 94.

58. Pierre Bayle, *A General Dictionary, Historical and Critical*, 10 vols. (London: J. Bettenham, 1734–41), 'Shaftesbury', note Q, vol. 9, p. 186, quoted in Rivers, *Reason, Grace, and Sentiment*, vol. 2, pp. 91–92. (The entry and notes on Shaftesbury were supplied by the English editors and are not by Bayle.)

59. Shaftesbury, *Life, Unpublished Letters . . .* , p. xii.

60. Esther A. Tiffany, 'Shaftesbury as Stoic', *Proceedings of the Modern Language Association*, vol. 38, no. 3 (September 1923), pp. 642–84. Alfred Owen Aldridge, 'Shaftesbury and the Deist Manifesto', *Transactions of the American Philosophical Society*, n.s., vol. 41, no. 2 (1951), pp. 297–385.

61. Parkin, *Science, Religion and Politics*, pp. 218–19.

62. See Darwall, *British Moralists*, pp. 37–41. See also J. B. Schneewind, 'Locke's Moral Philosophy', in Vere Chappell, ed., *The Cambridge Companion to Locke* (Cambridge: Cambridge University Press, 1994), esp. p. 215.

63. Klein, *Shaftesbury and the Culture of Politeness*, p. 65.

64. Shaftesbury, letter to Michael Ainsworth, 3 June 1709, in *Life, Unpublished Letters . . .* , p. 403.

65. Darwall, *British Moralists*, p. 183.

66. Shaftesbury, *An Inquiry Concerning Virtue or Merit*, in *Characteristics*, pp. 167, 168, 169.

67. Ibid., p. 171, italics in original.

68. Ibid., p. 172.

69. Ibid., p. 180.

70. Ibid., p. 185; see also p. 179; also Daniel Carey's discussion in his *Locke, Shaftesbury, and Hutcheson: Contesting Diversity in the Enlightenment and Beyond* (Cambridge: Cambridge University Press, 2006), esp. p. 111.

71. Shaftesbury, *An Inquiry Concerning Virtue or Merit*, p. 173.

72. Carey, *Locke, Shaftesbury and Hutcheson*, p. 112.

73. Ibid., pp. 113–14.

74. Ibid., p. 115.

75. Ibid., pp. 9, 115–16.

76. Shaftesbury, *Life, Unpublished Letters . . .* , p. 171; Shaftesbury, *Exercices*, Laurent Jaffro, ed. and trans. (Paris: Aubier, 1993), p. 164.

77. Darwall, *British Moralists*, p. 191.

78. Shaftesbury, *An Inquiry Concerning Virtue or Merit*, p. 173.

79. Ibid., p. 174. For discussion, see Darwall, *British Moralists,* pp. 190–91.

80. Shaftesbury, *An Inquiry Concerning Virtue or Merit*, pp. 174–75.

81. Epictetus, *Encheiridion*, § 1, *Discourses*, 1.1.

82. Darwall, *British Moralists*, p. 192.

83. Stanley Green, *Shaftesbury's Philosophy of Religion and Ethics: A Study in Enthusiasm* (Athens: University of Ohio Press, 1967), p. 7.

84. Ibid., pp. 137, 161.

85. Margaret Graver, *Stoicism and Emotion* (Chicago: University of Chicago Press, 2007), especially pp. 51–53.

86. Grean, *Shaftesbury's Philosophy of Religion and Ethics*, p. 149; Epictetus, *Epictetus his morals, with Simplicius his comment*, 3rd ed., George Stanhope, ed. (London: Richard Sare, 1704), preface, A4.

87. On this, see J. B. Schneewind, *The Invention of Autonomy* (Cambridge: Cambridge University Press, 1998), pp. 298–99.

88. Shaftesbury, *An Inquiry Concerning Virtue or Merit*, p. 175.

89. Ibid., p. 192.

90. Darwall, *British Moralists*, p. 194. Emphasis in original.

91. See ibid, pp. 195–96.

92. Schneewind, *The Invention of Autonomy*, p. 295.

93. Ibid., p. 306.

94. Shaftesbury, *Miscellany 3*, in *Characteristics*, p. 407.

95. Tim Harris, 'Cooper, Anthony Ashley, First Earl of Shaftesbury (1621–1683)', in *Oxford Dictionary of National Biography* (Oxford: Oxford University Press, 2004), vol. 13, pp. 199–217.

96. John Dryden, 'Absalom and Achitophel', ll. 152–55, in *The Major Works*, Keith Walker, ed. (Oxford: Oxford University Press, 2003), p. 182.

97. Shaftesbury, *Sensus communis*, in *Characteristics*, p. 52.

98. Ibid.

99. Ibid.

100. Ibid., pp. 52–53.

101. Ibid., p. 53.

102. Ibid.. See also Julie K. Ellison, *Cato's Tears and the Making of Anglo-American Emotion* (Chicago: University of Chicago Press, 1999), chap. 1, esp. pp. 23–29.

103. Klein, *Shaftesbury and the Culture of Politeness*, chap. 4.

104. Ibid., p. 71.

105. Pierre Hadot, *Philosophy as a Way of Life: Spiritual Exercises from Socrates to Foucault* (Oxford: Blackwell, 1995), chap. 6. Also Hadot, *The Inner Citadel: The* Meditations *of Marcus Aurelius* (Cambridge, MA: Harvard University Press, 1998).

106. Marcus Aurelius, *Meditations*, 6.13.

107. Hadot, *Philosophy as a Way of Life*, p. 193.

108. Shaftesbury, *Exercices*, Jaffro ed.

109. Epictetus, *Discourses*, W. A. Oldfather, trans. (Cambridge, MA: Harvard University Press, 1985–89), 3.12.16, quoted in Greek in Shaftesbury, *Exercices*, Jaffro ed., p. 47. (This quotation does not appear in the Rand edition of the *Philosophical Regimen*.)

110. Mentioned in Rivers, *Reason, Grace, and Sentiment*, vol. 2, p. 118.

111. Shaftesbury, *Soliloquy, or Advice to an Author*, in *Characteristics*, p. 143. Christopher J. Berry, 'Smith under Strain', *European Journal of Political Theory*, vol. 3, no. 4 (October 2004), p. 456.

112. Shaftesbury, *Miscellany 4*, in *Characteristics*, p. 423.

113. Ibid., p. 422.

114. Shaftesbury, *Miscellany 5*, in *Characteristics*, p. 467.

115. Istvan Hont, 'The Early Enlightenment Debate on Commerce and Luxury', in *The Cambridge History of Eighteenth-Century Political Thought*, Mark Goldie and Robert Wokler, eds. (Cambridge: Cambridge University Press, 2006), pp. 396–97.

116. Rivers, *Reason, Grace, and Sentiment*, vol. 2, pp. 136–37.

117. Ibid., vol. 2, pp. 137–38.

118. Darwall, *British Moralists*, p. 188.

119. Rivers, *Reason, Grace, and Sentiment*, vol. 2, p. 133.

120. Jonathan Israel, *Radical Enlightenment: Philosophy and the Making of Modernity 1650–1750* (Oxford: Oxford University Press, 2001), p. 618.

121. Anthony Collins, *A Philosophical Inquiry Concerning Human Liberty* (London: Routledge / Thoemmes Press, 1997), pp. 40–41.

122. John Toland, *Pantheisticon: or, the form of celebrating the Socratic-Society* (London: Samuel Paterson, 1751), pp. 73f.

123. Samuel Clarke, *A Discourse Concerning the Unchangeable Obligations of Natural Religion, and the Truth and Certainty of the Christian Revelation* (London: W. Botham, 1706), pp. 170–71.

124. Ibid., p. 171.

125. Ibid., p. 172.

Chapter Six
How the Stoics Became Atheists

1. All quotations from Pierre Bayle's *Dictionary* in what follows are taken from the second English translation, *A General Dictionary, Historical and Critical*, 10 vols. (London: J. Bettenham, 1734–41). Alternative treatments of Bayle's critique of the Stoics can be found in Jacqueline Lagrée, 'La critique du stoïcisme dans le *Dictionnaire* de Bayle', in Michelle Magdelaine et al., eds., *De l'humanisme aux Lumières, Bayle et le protestantisme: mélanges en l'honneur d'Elisabeth Labrousse* (Oxford: Voltaire Foundation, 1996), esp. pp. 583, 588–90; and Giovanni Bonacina, *Filosofia ellenistica e cultura moderna: Epicureismo, stoicismo e scetticismo da Bayle a Hegel* (Firenze: Casa Editrice Le Lettere, 1996), pp. 26–32.

2. Bayle, *Dictionary*, 'Lipsius', note A.

3. Ibid., 'Ovid', note H.

4. Justus Lipsius, *On Constancy*, John Stradling, trans., John Sellars, ed. (Exeter: Bristol Phoenix Press, 2006), 1.18, p. 65. Bayle, *Dictionary*, 'Chrysippus', note E.

5. Marcus Aurelius, *Réflexions morales avec des remarques de Mr. & de Mad. Dacier*, 2nd ed. (Amsterdam: Abraham Wolfgang, 1691), sig. *A4v.

6. Bayle, *Dictionary*, 'Jupiter' note C.

7. Ibid., 'Chrysippus', main text; 'Hipparchia', note D.

8. Jean Barbeyrac, 'An historical and critical account of the science of morality', in Samuel Pufendorf, *The Law of Nature and Nations*, Jean Barbeyrac, ed., Basil Kennet, trans. (London: J. & J. Bonwicke, 1749), p. 62.

9. Bayle, *Dictionary*, 'Epicurus', main text and note N; see also 'Hipparchia', note D.

10. E. D. James, 'Scepticism and Fideism in Bayle's *Dictionnaire*', *French Studies*, vol. 16, no. 4 (1962), p. 308.

11. Bayle, *Dictionary*, 'Chrysippus', note E.

12. Ibid., 'Chrysippus', note G. Plutarch, 'On Stoic Self-Contradictions', in *Moralia*, vol. 13, pt. 2, Harold Cherniss, trans. (Cambridge, MA: Harvard University Press, 1976), 1035F.

13. Bayle, *Dictionary*, 'Chrysippus', main text and note F, quoting Cicero, *Academica*, 4.27.

14. Bayle, *Dictionary*, 'Chrysippus', note E.

15. The discussion continues in Bayle, *Dictionary*, note E of 'Euclid' and note S of 'Loyola'.

16. Ibid., 'Chrysippus', note G.

17. Ibid.

18. Ibid., 'Lipsius', note C.

19. Ibid., 'Chrysippus', note O.

20. Ibid., 'Lingelsheim', note A.

21. Ibid., 'Chrysippus', note O; see Cicero, *Academica*, 2.92–96.

22. Bayle, *Dictionary*, 'Chrysippus', note H.

23. Ibid., 'Arcesilaus', note E.

24. Ibid., 'Heracleotes', note C.

25. Lipsius, *Physiologiae Stoicorum libri tres* (Antwerp: J. Moretus, 1604), 1.14.

26. Bayle, *Dictionary*, 'Chrysippus', note H.

27. Ibid., 'The Paulicians', note G.

28. Ibid., e.g., 'Spinoza', note A; 'Jupiter'.

29. From the Epistle Dedicatory of Guillaume du Vair, *The Moral Philosophie of the Stoicks*, Thomas James, trans. (London: F. Kingston, 1598).

30. Lipsius, *Physiologiae Stoicorvm*, I.8. A. A. Long, 'Stoicism in the Philosophical Tradition: Spinoza, Lipsius, Butler', in Brad Inwood, ed., *The Cambridge Companion to the Stoics* (Cambridge: Cambridge University Press, 2003), pp. 379–82. See also Jan Papy, 'Lipsius' (neo-) Stoicism: Constancy between Christian Faith and Stoic Virtue', in Hans W. Blom and Laurens C. Winkel, eds., *Grotius and the Stoa*, (Assen: Van Gorcum, 2004), pp. 52–56.

31. Thomas Gataker, quoted in Marcus Aurelius, *The Emperor Marcus Antoninus his Conversation with Himself*, Jeremy Collier, ed. (London: Richard Sare, 1701), sig. b4–b4v.

32. Thomas Gataker, in *The Meditations of the Emperor Marcus Aurelius Antoninus*, Francis Hutcheson and James Moor, trans., James Moore and Michael Silverthorne, eds. (Indianapolis, IN: Liberty Fund, 2008), pp. 161–62.

33. Ralph Cudworth, *The True Intellectual System of the Universe*, 3 vols. (London, 1845), vol. 2, p. 97.

34. Ibid., vol. 3, p. 83.

35. Ibid., vol. 1, p. 98.

36. Ibid., vol. 1, p. 98. On this point, Leibniz agreed. G. W. Leibniz, *Textes inédits*, Gaston Grua, ed. (Paris: Presses Universitaires de France, 1948), vol. 1, p. 328.

37. Cudworth, *True Intellectual System*, vol. 1, pp. 117–19.

38. Jonathan Israel, *Enlightenment Contested: Philosophy, Modernity, and the Emancipation of Man 1670–1752* (Oxford: Oxford University Press, 2006), p. 463.

39. Cudworth, *True Intellectual System*, vol. 1, p. 196.

40. Ibid., vol. 1, pp. 197–8.

41. Ibid., vol. 1, p. 198.

42. Israel, *Enlightenment Contested*, p. 458.

43. Benedict Spinoza, *Tractatus theologico-politicus*, Samuel Shirley, trans., Brad S. Gregory, ed. (Leiden: E. J. Brill, 1989), p. 132, cited in Jonathan Israel, *Radical Enlightenment: Philosophy and the Making of Modernity 1650–1750* (Oxford: Oxford University Press, 2001), p. 221.

44. E.g., Jonathan Israel, *Radical Enlightenment*, p. 9.

45. Israel, *Radical Enlightenment*, pp. 281–82. Also Margaret C. Jacob, *The Radical Enlightenment: Pantheists, Freemasons and Republicans* (London: George Allen & Unwin, 1981), p. 53.

46. Jacob Thomasius, *Exercitatio de stoica mundi exustione* (Leipzig: F. Lanckisius, 1676), quoted in Giovanni Santinello et al., eds., *Models of the History of Philosophy* (Dordrecht: Kluwer/Springer, 1993–2010), vol. 1, p. 416.

47. For discussion, see Jacqueline Lagrée, 'Théorie des principes et théologie naturelle', in Christian Mouchel, ed., *Juste Lipse (1547–1606) en son temps: actes du colloque de Strasbourg, 1994* (Paris: H. Champion, 1996), pp. 43–44.

48. Cudworth, *True Intellectual System*, vol. 1, pp. 106–7.

49. J. A. Passmore, *Ralph Cudworth: An Interpretation* (Cambridge: Cambridge University Press, 1951), pp. 5–6, quoting Cudworth, *True Intellectual System*, preface, xl.

50. These and other parallels are set out in Israel, *Enlightenment Contested*, pp. 459–62, and in Susan James, 'Spinoza the Stoic', in Tom Sorell, ed., *The Rise of Modern Philosophy* (Oxford: Clarendon Press, 1993), pp. 289–316. A. A. Long makes a similar case in 'Stoicism in the Philosophical Tradition', pp. 369–79. See also Alexandre Matheron, 'Le moment stoïcien de l'*Éthique* de Spinoza', in *Le Stoïcisme aux XVIe et XVIIe siècles: Actes du Colloque CERPHI (4–5 juin 1993)*, Pierre-François Moreau and Jacqueline Lagrée, eds. (Caen: Presses Universitaires de Caen, 1994), pp. 147-61.

51. James, 'Spinoza the Stoic', pp. 292, 310–16.

52. Firmin deBrabander, *Spinoza and the Stoics: Power, Politics and the Passions* (London: Continuum, 2007). Justin B. Jacobs, 'The ancient notion of self-preservation in the theories of Hobbes and Spinoza', PhD thesis (University of Cambridge, 2010). Jon Miller, *Spinoza and the Stoics* (Cambridge: Cambridge University Press, forthcoming).

53. Giambattista Vico, *The New Science of Giambattista Vico*, Thomas Goddard Bergin and Max Harold Fisch, trans. (Ithaca, NY: Cornell University Press, 1984), § 335.

54. Johann Franz Buddeus, 'De erroribus Stoicorum in philosophia morali', presented at Halle in 1695 and published in Buddeus, *Analecta historiae philosophicae* (Halle: Orphanotrophius, 1706), pp. 87–203. See also Alan C. Kors, *Atheism in France, 1650–1729* (Princeton, NJ: Princeton University Press, 1990), vol. 1, p. 231.

55. Johann Franz Buddeus, *De Spinozismo ante Spinozam* (Halle: Henckel, 1701).

56. Johann Franz Buddeus, *Theses theologicae de atheismo et superstitione* (Jena: Johann Felix Bielcke, 1717), more widely read in its French translation, *Traité de l'athéisme et de la superstition* (Amsterdam: P. Motier, 1740). See Israel, *Radical Enlightenment*, pp. 634–35; Kors, *Atheism in France*, vol. 1, p. 232.

57. Johann Franz Buddeus, *Introductionem ad philosophiam stoicam ex mente M. Antonini* (Leipzig: Samuel Benjamin Walther, 1729).

58. Buddeus, *Analecta historiae philosophicae*, and idem, *Compendium historiae philosophicae, observationibus illustratum*, J. G. Walch, ed. (Halle: Orphanotrophius, 1731), published posthumously.

59. For detailed descriptions of the contents of many such works, see Santinello, *Models of the History of Philosophy*.

60. Thomas Stanley, *The History of Philosophy*, 3 vols. (London: Humphrey Moseley & Thomas Dring, 1655–61).

61. For some remarks on Stanley's treatment of different periods of ancient

philosophy, see Santinello et al., *Models of the History of Philosophy*, vol. 1, pp. 200–201.

62. Stanley, *History of Philosophy*, pp. 481–83.

63. Ibid., pp. 483–87.

64. Ibid., p. 478.

65. Ibid. See also Santinello et al., *Models of the History of Philosophy*, vol. 1, pp. 200–201.

66. On the historiography, see Richard Tuck, 'The "Modern" Theory of Natural Law', in Anthony Pagden, ed., *The Languages of Political Theory in Early-Modern Europe* (Cambridge: Cambridge University Press, 1987), pp. 102–7; T. J. Hochstrasser, *Natural Law Theories in the Early Enlightenment* (Cambridge: Cambridge University Press, 2000), esp. pp. 150–59 on Buddeus; also Johann Jakob Brucker, *Historia critica philosophiae* (Leipzig: Bernhard Christoph. Breitkopf, 1742–44). There are also brief remarks in Pierluigi Donini, 'The History of the Concept of Eclecticism', in A. A. Long and John M. Dillon, eds., *The Question of 'Eclecticism* (Berkeley: University of California Press, 1988), pp. 15–33. See also Diderot's article, 'Eclectisme', in Denis Diderot and Jean le Rond d'Alembert, eds., *Encyclopédie, ou dictionnaire raisonné des sciences, des arts et des metiers*, 28 vols. (Geneva, Paris, Neuchâtel: Chez Briasson et al., 1754–72), vol. 5, pp. 270–93.

67. Santinello et al., *Models of the History of Philosophy*, vol. 2, pp. 361–62.

68. Ibid., vol. 2, pp. 358, 361–62, 365.

69. Ibid., vol. 2, p. 358, which refers to Buddeus, *Compendium historiae philosophiae*, Walch ed., p. 265.

70. Buddeus, *Traité de l'athéisme*, preface. (My translation.)

71. Ibid., p. 28 n. 2.

72. Ibid., p. 28 n. 1.

73. Ibid., p. 44 n. 1.

74. Israel, *Radical Enlightenment*, pp. 544ff.

75. Barbeyrac, 'Historical and critical account', pp. 59–63.

76. Ibid., p. 63.

77. Ibid., p. 59.

78. Ibid., p. 60.

79. Ibid., p. 63.

80. Ibid., chap. 28, esp. p. 63.

81. Ibid., p. 64.

82. For Montesquieu, see especially his replies to Objection 1 in *A Defence of The Spirit of the Laws*, in Montesquieu, *The Complete Works of M. de Montesquieu*, 4 vols. (London: T. Evans and W. Davis, 1777), vol. 4, p. 230.

83. Ralph Cudworth, *Systema intellectuale hujus universi*, J. L. Mosheim, ed., 2 vols (Jena: Meyer, 1733). Mosheim's notes are translated in Cudworth, *True Intellectual System*.

84. Mosheim, in Cudworth, *True Intellectual System*, vol. 2, p. 119.

85. For examples of this dialogue on the proper understanding of Stoicism, see in particular Cudworth, *True Intellectual System*, vol. 1, pp. 62, 118, 195, 211, 300, 331; vol. 2, pp. 97–98, 105–7, 112–13, 119–22, pp. 142–44, 270, 289–91; vol. 3, pp. 82, 145.

86. Ibid., vol. 2, p. 119.

87. Ibid., vol. 2, p. 120.

88. Ibid.

89. Brucker, *Historia critica philosophiae*. For an English version of Brucker's discussions, see William Enfield, *The History of Philosophy from the Earliest Times to the Beginning of the Present Century Drawn up from Brucker's* Historia Critica Philosophia, 2 vols. (Dublin: P. Wogan, 1792).

90. Santinello, *Models of the History of Philosophy*, vol.2, pp. 324, 342.

91. Brucker, in Enfield, *History of Philosophy*, vol. 1, p. 342.

92. Ibid., vol. 1, p. 339.

93. Ibid., vol. 1, p. 339–40.

94. Ibid., vol. 1, p. 340.

95. Ibid., vol. 1, p. 341.

96. Ibid., vol. 1, p. 343.

97. Brucker, *Historia critica philosophiae*, vol. 4, p. 500.

98. Diderot, 'Stoïcisme', in Diderot and d'Alembert, *Encyclopédie*, vol. 15, pp. 525–32.

Chapter Seven
From Fénelon to Hume

1. Jean Lafond, 'Augustinisme et épicurisme au XVII siècle', in his *L'homme et son image: Morales et littérature de Montaigne à Mandeville* (Paris: H. Champion, 1996), pp. 345–68. John Robertson, *The Case for the Enlightenment: Scotland and Naples, 1680–1760* (Cambridge: Cambridge University Press, 2005), esp. pp. 123–30. Pierre Force, *Self-Interest before Adam Smith: A Genealogy of Economic Science* (Cambridge: Cambridge University Press, 2003), esp. pp. 48–63.

2. François, duc de La Rochefoucauld, *Maxims*, Stuart D. Warner and Stéphane Douard, eds. (South Bend, IN: St Augustine's Press, 2001); Nannerl O. Keohane, *Philosophy and the State in France: The Renaissance to the Enlightenment* (Princeton, NJ: Princeton University Press, 1980), pp. 289–93.

3. Ben Rogers, *Pascal: In Praise of Vanity* (New York: Routledge, 1999), esp. pp. 30–33, 49–54; for his more extended argument, see Rogers, 'In Praise of Vanity: The Augustinian Analysis of the Benefits of Vice from Port-Royal to Mandeville', DPhil thesis (University of Oxford, 1994).

4. Pierre Nicole, 'Of Charity, and Self-Love', in *Moral Essays* (London: Samuel Manship, 1696), vol. 3, pp. 78–112; John M. Parrish, *Paradoxes of Political Ethics: From Dirty Hands to the Invisible Hand* (Cambridge: Cambridge University Press, 2007), pp. 187–204; Keohane, *Philosophy and the State in France*, pp. 293–303.

5. Nicolas Malebranche, *The Search after Truth*, Thomas M. Lennon and Paul J. Olscamp, eds. (Cambridge: Cambridge University Press, 1997), 1.17.2, p. 77, quoted in Force, *Self-Interest before Adam Smith*, pp. 190–91.

6. Jacques Abbadie, *L'art de se connoître soy-mesme* (Rotterdam: Pierre vander Slaart, 1693); Isaac Nakhimovsky, 'The Enlightened Epicureanism of Jacques Abbadie: *L'Art de se connoître soi-même* and the morality of self-interest', *History of European Ideas*, vol. 29, no. 1 (2003), pp. 1–14.

7. Pierre Bayle, *A General Dictionary, Historical and Critical* (London: J. Bettenham, 1734–41), 'Epicurus'; Robertson, *Case for the Enlightenment*, p. 130.

8. John Robertson, 'The Case for the Enlightenment: A Comparative Approach', in Joseph Mali and Robert Wokler, eds., *Isaiah Berlin's Counter-Enlightenment* (Philadelphia, PA: American Philosophical Society, 2003), p. 80.

9. Both this section and the one that follows on Mandeville are strongly indebted to Istvan Hont, 'The Early Enlightenment Debate on Commerce and Luxury', in Mark Goldie and Robert Wokler, eds., *The Cambridge History of Eighteenth-Century Political Thought* (Cambridge: Cambridge University Press, 2006), pp. 379–418.

10. François de Salignac de la Mothe-Fénelon, *Instruction pastorale de monseigneur l'archevesque duc de Cambray, au clergé & au peuple de son diocese, en forme de dialogues* (Cambrai: N. J. Douilliez, 1714), quoted in Force, *Self-Interest before Adam Smith*, p. 188.

11. François de Salignac de la Mothe-Fénelon, 'Sur le pur amour', in *Oeuvres*, Jacques Le Brun, ed. (Paris: Gallimard, 1983), vol. 1, pp. 656–70, cited in the introduction to *Telemachus, Son of Ulysses*, Patrick Riley, ed. (Cambridge: Cambridge University Press, 1994), p. xxi.

12. Ibid., p. xxii.

13. Andrew Michael Ramsay, *An Essay upon Civil Government* (London: Randal Minshull, 1722), pp. 22–23, 24, citing Cicero, *De legibus* 1 and Marcus Aurelius, 4.4.

14. Fénelon, *Telemachus*, Riley ed., pp. 161, 165–66.

15. Ibid., p. 297.

16. Christopher J. Berry, *The Idea of Luxury: A Conceptual and Historical Investigation* (Cambridge: Cambridge University Press, 1994), p. 64.

17. Ibid., esp. pp. 64–65.

18. Fénelon, *Telemachus*, Riley ed., p. 110.

19. For a more detailed history of the text, see Bernard Mandeville, *The Fable of the Bees, or, private vices, publick benefits*, F. B. Kaye, ed. (Oxford: Clarendon Press, 1924), vol. 1, pp. xxxiii–xxxvii.

20. Hont, 'The Early Enlightenment Debate on Commerce and Luxury', pp. 388–89.

21. François de Salignac de la Mothe-Fénelon, *Dialogues des morts anciens et modernes, avec quelques fables* (Paris: J. Estienne, 1718); Fénelon, *Fables and dialogues of the dead* (London: W. Chetwood & S. Chapman, 1722), p. 97.

22. François de Salignac de la Mothe-Fénelon, *The adventures of Telemachus the son of Ulysses*, 8th ed. (London: A. & J. Churchill, 1713); Fénelon, *The adventures of Telemachus. In English verse. Book I* (London: J. Morphew, 1712).

23. Fénelon, *Telemachus*, Riley ed., p. 134.

24. Agnès de la Gorce, *Le vrai visage de Fénelon* (Paris: Hachette, 1958), p. 285.

25. Mandeville, *The Fable of the Bees*, Remark L, vol. 1, p. 119.

26. Mandeville, 'The Moral' to 'The Grumbling Hive', ibid., vol. 1, p. 36.

27. Ibid., Remark L, vol. 1, p. 107.

28. Ibid., Remark L, vol. 1, p. 108.

29. Ibid., Remark O, vol. 1, p. 150.

30. Ibid., Remark O, vol. 1, pp. 150–51.

31. Ibid., Remark O, vol. 1, pp. 161–62.

32. Ibid., Remark O, vol. 1, pp. 162–63.

33. Lawrence E. Klein, *Shaftesbury and the Culture of Politeness: Moral Discourse and Cultural Politics in Early 18th-Century England* (Cambridge: Cambridge University Press, 1994), passim.

34. F. B. Kaye, introduction to Mandeville, *The Fable of the Bees*, vol. 1, p. lxxii.

35. Mandeville, 'A Search into the Nature of Society', in *The Fable of the Bees*, vol. 1, p. 324.

36. Ibid., vol. 1, p. 331; 'The Third Dialogue', pt. 2 of *The Fable of the Bees*, vol. 2, p. 109. For discussion of Mandeville on hypocrisy in politics, see David Runciman, *Political Hypocrisy: The Mask of Power from Hobbes to Orwell and Beyond* (Princeton, NJ: Princeton University Press, 2008), chap. 2.

37. Mandeville, 'A Search into the Nature of Society', p. 331.

38. Mandeville, 'The Second Dialogue', pt. 2 of *The Fable of the Bees*, vol. 2, pp. 47–48.

39. Joseph Addison, *Cato: A Tragedy*, 4.4, l. 82, in *Cato: A Tragedy, and Selected Essays*, Christine Dunn Henderson and Mark E. Yellin, eds. (Indianapolis, IN: Liberty Fund, 2004), p. 84; John Trenchard and Thomas Gordon, *Cato's Letters*, Ronald Hamowy, ed. (Indianapolis, IN: Liberty Fund, 1995).

40. Mandeville, 'A Search into the Nature of Society', pp. 385–86.

41. Francis Hutcheson, *An Inquiry into the Original of Our Ideas of Beauty and Virtue in Two Treatises*, Wolfgang Leidhold, ed. (Indianapolis, IN: Liberty Fund, 2004).

42. Francis Hutcheson, 'On the Natural Sociability of Mankind', in *Logic, Metaphysics, and the Natural Sociability of Mankind*, James Moore and Michael Silverthorne, eds. (Indianapolis, IN: Liberty Fund, 2006), p. 193.

43. Ibid., p. 202.

44. Ibid., p. 202.

45. Francis Hutcheson, *An Essay on the Nature and Conduct of the Passions and Affections, with Illustrations on the Moral Sense*, Aaron Garrett, ed. (Indianapolis, IN: Liberty Fund, 2002), p. 134.

46. Francis Hutcheson, *Reflections upon Laughter and Remarks upon the Fable of the Bees* (Glasgow: R. Urie, 1750), p. 53.

47. Hutcheson, 'On the Natural Sociability of Mankind', p. 203.

48. Ibid., pp. 203–4.

49. Ibid., p. 205.

50. Ibid., p. 203.

51. Ibid., p. 199.

52. Ibid., p. 204.

53. Ibid., pp. 193–94.

54. Ibid., p. 199.

55. Ibid., p. 209.

56. Ibid., p. 206.

57. Hutcheson, *Reflections upon Laughter*, p. 58.

58. Hutcheson, *An Essay on the Nature and Conduct of the Passions*, p. 83.

59. Ibid.; Marcus Aurelius, *The Meditations of the Emperor Marcus Aurelius Antoninus*, Francis Hutcheson and James Moor, trans., James Moore and Michael Silverthorne, eds. (Indianapolis, IN: Liberty Fund, 2008), p. 33.

60. Hutcheson, *An Essay on the Nature and Conduct of the Passions* p. 84.

61. Christian Maurer, 'Self-Love in Early Eighteenth-Century British Moral Philosophy', PhD thesis (Université de Neuchâtel, 2009), pp. 205–9, 255–58.

62. Terence Irwin, *The Development of Ethics: A Historical and Critical Study*, vol. 2, *From Suarez to Rousseau* (Oxford: Oxford University Press, 2008), § 637, p. 408.

63. On Hutcheson's attempt to fit his account of conscience into his sentimentalist theory, see Irwin, *The Development of Ethics*, vol. 2, § 715, pp. 543–45.

64. Hutcheson, *An Inquiry into the Original of Our Ideas of Beauty and Virtue*, p. 134.

65. James Moore, 'Hume and Hutcheson', in M. A. Stewart and John P. Wright, eds., *Hume and Hume's Connexions* (University Park: Pennsylvania State University Press, 1994), pp. 23–57.

66. David Fate Norton, 'Hume and Hutcheson: The Question of Influence', *Oxford Studies in Early Modern Philosophy*, vol. 2 (Oxford: Oxford University Press, 2005), pp. 211–56.

67. James Moore, 'The Eclectic Stoic, the Mitigated Skeptic', in E. Mazza and E. Ronchetti, eds., *New Essays on David Hume* (Milan: Franco Angeli, 2007), pp. 133–69.

68. Stephen Darwall, *The British Moralists and the Internal 'Ought': 1640–1740* (Cambridge: Cambridge University Press, 1995), p. 36.

69. Hutcheson, *An Inquiry into the Original of Our Ideas of Beauty and Virtue*, p. 8.

70. Ibid., p. 125.

71. Joseph Butler, preface to the *Fifteen Sermons*, in *The Works of Bishop Butler*, David E. White, ed. (Rochester, NY: University of Rochester Press, 2006), § 35, p. 42.

72. Butler, preface to *Works*, § 14, p. 37, referring to William Wollaston, *The Religion of Nature Delineated* (London: Samuel Palmer, 1724), pp. 22–23.

73. Butler, preface to *Works*, § 15, p. 38.

74. Ibid., p. 38.

75. Ibid., p. 38.

76. Ibid., p. 39.

77. Ibid., p. 39.

78. Terence Irwin, 'Stoic Naturalism in Butler', in Jon Miller and Brad Inwood, eds., *Hellenistic and Early Modern Philosophy* (Cambridge: Cambridge University Press, 2003), pp. 289–91.

79. Butler, Sermon 1, in *Works*, § 4, p. 48.

80. Irwin, 'Stoic Naturalism in Butler', p. 275.

81. A. A. Long, 'Stoicism in the Philosophical Tradition: Spinoza, Lipsius, Butler', in Brad Inwood, ed., *The Cambridge Companion to the Stoics* (Cambridge: Cambridge University Press, 2003), p. 385.

82. Butler, Sermon 1, in *Works*, § 9, p. 50.

83. Ibid., § 8, p. 49.

84. Darwall, *British Moralists*, p. 247.

85. Irwin, *Development of Ethics*, vol. 2, § 677, p. 480.

86. Butler, preface to *Works*, §24, p. 40. Darwall, *British Moralists*, p. 246. Irwin is good on Butler's objection to Shaftesbury, *Development of Ethics*, vol. 2, § 714, pp. 542–43.

87. Butler, 'Of the Nature of Virtue', Dissertation II, § 1 and note, in *Works*, pp. 309, 314 n. 1; Long, 'Stoicism in the Philosophical Tradition', p. 387.

88. Richard B. Sher, *Church and University in the Scottish Enlightenment: The Moderate Literati of Edinburgh* (Edinburgh: Edinburgh University Press, 1985), pp. 175–86.

89. Isabel Rivers, *Reason, Grace, and Sentiment: A Study of the Language of Religion and Ethics in England, 1660–1780*, vol. 2, *Shaftesbury to Hume* (Cambridge: Cambridge University Press, 2000), pp. 185, 186.

90. Marcus Aurelius, *The Meditations of the Emperor Marcus Aurelius Antoninus*, pp. x–xi.

91. Ibid., p. 3.

92. Ibid., p. 4.

93. Ibid., p. 35.

94. Ibid., p. 91.

95. Ibid., p. 42.

96. Ibid., p. 53.

97. Ibid., p. 19.

98. Ibid., p. 21.

99. Ibid., p. 22.

100. *A Vindication of Mr. Hutcheson from the Calumnious Aspersions of a late Pamphlet*, by 'several of his scholars' (Glasgow, 1738), preface. Marcus Aurelius, *The Meditations of the Emperor Marcus Aurelius Antoninus*, p. xxv.

101. Elizabeth Carter, *All the works of Epictetus, which are now extant; consisting of his Discourses, preserved by Arrian, in four books, the Enchiridion, and fragments* (London, printed by S. Richardson, 1758).

102. Epictetus, *Les morales d'Epictete de Socrate de Plvtarqve et de Seneqve*, Desmarets de Saint Sorlin, trans. (Paris: Estienne Migon, 1653).

103. Montagu Pennington, *Memoirs of the Life of Mrs Elizabeth Carter* (London: F. C. & J. Rivington, 1808), vol. 1, p. 187. On Secker, see Robert G. Ingram, *Religion, Reform and Modernity in the Eighteenth Century: Thomas Secker and the Church of England* (Woodbridge: Boydell Press, 2007).

104. Ingram, *Religion, Reform and Modernity*, p. 36.

105. Letter from Catherine Talbot to Elizabeth Carter, 31 March, 1753, in Pennington, *Memoirs*, vol. 1, p. 180.

106. Pennington, *Memoirs*, vol. 1, p. 187.

107. Letter from Elizabeth Carter to Catherine Talbot, July 1755, in ibid., vol. 1, p. 189.

108. Ibid., vol. 1, pp. 195–96.

109. Carter, *Epictetus*, Introduction, § 2, pp. i–ii.

110. Ibid., § 3, p. ii.

111. Ibid., § 8, p. v.

112. Ibid., § 10, p. vi.

113. Ibid., § 11, p. vi.

114. Ibid., § 12, p. vii.

115. Ibid., §§ 13–19.

116. Ibid., § 19.

117. Ibid., § 20 and § 23.

118. Ibid., § 24, pp. xvi–xvii.

119. Ibid., § 25, p. xviii.

120. Ibid., § 26, pp. xviii–xx.

121. Ibid., § 31, p. xxii.

122. Ibid., § 31, p. xxiii.

123. Ibid., § 34, p. xxv.

124. Ibid., § 35, p. xxv.

125. Ibid., § 35, pp. xxv–xxvi.

126. Ibid., § 36, p. xxvi.

127. Ibid., § 37, p. xxvi.

128. David Hume, 'Letter to a Physician', in *The Letters of David Hume*, J. Y. T. Greig, ed. (Oxford: Clarendon Press, 1932), vol. 1, pp. 12–18.

129. Ibid., vol. 1, p. 13.

130. Ibid.

131. Ibid., vol. 1, pp. 13–14.

132. Ibid., vol. 1., p. 17.

133. Ibid., vol. 1, p. 16.

134. Irwin, *The Development of Ethics*, vol. 2, § 724, p. 566.

135. Letter from Hume to Hutcheson, 17 September 1739, in *Letters of David Hume*, vol. 1, p. 34. For a good account of the relationship between Stoic philosophy and the catalogue of the virtues in *De officiis*, see Long, 'Cicero's politics in *De officiis*', in his *From Epicurus to Epictetus: Studies in Hellenistic and Roman Philosophy* (Oxford: Oxford University Press, 2006), pp. 307–34.

136. Moore, 'Hume and Hutcheson', p. 26. Irwin also juxtaposes 'hypothetical' and 'experimental', *The Development of Ethics*, vol. 2, § 724, p. 566.

137. David Hume, *A Treatise of Human Nature*, L. A. Selby-Bigge and P. H. Nidditch, eds. (Oxford: Oxford University Press, 1978), 3, 1, 2, p. 475.

138. Irwin, *The Development of Ethics*, vol. 2, § 728, p. 573.

139. Ibid., vol. 2, § 730, p. 575.

140. Moore, 'The Eclectic Stoic, the Mitigated Skeptic', p. 145.

141. Hume, *Treatise*, 3, 3, 1, pp. 579–80.

142. Ibid., 3, 2, 1, p. 477.

143. Moore, 'The Eclectic Stoic, the Mitigated Skeptic', p. 145.

144. Hume, 'The Platonist', in *Essays Moral, Political, and Literary*, Eugene F. Miller, ed. (Indianapolis, IN: Liberty Fund, 1985), p. 157.

145. On these essays, see Rivers, *Reason, Grace, and Sentiment*, vol. 2, p. 248; Moore, 'The Eclectic Stoic, the Mitigated Skeptic', p. 157; M. A. Stewart, 'The Stoic Legacy in the Early Scottish Enlightenment', in Margaret J. Osler, ed., *Atoms, Pneuma, and Tranquillity: Epicurean and Stoic Themes in European Thought* (Cambridge: Cambridge University Press, 1991), pp. 273–96.

146. Hume, 'Of Moral Prejudices', in *David Hume, Essays*, p. 539.

147. David Hume, *Enquiries concerning Human Understanding and concern-*

ing the Principles of Morals, L. A. Selby-Bigge and P. H. Nidditch, eds. (Oxford: Oxford University Press, 1975), p. 40.

148. Christopher J. Berry 'What's Wrong with Epictetus' Slippers? Or Hume and Superfluous Value', in M. Schabas and C. Wennerlind, eds., *Hume's Political Economy* (New York: Routledge, 2007), pp. 49–64.

149. Hume, 'Of Refinement in the Arts', in *Essays*, pp. 269, 272.

150. Carter, *Epictetus, Enchiridion*, § 39, p. 457.

151. Berry, 'What's Wrong with Epictetus' Slippers?', p. 49.

152. Ibid., pp. 52ff.

153. David Hume, *The Natural History of Religion* in *Principal Writings on Religion*, J. C. A. Gaskin, ed. (Oxford: Oxford University Press, 1993), p. 149.

154. Ibid., p. 174.

155. Cicero, *De natura deorum*, H. Rackham, trans. (Cambridge, MA: Harvard University Press, 1933), 3.40, p. 383.

Chapter Eight
Jean-Jacques Rousseau

1. Adam Smith, 'Letter to the Authors of the *Edinburgh Review*', printed in Smith, *Essays on Philosophical Subjects*, W. P. D. Wightman and J. C. Bryce, eds. (Oxford: Oxford University Press, 1980), p. 244.

2. Ibid., p. 250.

3. Ibid.

4. Ibid. Bernard Mandeville, 'A Search into the Nature of Society', in *The Fable of the Bees, private vices, publick benefits*, F. B. Kaye, ed. (Oxford: Clarendon Press, 1924), vol. 1, pp. 340–41: 'men desire the company of other men for its own sake'. Cf. Francis Hutcheson, 'On the Natural Sociability of Mankind', in *Logic, Metaphysics, and the Natural Sociability of Mankind*, James Moore and Michael Silverthorne, eds. (Indianapolis, IN: Liberty Fund, 2006), p. 201.

5. Smith, 'Letter', pp. 250–51.

6. Mandeville, *The Fable of the Bees*, vol. 2, p. 129.

7. Ibid., vol. 2, pp. 131–32.

8. Ibid., vol. 2, p. 130.

9. Ibid., vol. 2, p. 133.

10. Ibid., vol. 2, p. 132.

11. Bernard Mandeville, *La fable des abeilles, ou les fripons devenus honnetes gens* (Amsterdam?, 1740), vol. 3, pp. 143, 188.

12. Jean-Baptiste Dubos, *Réflexions critiques sur la poésie et de la peinture* (Paris: Jean Mariette, 1719), on which see Michael Sonenscher, *Sans-Culottes: An Eighteenth-Century Emblem in the French Revolution* (Princeton, NJ: Princeton University Press, 2008), pp. 86–90, 153.

13. Jean-Jacques Rousseau, *Discourse on the Origins of Inequality* (hereafter 'Second Discourse'), Note XV, in *The Collected Writings of Rousseau*, Roger D. Masters and Christopher Kelly, eds., 13 vols. (Hanover, NH: University Press of New England, 1990–2009), vol. 3, p. 91. Rousseau, *Oeuvres complètes* (hereafter OC), Bernard Gagnebin and Marcel Raymond, eds., 5 vols. (Paris: Gallimard, 1959–1995), vol. 3, p. 219.

14. Rousseau, *Second Discourse*, in *Collected Writings*, vol. 3, p. 44 (OC vol. 3, pp. 165–66).

15. Arthur O. Lovejoy and George Boas, *Primitivism and Related Ideas in Antiquity* (Baltimore, MD: Johns Hopkins University Press, 1935), esp. pp. 240–42; James H. Nichols, Jr., *Epicurean Political Philosophy: The* De rerum natura *of Lucretius* (Ithaca, NY: Cornell University Press, 1976), esp. pp. 198–201.

16. Lovejoy and Boas, *Primitivism*, p. 241.

17. Nichols, *Epicurean Political Philosophy*, p. 199.

18. Lovejoy and Boas, *Primitivism*, p. 241.

19. Ibid.

20. Nichols, *Epicurean Political Philosophy*, p. 199.

21. Lucretius, *On the Nature of Things*, W. H. D. Rouse trans., revised by Martin F. Smith (Cambridge, MA: Harvard University Press, 1992), p. 467.

22. Lovejoy and Boas, *Primitivism*, p. 232–33, esp. n. 16 (emphasis added).

23. Nichols, *Epicurean Political Philosophy*, p. 199.

24. Lovejoy and Boas, *Primitivism*, p. 242.

25. Smith, 'Letter', p. 250.

26. Mandeville, 'An Essay on Charity, and Charity-Schools', in *The Fable of the Bees*, vol. 1, p. 255.

27. Ibid.

28. Rousseau, *Second Discourse*, in *Collected Writings*, vol. 3, p. 37 (OC vol. 3, p. 154).

29. Ibid., vol. 3, p. 37 (OC vol. 3, p. 155).

30. Pierre Force, *Self-interest before Adam Smith: A Genealogy of Economic Science* (Cambridge: Cambridge University Press, 2003), p. 63. This sentence is italicised in Force's text.

31. Ibid., p. 5.

32. E.g., ibid., pp. 91ff.

33. David Hume, *A Treatise of Human Nature*, L. A. Selby-Bigge and P. H. Nidditch, eds. (Oxford: Oxford University Press, 1978), 3, 3, 1., p. 578.

34. Catherine Wilson, *Epicureanism at the Origins of Modernity* (Oxford: Oxford University Press, 2008), pp. 197–99; James Moore, 'Hume and Hutcheson', in M. A. Stewart and John P. Wright, eds., *Hume and Hume's Connexions* (University Park: Pennsylvania State University Press, 1994), pp. 23–57; John Robertson, *The Case for the Enlightenment: Scotland and Naples, 1680–1760* (Cambridge: Cambridge University Press, 2005), chap. 6, esp. pp. 291–96. Cf. James Harris, 'The Epicurean in Hume', in Neven Leddy and Avi S. Lifschitz, eds., *Epicurus in the Enlightenment* (Oxford: Voltaire Foundation, 2009), pp. 161–81.

35. Adam Potkay, *The Passion for Happiness: Samuel Johnson and David Hume* (Ithaca, NY: Cornell University Press, 2000), esp. p. 77.

36. Jean de Castillon, *Discours sur l'origine de l'inegalité parmi les hommes, pour servir de réponse au Discours que M. Rousseau, Citoyen de Géneve, a publié sur le même sujet* (Amsterdam: J. F. Jolly, 1756), pp. vi–vii. (My translation.) See also his remarks about Rousseau and Lucretius on, especially, pp. 261 and 265.

37. Rousseau, *Second Discourse*, in *Collected Writings*, vol. 3, p. 66 (OC vol. 3, p. 192).

38. Ibid., vol. 3, p. 43 (*OC* vol. 3, p. 164).

39. Note XV in ibid,, vol. 3, p. 91 (*OC* , vol. 3, p. 219).

40. Ibid., vol. 3, p. 37 (*OC* vol. 3, p. 155).

41. Preface to ibid., vol. 3, pp. 14–15 (*OC* vol. 3, pp. 125–26).

42. Both opinions are reported in Rousseau's *Confessions*, in *Collected Writings*, vol. 5: for Diderot, p. 326 (*OC* vol. 1, p. 389); for Rousseau, p. 480 (*OC*, vol. 1, p. 573).

43. 'Sanabilibus aegrotamus malis; ipsaque nos in rectum genitos natura, si emendari velimus, iuvat.' Seneca, *De ira*, 2.13; Rousseau, *Emile*, in *Collected Writings*, vol. 13, pp. 155, 739 Preface n. 2.

44. Rousseau, *Emile*, bk. 1, in *Collected Writings*, vol. 13, p. 162 (*OC* vol. 4, p. 247).

45. Ibid., bk. 1, vol. 13, p. 163 (*OC* vol. 4, p. 247).

46. Ibid., bk. 2, vol. 13, p. 211 (*OC*, vol. 4, p. 304).

47. Ibid.

48. Ibid., bk. 2, vol. 13, pp. 216–17 (*OC* vol. 4, p. 311).

49. Ibid., bk. 2, vol. 13, p. 217 (*OC* vol. 4, p. 312).

50. Seneca, Letter 121, in *Selected Philosophical Letters*, Brad Inwood, ed. (Oxford: Oxford University Press, 2007), p. 87.

51. Dom Joseph Cajot, *Les Plagiats de M. J-J Rousseau de Genève sur l'éducation* (La Haye: Durand, 1766), pp. 33–37.

52. Rousseau, *Emile*, bk. 4, in *Collected Writings*, vol. 13, p. 362 (*OC* vol. 4, pp. 490–91).

53. Ibid, bk. 4, vol. 13, pp. 362–3 (*OC* vol. 4, p. 491).

54. Ibid, bk. 4, vol. 13, p. 363 (*OC* vol. 4, p. 491).

55. Ibid.

56. Ibid, bk. 4, vol. 13, p. 363 (*OC* vol. 4, p. 492).

57. Ibid., bk. 4, vol. 13, p. 364 (*OC* vol. 4, pp. 492–3).

58. Ibid., bk. 4, vol. 13, p. 389 (*OC* vol. 4, p. 523).

59. Ibid., bk. 4, vol. 13, p. 364 (*OC* vol. 4, p. 493).

60. Ibid., bk. 4, vol. 13, p. 365 (*OC* vol. 4, p. 494).

61. Ibid., bk. 4, vol. 13, p. 370 (*OC* vol. 4, pp. 500–1).

62. Ibid., bk. 4, vol. 13, pp. 370–71 (*OC* vol. 4, p. 501).

63. Ibid., bk. 4, vol. 13, p. 372 (*OC* vol. 4, p. 502).

64. Ibid., bk. 4, vol. 13, pp. 372–73 (*OC* vol 4, p. 503).

65. For some of the contemporary criticisms of Rousseau's argument about pity in the *Second Discourse* and the difficulties these caused him, see Sonenscher, *Sans-Culottes*, pp. 29–32.

66. Rousseau, *Emile*, bk. 4, in *Collected Writings*, vol. 13, p. 374 (*OC* vol. 4, p. 505).

67. Ibid., bk. 4, vol. 13, pp. 374–75 (*OC* vol. 4, p. 506).

68. Ibid., bk. 4, vol. 13, p. 375 (*OC* vol. 4, p. 506).

69. Ibid., bk. 3, vol. 13, p. 353 (*OC* vol. 4, p. 481)..

70. For textual citations, see Keith Ansell-Pearson, *Nietzsche* contra *Rousseau* (Cambridge: Cambridge University Press, 1991), p. 234 n. 1. Cf. Friedrich Nietzsche, *The Gay Science*, Bernard Williams, ed. (Cambridge: Cambridge University Press, 2001), § 91, p. 89; 'Assorted Opinions and Maxims', § 408, in

Human, All Too Human, R. J. Hollingdale, trans. (Cambridge: Cambridge University Press, 1996), p. 299; *Beyond Good and Evil*, Rolf-Peter Horstmann and Judith Norman, eds. (Cambridge: Cambridge University Press, 2002), § 245, p. 137.

71. See, e.g., Michael Ure, 'The Irony of Pity: Nietzsche contra Schopenhauer and Rousseau', *Journal of Nietzsche Studies*, no. 32 (Autumn 2006), pp. 68–91; Martha C. Nussbaum, 'Pity and Mercy: Nietzsche's Stoicism', in Richard Schacht, ed., *Nietzsche, Genealogy, Morality: Essays on Nietzsche's Genealogy of Morals* (Berkeley: University of California Press, 1994).

72. Rousseau, *Emile*, bk. 4, in *Collected Writings*, vol. 13, p. 389 (OC vol. 4, p. 523).

73. Christopher Brooke, 'Rousseau's Political Philosophy: Stoic and Augustinian Origins', in Patrick Riley, ed., *The Cambridge Companion to Rousseau* (Cambridge: Cambridge University Press, 2001), pp. 94–123.

74. Blaise Pascal, *Pensées*, Léon Brunschvicg, ed. (Paris: Hachette, 1976), p. 183.

75. Nicholas Dent, *Rousseau: An Introduction to His Psychological, Social and Political Theory* (Oxford: Blackwell, 1988); *A Rousseau Dictionary* (Oxford: Blackwell, 1992), esp. '*amour de soi*', '*amour-propre*', and 'denaturing'; *Rousseau* (London: Routledge, 2005); Timothy O'Hagan, *Rousseau* (London: Routledge, 1999); John Rawls, *Lectures on the History of Political Philosophy* (Cambridge, MA: Harvard University Press, 2007); Frederick Neuhouser, *Rousseau's Theodicy of Self-Love* (Oxford: Oxford University Press, 2008).

76. Dent, *Rousseau Dictionary*, p. 35.

77. Frederick Neuhouser, *Foundations of Hegel's Social Theory: Actualizing Freedom* (Cambridge, MA: Harvard University Press, 2000), p. 68.

78. Rousseau, *Emile*, bk. 4, in *Collected Writings*, vol. 13, p. 389 (OC vol. 4, pp. 523–24). Michael Rosen has challenged Bloom's translation here, arguing that 'this one' (i.e., *amour-propre*) is wrong and should be replaced by 'the former' (i.e., *amour de soi*) on the ground that this is a better rendering of Rousseau's '*celle-là*'. (The full sentence is 'Voilà le point où l'amour de soi se change en amour-propre, et où commencent à naître toutes les passions qui tiennent à celle-là.') But this would only be preferable if there were a '*celle-ci*' ('the latter') or similar to balance the '*celle-là*' (which would then become 'the former'), but there isn't, so it isn't; and, in its absence, Bloom's translation is to be preferred. See Rosen, *On Voluntary Servitude: False Consciousness and the Theory of Ideology* (Cambridge: Polity Press, 1996), p. 85 n. 77; Dent, *Rousseau: An Introduction*, p. 54; cf. Neuhouser, *Rousseau's Theodicy of Self-Love*, p. 16 n. 27.

79. Rousseau, *Emile*, bk. 4, in *Collected Writings*, vol. 13, p. 409 (OC vol. 4, p. 547), quoted in, e.g., Dent, *Rousseau: An Introduction*, p. 55 (though the reference is given incorrectly there).

80. Ibid.

81. Ibid., p. 144.

82. Rousseau, *Second Discourse*, in *Collected Writings*, vol. 3, p. 37 (OC vol. 3, p. 156).

83. Neuhouser, *Rousseau's Theodicy of Self-Love*, chap. 7.

84. See Amélie Oksenberg Rorty, 'Rousseau's Therapeutic Experiments'", *Philosophy*, vol. 66, no. 258. (October 1991), pp. 413–34.

85. Rousseau, *Emile*, bk. 4, in *Collected Writings*, vol. 13, pp. 451–2 (*OC* vol. 4, p. 598).

86. Ibid., bk. 4, vol. 13, p. 453 (*OC* vol. 4, p. 599).

87. Ibid., bk. 4, vol. 13, p. 455 (*OC* vol. 4, p. 602).

88. Dent, *Rousseau Dictionary*, 'conscience', p. 60.

89. Ibid., 'amour de soi', p. 32.

90. Rousseau, *Emile and Sophie; or, the Solitaries* in *Collected Writings*, vol. 13, p. 686 (*OC* vol. 4, p. 883).

91. Ibid., vol. 13, p. 715 (*OC* vol. 4, pp. 916–8).

92. Rousseau, *Reveries of the Solitary Walker*, 'Second Walk', in *Collected Writings*, vol. 8, pp. 11–12 (*OC* vol. 1, pp. 1004–6). Pierre Hadot, *Philosophy as a Way of Life* (Oxford: Blackwell, 1995), chap. 8.

93. Epictetus, *Discourses*, W. A. Oldfather, trans. (Cambridge, MA: Harvard University Press, 1985–89), 1.2.17–18.

Epilogue

1. V. I. Lenin, 'The Three Sources and Component Parts of Marxism', in *Collected Works* (Moscow: Progress Publishers, 1977), vol. 19, p. 21.

2. Karl Marx, 'The Difference Between the Democritean and Epicurean Philosophy of Nature', in *Marx Engels Collected Works* (London: Lawrence & Wishart, 1975–2005), vol. 1, pp. 25–108; 'Notebooks on Epicurean Philosophy', ibid., pp. 403–509.

3. Karl Marx, 'A Contribution to the Critique of Hegel's *Philosophy of Right*', in *Marx Engels Collected Works*, vol. 3, pp. 3–129. David Leopold, *The Young Karl Marx: German Philosophy, Modern Politics, and Human Flourishing* (Cambridge: Cambridge University Press, 2007), chap. 2. Gareth Stedman Jones, introduction to Karl Marx and Friedrich Engels, *The Communist Manifesto*, Gareth Stedman Jones, ed. (London: Penguin, 2002), pp. 103–13.

4. Allan Megill, *Karl Marx: The Burden of Reason (Why Marx Rejected Politics and the Market)* (Lanham, MD: Rowman & Littlefield, 2002), pp. 106–10.

5. Karl Marx, 'Notes on James Mill', in *Marx Engels Collected Works*, vol. 3, pp. 211–28.

6. Jean-Jacques Rousseau, *Confessions*, in *The Collected Writings of Rousseau*, Roger D. Masters and Christopher Kelly, eds. (Hanover, NH: University Press of New England, 1990–2009), vol. 5, pp. 339–40; *Oeuvres complètes* (hereafter *OC*), Bernard Gagnebin and Marcel Raymond, eds. (Paris: Gallimard, 1959–1995), vol. 1, p. 404.

7. Rousseau, *The Social Contract*, bk. 4, ch. 9, in *Collected Writings*, vol. 4, p. 224 (*OC*, vol. 3, p. 470).

8. Rousseau, *Considerations on the Government of Poland and on Its Planned Reformation*, in *Collected Writings*, vol. 11, pp. 167–240 (*OC*, vol. 3, pp. 954–1041); *Plan for a Constitution for Corsica*, ibid., pp. 123–65 (*OC*, vol. 3, pp. 901–50).

9. Rousseau, 'Letter to Mirabeau', 26 July 1767, in *The Social Contract and Other Late Political Writings*, Victor Gourevitch, ed. (Cambridge: Cambridge University Press, 1997), p. 270.

10. Céline Spector, 'Le *Projet de paix perpétuelle*: de Saint-Pierre à Rousseau', in Jean-Jacques Rousseau, *Principes du droit de la guerre: Ecrits sur la paix perpétuelle*, Blaise Bachofen and Céline Spector, eds. (Paris: Vrin, 2008), pp. 229–94.

11. Immanuel Kant, 'Remarks on the Observations of the Beautiful and Sublime', quoted in Manfred Kuehn, *Kant: A Biography* (Cambridge: Cambridge University Press, 2001), p. 131.

12. Ibid., pp. 272, 483 n. 89.

13. Rousseau, *The Social Contract*, bk. 1, ch. 8, in *Collected Writings*, vol. 4, p. 142 (*OC*, vol. 3, p. 365).

14. Cicero, *Paradoxa Stoicorum*, in *Cicero* 4, H. Rackham, trans. (Cambridge, MA: Harvard University Press, 1942). For discussion, see John M. Cooper, 'Stoic Autonomy', *Social Philosophy and Policy*, vol. 20, no. 2 (2003), pp. 1–29.

15. Immanuel Kant, *The Moral Law: Groundwork of the Metaphysic of Morals*, H. J. Paton, trans. (London: Routledge, 2005).

16. Joshua Cohen, *Rousseau: A Free Community of Equals* (Oxford: Oxford University Press, 2010), p. 94; see also Frederick Neuhouser, *Foundations of Hegel's Social Theory: Actualizing Freedom* (Cambridge, MA: Harvard University Press, 2000), p. 319 n. 15.

17. Neuhouser, *Foundations of Hegel's Social Theory*, p. 81.

18. Ferdinand, Baron d'Eckstein, 'De l'Industrialisme', *Le Catholique*, vol. 5 (1827), pp. 239–42; Isaac Nakhimovsky, *The Closed Commercial State: Perpetual Peace and Commercial Society from Rousseau to Fichte* (Princeton, NJ: Princeton University Press, 2011), p. 156.

19. Adam Smith, *The Theory of Moral Sentiments*, D. D. Raphael and Alec Macfie, eds. (Oxford: Clarendon Press, 1976), 4.1.10, p. 185.

20. John Robertson, *The Case for the Enlightenment: Scotland and Naples, 1680–1760* (Cambridge: Cambridge University Press, 2005), p. 394.

21. Neven Brady Leddy, 'Adam Smith's *Theory of Moral Sentiments* in 1759, 1790 and 1976', paper presented at the International Adam Smith Society's conference, 'The Philosophy of Adam Smith', Balliol College, Oxford, January 2009.

22. D. D. Raphael and Alec Macfie, introduction to Adam Smith, *Theory of Moral Sentiments*, p. 5.

23. Adam Smith, *Theory of Moral Sentiments*, 6.3.11, p. 241, cited in Raphael and Macfie's introduction, p. 6.

24. Raphael and Macfie, introduction to Smith, *Theory of Moral Sentiments*, p. 7.

25. Norbert Waszek, 'Two Concepts of Morality: A Distinction of Adam Smith's Ethics and Its Stoic Origin', *Journal of the History of Ideas*, vol. 45 (1984), pp. 591–606; Stewart Justman, *The Autonomous Male of Adam Smith* (Norman: University of Oklahoma Press, 1993); Athol Fitzgibbons, *Adam Smith's System of Liberty, Wealth and Virtue* (Oxford: Clarendon Press, 1995). See also Vivienne Brown, *Adam Smith's Discourse: Canonicity, Commerce, and Conscience* (London: Routledge, 1994); Ryan Patrick Hanley, *Adam Smith and the*

Character of Virtue (Cambridge: Cambridge University Press, 2009); and Fonna Forman-Barzilai, *Adam Smith and the Circles of Sympathy: Cosmopolitanism and Moral Theory* (Cambridge: Cambridge University Press, 2010).

26. Smith, *Theory of Moral Sentiments*, 7.2.1, p. 292.

27. Robertson, *Case for the Enlightenment*, pp. 395–96. See also Neven Brady Leddy, 'Adam Smith's Moral Philosophy at the Nexus of National and Philosophical Contexts: French Literature and Epicurean Philosophy in the Scottish Enlightenment', DPhil thesis (University of Oxford, 2009).

28. Gloria Vivenza, *Adam Smith and the Classics* (Oxford: Oxford University Press, 2001), p. 61.

29. Emma Rothschild, *Economic Sentiments: Adam Smith, Condorcet and the Enlightenment* (Cambridge, MA: Harvard University Press, 2001), esp. pp. 131–34.

30. J. Dautry, ed., *Gilbert Romme et son temps* (Paris: Presses Universitaires de France, 1966), p. 204.

31. Martin Thom, *Republics, Nations and Tribes* (London: Verso, 1995), pp. 26–29.

32. Karl Marx, *The Eighteenth Brumaire of Louis Bonaparte*, in *Marx Engels Collected Works*, vol. 11, p. 104.

33. Thom, *Republics, Nations and Tribes*, p. 312 n. 59.

34. Dorinda Outram, *The Body and the French Revolution: Sex, Class, and Political Culture* (New Haven, CT: Yale University Press, 1989), p. 103.

35. Ibid., p. 84.

36. See Sarah Hutton, 'Virtue, God, and Stoicism in the Thought of Elizabeth Carter and Catharine Macaulay', in J. Broad and K. Green, eds., *Virtue, Liberty and Toleration: Political Ideas of European Women, 1400–1800* (Dordrecht: Springer, 2007), p. 142.

37. Mary Wollstonecraft, review of Catharine Macaulay, *Letters on Education*, *Analytical Review,* vol. 8, no. 3 (1790), p. 253.

38. For Wollstonecraft as a Stoic, see Richard Vernon, *Friends, Citizens, Strangers: Essays on Where We Belong* (Toronto, ON: University of Toronto Press, 2005), chap. 3. For some caution with this identification of Wollstonecraft, see Elizabeth Wingrove, 'Getting Intimate with Wollstonecraft: In the Republic of Letters', *Political Theory,* vol. 33 (2005), pp. 344–69.

39. Mary Wollstonecraft, *A Vindication of the Rights of Woman*, in *A Vindication of the Rights of Men . . .* , Sylvana Tomaselli, ed. (Cambridge: Cambridge University Press, 1995), pp. 240–41.

Bibliography

Primary

Jacques Abbadie, *L'art de se connoître soy-mesme* (Rotterdam: Pierre vander Slaart, 1693).

Joseph Addison, *Cato: A Tragedy, and Selected Essays*, Christine Dunn Henderson and Mark E. Yellin, eds. (Indianapolis, IN: Liberty Fund, 2004).

John Aubrey, 'Brief Life' of Thomas Hobbes, in Hobbes, *Human Nature and De Corpore Politico*, J. C. A. Gaskin, ed. (Oxford: Oxford University Press, 1999), pp. 231–45.

Augustine, *Confessions*, William Watts, trans., 2 vols. (Cambridge, MA: Harvard University Press, 1989).

————, *The City of God against the Pagans*, R. W. Dyson, ed. (Cambridge: Cambridge University Press, 1998).

————, *On Christian Doctrine*, D. W. Robertson, trans. (New York: Liberal Arts Press, 1958).

————, *St. Augustine on the Psalms*, Scholastica Hebgin and Felicitas Corrigan, trans., 2 vols. (Westminster, MD: Newman Press, 1960).

————, *Letters*, Sister Wilfrid Parsons, trans., 6 vols. (Washington, DC: Catholic University of America Press, 1964–89).

————, *Against Julian*, Matthew A. Schumacher, trans. (Washington, DC: Catholic University of America Press, 1977).

Francis Bacon, *Of the advancement and proficience of learning*, Gilbert Watts, trans. (Oxford: Leonard Lichfield, 1640).

Jean Barbeyrac, 'An Historical and Critical Account of the Science of Morality,' in Samuel Pufendorf, *The Law of Nature and Nations*, Jean Barbeyrac, ed., Basil Kennet, trans. (London: J. & J. Bonwicke, 1749).

Barnabe Barnes, *Foure bookes of offices enabling privat persons for the speciall seruice of all good princes and policies* (London: G. Bishop, J. Adams & C. Burbie, 1606).

Pierre Bayle, *A General Dictionary, Historical and Critical*, 10 vols. (London: J. Bettenham, 1734–41).

Aphra Behn, ed., *Miscellany, being a collection of poems by several hands; together with Reflections on morality, or, Seneca unmasqued* (London: J. Hindmarsh, 1685).

Trajano Boccalini, *Advertisements from Parnassus* (London: Richard Smith, 1704).

Johann Heinrich Böcler, *In Hugonis Grotii Jus belli et pacis, ad illustrissimum baronem Boineburgium commentatio* (Giessen: Caspar Wächtler, 1687).

John Bramhall, *Castigations of Mr. Hobbes, his last animadversions, in the case concerning liberty and universal necessity* (London: John Crook, 1658).

————, *A Defence of True Liberty from Antecedent and Extrinsecall Necessity, being an answer to a late book of Mr. Thomas Hobbs of Malmsbury, intituled, A Treatise of Liberty and Necessity* (London: John Crook, 1655).

————, *Works* (Dublin: His Majesty's Printing-house, 1676).

Johann Jakob Brucker, *Historia critica philosophiae* (Leipzig: Bernhard Christoph Breitkopf 1742–44).

Johann Franz Buddeus, *Analecta historiae philosophicae* (Halle: Orphanotrophius, 1706).

————, *Compendium historiae philosophicae, observationibus illustratum*, J. G. Walch, ed. (Halle: Orphanotrophius, 1731).

————, 'De erroribus Stoicorum in philosophia morali', in *Analecta historiae philosophicae* (Halle: Orphanotrophius, 1706), pp. 87–203.

————, *De Spinozismo ante Spinozam* (Halle: Henckel, 1701).

————, *Introductionem ad philosophiam stoicam ex mente M. Antonini* (Leipzig: Samuel Benjamin Walther, 1729).

————, *Theses theologicae de atheismo et superstitione* (Jena: Johann Felix Bielcke, 1717).

————, *Traité de l'athéisme et de la superstition*, Louis Philon, trans. (Amsterdam: P. Motier, 1740).

Joseph Butler, preface to the *Fifteen Sermons*, in *Works*, pp. 35–46.

————, *The Works of Bishop Butler*, David E. White, ed. (Rochester, NY: University of Rochester Press, 2006).

Dom Joseph Cajot, *Les Plagiats de M. J-J Rousseau de Genève sur l'éducation* (La Haye: Durand, 1766).

Elizabeth Carter, *All the works of Epictetus: which are now extant; consisting of his Discourses, preserved by Arrian, in four books, the Enchiridion, and fragments* (London: S. Richardson, 1758).

Jean de Castillon, *Discours sur l'origine de l'inegalité parmi les hommes, pour servir de réponse au Discours que M. Rousseau, Citoyen de Géneve, a publié sur le même sujet* (Amsterdam: J. F. Jolly, 1756).

Cicero, *De natura deorum*, H. Rackham, trans. (Cambridge, MA: Harvard University Press, 1933).

————, *On Duties*, M. T. Griffin and E. M. Atkins, eds. (Cambridge: Cambridge University Press, 1991).

————, *On Moral Ends*, Julia Annas, ed. (Cambridge: Cambridge University Press, 2001).

————, *Paradoxa Stoicorum*, in *Cicero* 4, H. Rackham, trans. (Cambridge, MA: Harvard University Press, 1942).

————, *Tusculan Disputations*, J. E. King, trans. (Cambridge, MA: Harvard University Press, 1989).

Samuel Clarke, *A Discourse Concerning the Unchangeable Obligations of Natural Religion, and the Truth and Certainty of the Christian Revelation* (London: W. Botham, 1706).

Anthony Collins, *A Philosophical Inquiry Concerning Human Liberty* (London: Routledge / Thoemmes Press, 1997).

Hermann Conring, *De civili prudentia* (Helmstedt, 1662).

Ralph Cudworth, *Systema intellectuale hujus universi*, J. L. Mosheim ed., 2 vols. (Jena: Meyer, 1733).

————, *The True Intellectual System of the Universe*, 3 vols. (London: Thomas Tegg, 1845).

Nathaniel Culverwell, *An Elegant and Learned Discourse of the Light of Nature* (Indianapolis, IN: Liberty Fund, 2001).

Richard Cumberland, *A Treatise of the Laws of Nature*, Jon Parkin, ed., James Maxwell, trans. (Indianapolis, IN: Liberty Fund, 2005).

Denis Diderot, "Eclectisme," in Diderot and d'Alembert, *Encyclopédie*, vol. 5, pp. 270–93.

————, "Stoïcisme", in Diderot and d'Alembert, *Encyclopédie*, vol. 15, pp. 525–32.

Denis Diderot and Jean le Rond d'Alembert, eds., *Encyclopédie, ou dictionnaire raisonné des sciences, des arts et des metiers*, 28 vols. (Geneva, Paris, Neuchâtel: Chez Briasson et al., 1754–72).

Diogenes Laertius, *Lives of Eminent Philosophers*, R. D. Hicks, trans. (Cambridge, MA: Harvard University Press, 1975), 2 vols.

John Dryden, 'Absalom and Achitophel', in *The Major Works*, Keith Walker, ed. (Oxford: Oxford University Press, 2003).

Jean-Baptiste Dubos, *Réflexions critiques sur la poésie et de la peinture* (Paris: Jean Mariette, 1719).

Guillaume du Vair, *Le Manuel d'Epictète* (Paris: Langelier, 1591).

————, *The Moral Philosophie of the Stoicks*, Thomas James, trans. (London: F. Kingston, 1598).

————, *Traité de la constance et consolation ès calamitez publiques* (Paris: Libraire de la Société du Recueil Sirey, 1915).

Ferdinand, Baron d'Eckstein, 'De l'Industrialisme', *Le Catholique*, vol. 5 (1827), pp. 233–63.

William Enfield, *The History of Philosophy from the Earliest Times to the Beginning of the Present Century Drawn up from Brucker's* Historia Critica Philosophia, 2 vols. (Dublin: P. Wogan, 1792).

Epictetus, *The Discourses as reported by Arrian, the Manual, and fragments*, W. A. Oldfather, trans., 2 vols. (Cambridge, MA: Harvard University Press, 1985–9).

————, *Epictetus his morals, with Simplicius his comment*, George Stanhope, ed., 3rd ed. (London: Richard Sare, 1704).

————, *Les morales d'Epictete de Socrate de Plvtarqve et de Seneqve*, Desmarets de Saint Sorlin, trans. (Paris: Estienne Migon, 1653).

François de Salignac de la Mothe-Fénelon, *The adventures of Telemachus. In English verse. Book I* (London: J. Morphew, 1712).

————, *The adventures of Telemachus the son of Ulysses*, 8th ed. (London: A. & J. Churchill, 1713).

————, *Dialogues des morts anciens et modernes, avec quelques fables* (Paris: J. Estienne, 1718).

————, *Fables and dialogues of the dead* (London: W. Chetwood & S. Chapman, 1722).

————, *Instruction pastorale de monseigneur l'archevesque duc de Cambray, au clergé & au peuple de son diocese, en forme de dialogues* (Cambrai: N. J. Douilliez, 1714).

————, 'Sur le pur amour', in Fénelon, *Oeuvres*, Jacques Le Brun, ed. (Paris: Gallimard, 1983), vol. 1, pp. 656–70.

———, *Telemachus, Son of Ulysses*, Patrick Riley, ed. (Cambridge: Cambridge University Press, 1994).

Simon Goulart, 'Ample discours sur la doctrine des Stoïques', in *Oeuvres morales et mêlées* (Geneva, 1606), vol. 3.

Hugo Grotius, *De Iure Belli ac Pacis Libri Tres* (Paris: Nicholas Buon, 1625).

———, *De Iure Belli ac Pacis Libri Tres* (Amsterdam: Willem Jansz Blaeu, 1631).

———, *De Iure Belli ac Pacis Libri Tres* (Amsterdam: Johannes & Cornelius Blaeu, 1642).

———, *The Rights of War and Peace*, Richard Tuck and Jean Barbeyrac, eds., 3 vols. (Indianapolis, IN: Liberty Fund, 2005).

Joseph Hall, *Heaven upon Earth, and Characters of Vertues and Vices*, Rudolf Kirk, ed. (New Brunswick, NJ: Rutgers University Press, 1939).

Thomas Hobbes, *An answer to a book published by Dr. Bramhall, late bishop of Derry; called the Catching of the leviathan. Together with an historical narration concerning heresie, and the punishment thereof* (London: W. Crooke, 1682).

———, *Human Nature and De corpore politico*, J. C. A. Gaskin, ed. (Oxford: Oxford University Press, 1999).

———, *The Elements of Law, Natural and Politic*, in *Human Nature and De corpore politico*, pp. 1–182.

———, *Leviathan*, Richard Tuck, ed. (Cambridge: Cambridge University Press, 1991).

———, *Of libertie and necessitie a treatise: wherein all controversie concerning predestination, election, free-will, grace, merits, reprobation, &c. is fully decided and cleared in answer to a treatise written by the Bishop of London-derry, on the same subject* (London: F. Eaglesfield, 1654).

———, *On the Citizen*, Richard Tuck and Michael Silverthorne, eds. (Cambridge: Cambridge University Press, 1998).

———, *Philosophicall rudiments concerning government and society* (London: Royston, 1651).

———, *The questions concerning liberty, necessity, and chance: clearly stated and debated between Dr. Bramhall, Bishop of Derry, and Thomas Hobbes of Malmesbury* (London: Andrew Crook, 1656).

———, *Three Discourses*, Noel B. Reynolds and Arlene W. Saxonhouse, eds. (Chicago: University of Chicago Press, 1995).

Horae subseciuae: Observations and discourses (London: Edward Blount, 1620).

David Hume, *Enquiries concerning Human Understanding and concerning the Principles of Morals*, L. A. Selby-Bigge and P. H. Nidditch, eds. (Oxford: Oxford University Press, 1975).

———, *The Letters of David Hume*, J. Y. T. Greig, ed., 2 vols. (Oxford: Clarendon Press, 1932).

———, *The Natural History of Religion*, in *Principal Writings on Religion*, pp. 134–96.

———, 'Of Moral Prejudices', in *Essays Moral, Political, and Literary*, pp. 538–44.

———, 'The Platonist', in *Essays Moral, Political, and Literary*, 155–58.

———, 'Of Refinements in the Arts', in *Essays Moral, Political, and Literary*, pp. 268–80.

————, *Principal Writings on Religion*, J. C. A. Gaskin, ed. (Oxford: Oxford University Press, 1993).

————, *A Treatise of Human Nature*, L. A. Selby-Bigge and P. H. Nidditch, eds. (Oxford: Oxford University Press, 1978).

————, *Essays Moral, Political, and Literary*, Eugene F. Miller, ed. (Indianapolis, IN: Liberty Fund 1985).

Francis Hutcheson, *An Essay on the Nature and Conduct of the Passions and Affections, with Illustrations on the Moral Sense*, Aaron Garrett, ed. (Indianapolis, IN: Liberty Fund, 2002).

————, *An Inquiry into the Original of Our Ideas of Beauty and Virtue in Two Treatises*, Wolfgang Leidhold, ed. (Indianapolis, IN: Liberty Fund, 2004).

————, 'On the Natural Sociability of Mankind', in *Logic, Metaphysics, and the Natural Sociability of Mankind*, James Moore and Michael Silverthorne, eds. (Indianapolis, IN: Liberty Fund, 2006), pp. 189–216.

————, *Reflections upon Laughter and Remarks upon the Fable of the Bees* (Glasgow: R. Urie, 1750).

King James, *Basilikon Doron* (Edinburgh: Robert Waldegrave, 1599).

————, *Basilikon Doron* (London: Richard Field, 1603).

Corneille Jansen, *Augustinus* (Paris: Guillemot, 1641).

Immanuel Kant, *Immanuel Kant's Critique of Pure Reason*, Norman Kemp Smith, trans. (London: Macmillan, 1964).

————, *The Moral Law: Groundwork of the Metaphysic of Morals*, H. J. Paton, trans. (London: Routledge, 2005).

François, duc de La Rochefoucauld, *Maxims*, Stuart D. Warner and Stéphane Douard, eds. (South Bend, IN: St Augustine's Press, 2001).

————, *Maximes et mémoires*, Jean Starobinski, ed. (Paris: Union Générale d'Éditions, 1964).

Lactantius, *Divine Institutes*, Anthony Bowen and Peter Garnsey, trans. (Liverpool: Liverpool University Press, 2003).

Antoine Le Grand, *The Entire Body of Philosophy* (London: Samuel Roycroft, 1694).

————, *Le Sage des Stoiques* (The Hague: Sam Browne & Jean L'Escluse, 1662).

————, *Man Without Passion* (London: C. Harper & J. Amery, 1675).

G. W. Leibniz, *Textes inédits*, Gaston Grua, ed. (Paris: Presses Universitaires de France, 1948).

V. I. Lenin, 'The Three Sources and Component Parts of Marxism', in *Collected Works* (Moscow: Progress Publishers, 1977), vol. 19.

Justus Lipsius, C. *Cornelii Taciti Opera quae exstant* (Louvain: Plantin, 1588).

————, *De constantia libri duo* (London: George Bishop, 1586).

————, *De recta pronuntatione Latinae linguae dialogus* (Antwerp, 1586).

————, *Iusti Lipsi Epistolae*, A. Gerlo, M. A. Nauwelaerts and H. D. L. Vervliet, eds. (Brussels: Koninklijke Academie voor Wetenschappen, Letteren, en Schone Kunsten van Belgie, 1978–).

————, *Manuductionis ad Stoicam philosophiam libri tres*, 1.19, in *Opera omnia* (Wesel: Andreas van Hoogenhuysen, 1675), vol. 4.

————, *On Constancy*, John Stradling, trans., John Sellars, ed. (Exeter: Bristol Phoenix Press, 2006).

————, *Physiologiae Stoicorum libri tres* (Antwerp: J. Moretus, 1604).

————, *Politica: Six Books of Politics or Political Instruction*, Jan Waszink, ed. (Assen: Van Gorcum, 2004).

————, *Sixe bookes of politickes or ciuil doctrine*, William Jones, trans. (London: Richard Field, 1594).

————, *War and peace reconciled, or, A discourse of constancy in inconstant times*, Nathaniel Wanley, trans. (London: Royston, 1672).

Lucretius, *On the Nature of Things*, W. H. D. Rouse trans., revised by Martin F. Smith (Cambridge, MA: Harvard University Press, 1992).

Niccolò Machiavelli, *Discourses on Livy*, Harvey C. Mansfield and Nathan Tarcov, trans. (Chicago: University of Chicago Press: 1996).

————, *The Prince*, Harvey C. Mansfield, trans. (Chicago: University of Chicago Press, 1998).

Nicolas Malebranche, *The Search After Truth*, Thomas M. Lennon and Paul J. Olscamp, eds. (Cambridge: Cambridge University Press, 1997).

————, *Treatise on Ethics (1684)*, Craig Walton, trans. (Dordrecht: Kluwer Academic, 1993).

Bernard Mandeville, *La fable des abeilles, ou les fripons devenus honnetes gens*, 4 vols. (Amsterdam?: 1740), 4 vols.

————, *The Fable of the Bees, or, private vices, publick benefits*, F. B. Kaye, ed., 2 vols. (Oxford: Clarendon Press, 1924).

————, 'An Essay on Charity, and Charity-Schools', in *The Fable of the Bees*, vol. 1, p. 253–322.

————, 'A Search into the Nature of Society', in *The Fable of the Bees*, vol. 1, pp. 323–69.

Marcus Aurelius, *The Emperor Marcus Antoninus his Conversation with Himself*, Jeremy Collier, ed. (London: Richard Sare, 1701).

————, *His Meditations concerning Himself*, Meric Casaubon, trans., 3rd ed. (London: James Flesher, 1663).

————, *Marci Antonini Imperatoris De Rebus Suis*, 2nd ed., Thomas Gataker, trans. (London: Edward Millington, 1697).

————, *The Meditations of the Emperor Marcus Aurelius Antoninus*, Francis Hutcheson and James Moor, trans., James Moore and Michael Silverthorne, eds. (Indianapolis, IN: Liberty Fund, 2008).

————, *Réflexions morales avec des remarques de Mr. & de Mad. Dacier*, 2nd ed. (Amsterdam: Abraham Wolfgang, 1691).

Karl Marx, 'Difference Between the Democritean and Epicurean Philosophy of Nature', in Marx and Engels, *Marx Engels Collected Works*, vol. 1, pp. 25–108.

————, 'A Contribution to the Critique of Hegel's *Philosophy of Right*', in Marx and Engels, *Marx Engels Collected Works*, vol. 3, pp. 3–129.

————, *The Eighteenth Brumaire of Louis Bonaparte*, in Marx and Engels, *Marx Engels Collected Works*, vol. 11.

————, 'Notebooks on Epicurean Philosophy', in Marx and Engels, *Marx Engels Collected Works*, vol. 1, pp. 403–509.

————, 'Notes on James Mill', in Marx and Engels, *Marx Engels Collected Works*, vol. 3, pp. 211–28.

Karl Marx and Friedrich Engels, *Marx Engels Collected Works*, 50 vols. (London: Lawrence & Wishart, 1975–2005).

Fulgenzio Micanzio, *Lettere a William Cavendish*, Roberto Ferrini, ed. (Rome: Istituto storico O. S. M, 1987).

Michel de Montaigne, *The Complete Essays*, M. A. Screech, trans. (Harmondsworth: Penguin, 1993).

———, 'De l'institution des enfans', Essais, 1.26, in *Oeuvres complètes*, Albert Thibaudet and Maurice Rat, eds. (Paris: Gallimard, 1962), pp. 144–77.

Montesquicu, *The Complete Works of M. de Montesquieu*, 4 vols. (London: T. Evans and W. Davis, 1777).

Henry More, *An Account of Virtue* (London: Benjamin Tooke, 1690).

———, *Enchiridion Ethicum* (London: James Flesher, 1668).

Pierre Nicole, 'Of Charity, and Self-Love', in *Moral Essayes* (London: Samuel Manship, 1696), vol. 3, pp. 78–112.

Friedrich Nietzsche, *The Anti-Christ, Ecce Homo, Twilight of the Idols and Other Writings*, Aaron Ridley and Judith Norman, eds. (Cambridge: Cambridge University Press, 2005).

———, *Beyond Good and Evil*, Rolf-Peter Horstmann and Judith Norman, eds. (Cambridge: Cambridge University Press, 2002).

———, *The Gay Science*, Bernard Williams, ed. (Cambridge: Cambridge University Press, 2001).

———, *Human, All Too Human*, R. J. Hollingdale, trans. (Cambridge: Cambridge University Press, 1996).

Samuel Parker, *A Demonstration of the Divine Authority of the Law of Nature and of the Christian Religion in two parts* (London: M. Flesher, 1681).

Blaise Pascal, 'Discussion with Monsieur de Sacy', in *Pensées and Other Writings*, Honor Levi, trans. (Oxford: Oxford University Press, 1995), pp. 182–92.

———, *Pensées*, Léon Brunschvicg, ed. (Paris: Hachette, 1976).

Montagu Pennington, *Memoirs of the Life of Mrs Elizabeth Carter*, 2 vols. (London: F. C. & J. Rivington, 1808).

Plutarch, *The lives of the noble Grecians and Romanes compared together*, Thomas North, trans. (London: Thomas Vautroullier and John Wight, 1579).

———, 'On Stoic Self-Contradictions', in *Moralia*, vol. 13, pt. 2, Harold Cherniss, trans. (Cambridge, MA: Harvard University Press, 1976).

Samuel Pufendorf, *De jure naturae et gentium* (Amsterdam: Andreas van Hoogenhuysen, 1688).

———, *The Law of Nature and of Nations*, Jean Barbeyrac, ed., Basil Kennet, trans. (London: J. & J. Bonwicke, 1749.

———, *De origine et progressu disciplinae juris naturalis*, in Pufendorf, *Eris Scandica und andere polemische Schriften über das Naturrecht*, Fiammetta Palladini, ed. (Berlin: Akademie Verlag, 2002), pp. 124–28.

Andrew Michael Ramsay, *An Essay upon Civil Government* (London: Randal Minshull, 1722).

Jean-Jacques Rousseau, *Oeuvres complètes*, Bernard Gagnebin and Marcel Raymond, eds., 5 vols. (Paris: Gallimard, 1959–1995).

———, *The Collected Writings of Rousseau*, Roger D. Masters and Christopher

Kelly, eds., 13 vols. (Hanover, NH: University Press of New England, 1990–2009).

———, *Confessions*, in Masters and Kelly, *Collected Writings*, vol. 5, pp. 1–550.

———, *Considerations on the Government of Poland and Its Planned Reformation*, in Masters and Kelly, *Collected Writings*, vol. 11, pp. 167–240.

———, *Discourse on the Origins of Inequality (Second Discourse)*, in Masters and Kelly, *Collected Writings*, vol. 3, pp. 1–95.

———, *Emile*, in Masters and Kelly, *Collected Writings*, vol. 13, pp. 155–678.

———, *Emile and Sophie; or, the Solitaries*, in Masters and Kelly, *Collected Writings*, vol. 13, pp. 685–721.

———, 'Letter to Mirabeau', 26 July 1767, in *The Social Contract and Other Late Political Writings*, Victor Gourevitch, ed. (Cambridge: Cambridge University Press, 1997), pp. 268–71.

———, *Plan for a Constitution for Corsica*, in Masters and Kelly, *Collected Writings*, vol. 11, pp. 123–65.

———, *The Social Contract*, in Masters and Kelly, *Collected Writings*, vol. 4, pp. 127–224.

Jean-François Senault, *The Use of Passions*, trans. Henry Carey, Earl of Monmouth (London: J. L. & Humphrey Moseley, 1649).

———, *L'homme criminel* (Paris: Camusat, 1644).

———, *L'homme Chrestien* (Paris: Camusat, 1648).

———, *De l'usage des passions* (Paris: Journel, 1641).

———, *The Christian man: or, The reparation of nature by grace* (London: M.M. G. Bedell, 1650).

———, *Man become guility, or, The corruption of nature by sinne, according to St. Augustines sense*, Henry Carey, Earl of Monmouth, trans. (London: William Leake, 1650).

Seneca, *Selected Philosophical Letters*, Brad Inwood, ed. (Oxford: Oxford University Press, 2007).

Anthony Ashley Cooper, Third Earl of Shaftesbury, *Characteristics of Men, Manners, Opinions, Times*, Lawrence E. Klein, ed. (Cambridge: Cambridge University Press, 1999).

———, *Exercices*, Laurent Jaffro, ed. and trans. (Paris: Aubier, 1993).

———, *An Inquiry Concerning Virtue or Merit*, in *Characteristics*, pp. 163–230.

———, *Miscellaneous Reflections*, in *Characteristics*, pp. 339–483.

———, *Soliloquy, or Advice to an Author*, in *Characteristics*, pp. 70–162.

———, *The Life, Unpublished Letters and Philosophical Regimen of Anthony, Earl of Shaftesbury*, Benjamin Rand, ed. (London: Swan Sonnenschein, 1900).

William Shakespeare, *Coriolanus*, Philip Brockbank, ed. (London: Arden Shakespeare, 2001).

Robert Sharrock, *Hypothesis ethike: de officiis secundum naturae jus* (Oxford: Lichfield, 1660).

Adam Smith, 'Letter to the Authors of the *Edinburgh Review*', *Essays on Philosophical Subjects*, W. P. D. Wightman and J. C. Bryce, eds. (Oxford: Oxford University Press, 1980).

———, *The Theory of Moral Sentiments*, D. D. Raphael and Alec Macfie, eds. (Oxford: Clarendon Press, 1976).

Benedict Spinoza, *Tractatus theologico-politicus*, Samuel Shirley, trans., Brad S. Gregory, ed. (Leiden: E. J. Brill, 1989).

Thomas Stanley, *The History of Philosophy*, 3 vols. (London: Humphrey Moseley & Thomas Dring, 1655–61).

Tacitus, *Agricola and Germany*, Anthony R. Birley, trans. (Oxford: Oxford University Press, 1999).

———, *The Annals*, A. J. Woodman, trans. (Indianapolis, IN: Hackett, 2004).

———, *The Annals of Tacitus*, George Gilbert Ramsay, ed., 2 vols. (London: John Murray, 1909).

Jacob Thomasius, 'De statu naturali adversus Hobbesium. Programma XIX, 16. Januar 1661', *Dissertationes LXIII varii argumenti magnam partem ad historiam philosophicam et ecclesiasticam pertinentes* (Halle, 1693),

———, *Exercitatio de stoica mundi exustione* (Leipzig: F. Lanckisius 1676).

John Toland, *Pantheisticon: or, the form of celebrating the Socratic-Society* (London: Samuel Paterson, 1751).

John Trenchard and Thomas Gordon, *Cato's Letters*, Ronald Hamowy, ed. (Indianapolis, IN: Liberty Fund, 1995).

Giambattista Vico, *The New Science of Giambattista Vico*, Thomas Goddard Bergin and Max Harold Fisch, trans. (Ithaca, NY: Cornell University Press, 1984).

A Vindication of Mr. Hutcheson from the Calumnious Aspersions of a late Pamphlet [by 'several of his scholars'] (Glasgow: 1738).

John Webster, *The Duchess of Malfi*, Leah S. Marcus, ed. (London: Arden Shakespeare, 2009).

John Wesley, *The Works of the Rev. John Wesley* (New York: J. & J. Harper, 1826), 10 vols.

Benjamin Whichcote, *Select Sermons of Dr. Whichcot* (London: Printed for Awnsham and John Churchill, 1698).

William Wollaston, *The Religion of Nature Delineated* (London: Samuel Palmer, 1724).

Mary Wollstonecraft, review of Catharine Macaulay, *Letters on Education*, *Analytical Review*, vol. 8, no. 3 (1790), pp. 241–54.

———, *Vindication of the Rights of Woman*, in *A Vindication of the Rights of Men* . . . , Sylvana Tomaselli, ed. (Cambridge: Cambridge University Press, 1995).

Secondary

Nigel Abercrombie, *The Origins of Jansenism* (Oxford: Clarendon Press, 1936).

Alfred Owen Aldridge, 'Shaftesbury and the Deist Manifesto', *Transactions of the American Philosophical Society*, n.s., vol. 41, no. 2 (1951), pp. 297–385.

J. W. Allen, *A History of Political Thought in the Sixteenth Century* (London: Methuen, 1977).

Julia Annas, 'Ethics in Stoic Philosophy', *Phronesis*, vol. 52, no. 1 (2007), pp. 58–87.

———, *The Morality of Happiness* (Oxford: Oxford University Press, 1993).

———, 'Reply to Cooper', *Philosophy and Phenomenological Research*, vol. 55, no. 3 (September 1995), pp. 599–610.

Keith Ansell-Pearson, *Nietzsche* contra *Rousseau* (Cambridge: Cambridge University Press, 1991).

Reid Barbour, *English Epicures and Stoics: Ancient Legacies in Early Stuart Culture* (Amherst: University of Massachusetts Press, 1998).

Paul Bénichou, *Morales du Grand Siècle* (Paris: Gallimard, 1948).

Matija Berljak, *Il diritto naturale e il suo rapporto con la divinità in Ugo Grozio* (Rome: Università Gregoriana Editrice, 1978).

Christopher J. Berry, *The Idea of Luxury: A Conceptual and Historical Investigation* (Cambridge: Cambridge University Press, 1994).

———, 'Smith under Strain', *European Journal of Political Theory*, vol. 3, no. 4 (October 2004), pp. 455–63.

———, 'What's Wrong with Epictetus' Slippers? Or Hume and Superfluous Value', in M. Schabas and C. Wennerlind, eds., *Hume's Political Economy* (New York: Routledge, 2007), pp. 49–64.

Robert Bireley, SJ, *The Counter-Reformation Prince: Anti-Machiavellianism or Catholic Statecraft in Early Modern Europe* (Chapel Hill: University of North Carolina Press, 1990).

Hans W. Blom, *Morality and Causality in Politics: The Rise of Naturalism in Dutch Seventeenth-Century Political Thought* (Utrecht: Universiteit Utrecht, 1995).

Giovanni Bonacina, *Filosofia ellenistica e cultura moderna: Epicureismo, stoicismo e scetticismo da Bayle a Hegel* (Firenze: Casa Editrice Le Lettere, 1996).

William J. Bouwsma, 'The Two Faces of Humanism: Stoicism and Augustinianism in Renaissance Thought', in Heiko A. Oberman and Thomas A. Brady, Jr., eds., *Itinerarium Italicum: The Profile of the Italian Renaissance in the Mirror of Its European Transformation* (Leiden: E. J. Brill, 1975).

Reinhard Brandt, 'Self-Consciousness and Self-Care: On the Tradition of *Oikeiosis* in the Modern Age', in Hans W. Blom and Laurens C. Winkel, eds., *Grotius and the Stoa* (Assen: Van Gorcum, 2004), pp. 73–91.

Tad Brennan, *The Stoic Life: Emotions, Duties, and Fate* (Oxford: Clarendon Press, 2005).

Annabel Brett, 'Natural Right and Civil Community: The Civil Philosophy of Hugo Grotius', *Historical Journal*, vol. 45, no. 1 (2002), pp. 31–51.

Christopher Brooke, 'Rousseau's Political Philosophy: Stoic and Augustinian Origins', in Patrick Riley, ed., *The Cambridge Companion to Rousseau* (Cambridge: Cambridge University Press, 2001), pp. 94–123.

Vivienne Brown, *Adam Smith's Discourse: Canonicity, Commerce, and Conscience* (London: Routledge, 1994).

Peter Brunt, 'Stoicism and the Principate', *Papers of the British School at Rome*, vol. 43 (1975), pp. 7–35.

Stephen Buckle. *Natural Law and the Theory of Property: Grotius to Hume* (Oxford: Clarendon Press, 1991).

David Burchell, 'The Disciplined Citizen: Thomas Hobbes, Neostoicism and the Critique of Classical Citizenship', *Australian Journal of Politics & History*, vol. 45, no. 4 (December 1999), pp. 506–24.

Peter Burke, 'Tacitism', in T. A. Dorey, ed., *Tacitus* (London: Routledge & Kegan Paul, 1969), pp. 149–71.

Daniel Carey, *Locke, Shaftesbury, and Hutcheson: Contesting Diversity in the Enlightenment and Beyond* (Cambridge: Cambridge University Press, 2006).

Ernst Cassirer, *The Myth of the State* (New Haven, CT: Yale University Press, 1961).

Isabelle Chariatte, 'Le frontispice des *Réflexions ou sentences et maximes morales de La Rochefoucauld*: Une clé de lecture à plusieurs niveaux', *Revue d'Histoire Littéraire de la France*, vol. 102 (2002), pp. 637–43.

Joshua Cohen, *Rousseau: A Free Community of Equals* (Oxford: Oxford University Press, 2010).

Marcia L. Colish, *The Stoic Tradition from Antiquity to the Early Middle Ages*, 2 vols. (Leiden: E. J. Brill, 1985).

John Cooper, 'Eudaimonism and the Appeal to Nature in the Morality of Happiness: Comments on Julia Annas, *The Morality of Happiness*', *Philosophy and Phenomenological Research*, vol. 55, no. 3 (September 1995), pp. 587–98.

———, 'Stoic Autonomy', *Social Philosophy and Policy*, vol. 20 (2003), no. 2, pp. 1–29.

Julien-Eymard d'Angers, *Récherches sur le stoicisme aux XVIᵉ et XVIIᵉ siècles* (New York: G. Olms, 1976).

Stephen Darwall, *The British Moralists and the Internal 'Ought': 1640–1740* (Cambridge: Cambridge University Press, 1995).

J. Dautry, ed., *Gilbert Romme et son temps* (Paris: Presses Universitaires de France, 1966).

Firmin deBrabander, *Spinoza and the Stoics: Power, Politics and the Passions* (London: Continuum, 2007).

Nicholas Dent, *Rousseau* (London: Routledge, 2005).

———, *Rousseau: An Introduction to His Psychological, Social and Political Theory* (Oxford: Blackwell, 1988).

———, *A Rousseau Dictionary* (Oxford: Blackwell, 1992).

Horst Denzer, *Moralphilosophie und Naturrecht bei Samuel Pufendorf* (Munich: Beck, 1972).

Pierluigi Donini, 'The History of the Concept of Eclecticism', in A. A. Long and John M. Dillon, eds., *The Question of 'Eclecticism* (Berkeley: University of California Press, 1988), pp. 15–33.

Horst Dreitzel, 'The Reception of Hobbes in the Political Philosophy of the Early German Enlightenment', *History of European Ideas*, vol. 29, no. 3 (September 2003), pp. 255–89.

John Dunn, 'The Identity of the History of Ideas', in *Political Obligation in Historical Context* (Cambridge: Cambridge University Press, 1980), pp. 13–28.

T. S. Eliot, 'Shakespeare and the Stoicism of Seneca' (1927), in *Selected Essays* (London: Faber & Faber, 1951), pp. 126–40.

Julie K. Ellison, *Cato's Tears and the Making of Anglo-American Emotion* (Chicago: University of Chicago Press, 1999).

Athol Fitzgibbons, *Adam Smith's System of Liberty, Wealth and Virtue* (Oxford: Clarendon Press, 1995).

Pierre Force, *Self-interest before Adam Smith: A Genealogy of Economic Science* (Cambridge: Cambridge University Press, 2003).

Fonna Forman-Barzilai, *Adam Smith and the Circles of Sympathy: Cosmopolitanism and Moral Theory* (Cambridge: Cambridge University Press, 2010).

Michel Foucault, *Discipline and Punish: The Birth of the Prison*, Alan Sheridan, trans. (New York: Pantheon Books, 1979).

———, *Security, Territory, Population: Lectures at the Collège de France, 1977–1978*, Michael Senellart, ed. (Basingstoke: Palgrave Macmillan, 2007).

Larry Frohman, 'Neo-Stoicism and the Transition to Modernity in Wilhelm Dilthey's Philosophy of History', *Journal of the History of Ideas*, vol. 56, no. 2 (1995), pp. 263–87.

Martin van Gelderen, 'The Machiavellian Moment and the Dutch Revolt: The Rise of Neostoicism and Dutch Republicanism', in Gisela Bock, Quentin Skinner, and Maurizio Viroli, eds., *Machiavelli and Republicanism* (Cambridge: Cambridge University Press, 1990), pp. 205–23.

Felix Gilbert, ed., *The Historical Essays of Otto Hintze* (New York: Oxford University Press, 1975).

Mark Goldie and Robert Wokler, eds., *The Cambridge History of Eighteenth-Century Political Thought* (Cambridge: Cambridge University Press, 2006).

Agnès de la Gorce, *Le vrai visage de Fénelon* (Paris: Hachette, 1958).

Philip S. Gorski, *The Disciplinary Revolution: Calvinism and the Rise of the State in Early Modern Europe* (Chicago: University of Chicago Press, 2003).

Margaret Graver, *Stoicism and Emotion* (Chicago: University of Chicago Press, 2007).

Stanley Green, *Shaftesbury's Philosophy of Religion and Ethics: A Study in Enthusiasm* (Athens: University of Ohio Press, 1967).

Miriam Griffin, 'The Flavians', in Alan K. Bowman, Peter Garnsey, and Dominic Rathbone, eds., *The Cambridge Ancient History*, vol. 11, *The High Empire, AD 70–192* , 2nd ed. (Cambridge: Cambridge University Press, 2000), pp. 1–83.

———, *Nero: The End of a Dynasty* (London: Batsford, 1984).

———, 'Philosophy, Cato, and Roman Suicide: I', *Greece & Rome*, 2nd ser., vol. 33, no. 1 (April 1986), pp. 64–77.

Knud Haakonssen, *Natural Law and Modern Philosophy: From Grotius to the Scottish Enlightenment* (Cambridge: Cambridge University Press, 1996).

Thomas Habinek, 'Seneca's Renown: *Gloria*, *Claritudo*, and the Replication of the Roman Elite', *Classical Antiquity*, vol. 19, no. 2 (2000), pp. 264–303.

Pierre Hadot, *The Inner Citadel: The Meditations of Marcus Aurelius* (Cambridge, MA: Harvard University Press, 1998).

———, *Philosophy as a Way of Life: Spiritual Exercises from Socrates to Foucault* (Oxford: Blackwell, 1995).

Ryan Patrick Hanley, *Adam Smith and the Character of Virtue* (Cambridge: Cambridge University Press, 2009).

James Harris, 'The Epicurean in Hume', in Neven Leddy and Avi S. Lifschitz, eds., *Epicurus in the Enlightenment* (Oxford: Voltaire Foundation, 2009), pp. 161–81.

Tim Harris, 'Cooper, Anthony Ashley, first earl of Shaftesbury (1621–1683)', in *Oxford Dictionary of National Biography* (Oxford: Oxford University Press, 2004), vol. 13, pp. 199–217.

Ross Harrison, *Hobbes, Locke, and Confusion's Masterpiece: An Examination of*

Seventeenth-Century Political Philosophy (Cambridge: Cambridge University Press, 2003).

T. J. Hochstrasser, *Natural Law Theories in the Early Enlightenment* (Cambridge: Cambridge University Press, 2000).

Istvan Hont, 'The Early Enlightenment Debate on Commerce and Luxury', in *The Cambridge History of Eighteenth-Century Political Thought*, Mark Goldie and Robert Wokler, eds. (Cambridge: Cambridge University Press, 2006), pp. 379–418.

———, *Jealousy of Trade: International Competition and the Nation-State in Historical Perspective* (Cambridge, MA: Harvard University Press, 2005).

Sarah Hutton, 'Liberty and Self-Determination: Ethics, Power and Action in Ralph Cudworth', in Luisa Simonutti, ed., *Dal necessario al possibile: Determinismo e libertà nel pensiero anglo-olandese del XVII secolo* (Milan: Franco Angeli, 2001).

———, 'Virtue, God, and Stoicism in the Thought of Elizabeth Carter and Catharine Macaulay', in J. Broad and K. Green, eds., *Virtue, Liberty and Toleration: Political Ideas of European Women, 1400–1800* (Dordrecht: Springer, 2007), pp. 137–48.

Katherine Ibbett, *The Style of the State in French Theater, 1630–1660: Neoclassicism and Government* (Farnham: Ashgate, 2009).

Robert G. Ingram, *Religion, Reform and Modernity in the Eighteenth Century: Thomas Secker and the Church of England* (Woodbridge: Boydell Press, 2007).

Terence Irwin, *The Development of Ethics: A Historical and Critical Study*, vol. 2, *From Suarez to Rousseau* (Oxford: Oxford University Press, 2008).

———, 'Stoic Naturalism in Butler', in *Hellenistic and Early Modern Philosophy*, Jon Miller and Brad Inwood, eds. (Cambridge: Cambridge University Press, 2003), pp. 274–300.

Jonathan Israel, *Enlightenment Contested: Philosophy, Modernity, and the Emancipation of Man 1670–1752* (Oxford: Oxford University Press, 2006).

———, *Radical Enlightenment: Philosophy and the Making of Modernity 1650–1750* (Oxford: Oxford University Press, 2001).

Margaret C. Jacob, *The Radical Enlightenment: Pantheists, Freemasons and Republicans* (London: George Allen & Unwin, 1981).

Justin B. Jacobs, 'The ancient notion of self-preservation in the theories of Hobbes and Spinoza', PhD thesis (University of Cambridge, 2010).

E. D. James, *Pierre Nicole, Jansenist and Humanist: A Study of His Thought* (The Hague: Martinus Nijhoff, 1973).

———, 'Scepticism and Fideism in Bayle's *Dictionnaire*', *French Studies*, vol. 16, no. 4 (1962), pp. 307–23.

Susan James, 'Spinoza the Stoic', in Tom Sorell, ed., *The Rise of Modern Philosophy* (Oxford: Clarendon Press, 1993), pp. 289–316.

Stewart Justman, *The Autonomous Male of Adam Smith* (Norman: University of Oklahoma Press, 1993).

Victoria Kahn, *Rhetoric, Prudence and Skepticism* (Ithaca, NY: Cornell University Press, 1985).

Nannerl O. Keohane, *Philosophy and the State in France: The Renaissance to the Enlightenment* (Princeton, NJ: Princeton University Press, 1980).

Lawrence E. Klein, *Shaftesbury and the Culture of Politeness: Moral Discourse and Cultural Politics in Early 18th-Century England* (Cambridge: Cambridge University Press, 1994).

Leszek Kolakowski, *God Owes Us Nothing* (Chicago: University of Chicago Press, 1995).

Alan C. Kors, *Atheism in France, 1650–1729*, vol. 1 (Princeton, NJ: Princeton University Press, 1990).

Jill Kraye, '"Ethnicorum omnium sanctissimus": Marcus Aurelius and His *Meditations* from Xylander to Diderot', in Jill Kraye and M. W. F. Stone, eds., *Humanism and Modern Philosophy* (London: Routledge, 2000), pp. 107–34.

Manfred Kuehn, *Kant: A Biography* (Cambridge: Cambridge University Press, 2001).

Jean Lafond, 'Augustinisme et épicurisme au XVII siècle', in *L'homme et son image: Morales et littérature de Montaigne à Mandeville* (Paris: H. Champion, 1996), pp. 345–68.

——, *La Rochefoucauld, Augustinisme et littérature* (Paris: Klincksieck, 1977).

Jacqueline Lagrée, 'Constancy and Coherence', in Steven K. Strange and Jack Zupko, eds., *Stoicism: Traditions and Transformations* (Cambridge: Cambridge University Press: 2004), pp. 148–76.

——, 'La critique du stoïcisme dans le *Dictionnaire* de Bayle', in *De l'humanisme aux Lumières, Bayle et le protestantisme: Mélanges en l'honneur d'Elisabeth Labrousse*, ed. Michelle Magdelaine et al. (Oxford: Voltaire Foundation, 1996), pp. 581–93.

——, 'Théorie des principes et théologie naturelle' in Christian Mouchel, ed., *Juste Lipse (1547–1606) en son temps: Actes du colloque de Strasbourg, 1994* (Paris: H. Champion, 1996), pp. 31–47.

Neven Brady Leddy, 'Adam Smith's Moral Philosophy at the Nexus of National and Philosophical Contexts: French literature and Epicurean Philosophy in the Scottish Enlightenment', DPhil thesis (University of Oxford, 2009).

——, 'Adam Smith's *Theory of Moral Sentiments* in 1759, 1790 and 1976', paper presented at the International Adam Smith Society's conference, 'The Philosophy of Adam Smith', Balliol College, Oxford, January 2009.

Thomas M. Lennon, 'The Contagious Communication of Strong Imaginations: History, Modernity, and Scepticism in the Philosophy of Malebranche', in Tom Sorell, ed., *The Rise of Modern Philosophy* (Oxford: Clarendon Press, 1993), pp. 197–212.

David Leopold, *The Young Karl Marx: German Philosophy, Modern Politics, and Human flourishing* (Cambridge: Cambridge University Press, 2007).

A. H. T. Levi, 'The Relationship of Stoicism and Scepticism: Justus Lipsius', in Jill Kraye and M. W. F. Stone, eds., *Humanism and Early Modern Philosophy* (London: Routledge, 2000), pp. 91-106.

Anthony Levi, SJ, *French Moralists: The Theory of the Passions 1585–1649* (Oxford: Clarendon Press, 1964).

A. A. Long, *Epictetus: A Stoic and Socratic Guide to Life* (Oxford: Oxford University Press, 2002).

——, *From Epicurus to Epictetus: Studies in Hellenistic and Roman Philosophy* (Oxford: Oxford University Press, 2006).

——, 'Stoicism in the Philosophical Tradition: Spinoza, Lipsius, Butler', in Brad Inwood, ed., *The Cambridge Companion to the Stoics* (Cambridge: Cambridge University Press, 2003), pp. 365-92.

A. A. Long and D. N. Sedley, *The Hellenistic Philosophers*, 2 vols. (Cambridge: Cambridge University Press, 1987).

Arthur O. Lovejoy and George Boas, *Primitivism and Related Ideas in Antiquity* (Baltimore, MD: Johns Hopkins University Press, 1935).

Noel Malcolm, *De Dominis, 1560–1624: Venetian, Anglican, Ecumenist, and Relapsed Heretic* (London: Strickland & Scott Academic Publications, 1984).

——, *Reason of State, Propaganda, and the Thirty Years' War: An Unknown Translation by Thomas Hobbes* (Oxford: Clarendon Press, 2007).

Henri Maleprade, *Léontine Zanta: Vertueuse aventurière du feminisme* (Paris: Rive droit, 1997).

Alexandre Matheron, 'Le moment stoïcien de l'*Éthique* de Spinoza' in *Le Stoïcisme aux XVIe et XVIIe siècles: Actes du Colloque CERPHI* (4–5 June 1993), Pierre-François Moreau and Jacqueline Lagrée, eds. (Caen: Presses Universitaires de Caen, 1994), pp. 147-61.

Christian Maurer, 'Self-Love in Early Eighteenth-Century British Moral Philosophy: Shaftesbury, Mandeville, Hutcheson, Butler and Campbell', PhD diss. (Université de Neuchâtel, 2009).

Thomas Mautner, 'Grotius and the Skeptics', *Journal of the History of Ideas*, vol. 66, no. 4 (2005), pp. 577–601.

——, 'Not a Likely Story', *British Journal for the History of Philosophy*, vol. 11, no. 2 (2003), pp. 303–7.

Adriana McCrea, *Constant Minds: Political Virtue and the Lipsian Paradigm in England, 1584–1650* (Toronto, ON: University of Toronto Press, 1997).

D. McKitterick, *A History of Cambridge University Press*, 3 vols. (Cambridge: Cambridge University Press, 1992–2004).

Allan Megill, *Karl Marx: The Burden of Reason (Why Marx Rejected Politics and the Market)* (Lanham, MD: Rowman & Littlefield, 2002).

Geoffrey Miles, *Shakespeare and the Constant Romans* (Oxford: Clarendon Press, 1996).

Jon Miller, 'Grotius and Stobaeus', *Grotiana*, vols. 26–8 (2005–7), pp. 104–26.

——, 'Innate Ideas in Stoicism and Grotius', in Hans W. Blom and Laurens C. Winkel, eds., *Grotius and the Stoa* (Assen: Van Gorcum, 2004), pp. 157–75.

——, 'Stoics, Grotius and Spinoza on Moral Deliberation', in Jon Miller and Brad Inwood, eds., *Hellenistic and Early Modern Philosophy* (Cambridge: Cambridge University Press, 2003).

——, *Spinoza and the Stoics* (Cambridge: Cambridge University Press, forthcoming).

Peter N. Miller, 'Nazis and Neostoics: Otto Brunner and Gerhard Oestreich before and after the Second World War', *Past & Present*, vol. 176 (2002), pp. 144–86.

Toril Moi, *Simone de Beauvoir: The Making of an Intellectual Woman* (Oxford: Blackwell, 1994).

James Moore, 'The Eclectic Stoic, the Mitigated Skeptic', in E. Mazza and E. Ronchetti, eds., *New Essays on David Hume* (Milan: Franco Angeli, 2007).

———, 'Hume and Hutcheson', in M. A. Stewart and John P. Wright, eds., *Hume and Hume's Connexions* (University Park: Pennsylvania State University Press, 1994), pp. 23–57.

Joseph Moreau, 'Sénèque et Malebranche', *Crisis*, vol. 12 (1965), pp. 345–52.

Mark Morford, *Stoics and Neostoics: Rubens and the Circle of Lipsius* (Princeton, NJ: Princeton University Press: 1991).

———, 'Tacitean *Prudentia* and Lipsius', in T. J. Luce and A. J. Woodman, eds., *Tacitus and the Tacitean Tradition* (Princeton, NJ: Princeton University Press, 1993), pp. 129–51.

Isaac Nakhimovsky, *The Closed Commercial State: Perpetual Peace and Commercial Society from Rousseau to Fichte* (Princeton, NJ: Princeton University Press, 2011).

———, 'The Enlightened Epicureanism of Jacques Abbadie: *L'Art de se connoître soi-même* and the Morality of Self-interest', *History of European Ideas*, vol. 29, no.1 (2003), pp.1–14.

Frederick Neuhouser, *Foundations of Hegel's Social Theory: Actualizing Freedom* (Cambridge, MA: Harvard University Press, 2000).

———, *Rousseau's Theodicy of Self-Love* (Oxford: Oxford University Press, 2008).

James H. Nichols, Jr., *Epicurean Political Philosophy: The* De rerum natura *of Lucretius* (Ithaca, NY: Cornell University Press, 1976).

David Fate Norton, 'Hume and Hutcheson: The Question of Influence', *Oxford Studies in Early Modern Philosophy* (Oxford: Oxford University Press, 2005), vol. 2, pp. 211–56.

Robert Nozick, *Anarchy, State, and Utopia* (New York: Basic Books, 1974).

Martha C. Nussbaum, 'Patriotism and Cosmopolitanism', in Joshua Cohen, ed., *For Love of Country: Debating the Limits of Patriotism* (Boston: Beacon Press, 1998), pp. 2–17.

———, 'Pity and Mercy: Nietzsche's Stoicism', in Richard Schacht, ed., *Nietzsche, Genealogy, Morality: Essays on Nietzsche's Genealogy of Morals* (Berkeley: University of California Press, 1994).

Oliver O'Donovan, *The Problem of Self-Love in Augustine* (New Haven, CT: Yale University Press, 1980).

Timothy O'Hagan, *Rousseau* (London: Routledge, 1999).

Gerhard Oestreich, *Neostoicism and the Early Modern State* (Cambridge: Cambridge University Press, 1982).

R. M. Ogilvie, *A Commentary on Livy, Books 1–5* (Oxford: Clarendon Press, 1965).

Dorinda Outram, *The Body and the French Revolution: Sex, Class, and Political Culture* (New Haven, CT: Yale University Press, 1989).

Jürgen Overhoff, *Hobbes's Theory of the Will: Ideological Reasons and Historical Circumstances* (Lanham, MD: Rowman & Littlefield, 2000).

Jan Papy, 'Justus Lipsius', *Stanford Encyclopedia of Philosophy*, http://plato.stanford.edu/entries/justus-lipsius/.

———, 'Lipsius' (neo-)Stoicism: Constancy between Christian Faith and Stoic Virtue', in Hans W. Blom and Laurens C. Winkel, eds., *Grotius and the Stoa* (Assen: Van Gorcum, 2004), pp. 47–71.

Jon Parkin, *Science, Religion and Politics in Restoration England: Richard Cumberland's* De Legibus Naturae (Woodbridge: Boydell Press, 1999).

——, *Taming the Leviathan: the Reception of the Political and Religious Ideas of Thomas Hobbes in England, 1640–1700* (Cambridge: Cambridge University Press, 2007).

John M. Parrish, *Paradoxes of Political Ethics: From Dirty Hands to the Invisible Hand* (Cambridge: Cambridge University Press, 2007).

J. A. Passmore, *Ralph Cudworth: An Interpretation* (Cambridge: Cambridge University Press, 1951).

Christopher Pelling, 'The Shaping of *Coriolanus*: Dionysius, Plutarch and Shakespeare', in *Plutarch and History* (Swansea: Duckworth, 2002), pp. 387–411.

S. G. Pembroke, '*Oikeiosis*', in A. A. Long, ed., *Problems in Stoicism* (London: Athlone Press, 1971), pp. 114–49.

Max Pohlenz, *Die Stoa: Geschichte einer geistigen Bewegung* (Göttingen: Vandenhoeck & Ruprecht, 1978).

Adam Potkay, *The Passion for Happiness: Samuel Johnson and David Hume* (Ithaca, NY: Cornell University Press, 2000).

Anthony R. Pugh, *The Composition of Pascal's Apologia* (Toronto, ON: University of Toronto Press, 1984).

John Rawls, *Lectures on the History of Political Philosophy* (Cambridge, MA: Harvard University Press, 2007)

Isabel Rivers, *Reason, Grace, and Sentiment: A Study of the Language of Religion and Ethics in England, 1660–1780*, vol. 1, *Whichcote to Wesley* (Cambridge: Cambridge University Press, 1991).

——, *Reason, Grace, and Sentiment: A Study of the Language of Religion and Ethics in England, 1660–1780*, vol. 2, *Shaftesbury to Hume* (Cambridge: Cambridge University Press, 2000).

John Robertson, 'The Case for the Enlightenment: A Comparative Approach', in Joseph Mali and Robert Wokler, eds., *Isaiah Berlin's Counter-Enlightenment* (Philadelphia, PA: American Philosophical Society, 2003).

——, *The Case for the Enlightenment: Scotland and Naples, 1680–1760* (Cambridge: Cambridge University Press, 2005).

Geneviève Rodis-Lewis, 'L'anti-stoïcisme de Malebranche', *7ᵉ Congres de l'Association Guillaume Budé, Aix-en-Provence, 1963* (1964).

Ben Rogers, 'In Praise of Vanity: The Augustinian Analysis of the Benefits of Vice from Port-Royal to Mandeville', DPhil thesis (University of Oxford, 1994).

——, *Pascal: In Praise of Vanity* (New York: Routledge, 1999).

Amélie Oksenberg Rorty, 'Rousseau's Therapeutic Experiments', *Philosophy*, vol. 66, no. 258 (October 1991), pp. 413–34.

Michael Rosen, *On Voluntary Servitude: False Consciousness and the Theory of Ideology* (Cambridge: Polity, 1996).

Emma Rothschild, *Economic Sentiments: Adam Smith, Condorcet and the Enlightenment* (Cambridge, MA: Harvard University Press, 2001).

David Runciman, *Political Hypocrisy: The Mask of Power, from Hobbes to Orwell and Beyond* (Princeton, NJ: Princeton University Press, 2008).

J.H.M. Salmon, *Cardinal de Retz: The Anatomy of a Conspirator* (London: Weidenfeld & Nicolson, 1969).

———, 'Stoicism and Roman Example: Seneca and Tacitus in Jacobean England', *Journal of the History of Ideas*, vol. 50, no. 2 (1989), pp. 199–225.

Giovanni Santinello et al., eds., *Models of the History of Philosophy*, 2 vols. (Dordrecht: Kluwer/Springer, 1993–2010), vol. 1 'From its origins in the Renaissance to the "Historia Philosophica"; vol. 2 'From the Cartesian Age to Brucker'.

Giovanni Santinello et al., eds., *Storia della storie generali della filosofia*, vol. 2, *Dall'éta cartesiana a Brucker* (Brescia: La Scuola, 1979).

Jason Lewis Saunders, *Justus Lipsius: The Philosophy of Renaissance Stoicism* (New York: Liberal Arts Press, 1955).

J. B. Schneewind, *The Invention of Autonomy* (Cambridge: Cambridge University Press, 1998).

———, 'Locke's Moral Philosophy', in Vere Chappell, ed., *The Cambridge Companion to Locke* (Cambridge: Cambridge University Press, 1994), pp. 199–225.

Robert Shaver, 'Grotius on Scepticism and Self-Interest', *Archiv für Geschichte der Philosophie*, vol. 78, no. 1 (1996), pp. 27–47.

Richard B. Sher, *Church and University in the Scottish Enlightenment: The Moderate Literati of Edinburgh* (Edinburgh: Edinburgh University Press, 1985).

Andrew Shifflett, *Stoicism, Politics and Literature in the Age of Milton: War and Peace Reconciled* (Cambridge: Cambridge University Press, 1998).

Quentin Skinner, *The Foundations of Modern Political Thought*, 2 vols. (Cambridge: Cambridge University Press, 1978).

Robert Sleigh, Jr., Vere Chappell, and Michael Della Rocca, 'Determinism and Human Freedom', in Daniel Garber and Michael Ayers, eds., *The Cambridge History of Seventeenth-Century Philosophy* (Cambridge: Cambridge University Press, 1998), pp. 1195–1270.

Gabriella Slomp, *Thomas Hobbes and the Political Philosophy of Glory* (Basingstoke: Palgrave Macmillan, 2000).

Michael Sonenscher, *Sans-Culottes: An Eighteenth-Century Emblem in the French Revolution* (Princeton, NJ: Princeton University Press, 2008).

Richard Sorabji. *Emotion and Peace of Mind: From Stoic Agitation to Christian Temptation* (Oxford: Oxford University Press, 2000).

Céline Spector, 'Le *Projet de paix perpétuelle*: De Saint-Pierre à Rousseau', in Jean-Jacques Rousseau, *Principes du droit de la guerre—Ecrits sur la paix perpétuelle*, Blaise Bachofen and Céline Spector, eds. (Paris: Vrin, 2008), pp. 229–94.

Peter Stacey, *Roman Monarchy and the Renaissance Prince* (Cambridge: Cambridge University Press: 2007).

Gareth Stedman Jones, introduction to Karl Marx and Friedrich Engels, *The Communist Manifesto*, Gareth Stedman Jones, ed. (London: Penguin, 2002).

M. A. Stewart, 'The Stoic legacy in the Early Scottish Enlightenment', in Margaret J. Osler, ed., *Atoms, Pneuma, and Tranquillity: Epicurean and Stoic Themes in European Thought* (Cambridge: Cambridge University Press, 1991).

Benjamin Straumann, *Hugo Grotius und die Antike: Römisches Recht und römische Ethik im frühneuzeitlichen Naturrecht* (Baden-Baden: Nomos Verlagsgesellschaft, 2007).

———, '*Oikeiosis* and *appetitus societatis*: Hugo Grotius' Ciceronian argument for Natural Law and Just War', *Grotiana*, vol. 24–25 (2003–4), pp. 41–66.

Leo Strauss, *The Political Philosophy of Hobbes* (Chicago: University of Chicago Press, 1952).

Fortunat Strowski, *Pascal et son temps*, vol. 1, *De Montaigne à Pascal* (Paris: Plon-Nourrit, 1907).

Charles Taylor, *A Secular Age* (Cambridge, MA: Belknap Press of Harvard University Press, 2007).

Pierre Teilhard de Chardin, *Letters to Leontine Zanta*, Bernard Wall, trans. (London: Collins, 1969).

Martin Thom, *Republics, Nations and Tribes* (London: Verso, 1995).

Brian Tierney, *The Idea of Natural Rights: Studies on Natural Rights, Natural Law and Church Law, 1150–1625* (Atlanta, GA: Scholars Press, 1997).

Esther A. Tiffany, 'Shaftesbury as Stoic', *Proceedings of the Modern Language Association*, vol. 38, no. 3 (September 1923), pp. 642–84.

Giuseppe Toffanin, *Machiavelli e il tacitismo* (Padova: A. Draghi, 1921).

Richard Tuck, 'Grotius, Carneades and Hobbes', *Grotiana*, vol. 4 (1983), pp. 43–62.

———, 'Grotius and Selden', in J. H. Burns and Mark Goldie, eds., *The Cambridge History of Political Thought, 1450–1700* (Cambridge: Cambridge University Press, 1991), pp. 499–529.

———, 'Hobbes and Tacitus', in G. A. J. Rogers and Tom Sorell, eds., *Hobbes and History* (London: Routledge, 2000), pp. 99–111.

———, 'The "Modern" Theory of Natural Law', in Anthony Pagden, ed., *The Languages of Political Theory in Early-Modern Europe* (Cambridge: Cambridge University Press, 1987), pp. 99–119.

———, *Natural Rights Theories: Their Origin and Development* (Cambridge: Cambridge University Press, 1979).

———, *Philosophy and Government, 1572–1651* (Cambridge: Cambridge University Press, 1993).

———, *The Rights of War and Peace: Political Thought and the International Order from Grotius to Kant* (Oxford: Oxford University Press, 1999).

———, 'The Utopianism of *Leviathan*', in Tom Sorell and Luc Foisneau, eds., *Leviathan after 350 Years* (Oxford: Clarendon Press, 2004), pp. 125–39.

Michael Ure, 'The Irony of Pity: Nietzsche contra Schopenhauer and Rousseau', *Journal of Nietzsche Studies*, vol. 32 (2006), pp. 68–91

Gérard Verbeke, *The Presence of Stoicism in Medieval Thought* (Washington, DC: Catholic University of America Press, 1983).

Richard Vernon, *Friends, Citizens, Strangers: Essays on Where We Belong* (Toronto, ON: University of Toronto Press, 2005).

Gloria Vivenza, *Adam Smith and the Classics* (Oxford: Oxford University Press, 2001).

Maurizio Viroli, *For Love of Country* (Oxford: Clarendon Press, 1995).

Ira O. Wade, *The Intellectual Origins of the French Enlightenment* (Princeton, NJ: Princeton University Press, 1971).

Norbert Waszek, 'Two Concepts of Morality: A Distinction of Adam Smith's Ethics and its Stoic Origin', *Journal of the History of Ideas*, vol. 45 (1984), pp. 591–606.

Max Weber, *The Protestant Ethic and the Spirit of Capitalism*, Talcott Parsons, trans. (London: George Allen & Unwin, 1930).

Catherine Wilson, *Epicureanism at the Origins of Modernity* (Oxford: Clarendon Press, 2008).

Elizabeth Wingrove, 'Getting Intimate with Wollstonecraft: In the Republic of Letters', *Political Theory* vol. 33 (2005), pp. 344–69.

Laurens C. Winkel, 'Les origines antiques de l'*appetitus societatis* de Grotius', *Tijdschrift voor Rechtsgeschiedenis*, vol. 68 (2000), pp. 393–403.

Perez Zagorin, 'Hobbes without Grotius', *History of Political Thought*, vol. 21, no. 1 (2000), pp. 16–40.

Léontine Zanta, *La renaissance du stoïcisme au XVIᵉ siècle* (Paris: H. Champion, 1914).

Index

Abbadie, Jacques, 149, 150
Abercrombie, Nigel, 79
Academics, 41, 100, 107, 112, 114, 130, 178. *See also* scepticism
Adam and Eve, xiv, xv, 1, 3, 8–11, 78, 79, 81, 90, 96, 102. *See also* original sin
Addison, Joseph, 158
affections, 6, 47, 76, 98, 165, 173, 208; Hutcheson on, 160–61, 162–63, 164, 168, 169; Rousseau on, 193, 194, 195; Shaftesbury on, 115–16, 117, 118–19, 122, 163. *See also* passions
Agricola, Gnaeus Julius, 64
Agrippina, Julia, 63–64
Ainsworth, Michael, 114
Alcibiades, 6
Aldridge, Alfred Owen, 113, 118
Alembert, Jean le Rond d', xx, 181
alienation, 43
Allen, J. W., 14
amour de soi-même. See self-love
amour-propre. See self-love
Amyot, Jacques, 62
Anaxarchus, 61
Annas, Julia, xviii, 41, 42, 43, 44, 45, 51, 52
Antipater of Sidon, 140
apatheia, xii, 6–7, 8–9, 10–11, 62, 79, 188
appropriation. See *oikeiosis*
Arcesilaus, 127, 131, 132
Aristotle, xii, xiv, 27, 105, 110, 137, 138, 142, 207
Arius Didymus, 53
Arrian, 113
Ashcham, Roger, 68
atheism, xvi, 102, 109, 125–26, 133, 135, 136, 137, 138, 139, 141–42, 146, 148, 174
Aubrey, John, 71
Augustine, Saint, xiv, xv, 1–11, 27, 59, 60, 69, 78, 79, 81, 82, 83, 87, 89, 95, 130, 225n16
Augustinianism, xiv–xv, xvi, 59–61, 69, 70, 75, 76–96, 99–100, 101, 127, 129, 149–

51, 155, 156, 158, 160, 169, 178, 187, 196, 200–201. *See also* Jansenism
Augustus, 22, 71
Aulus Gellius, 63, 130

Bacon, Francis, 67–68, 71
Baglioni, Giovampagolo, 33
Barbeyrac, Jean, 54, 55, 129, 142, 143–45, 165
Barbin, Claude, 99
Barea Soranus, 65
Barnes, Barnabe, 67
Bayle, Pierre, xx, 113, 127–33, 139, 143, 149, 150, 158
beavers, republic of, 205
Beauvoir, Simone de, 14
Becker, Gary, 187
bees, 153
Behn, Aphra, 93
Bellarmine, Cardinal Robert, 20
benevolence, 24, 158, 167; Hume on, 177; Hutcheson on, 160, 162, 163, 164, 166, 167, 169; Rousseau on, 186, 193, 198
Bénichou, Paul, 77
Berljak, Matija, 40
Berry, Christopher J., xvii, 152, 178, 179
Bertrand, Jean, 183
Binet, Etienne, 77
Bireley, Robert, 18–20
Bloom, Allan, 248n78
Boas, George, 184–85
Bobzien, Susanne, xviii
Boccalini, Trajano, 66
Böcler, Johann Heinrich, 104–5
Boethius, 140
Boethus, 136
Boineburg, Johann Christian von, 104
Bossuet, Jacques-Bénigne, 151
Botero, Giovanni, 18
Bourbotte, Pierre, 207
Bouwsma, William J., xiv
Bramhall, John, xvi, 101–4, 132
Brandt, Reinhard, 40
Brennan, Tad, 45–46, 57